CLASSICS
OF
CHRISTIAN
MISSIONS

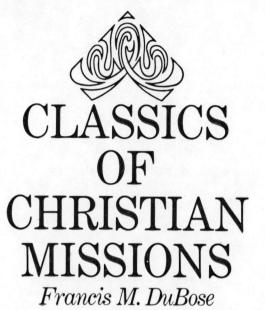

CLASSICS
OF
CHRISTIAN
MISSIONS

Francis M. DuBose
EDITOR

BROADMAN PRESS
Nashville, Tennessee

© Copyright 1979 • Broadman Press.
All rights reserved.
4263-13
ISBN: 0-8054-6313-5

Dewey Decimal Classification: 266
Subject heading: MISSIONS

Library of Congress Catalog Card Number: 78-53147
Printed in the United States of America.

Dedicated in loving memory
of my parents
Hansford Arthur DuBose, Sr.
Mayde Frances Owen DuBose

CONTENTS

Part III. Missionary Biographies

Part IV. Missionary Journals and Diaries

Part V. Missionary Letters

Part VI. Mission Theory and Practice

Foreword

The purpose of this book is to provide in a single volume an introduction to the classics of Christian missions. The motivation stems from a strong and widespread plea for such a work. The desire for such a work is a part of a remarkable resurgence of interest in Christian missions in recent years.

This renewed interest in missions is expressing itself in a number of significant ways. There are some forty thousand North American missionaries serving around the world, the largest number ever. Moreover, there is a growing company of missionaries from Third World countries in places of service over the globe. The International Association for Mission Study has had a significant increase in its membership since its inception a few years ago. Its American counterpart, the American Society of Missiology (A.S.M.) likewise has enjoyed encouraging growth in its brief history. It is a member of the prestigious Council on the Study of Religion along with such significant learned societies as the American Academy of Religion and the Society of Biblical Literature. There are over two hundred schools in the United States alone which teach courses in missions, over sixty of which offer ten or more courses on the subject. Some schools offer between twenty and fifty missions courses.

Missionary journals enjoy a growing reception today. The *International Review of Missions* has a healthy worldwide circulation, and the prestigious *Missiology,* the official organ of the A.S.M., enjoys a growing audience in North America. The *Occasional Bulletin of Missionary Research* has recently experienced a phenomenal increase in subscriptions. There are many denominational and other specialized mission journals serving large and growing audiences. Mission centers such as the Fuller School of World Mission in Pasadena, California, and the Overseas Ministry Study Center (O.M.S.C.) in Ventnor, New Jersey, have had unusual

13

success and have attracted a wide constituency from around the world in recent years. New centers such as the United States Center for World Missions in Pasadena and the World Mission Center of Golden Gate Baptist Theological Seminary in Mill Valley (San Francisco) are further indications of this mounting new interest in missions.

A vital concern of the above groups is the location and preservation of all mission data possible in every existing literary form. Related to this is the effort to publish as much of this material as possible. This work seeks to address itself to this vital concern.

The task of selecting appropriate classical writings from the field of Christian missions to fill a volume of this size is a frustrating experience. The frustration stems from a number of sources. One is the necessity of having to choose from a wealth of biblical studies, histories, biographies, journals, diaries, letters, tracts, sermons, findings of historic mission conferences, and definitive studies in mission philosophy from both the so-called "sending" and "younger" churches. Another source of frustration is the necessity of having to condense most of the material. A volume of this length could accommodate the full text of only a dozen classic documents the size of William Carey's famous "An Enquiry." Moreover, it would accommodate only a single work by such a man as Hendrick Kraemer or Kenneth Scott Latourette or a single biography of a Livingstone or a Judson. Another frustration comes from having to decide on only one work of a personality who himself or herself is a "missionary classic." Which of Roland Allen's studies should be included: *Missionary Methods, Saint Paul's Ours,* or *The Spontaneous Expansion of the Church?* What portion of Harnack's classic study should be selected? Which missionary biography or journal should be chosen?

Besides a few unquestioned works, the selections have to be representative. Moreover, at best they can only serve as introductions to the vast reservoir of mission literature which has come to be standard.

What constitutes a classic of Christian missions? It is only a specialized way of judging any kind of Christian literature as being worthy of such a designation. It largely awaits the verdict of history. When a given work comes to be recognized over a considerable period of time by a broad spectrum of the Christian community, especially by later writers who repeatedly draw from it, it comes to be regarded as a classic.

In every field of Christian literature, certain works have been regarded as classics in that field when they may not necessarily be so regarded within the larger Christian community. Although such works as Origen's *Against Celsus* and David Livingstone's *Journal* would be recognized broadly as classics, the definitive studies on mission theory and practice by Henry Venn and Rufus Anderson may be recognized as classics only within mission circles.

The same principle applies to different segments of the larger Christian community. Works regarded as classics in one segment of the faith may not be so regarded in another. Moreover, any range of selection is limited by the orientation and perspective (indeed the bias) of any given author. This work is essentially a Protestant view. A Roman Catholic writer would no doubt have a different selection, especially as it concerns the last few centuries. However, any writer who seeks to discern the thinking of the larger Christian community and to be as objective as possible in his choices will be disciplined by that discernment and objectivity. That principle has been a part of the philosophy behind this work. Because of the wealth of sources from which to choose, some limitation has to be imposed. Consequently, the decision was made to include only post-biblical sources and material by authors who are not living, that is, at the time of this writing. The former seemed to be a wise choice for such a volume, and the later was dictated by the vast amount of significant mission material produced by authors who are still living. This means, of course, that this arbitrary principle will eliminate one whose birthday actually antedates someone included in this volume. There seems to be little doubt that some of the current mission studies will in time be regarded as classics.

The general format for this study is topical, covering the broad range of mission literature in eleven categories. Within each major part, however, the arrangement is chronological, that is, as it concerns the person who is the focal point, whether the work is by that person or about him or her.

In the selection of these mission classics, the concern has been with writings which have been accessible to the English-speaking world, regardless of the original linguistic source. Although a significant number of these works obviously have been translated, no effort has been made to translate works for the purpose of inclusion in this volume, except in the one case of Juan C. Varetto. Admittedly, therefore, this work in English reflects mission documents which for the most part have existed in English long enough to be read and loved by the English-speaking world to the extent that they have become classics (for this and other reasons, regrettably, we have not included any material from the Greek and Russian Orthodox Church). The spellings of names, therefore, will usually be in the English form unless a given text reflects an original spelling.

No effort has been made to change any of the given texts even when they contain terminology which obviously is offensive to the modern mind. For example, a particularly objectable term to the modern mind is the word *heathen*. It was used in the past in much the same way we use the designation *non-Christian*. The word is retained in all references where it originally appeared. Therefore no effort has been made in this work to change the form of the text as it has originally appeared or as it appears in standard translation form. Even though the introductions will include the most widely accepted current spelling of words, the spelling in the original texts is retained.

Realizing that even the most careful scholar writes from the vantage point of his own limitation and bias, I sought the advice of scholars, most of them missiologists actively engaged in teaching, both as an aid to my own understanding and as a test of my own assessment of the relative value of the significant mission literature of the past. I wish to express my appreciation to the following persons who were very helpful in personal conversation: Gerald H. Anderson, Overseas Ministries Service Center; W. Richey Hogg, Southern Methodist University; Walter T. Davis, Missionary Teacher, Nigeria; E. A. Adeolu Adegbola, Institute of Church and Society, Ibadan, Nigeria; Henri J. Schutte, Missiological Institute, Natal, South Africa; Orlando Costas, Latin America Evangelical Center for Pastoral Studies, San José, Costa Rica; René Padilla, International Fellowship of Evangelical Students, Buenos Aires, Argentina; Andrew Walls, University of Aberdeen, Scotland.

In addition I wrote to a large number of scholars most of whom have been active in the Association of Professors of Missions and the A.S.M. I wish to express my appreciation to the following persons who wrote and expressed a special interest in this project: R. Pierce Beaver, professor emeritus University of Chicago; Ralph Winter, United

States Center for World Mission; Stephen L. Peterson, Yale University Divinity School; Gary Pinter, Chicago Research and Trading; Lavell Seats, Midwestern Baptist Theological Seminary, Kansas City; Sister Ann Gormly, United States Catholic Mission Council; Robert J. Schreiter, Catholic Theological Union; Wi Jo Kann, Seminex, Saint Louis.

I wish especially to thank the following persons who took the time to write (some at length) and who offered valuable suggestions: Hugo H. Culpepper, Southern Baptist Theological Seminary, Louisville; Justice Anderson, Cal Guy, L. Jack Gray, Leon McBeth, Robert A. Baker, Southwestern Baptist Theological Seminary, Fort Worth; Charles Corwin, Talbot Seminary, Los Angeles; Waldo J. Werning, Concordia Theological Seminary, Fort Wayne; M. Douglas Swendseid, Division of World Mission, The American Lutheran Church; Richard R. De Ridder, Calvin Theological Seminary, Grand Rapids; Wilbert R. Shenk, Mennonite Board of Missions; Hans Kasdorf, Biblical Seminary, Mennonite Brethren, Fresno; James A. Bergquist, Lutheran Theological Seminary, Columbus, Ohio; Henry M. Goodpasture, Union Theological Seminary, Richmond; James H. Pyke, Wesley Seminary, Washington; Philip Slate, Harding Graduate School of Religion, Memphis; Franklin J. Woo, National Council of Churches; John Gration, Wheaton College, Illinois; J. Herbert Kane, Trinity Evangelical Seminary, Deerfield, Ill.; Ralph H. Covell, Conservative Baptist Theological Seminary, Denver; Charles W. Foreman, Yale University Divinity School; J. Christy Wilson, Gordon-Conwell Theological Seminary, South Hamilton, Mass.; C. L. Boughter, Lancaster Bible College, Pennsylvania; Norman A. Horner, O.M.S.C.; Arthur F. Glasser, Fuller Theological Seminary; Charles R. Taber, Milligan College, Tennessee; David Steward, M.D., Louisville; Irven Paul, Hartford, Connecticut; Simon J. Smith, Jesuit Missions, Washington; John S. Conner, Vincentian Fathers, Brooklyn; Thomas F. Stransky, Paulist Fathers, New York; Calvin Anderson, Washington Theological Union; Jim Seunarine, Division of World Outreach, United Church of Canada; Katherine Hockin, Ecumenical Forum of Canada.

I also wish to express my appreciation for the courtesy of the libraries and their staffs from which sources were drawn for this work. In California they are: Golden Gate Baptist Seminary, Mill Valley; San Francisco Theological Seminary, San Anselmo; Pacific School of Religion, Graduate Theological Union, Berkeley; Fuller Theological Seminary,

Pasadena; University of San Francisco. Other libraries where facilities and resources were used are the Maryknoll Seminary, New York and the Gulf Coast Bible College, Houston. Two schools which provided sources through library loans are Southwestern Baptist Seminary, Fort Worth, and Church Divinity School of the Pacific, Berkeley.

Finally, I wish to express special appreciation to Justice Anderson of Southwestern Baptist Seminary and formerly of the International Seminary in Buenos Aires for translating the material from *Heroes and Martyrs* by Juan C. Varetto.

This volume is sent forth with a sincere prayer that it will serve to whet the appetite of those who read it to delve further into the riches of the great missionary literature of the centuries, which by divine providence has been preserved for our spiritual enrichment and as a challenge to lead us into a more faithful life of service.

Francis M. DuBose

I

The Biblical and Theological Basis of Missions

General Introduction

The Christian mission as *event* and *idea* has its roots in the Scriptures. It is not surprising, therefore, that Christian writers from the early church fathers to the modern period have been preoccupied with the biblical basis of the missionary enterprise and the theological foundations which must form the basis of mission theory and practice. For example, Origen in a letter to his protégé, Gregory Thaumaturgus, about the year 230, appealed to the Scriptures in his vocational advice to his young admirer, who within a decade would become Bishop of Pontus and who in time would become the greatest missionary of his day (see part V, 18).

Recent works have ranged from such popular studies as Julian Price Love's, *The Missionary Message of the Bible* (1941), and Robert Hall Glover's, *The Bible Basis of Missions* (1964), to more scholarly works such as Johannes Blauw's *The Missionary Nature of the Church* (1962), and Ferdinand Hahn's *Mission in the New Testament* (1965). Writers continue to produce works on this vital theme. Two good examples are George W. Peters' *A Biblical Theology of Missions* (1972) and J. Herbert Kane's *Christian Missions in Biblical Perspective* (1976). An excellent example of a work which deals with the broader theological dimensions is a volume edited by Gerald H. Anderson entitled *The Theology of the Christian Mission* (1961).

The following selections illustrate the significance of biblical and theological principles in determining the nature of mission thought and practice. The four works are by a great missionary, a distinguished professor of missions, a renowned Old Testament scholar who began his teaching career in China, and one of the leading theologians of modern times.

1

"An Enquiry into the Obligations of Christians to Use Means for the Conversion of the Heathens" [1] William Carey

Introduction

Biblical and theological motivation was fuel for the fire which burned in the soul of William Carey and led to his revolutionary tract, "An Enquiry into the Obligations of Christians to Use Means for the Conversion of the Heathens." This document became the manifesto of the modern mission movement.

William Carey (1761-1834) was born in Paulerspury near Northampton, England. While he was an apprentice to a shoemaker and cobbler, he came under the influence of dissenters, had a deep conversion experience, and attached himself to the Baptists. Carey earned a living for his family by making and mending shoes, by teaching, and by serving as a pastor. He was an avid student, early acquiring the knowledge of several languages. His study of the Scriptures and knowledge of the work of John Eliot and David Brainerd among the American Indians led to a profound sense of mission. Although he was discouraged by the ultra-Calvinistic thinking of his Particular Baptist brethren, the example of the missionary labors of the Moravians challenged him. This led him in turn to challenge the then current hyper-Calvinism which advocated that God would save the heathen in his own time and in his own way. [2]

In 1792 Carey published his famous "An Enquiry." He argued convincingly that the New Testament command to "preach the gospel to every creature" was as binding upon the Christians of his day as it was upon the apostles. In addition to the scriptural argument which he gave, he surveyed the mission work which had been accomplished by Protestants and

Catholics up until that time, and he dealt in detail with all of the current objections to mission work. Later at a meeting of the Northampton Baptist Association in Nottingham in May of 1792, he preached a stirring sermon on Isaiah 44:2-3. It contained his famous statement, "Expect great things from God. Attempt great things for God." This sermon and the earlier tract "An Enquiry" were the main influences behind the meeting in Kettering on October 2, 1792, which convened for the purpose of organizing the Particular Baptist Society for Propagating the Gospel among the Heathen. The name was later shortened to the Baptist Missionary Society. Carey quite logically was the first to be sent out by the new society.[3]

Carey's field of labor was India. Early opposition by the empire-minded East India Company caused him to flee Calcutta and establish his headquarters in the Danish settlement of Serampore sixteen miles away. Joshua Marshman and William Ward joined him there, and the three constituted the remarkable "Serampore Trio." Apart from the phenomenal accomplishments of the team, Carey's feats as a missionary are almost unbelievable. He was an indefatigable worker, and his accomplishments are staggering to recount. Despite personal and domestic handicaps of health, he was able, in addition to his usual pastoral and preaching duties, to translate the Scriptures in whole or in part in thirty-seven different languages. Alone he produced a complete Bible in Sanskrit, Bengali, and Marathi. In addition to his work as a church planter, he founded Serampore College for the training of an indigenous Indian ministry. He founded the botanical gardens near Calcutta, which evoked the praise of all Asia. Carey also wrote Bengali colloquies which authorities have acknowledged as constituting the basis for modern Bengali prose. He distinguished himself both as a scholar and as a reformer. He became professor of Sanskrit and Bengali and played a significant leadership role in the abolition of Suttee, the practice of burning alive Hindu widows upon the pyres of their husbands.[4]

In addition to his incredible personal accomplishments as a missionary, Carey's influence upon the modern mission movement was profound. Whether he deserves to be called the father of modern missions may be open to question. Indeed he stood in a distinguished line of missionaries. He was not the first Protestant to go to India, and he drew inspiration from the Moravian missionaries who went before him. However, Carey's leadership marked a significant beginning. His spirit was contagious, and it was his vision more than any other that excited the whole international Christian community to a world missionary endeavor. His ideas and his model of missions in India inspired a long line of missionaries, missionary societies, and mission boards of denominations which spearheaded the greatest advance of missions in the history of Christianity.[5]

An Enquiry into the Obligations of Christians to Use Means for the Conversion of the Heathens

INTRODUCTION

As our blessed Lord has required us to pray that his kingdom may come, and his will be done on earth as it is in heaven, it becomes us not only to express our desires of that event by words but to use every lawful method to spread the knowledge of his name. In order to this, it is necessary that we should become, in some measure, acquainted with the religious state of the world; and as this is an object we should be prompted to pursue, not only by the gospel of our Redeemer, but even by the feelings of humanity, so an inclination to conscientious activity therein would form one of the strongest proofs that we are the subjects of grace, and partakers of that spirit of universal benevolence and genuine philanthropy which appears so eminent in the character of God himself.

Sin was introduced amongst the children of men by the fall of Adam, and has ever since been spreading its baneful influence. By changing its appearances to suit the circumstances of the times, it has grown up in ten thousand forms, and constantly counteracted the will and designs of God. One would have supposed that the remembrance of the deluge would have been transmitted from father to son, and have perpetually deterred mankind from transgressing the will of their Maker; but so blinded were they, that in the time of Abraham, gross wickedness prevailed wherever colonies were planted, and the iniquity of the Amorites was great, though not yet full. After this, idolatry spread more and more, till the seven devoted nations were cut off with the most signal marks of divine displeasure. Still, however, the progress of evil was not stopped, but the Israelites themselves too often joined with the rest of mankind against the God of Israel. In one period, the grossest ignorance and barbarism prevailed in the world; and afterwards, in a more enlightened age, the most daring infidelity, and contempt of God; so that the world, which was once overrun with ignorance, now *by wisdom knew not God, but changed the glory of the incorruptible God,* as much as in the most barbarous ages, into an image made like to corruptible man, and to birds, and four-footed beasts and creeping things. Nay, as they increased in science and politeness, they ran into more abundant and extravagant idolatries.

Yet God repeatedly made known his intention to prevail finally over all the power of the devil, and to destroy all his works, and set up his own kingdom and interest among men, and extend it as universally as Satan had extended his. It was for this purpose that the Messiah came and died, that God might be just, and the justifier of all that should believe in him. When he had laid down his life, and taken it up again, he sent forth his disciples to preach the good tidings to every creature, and to endeavor by all possible methods to bring over a lost world to God. They went forth according to their divine commission, and wonderful success attended their labors: the civilized Greeks, and uncivilized barbarians, each yielded to the cross of Christ, and embraced it as the only way of salvation. Since the apostolic age, many other attempts to spread the gospel have been made, which have been considerably successful, notwithstanding which a very considerable part of mankind are still involved in all the darkness of heathenism. Some attempts are still making, but they are inconsiderable in comparison of what might be done if the whole body of Christians entered heartily into the spirit of the divine command on this subject. Some think little about it, others are acquainted with the state of the world, and others love their wealth better than the souls of their fellow-creatures.

In order that the subject may be taken into more serious consideration, I shall enquire, whether the commission given by our Lord to his disciples be not still binding on us; take a short view of former undertakings; give some account of the present state of the world; consider the practicability of doing something more than is done; and the duty of Christians in general in this matter.

Section I

AN ENQUIRY WHETHER THE COMMISSION GIVEN BY OUR LORD TO HIS DISCIPLES BE NOT STILL BINDING ON US

Our Lord Jesus Christ, a little before his departure, commissioned his apostles to "Go, and teach all nations"; or, as another evangelist expresses it, "Go into all the world, and preach the gospel to every creature." This commission was as extensive as possible, and laid them under obligation to disperse themselves into every country of the habitable globe, and preach to all the inhabitants, without exception or limitation. They accordingly went forth in obedience to the command, and the power of God evidently wrought with them. Many attempts of the same kind have been made since their day, and which have been attended with various success; but the work has not been taken up, or prosecuted of late years (except by a few individuals) with that zeal and perseverance with which the primitive Christians went about it. It seems as if many thought the commission was sufficiently put in execution by what the apostles and others have done; that we have enough to do to attend to the salvation of our own countrymen; and that, if God intends the salvation of the heathen, he will some way or other bring them to the gospel, or the gospel to them. It is thus that multitudes sit at ease, and give themselves no concern about the far greater part of their fellow-sinners, who, to this day, are lost in ignorance and idolatry. There seems also to be an opinion existing in the minds of some, that because the apostles were extraordinary officers and have no proper successors, and because many things which were right for them to do would be utterly unwarrantable for us, therefore it may not be immediately binding on us to execute the commission, though it was so upon them. To the consideration of such persons I would offer the following observations:

First. If the command of Christ to teach all nations be restricted to the apostles, or those under the immediate inspiration of the Holy Ghost, then that of baptizing should be so too; and every denomination of Christians, except the Quakers, do wrong in baptizing with water at all.

Secondly. If the command of Christ to teach all nations be confined to the apostles, then all such ordinary ministers who have endeavored to carry the gospel to the heathens, have acted without a warrant, and run before they were sent. Yea, and though God has promised the most glorious things to the heathen world by sending his gospel to them, yet whoever goes first, or indeed at all, with that message, unless he have a new and special commission from heaven, must go without any authority for so doing.

Thirdly. If the command of Christ to teach all nations extend only to the apostles, then, doubtless, the promise of the divine presence in this work must be so limited; but this is worded in such a manner as expressly precludes such an idea: "Lo, I am with you alway, even to the end of the world."

That there are cases in which even a divine command may cease to be binding is admitted—as for instance: if it be *repealed,* as the ceremonial commandments of the Jewish law; or if there be *no subjects* in the world for the commanded act to be exercised upon, as in the law of Septennial Release, which might be dispensed with when there should be no poor in the land to have their debts forgiven (Deut. 15:4); or if, in any particular instance, we can produce a *counter-revelation,* of equal authority with the original command, as when Paul and Silas were forbidden of the Holy Ghost to preach the word in Bithynia (Acts 16:6, 7); or if, in any case, there be a *natural impossibility* of putting it in execution. It was not the duty of Paul to preach Christ to the inhabitants of Otaheite, because no such place was then discovered, nor had he any means of coming at them. But none of these things can be alleged by us in behalf of the neglect of the commission given by Christ. We cannot say that it is repealed, like the commands of the ceremonial law; nor can we plead that there are no objects for the command to be exercised upon. Alas! the far greater part of the world, as we shall see presently, is still covered with heathen darkness! Nor can we produce a counter-revelation, concerning any particular nation, like that to Paul and Silas, concerning Bithynia; and, if we could, it would not warrant our sitting still and neglecting all the other parts of the world. For Paul and Silas, when forbidden to preach to those heathens, went elsewhere, and preached to others. Neither can we allege a natural impossibility in the case. It has been said that we ought not to force our way, but to wait for the openings and leadings of providence; but it might with equal propriety be answered in this case, neither ought we to neglect embracing those openings in providence which daily present themselves to us. What openings of providence do we wait for? We can neither expect to be transported into the heathen world without ordinary means, nor to be endowed with the gift of tongues, etc., when we arrive there. These would not be providential interpositions, but miraculous ones. Where a command exists, nothing can be necessary to render it binding but a removal of those obstacles which render obedience impossible, and these are removed already. Natural impossibility can never be pleaded so long as facts exist to prove the contrary. Have not the popish missionaries surmounted all those difficulties which we have generally thought to be insuperable? Have not the missionaries of the Unitas Fratrum, or Moravian Brethren, encountered the scorching heat of Abyssinia, and the frozen climes of Greenland and Labrador, their difficult languages and savage manners? Or have not English traders, for the sake of gain, surmounted all those things which have generally been counted insurmountable obstacles in the way of preaching the gospel? Witness the trade to Persia, the East Indies, China and Greenland, yea, even the accursed slave trade on the coasts of Africa. Men can insinuate themselves into the favor of the most barbarous clans, and uncultivated tribes, for the sake of gain; and how different soever the circumstances of trading and preaching are, yet this will prove the possibility of ministers being introduced there; and if this is but thought a sufficient reason to make the experiment, my point is gained.

It has been said that some learned divines have proved from Scripture that the time is not yet come that the heathen should be converted, and that first the witnesses must be slain, and many other prophecies fulfilled. But admitting this to be the case (which I must doubt) yet if any objection is made from this against preaching to them immediately, it must be founded on one of these things: either that the secret purpose of God is the rule of our duty, and then it must be as bad to pray for them as to preach to them; or else that none shall be converted in the heathen world till the universal downpouring of the Spirit in the last days. But this objection comes too late; for the success of the gospel has been very considerable in many places already.

It has been objected that there are multitudes in our own nation, and within our immediate spheres of action, who are as ignorant as the South Sea savages, and that therefore we have work enough at home, without going into other countries. That there are thousands in our own land as far from God as possible, I readily grant, and that this ought to excite us to tenfold diligence in our work, and in attempts to spread divine knowledge amongst them, is a certain fact; but that it ought to supersede all attempts to spread the gospel in foreign parts seems to want proof. Our own countrymen have the means of grace, and many attend on the word preached if they choose it. They have the means of knowing the truth, and faithful ministers are placed in almost every part of the land, whose spheres of action might be much extended if their congregations were but more hearty and active in the cause. But with them the case is widely different, who have no Bible, no written language (which many of them have not), no ministers, no good civil government, nor any of those advantages which we have. Pity, therefore, humanity, and much more Christianity, call loudly for every possible exertion to introduce the gospel amongst them.

. . . .

2

Missions in the Plan of the Ages[6]
William Owen Carver

Introduction

William Owen Carver's *Missions in the Plan of the Ages,* first published in 1909, is more than a biblical rationale for the missionary enterprise.[7] It is a missionary interpretation of the biblical message. It is an interpretation of Christianity in terms of its missionary nature. The value of such a work lies in the fact that it places missions at the very heart of the faith. It is a biblical study in that it expounds the rich missionary ideas of the Scriptures. It is a theological study in that it defines mission not simply by prooftexts but on the basis of the very meaning of the Bible and the very nature of the faith it describes. Even though modern writers would use the singular *mission* rather than the plural *missions* to refer to the missionary idea, Carver's use of the less euphonious plural form ("missions is") does not take from the majesty of his definitions. He locates the origins of missions ultimately in the heart of God, historically in the life, work, and command of Jesus, and practically in the very essence and spirit of the Christian faith.

William Owen Carver (1868-1954) was born in Wilson County, Tennessee. He studied at Boyle College, Tennessee; Richmond College; and Southern Baptist Theological Seminary. He first served as a pastor and as a teacher of philosophy and languages. He began his teaching career at Southern Baptist Theological Seminary in 1896 in the fields of New Testament, homiletics, and theology. In 1899 he became professor of comparative religion and missions, a post he held until retirement in 1943. In 1907, he founded the Woman's Missionary Training School and taught there a number of years. After his death, the school became Carver School of Missions and Social Work. He was managing editor of the *Review and Expositor* from 1920 to 1942, and was one of the founders of the Southern Baptist Historical Society. He wrote twenty books, a number of which were directly on the subject of missions. Besides *Missions in the Plan of the Ages,* those related directly to missions are: *Missions and Modern Thought* (1910), *All the World in All the Word* (1918), *The Bible, a Missionary Message* (1921), *The Course of Christian Missions* (1932),

The Furtherance of the Gospel (1935), *Christian Missions in Today's World* (1942).[8]

In addition to his contribution as an author and missionary statesman, Carver holds the honor of occupying the first professorship of missions in the United States. It was established at Southern Baptist Theological Seminary in 1899.[9] The first professorship of Christian missions ever to be formed was in Edinburgh, Scotland in 1867. The second was established in 1896 (1897) at the University of Halle in Germany.[10] Only these two antedate the professorship at Southern Seminary.

The Missionary Idea in the Bible

I. DEFINITION

Missions mean the extensive realization of God's redemptive purpose in Christ by means of human messengers.

It is not possible closely to mark missions off from other work in that kingdom of God which it is ever the first duty of every disciple to seek. It will be suggestive to say that missions introduce the kingdom of heaven which other work deepens and develops in the extent and power of its influence in the whole life of man. Missions is the proclamation of the Good News of the kingdom where it is *news;* further evangelization and ministration make manifest the *goodness* of the news, emphasizing and applying it in the varied relations of our life. It is too common an error to mark off by geographical lines missionary work from other phases of evangelization.

Jehovah is "the Judge of all the earth" [11] and "His kingdom ruleth over all." [12] God's ideal includes all this and more. As expressed in the Christ it is that His kingdom shall rule *within* all. It is the spiritual ideal, wherein all shall know God, from the least to the greatest.[13] The Divine Logos was in the world and the world was made through Him and yet the world did not know Him. He was indeed the true Light lighting every man who comes into the world; and yet as the Life-light of men He shines in a darkness that not only fails to "apprehend" the Light, but even resists and seeks to "overcome" it.[14] Missions is the agency through which the people that walk in darkness come to see the Great Light and by which the Light shines upon them that are dwelling in the land of deep darkness.[15]

We shall see how fully the Scriptures teach that for this age the Father and the Son have appointed missions as the process for approaching the ideal of God's spiritual reign on earth.

II. ORIGIN

1. The origin of missions is *ultimately* to be found in the heart of God. His are the redemptive purpose and plan. No thought of God is true to His revelation of Himself that does not rest on the fact that He "so loved the world that He gave His only begotten Son" that by believing in Him "the world should be saved through Him." [16] It was God that was "in Christ reconciling the world unto Himself, not reckoning their trespasses unto them" [17]; and not so reckoning for the reason that this love-sent Son "is the propitiation for the whole world." [18] This attitude of God is eternal and is determinative in all His dealings with men. He is ever working towards the end that "they who have not heard" may have "the glad tidings preached unto them"; that "they who were no people may come to be a people of God's own possession." [19] So it is that when men come to be God's "ambassadors on behalf of Christ" they must go to all ignorant and erring men beseeching them "to be reconciled unto God." [20]

In our time this missionary idea of God is playing a large part in saving our theology and vitalizing it with a new life.

Modern missions more than all else have fostered the true idea of the Father love of God for sinful and incomplete men. In speculative theology two imperfect views have been in sharp conflict. One school has insisted on the judicial interpretation of God, to be moved in behalf of man only by the bloody persuasion of a crucified Christ. In this view God meets Christ for man only on Ascension day. Another school, as narrowly speculative as the first, interprets God sentimentally and finds the Christ practically serviceable for impressing men but not essential to man's redemption. The theology of missions—the theology that produces missions and is fostered by missions—interprets God as revealed in Christ: "God was in Christ reconciling the world unto *Himself.*" [21] It is missions that have done most, although, it may be, largely indirectly, to give currency to this conception of God, so vital in the Christianity of our time. It is sometimes thought that the Old Testament view of God is more largely judicial. But we must remember that in the Old Testament the Redeemer is not very clearly distinguishable from Jehovah God, and when a "Daysman" does stand between man and God he comes from Jehovah and as the Servant of Jehovah to redeem His people—all people. In the one Old Testament passage where the Redeemer is the Son of Jehovah this sonship is of the essence of Jehovah. The Old Testament bears elaborate evidence that God moves in universal love to men for centuries before He is manifest as Immanuel—God-with-us. Such is the theology of missions which take their rise in the heart of God. An exclusively "forensic theology" hindered the beginning of modern missions; an exclusively sentimental theology hampers the progress of missions.

2. The *historical* origin of missions is found in the work, the life, the command of Jesus Christ projected in the lives of His followers. Like every other "fact of Christ" missions have foundation and preparation in the prior history of God's dealing with men, recorded in the Old Testament. How abundantly this is true we hope in some measure to set forth in these studies. The culmination of the preparation for, and the historical beginning of, God's out-reaching for a lost world, as contrasted with what we may call His previous down-reaching, are to be found in the Christ.

In the fact of incarnation there lies already the implication of race conquest. And since God has become man to bring men to God it must be that as men become identified with this redeeming God they will extend and hasten His endeavor.

As the Light enlightens men they must themselves shine forth as luminaries among men.[22] In the Prologue of John's Gospel [23] there is the clearest identification of the Word with the entire race of men, and not with any one section of it. His preincarnate relations are presented with no limitations but with the most emphatic universalism. To be sure in His earthly life the Logos comes to "that which was His own"; but there is immediately revealed a deep contrast between this providential and potential ownership and that vital and actual ownership which alone He recognizes. Those of His own that received Him must have His "authority to become children of God," and as such children need a nature "not of blood, nor of the will of the flesh, nor of the will of man, but of God." "The Word became flesh," not Jew, nor Greek, nor Barbarian, but essential humanity. Again we read, "No man hath seen God at any time," Jewish man and Greek man included without distinction; and to all classes "the only begotten Son who is in the bosom of the Father hath declared Him."

Missions mean that every one who comes to the bosom of the Son, and so to the knowledge of the Father, in his turn also declares Him to mankind.

Various events connected with the advent of the Son of God, in the infancy of Jesus, proclaim the universalism of His mission. In the records of Matthew and Luke in the midst of simple-hearted Jewish people, cherishing the best elements of a too narrow Messianism, we seem to be moving in an atmosphere of universalism. The conscious concepts of Zecharias and Joseph, of Elizabeth and Mary, of the shepherds and of Anna may well enough have been limited to Jewish redemption; but they were spiritual conceptions and as such must needs express themselves in terms that most readily lead to universal applications. In these days of the Son of God to express their thoughts angels and men drew on the prophets of universal Messianism, Daniel and Isaiah, and the Messianic psalms. Mary discerns that in her Son God will fulfill His word of "mercy towards Abraham and his seed forever," [24] a word which God, certainly, meant to include blessing for all mankind.

The Angel Chorus [25] was of a universal peace, however it seemed to the shepherds. Simeon, by special warrant awaiting the sight of the Lord's Christ, when he held Him at length in his arms, blessed God and said:

". . . Mine eyes have seen Thy salvation
Which Thou hast prepared *before the face of all peoples,*
A light for revelation to the Gentiles
And the glory of Thy people Israel." [26]

He puts first the "revelation to the Gentiles," reversing the order of Isaiah, in both 42:6 and 49:6. In the visit of the Magi and their worship [27] there is universalism, in the fact itself, in the necessary antecedents of the fact and in the inevitable consequences of their visit and the knowledge with which they returned to their own lands.

The work of Jesus, although technically limited to "the lost sheep of the House of Israel," [28] nevertheless constantly transgressed current

Jewish ideals and in some examples, at once prophetic and characteristic, went beyond the limits of His assigned mission. Thus was His work true to the essential universalism of its spirit, a spirit that did not, because it could not, fail to impress all classes in His own generation. Jesus aroused the enmity of His opposers, the suspicions of His friends, and the hopes of the aliens, that in His thinking and work, man, and not Jew merely, was the aim.

In the teaching of Jesus, both in its general terms and principles and in specific precept, He laid the foundation for, and enjoined upon all His followers, universal missionary work. Leaving details for later exposition it will be sufficient now to note the general facts. The Jewish leaders had more than an instinctive feeling that in the word and work of this Teacher lay the germs of a universal love and aim incompatible with, and destructive of, exclusive privileges for themselves and their nation. It was in large measure His liberalism that inspired their hatred and urged them on to accomplish His death.

Jesus' favorite designation of Himself was "Son of Man." His choice may well have been influenced by the fact that this was the characteristic Messianic term. That it identified Him with every man and all men was a stronger reason and was also the explanation of the employment of the term by the prophets. Jesus has ever in mind the needs of man when He interprets the Law, the traditions, the obligation of the Sabbath, His own message, and His death that will draw all men unto Him.

It is in the effort of His followers to interpret their Master's mind that we have the four Gospels which set forth the universal Gospel distinctly conceived to be aggressively designed for all humanity.

3. The *practical* origin of missions. If ultimately missions arise from the heart of Him who is "Lord of all and rich unto all that call upon Him;" [29] if historically missions begin in the life and word of the Son of Man who is come to seek and to save that which was lost; continuously missions spring from the very spirit of our religion. In its very essence Christianity is a propaganda. It goes forth for conquest in the name of its Lord. The Christian is full of loving concern for men and emptied of selfish aims. In a world of need he is a channel of supply; in a world of darkness, himself some time darkness, he is now light in the Lord [30] and must illuminate the darkness; in a world of death he is an agent of Life.

The Christian life is a life begun and sustained by the Holy Spirit. But the Holy Spirit is first of all the witness-bearer of Jesus the Redeemer.[31] It cannot but be that Christians, too, bear witness when they know Jesus. Whenever Christianity has been true to its origin and faithful to its spirit, wherever it has been spiritual—marked by the Spirit's presence—it has been crying, in the wilderness, of the kingdom of God come among men. There is no separation of the missionary impulse from a true and vital Christianity. The antecedent conditions, the initial facts, the continuous experience of any one into whom the life of God has come all move him to make known his Saviour.

. . . .

3

The Missionary Message of the Old Testament[32]
H. H. Rowley

Introduction

The significance of H. H. Rowley's small book on *The Missionary Message of the Old Testament* is in the fact that it was written from the standpoint of critical Old Testament scholarship, though the style is somewhat popular. In this study Rowley deals with "The Foundations of the Message," "Visions of the Goal," "The Mission and Its Method," and "The Heirs of the Mission." In his understanding of "Foundations," he sees Moses not only as the first missionary but as the personality through whom the foundations were laid both for the missionary message of Israel and the missionary activity of the Christian church. G. Ernest Wright's definitive essay, "The Old Testament Basis for the Christian Mission," builds upon the concepts of Rowley expressed in his classic little volume.[33]

Harold Henry Rowley was born in Leicester, England in 1890. He studied at the Bristol Baptist College and the universities of Bristol and Oxford. He was a Baptist. In 1922, he became a missionary to China where he taught Old Testament at the Shantung Christian University until 1929. He returned to England in 1930, and distinguished himself as a scholar in the field of Semitic languages and the Old Testament. He was professor of Semitic language at the University College of North Wales, Bangor, and professor of Hebrew at the Victoria University of Manchester. He wrote fourteen books on themes relating to the Old Testament and Semitic languages. Among his works are: *The Aramaic of the Old Testament* (1929), *Israel's Mission to the World* (1939), and *The Rediscovery of the Old Testament* (1946).[34]

The Foundations of the Message

. . . .

Moses was the first missionary of whom we have any knowledge. Jehovah sent him to the Israelites in Egypt not alone to save them and to lead them out, but to bring them to worship Him. He was adopting them to be His people, and He needed Moses to be His messenger to them. We are told that hitherto they had worshipped El Shaddai, and did not know Jehovah as their God. But Moses claimed them for Jehovah by saying that He was really the same as the God of their fathers. This is what is called syncretism, and it is common in the history of religion. Sometimes it lifts a lower religion to the level of a higher; sometimes it brings a higher down to the level of a lower. Paul came to the people of Athens, and claimed for God the worship offered to the Unknown God, saying: "Whom therefore ye ignorantly worship, Him declare I unto you." And when missionaries went to China they identified God with the Shang Ti of Chinese religion, so that in the Bibles most widely used in China to-day Shang Ti stands everywhere instead of God, and Jehovah is declared to be Shang Ti. But Moses, Paul, and Christian missionaries came to bring a new and richer content to the old worship, and to lift it to a higher level. The exact opposite took place when the children of Israel reached Canaan, and identified Jehovah with Baal. For they brought the higher religion that Moses had given them down to the level of the religion of Canaan.

That Moses brought some of the Israelite tribes out of Egypt is allowed by everyone, and too often his work is thought of merely as the political achievement of leading them out and welding them together with a national consciousness that centered in the Kenite worship of Jehovah. This seems to me very inadequate. For he did not merely get them to adopt the Kenite religion. Though Jehovah was the Kenite God before Moses became His missionary to Israel, the Jehovah worship that Moses established was very different from that of the Kenites. It meant more to Israel than it had ever meant to the Kenites because of the very way it came to them, and the amazing experience of deliverance which they had. Moreover, the Jehovah worship which Moses established was higher in character than that of the Kenites. For it was mediated to Israel through the prophetic personality of Moses, who gave it a new quality.

His mission was fulfilled first of all in the great act of deliverance. Pharaoh was compelled by no human hand and by no strength of the Israelites to let them go, and when he repented and pursued them he was involved in a disaster of which the Israelites were but the spectators and not the agents. The wind blew the waters back and uncovered a wide stretch of sand across which the Israelites hastened; and when the Egyptians with their heavy chariots tried to follow, they sank into the soft sand, and the wind turned and swept the waters back upon them and overwhelmed them. The deliverance is attributed to the convenient action of wind and wave. But that does not eliminate God from it, or turn it into a natural coincidence from which all miracle is removed. Such a view is very shallow and inadequate. For while the timely action of wind and wave might be supposed to be no more than a coincidence, it could not possibly explain the confidence of Moses beforehand that deliverance would be achieved. For remember that he had gone into Egypt and promised the people deliverance in the name of Jehovah. The winds and waves did not merely respond to the need of Israel, therefore, but to the word of Moses. And Moses spoke that word as a prophet. That is to say, he profoundly believed that it was not his own word, but God's. Moreover, while the deliverance was wrought by no human hand, it was wrought for men who had faith in the prophetic word of Moses, and who had launched themselves in faith on the course to which he called them. Faith was necessary to their deliverance, yet it was not by their faith that they were delivered, but by the forces of Nature that were moved by the hand of God.

Nor did the mission of Moses end there. Rather did it begin there. For he led the people to the sacred mountain and there they pledged themselves in a solemn covenant to the God who had delivered them. That covenant was not a sordid bargain, or a legal contract. It was the pledge of undeviating loyalty to God made in gratitude by those whom He had delivered. And implicit in the making of that pledge was the conception of religion as man's response to the achieved salvation of God. That was something the Kenites had never known, and therefore at the heart of the Jehovah worship of these people whom Moses led was something new and unique. They chose the God Who had first chosen them, and found the divine initiative at the root of their religion.

To that religion Moses gave an ethical character in advance of that of the Kenites. It is probable that the Kenites had a Decalogue, but a much more primitive one than the familiar one of Exodus xx. It was concerned with ritual, rather than with ethical, duties. And when the southern tribes took over the worship of Jehovah by gradual penetration, they took over that primitive Decalogue, and modified it slightly to adapt it to the needs of a settled community. It is that primitive Decalogue, adapted to suit a settled community, that we find in Exodus xxxiv, though in its present form there are thirteen, instead of an original ten, words. But Moses was not content with such a Decalogue, and to the tribes he led he gave a new and higher Decalogue, which we have in an expanded form in Exodus xx and Deuteronomy v. It is frequently said that this Decalogue must be much later than the time of Moses, and that it reflects the teaching of the great eighth century prophets. I cannot see why. For, as I have said, Moses showed as ethical an indignation against oppression before he fled from Egypt as Amos did centuries later. But at first it was merely ethics, instead of ethics rooted and grounded in religion, ethics born of the vision of God and arising from the will of God. But in his call his indignation and sympathy were lifted into the service of God, and related to the character and will of God. And then Moses established the Covenant of Sinai on gratitude, which is an essentially ethical emotion. Why should it then be surprising that he gave an ethical character to the demands of this religion? He was not merely introducing Israel to the God of the Kenites. He was a great prophetic person, through whom this God was doing a new thing in the world, and a new quality was given to the religion he established in Israel.

That ethical religion reached greater heights in the prophets of the eighth and seventh centuries may be agreed. But that there was an ethical strain in Israelite religion before their day is patent to the reader of the Bible. Nathan's rebuke of David, and Elijah's of Ahab, cannot be pronounced unethical. There is no reason to suppose that ethical religion began with Nathan, but there is ample reason to credit the ascription of the familiar Decalogue to Moses, and to find there the beginnings of ethical religion in the first establishment of the religion of Jehovah amongst the tribes Moses led. And if the primitive Decalogue of Exodus xxxiv represents the quality of the Jehovah worship that was practised amongst the tribes that derived it from the Kenites apart from Moses, and the Decalogue of Exodus xx represents the quality of that which was established by Moses, we have a sufficient explanation of the difference between them.

There are some modern scholars who maintain that Moses attained full monotheism, but most deny this. In support of the view that he reached monotheism, it is sometimes pointed out that he would still not be the first monotheist of whom we have knowledge. In the age in which I have placed the going down into Egypt and the career of Joseph, there was a Pharaoh of Egypt who is famous for his religious reform. This was the Pharaoh Amenhotep IV, who forbade all worship in Egypt except the worship of the sun god of Heliopolis. This god was worshipped under the name of Aton, and his symbol was the disk of the sun with rays stretching downwards, each ending with a hand. The Pharaoh changed his name to Ikhnaton, confiscated all the revenues of the rich Theban priesthood of Amen, and moved his capital from Thebes to a new city which he built, and which he called Akhetaton. Hitherto the priests of Amen had provided most of the chief officers of state, and hence this is just the time when the king would look for other talent to help administer the kingdom. While there is no reference to Joseph in the Egyptian records, there is evidence that the Pharaoh employed Semites in the state service. It is also significant to note that the Bible says the Pharaoh gave Joseph the daughter of the priest of On, or Heliopolis, to wife. In no age would it be quite so great an honour to marry this priest's daughter as in the time of Ikhnaton.

That Ikhnaton was a monotheist is probable, though the fact that in the famous Hymn to Aton, which has been found at Tel el Amarna, the modern name of the ruined site of Akhetaton, Aton is addressed as "Thou sole God, whose powers no other possesseth" does not prove it. For similar phrases are found elsewhere without implying monotheism. That Ikhnaton desired to substitute the worship of a single god for the multiplicity of gods hitherto worshipped in Egypt is certain, and equally so that his idea of God was lofty and pure. Extravagant claims are sometimes made for him, and it is even suggested that in him religion reached a higher level than anywhere in the world before the time of our Lord. Such claims I am not disposed to endorse. His religious interest does not seem to have gone beyond the borders of his kingdom, or to have attained anything like the same fullness and richness that marked the Old Testament prophets. But that he was in all probability a monotheist may be allowed.

Yet it is improbable that Moses was in any way influenced by Ikhnaton, or thought of monotheism as a theological principle. He was only concerned with the group of tribes which he led out of Egypt, and he did for them something far higher and more significant than proclaim an abstract idea of the unity of God. He sought to establish the worship of Jehovah as the only worship practised by these tribes and to give to that worship an emotional and ethical quality of unique worth. Yet in his work there was an incipient monotheism, and he planted the seed that germinated and later produced the full flower of the monotheism at which we shall later look.

The first word of the Decalogue is "Thou shalt have none other gods before me." This is not a denial of the reality of any other gods beside Jehovah, but a declaration that no other god is a legitimate object of Israel's worship. He demands the exclusive worship of the people He has adopted. In the old primitive Decalogue to which I have already referred, the Decalogue employed by the group that Moses did not lead, we have this same word. For there we read: "Thou shalt worship no other god"; and the comment is added: "for Jehovah, Whose name is Jealous, is a jealous God." This demand for exclusive worship therefore appears to belong to Jehovah worship from before the time of Moses, and it does not involve monotheism. It does not question the legitimacy of the worship of other gods by other peoples, but simply demands that Jehovah should be the sole God of those who worshipped Him. And not seldom it is supposed that this is as far as the work of Moses carries us. Actually it carries us a long step beyond that on the road to monotheism.

For whether Moses regarded other gods as real or not, he certainly regarded them as negligible. Jehovah adopted Israel, and absorbed into His worship whatever religion they had hitherto practised, and manifested His power in Egypt. It was not merely that He was able to exercise His power upon the people He had chosen for Himself, or to protect them from their enemies. He was able to exercise His power over the Egyptians and over their land. All Nature lay in the hollow of His hand, and His was the only power that counted. His mighty acts are not presented as a trial of strength between Jehovah and the Egyptian gods. They do not figure in the story, save as subject to His judgement. The Egyptian magicians figure in the story, trying to match their skill against that of Moses and Aaron, but the gods are an irrelevance, and Jehovah does as He pleases in the land of Egypt. This is more than the demand that though other gods may be real, Israel must not worship them. It is rather the declaration that though other gods may be real they are unimportant.

Great theological ideas were therefore implicit in the work of Moses, and gradually, in the centuries that followed, those ideas were more clearly unfolded, and their corollaries were seen.

. . . .

While, therefore, it is improbable that Moses attained full monotheism, or that either he or any other Israelite of anything like such an age perceived the full implications of election, it is insufficient for us to rest satisfied with this negative position. We should ever view the Old Testament dynamically and not statically, and find in its ideas an impelling power which drove men forward to something richer and fuller. When we distinguish between the germ and the fruit let us not forget that it is from the germ that the fruit developed. And for the missionary message of the Old Testament it is desirable to start back here at the roots of Old Testament religion, with the man who was the first missionary known to history. For Moses was a giant amongst men, and the relevance of his work and of the ideas which lay at its root to the religion of men is far from exhausted. In him were the foundations laid, and not least the foundations of the missionary message of Israel, and the missionary activity of the Christian Church.

4

"An Exegetical Study of Matthew 28:16-20"[35]
Karl Barth

Introduction

The significance of Karl Barth's "An Exegetical Study of Matthew 28:16-20" lies in the fact that it is a profound piece of mission literature by one of the leading theologians of the twentieth century. As any student of Barth is well aware, he took seriously the missionary implication of Christian doctrine. This study is a microcosm of Barth's idea of mission. The exegesis is replete with striking sentences that reveal graphically Barth's creative understanding of the missionary nature of Christianity. Concerning verse 19 he says: "Make them what you yourselves are! . . . Call them unto the twelve of the eschatological Israel! . . . We have already noticed the strangeness of Biblical arithmetic. The twelve are designed to be countless . . . the apostles are called to make apostolic Christians of all others."

Karl Barth was born in Basel in 1886. He studied at the Universities of Bern, Berlin, Tuebingen, and Marburg. He was a pastor from 1909 to 1921, at which time he became a professor. While he was professor at Bonn, he was a leader in the resistance movement against Hitler. This led to his explusion in 1935. He then became professor of theology at Basel. Barth's theological work soon became widely recognized. He was the acknowledged leader of the movement in theology which sought to turn the tide of liberalism and call Christian theology back to its biblical roots. This movement, which has been variously known as the "theology of crisis," "dialectical theology," or "neoorthodoxy," was based in part upon Reformation confessions. However, Barth's rejection of Calvin's doctrine of predestination and views on eschatology, leaves him somewhat out of the main Reformation tradition. His voluminous works, especially his *Church Dogmatics,* have made a significant impact on modern theological thought.[36] Barth's influence upon the modern missionary enterprise has been both direct and indirect. His most conspicuous indirect influence has been upon such men as Hendrik Kraemer, whose definitive studies made a major impact upon mission thought (see part ix, 42).

An Exegetical Study of Matthew 28:16-20

Now the eleven disciples went to Galilee, to the mountain to which Jesus had directed them. And when they saw him they worshiped him; but some doubted. And Jesus came and said to them, "All authority in heaven and on earth has been given to me. Go therefore and make disciples of all nations, baptizing them in the name of the Father and of the Son and of the Holy Spirit, teaching them to observe all that I have commanded you; and lo, I am with you always, to the close of the age." MATTHEW 28:16-20

. . . .

Verses 19-20a

This is the crucial affirmation of the whole text. It is the charge and commission of the risen Jesus, the authority for which was asserted in verse 18.

"Go therefore and make disciples . . ." Make them what you yourselves are! Have them learn here, with me, where you yourselves have learned! Call them into the twelve of the eschatological Israel! Let them share in its place and task in the world!

We have already noticed the strangeness of Biblical arithmetic. The twelve are designed to be countless. In the same manner as Jesus "made" apostles from the first disciples (Mk. 3:14-15), the apostles are called to make apostolic Christians of all others. The kingly ministry of the Messiah is here entrusted to the first disciples constituting the king's troops.

The sweeping imperative, "Go therefore," rests on the authority which is given to Jesus. As soon as his authority is announced in verse 18 there follows the charge, "make disciples!" The reminiscence of the "sending" in Matthew 10 and of its parallel in Mark 16:15, " 'Go into all the world and preach the gospel to the whole creation,' " largely obscures the peculiarity of our text. The same reality is envisaged here as in chapter 10. Yet there it appears in its implicit and hidden form, while here in its explicit and visible form. In both instances the founding, through Jesus' word, of the *apostolic* Church is envisaged. It is the Church that receives the apostles' word and actively transmits it. " 'As the Father has sent me, even so I send you' " (Jn. 20:21). This apostolic Church, existing not for itself, but "for Christ," on behalf of him (2 Cor. 5:20), is the decisive event of the *eschaton* that has broken into time. The existence of the new community consists not only in the apostles' preaching of the Gospel and their fellow men's listening. It is constantly renewed as the listeners themselves become "apostolic" and, as new disciples, begin to proclaim the good news. Consequently the charge is not only κηρύξατε but μαθητεύσατε, "make disciples." John 17:20-23 might well be the appropriate commentary to this charge. " 'I do not pray for these only, but also for those who are to believe in me through their word, that they may all be one; even as thou, Father, art in me, and I in thee, that they also may be in us, so that the world may believe that thou hast sent me . . . and hast loved them even as thou hast loved me.' "

And now the great problem of our text:

". . . *all nations* . . ." πάντα τὰ ἔθνη. On the basis of these words the text is called "the great commission." What does "all nations" mean?

It means, first of all, *people* from among all nations who are received into discipleship. They become significant for the existence of their respective nations because the nations now come within reach of the apostolate and its proclamation and receive their concealed center through the Christian community living in their midst. Note the αὐτούς, which occurs twice. It cannot refer to ἔθνη. Not the nations as such are made disciples. This interpretation once infested missionary thinking and was connected with the painful fantasies of the German Christians. It is worthless.

"All nations" means, furthermore, people from Gentile lands, from the *goyim*. This does not exclude Israel. Her right of the firstborn, her *dignitas primogeniturae*, as Calvin called it, remains unimpaired. Yet the disciples are summoned to go out to the Gentile people and nations. For now the eschatological Israel shall appear, the people gathered by the Messiah who appeared at the end of time. This is the new eschatological community. It is gathered from among the Jews and Gentiles. The doors and windows of the house of Israel, so far closed, must open. The apostles' mission is "to the Jew first and also to the Greek" (Rom. 1:16). Accordingly, Mark 16:15 states, " 'Go into all the world and preach the gospel to the whole creation.' " Matthew expresses the same idea, only in more concrete terms, when he speaks of "all nations." Through this mission the community of Jesus becomes manifest in his resurrection as the universal community. It is the eschatological Israel, the Israel which receives into its life and history the chosen ones from among the Gentiles. In fact it had never been anything else. Even during his life before death Jesus had never given it any other foundation than that which now became apparent: not as a special community within Israel, and hence not as a new form of the previous Israel in history, but as the Israel of the end of time, fulfilling the destiny of the historical Israel, as "a covenant to the people, a light to the nations" (Is. 42:6, 49:8). It is important to see this. Already the relationship to verse 18 and its parallels rules out any limitation of Jesus' dominion. How could he, to whom all power is given, have ever intended founding a pious little Jewish club? The name of the "Son of man" is the name of him whom "all peoples, nations, and languages" shall serve (Dan. 7:14). The field where the Son of man sows the good seed is the world (Mt. 13:38). The ransom for many (ἀντὶ πολλῶν Mk. 10:45) and the shedding of blood for many (ὑπὲρ πολλῶν) certainly imply Jesus' identification with the suffering servant of God in Isaiah 53 (see in particular verses 11-12). Of him it is said, " 'It is too light a thing that you should be my servant to raise up the tribes of Jacob and to restore the preserved of Israel; I will give you as a light to the nations, that my salvation may reach to the end of the earth' " (Is. 49:6). "He shall be exalted and lifted up, and shall be very high. . . . So shall he startle many nations; kings shall shut their mouths because of him" (Is. 52:13 f.). From the very beginning Jesus calls his disciples "the salt of the earth" and "the light of the world" (Mt. 5:13-14). Already John the Baptist had proclaimed that God would raise up children to Abraham from the stones (Mt. 3:9). Jesus himself spoke of the many that will come from east and west and sit at table with the patriarchs (Mt. 8:11); of the angels whom the Son of man shall sent out at the Parousia to gather his elect from the four winds, from one end of heaven to the other (Mt. 24:31; see also 25:31 f.); of the servants that will go out to the streets and gather all they find, both bad and good (Mt. 22:9 f.); even of the testimony his disciples will bear also before the Gentiles (Mt. 10:18).

Jesus at first kept this universality of the new community relatively hidden, as he did with the power and authority given him (verse 18), and with the name of Messiah (Mt. 16:20). Why? The previous, historical, Israel had not yet run its course before Jesus' death. His life had not yet been spent as a ransom for many. Not everything was ready yet. The table had not been set. The guests could not yet be invited. Israel was not yet fully prepared to fulfill its eschatological mission. Aware of this "not yet," Jesus understood his mission to be—temporarily—to the lost sheep of the house of Israel. But even as he pronounced this rule, he made an exception (Mt. 15:24). In the very strange passage of Mark 4:10-12 an even stricter rule is announced. Initially he did "not yet" address himself directly and properly to the whole people of Israel, but only to his disciples. Aware of this "not yet" he charged his disciples to go—temporarily—nowhere among the Gentiles and to enter no town of the Samaritans (Mt. 10:5). This "not yet" again overshadows the relative seclusion of the primitive apostles in Jerusalem. They had first to overcome their reluctance to get in touch with the Gentiles (Act 10), and finally entrusted Paul with the mission to the Gentiles (Gal. 2). Nevertheless, while this "not yet" casts its shadows even over the time after Easter, it was in fact overcome. The great turning point in history had since been marked. The "delivering" of Jesus to the Gentiles, foretold in the second and third announcements of his imminent suffering, had taken place (Mt. 27:2). This event separates the times. Now the eschatological Israel begins. Jesus' rejection by the Jews becomes the offer of grace to the Gentiles. In the rejection and death of its Messiah, the history of Israel has reached its end and goal; the hidden church of Jews and Gentiles awaits its revelation. The messianic Israel is in fact revealed by the words of verse 19. What does it matter if the revelation was apparently not fully realized right away? The number twelve of the eschatological Israel is even externally again complete by the addition of Paul. The activity of the apostles must set in with this very revelation: "Make disciples of all nations."

This "all nations" in no way contradicts the earlier teaching and practice of Jesus. The narrow path within Israel had to branch out into the wide world of all nations, and the inroad into the wide world had to begin as the narrow path within Israel. "Salvation is from the Jews" (Jn. 4:22). From the *Jews*—this is the first, limited, and hidden form of the eschatological community, represented by the eleven. Salvation *comes* from the Jews—to the Gentiles—this is its second, unlimited, and manifest form, represented by the eleven plus one.

To say that the primitive apostles acted as if they had not heard the Great Commission (J. Weiss, Klostermann) is misleading. Already the eleven, as Jesus saw and addressed them, are the eleven plus one who shall carry out the mission. The Church as a body will obey the command: its proclamation, first exclusively addressed to Israel, is immediately understood by the Jews of all lands in their own language (Acts 2:6 f.). Spread by Paul, the twelfth apostle, it becomes the message to the Gentiles.

It is therefore not necessary to draw upon the assumption of a "backward projection on the part of the later Church" (Klostermann) in order to explain verse 19. Nor do we have to declare the commission as "interpolated," to justify the mission to the Gentiles by the "supra-Jewish substance of the Gospel," and to find its Magna Charta in the history of "early Christian missions" (J. Weiss). As recapitulation and anticipation, revealing the hidden reality of the eschatological community, the Great Commission is truly the most genuine utterance of the risen Jesus.

". . . baptizing them in the name of the Father and of the Son and of the Holy Spirit." The making of disciples is achieved by baptism and teaching.

Baptizing is the priestly function of objectively introducing others into the realm of God's reign. Initially it is the function of Jesus himself.

Yet here he transmits it to his first disciples after he had them taste in advance the fruit of his sacrificial death—at the Last Supper—and then had suffered death.

Baptizing in a *name* meant, in the Jewish custom of the day, to administer to someone a cleansing bath intended to certify a state to be attained. A Gentile slave, for instance, was administered baptism as a sign of his liberation when he left. Baptizing in the name of the Father and of the Son and of the Holy Spirit means to give to someone the cleansing bath which certifies to him and to others that he belongs to this God. Father, Son, and Holy Spirit, then, are for him what the name of the triune God really stands for. He in turn has to confess and to confirm that he belongs to this God.

Some special observations:

1. If the *BD* reading [37] βαπτίσαντες ("after having baptized them") were correct, the administering of baptism would only be a secondary task to laying the groundwork for the primary task of teaching.

2. The text does not propose a liturgical formula to be used for baptism (as maintained by Zahn). Baptism "in the name of Jesus Christ" (Acts 2:38) therefore does not speak against the authenticity of the text (as has been suggested by J. Weiss).

3. Stress is laid, not on the act of baptizing itself, since cleansing rites attesting initiation were a current Jewish practice of the time; rather, the emphasis is on the particular kind of baptism the disciples are asked to administer. A Gentile becomes a disciple when he is assured of his belonging to the Father, Son, and Holy Spirit.

4. The external act of baptizing is a *signum pro re*. The disciples are commanded, and therefore they expect to be able, to bring about the state of affairs to be certified. By the intermediary of the disciples the Gentiles shall be joined with those who belong to the Father, the Son, and the Holy Spirit, thereby becoming themselves disciples. Luke 24:47 explains the meaning of this incorporation. Repentance and the forgiveness of sin shall be preached to the Gentiles in Jesus' name. They become disciples as sinners who, set free by God and thankful to God, are wrenched from the separation from God.

The command to baptize is to be understood in the same light. It is the transferral of the messianic power of Jesus, the priest of all men, to Peter. "I will give you the keys of the kingdom of heaven" (Mt. 16:19), a most genuine word of the risen Lord. Genuine and very significant, furthermore, is the invocation of the name of the triune God at the very moment when the universal existence of the apostolic Church at the end of time is revealed. This is the only place in the New Testament where this name is invoked with such simplicity (cf. 1 Cor. 12:4-6; 2 Cor. 13:13; 2 Thess. 2:13-14; Eph. 4:4-6; 1 Pet. 1:2).

". . . teaching them to observe all that I have commanded you." As baptism constitutes the existence and the nature of discipleship, teaching constitutes the ways and works of the disciples.

"Teaching," διδάσκειν, is the function of the prophet and teacher by preaching and instruction. Now Jesus appoints his disciples to this teaching office. To become a Christian means to become a Christ to others by participating in Christ's kingly, priestly, and prophetic ministry. The apostles accede to this ministry after passing through the crisis, i.e., through their failure during the Passion when their apostleship, humanly speaking, had become utterly discredited. They had failed in τηρεῖν, in observing what Jesus had commanded them. Yet without inquiring into the validity of their conversion (see, however, Lk. 22:32), Jesus freely entrusts them, the undeserving, with teaching the Gentiles this "observance," and with guiding them in the ways and works of disciples. (τηρεῖν means "to keep," "to preserve," to protect something entrusted to one's care.)

". . . all that I have commanded you." What did Jesus command them to do? To follow him, in order "to be with him" (Mk. 3:14). They are to live within the earthly confines of the kingdom of God and to submit to the order of life established there. All this not as an end in itself, for the sake of their own personal morals and salvation or of the well-being of society, but that the order of service be preserved which he had given them, his heralds and apostles. All "baptized" become *eo ipso* subservient to this order of service, the very foundation of the Christian community. They in turn need to be called to acknowledge, to keep, and to confirm their belonging to the Father, the Son, and the Holy Spirit. They need to be nurtured in this service in order that their works may become those of disciples and a Christian community may exist in the world. It exists only where the things commanded by Jesus are "observed." This nurturing of the Gentiles who, by baptism, become servants of the triune God, is the task of the apostles. As the witnesses to Jesus' life and resurrection, they are entrusted with the task for all times and in all places. All others receive it only from them, secondhand. The apostles, and they alone, are called to teach in the Church. For there is no room in the Church for any other object of τηρεῖν but the one commanded by Jesus to the apostles. What they have been commanded, they must teach without omission, the whole content of the order of service. This is the New Testament affirmation of the self-sufficiency of the Scriptures, the crossroad where we must part from the Roman Catholic Church. Teaching in the Church can only be repetitive of apostolic teaching.

There remains one more question with regard to verses 19-20a. What about the explicitly stated task (Mt. 10:8 f.) to heal the sick, to raise the dead, to make clean the lepers, to cast out evil spirits? We know from Acts and from several Letters that such special "gifts," though not widespread, were not lacking in the later Church. Nevertheless, the part of Jesus' commandment dealing with doing signs has been fulfilled and become superfluous with the Resurrection of Jesus, the sign of signs. Signs may happen again. But they cannot be postulated as essential marks of the eschatological community. In its past, the forty days, as in its future, the Second Coming, this community is surrounded by the one "sign of the Son of man." When in Mark 16:17 ff. the gift of "accompanying" signs is declared to be an almost indispensable attribute of faith, it only shows the noncanonical character of that text. The task of the apostles, and therefore also of the apostolic Church, consists in baptizing and teaching in the light of this sign—in the light of Easter morning, in the light of "the hope laid up for you in heaven" (Col. 1:5).

Verse 20b

"And lo, I am with you . . . " The Church of the *eschaton* which broke into time and now is manifest and recognized is not left alone. Its founder possesses not in vain all authority in heaven and on earth (verse 18). "Where two or three are gathered in my name, there am I in the midst of them" (Mt. 18:20). Jesus himself, with all his power and authority, stands behind the apostles when they carry out his command and commission. "He who hears you hears me" (Lk. 10:16). "So every one who acknowledges me before man, I also will acknowledge before my Father who is in heaven" (Mt. 10:32). *Ergo nunquam*

plane exspirabit ecclesia christiana (Bengel). This is why the Christian Church can never speak or act on its own authority and for its own cause. The self-seeking and self-exalting idea of the Roman Catholic Church is thereby attacked at the very roots.

"I am with you" is, according to Genesis 28:15; Judges 6:12; Haggai 1:13, the affirmation of the immediate presence of God. In making it, Jesus once more says who he is. "I am *with you.*" This is not to say that he will always be with his people in the same way as he is now. These forty days are unique, only to be compared with the return in glory which, rightly understood, begins already with the forty days. However, the Church between Ascension and Second Coming is not without a master. And because the Church is in the world, the world is not without a master either. The Church has no right to consider the world as "masterless," merely neutral or even hostile, or else it has not grasped Jesus' "with you."

"I am with you": in remembrance of my past life, death and resurrection, I speak and act today. In the Holy Spirit I fill and rule the present, any present, with my word. I will come with the future, any future. I stand at the door and knock. With my past, my present, and my future I shall be with you evermore.

This is the *promise* of the risen Lord, covering the time beyond the forty days. It is the point of departure for the subsequent events at the end of time. As the apostles receive and grasp this promise and stand on this firm ground, they are the rock on which Jesus builds his church, stronger than the gates of Hades.

". . . *to the close of the age.*" We must reckon with three different times or ages. From creation to the appearance of Christ: the time as it passes, and is actually past, with the appearance of Christ. From Christ's appearance to his return in glory: the *eschaton* as revealed in Christ's resurrection. From his return in glory into eternity: God's own eternal time in which the temporal is suspended. Accordingly, "to the close of the age," of this age, must signify until the time when the *eschaton,* ushered in with the appearance of Christ, will have run its course, when the universe will be subjected to God's reign, when the distinct reign of Christ will come to an end, and God will be everything to everyone (1 Cor. 15:27 f.). Because of Jesus' presence, the sum and substance of our text, the Great Commission of the risen Lord to baptize and evangelize is valid throughout the days of this "last" age.

Notes

1. William Carey, "An Enquiry into the Obligations of Christians to Use Means for the Conversion of the Heathens," in *The Highway of Mission Thought,* T. B. Ray, ed. (Nashville: Sunday School Board, Southern Baptist Convention, 1907), pp. 9-17.

2. Kenneth Scott Latourette, *A History of the Expansion of Christianity,* Vol. IV, *The Great Century in Europe and the United States of America* (New York: Harper and Brothers, 1941), pp. 66-67.

3. Ibid., pp. 67-69.

4. Stephen Neill, "William Carey," *Concise Dictionary of the Christian World Mission,* Stephen Neill, Gerald H. Anderson, and John Goodwin, eds. (New York: Abingdon Press, 1971), pp. 82-83. S. Pearce Carey, *William Carey* (New York: George H. Doran, Co., 1923).

5. Latourette, pp. 69-70.

6. William Owen Carver, "The Missionary Idea in the Bible," *Missions in the Plan of the Ages* (Nashville: Broadman Press, 1951), pp. 11-20.

7. Fleming H. Revell Company.

8. William A. Mueller, "William Owen Carver," *Twentieth Century Encyclopedia of Religious Knowledge,* Vol. I, Lefferts A. Loetscher, ed. (Grand Rapids: Baker Book House, 1955), p. 215. J. Herbert Kane, "William Owen Carver," *Concise Dictionary of the Christian World Mission,* p. 90.

9. Theodore G. Tappert, "Mission Research," *Twentieth Century Encyclopedia,* Vol. II, pp. 743-744.

10. See "Missions," *Encyclopedia of Southern Baptists* (Nashville: Broadman Press, 1958), p. 868.

11. Genesis 18:25.

12. Psalm 103:19.

13. Jeremiah 31:34.

14. Cf. John 1:10, 4 f.

15. Isaiah 9:2; cf. marginal reading.

16. Cf. John 3:16-17.

17. 2 Corinthians 5:19.

18. See 1 John 2:2, original.

19. Isaiah 52:15; 1 Peter 2:10.

20. 2 Corinthians 5:20.

21. 2 Corinthians 5:19.

22. Cf. Philippians 2:15; Matthew 5:14.

23. John 1:1-18.

24. Luke 1:55.

25. Luke 2:14.

26. Luke 2:30-32.

27. Matthew 2:1 ff.

28. Matthew 15:24.

29. Romans 10:12.

30. Ephesians 5:8.

31. John 15:16; 16:13 f.

32. H. H. Rowley, "The Foundations of the Message," *The Missionary Message of the Old Testament* (London: The Carey Press, 1944), pp. 15-22, 27.

33. Ernest Wright, "The Old Testament Basis for the Christian Mission," *The Theology of the Christian Mission,* Gerald H. Anderson (New York: Abingdon Press, 1961), pp. 17-30.

34. "Harold Henry Rowley," *Twentieth Century Encyclopedia,* p. 984.

35. Karl Barth, "An Exegetical Study of Matthew 28:16-20," Thomas Wiser, trans. from *The Theology of the Christian Mission* by Gerald H. Anderson, pp. 63-71. Copyright © 1961 by Gerald H. Anderson. Used with permission of McGraw-Hill Book Company.

36. William J. Wolf, "Karl Barth," *Twentieth Century Encyclopedia,* pp. 110-111.

37. A reference to two Greek manuscripts: *B—Codex Vaticanus; D—Codex Bezae Cantabrigiensis.*

II
Mission Histories

General Introduction

Mission history is a vital part of church history. Its essential concern is to describe and interpret the spread of Christianity. Its purpose is to tell the story of the faith on the basis of the events and issues which surround its advance over the centuries.

Mission history is preoccupied with the growth of the church, its multiplication, and its geographical spread across the globe. It is therefore concerned with the men and women, the movements and methods, and the issues and the institutions that have been responsible for and have shaped the various styles of that advance.

The earliest church historians did not bother to write mission histories as such, but their accounts include much vital data concerning the growth of the church. This is true of both Eusebius and Bede. It was not until relatively modern times, however, that church historians undertook the task of mission histories as such. Gustav Warneck and Adolf Harnack were the pioneers. However, Harnack's classic study is limited to the first three centuries, and Warneck's standard work is a Protestant perspective, covering the period from the Reformation to the time of its writing. The final revision and edition came just after the turn of the century. There have been many histories of missions of a given country, of a given period, or of a given mission society or board. There have been Protestant histories and Catholic histories. In recent years, two excellent one-volume histories have appeared in English: *A History of Christian Missions* by Stephen Neill, and *A Global View of Missions* by J. Herbert Kane, based upon an earlier volume by Robert Hall Glover, *The Progress of World-Wide Missions.* However, the ultimate work of mission history came with the labors of Kenneth Scott Latourette. His seven-volume work, *A History of the Expansion of Christianity,* was the first multivolumed, exhaustive history of

57

the whole Christian movement from its beginning. It has become the standard in the field.

5

"The Evangelists that were still Eminent at that Time" "Pantaenus the Philosopher" [1] Eusebius

Introduction

The work of Eusebius is the most extensive document of sources on church history to come from the early period of the Christian movement. In this invaluable array of data on the early church are a number of items that describe the spread of the faith. Book III, chapter XXXVII speaks of the missionary pursuits of the successors of the apostles who "preached the Gospel more and more widely and scattered the saving seeds of the kingdom of heaven far and near throughout the whole world." He speaks of evangelists who went on long journeys, laying the foundations of the faith, appointing pastors to whom they entrusted the young work, "while they themselves went on again to other countries and nations." In book V, chapter X he speaks of the philosopher-missionary Pantaenus whose zeal carried him as far as India.

Ironically, as careful as Eusebius was to describe the biographical details of others, we know nothing of his parentage and can only assume that he was born soon after 260, apparently in Neocaesarea. It was there that he was baptized and received his first Christian instruction. He served first as a presbyter in that city and later was promoted to the episcopate. He did, of course, make numerous journeys to principal cities of his day, collecting data for his history. He visited such cities as Jerusalem, Caesarea Philippi, Tyre, and Antioch and traveled as far as Egypt in pursuit of sources for his history. He was a friend of the renowned scholar and martyr, Pamphilus, and in later years he was an intimate friend of Emperor Constantine. One of his most significant accomplishments was his participation in the historic Council of Nicaea. In addition to his famous history, he wrote *The Martyrs of Palestine*. A number of his letters, which contain helpful autobiographical data, are found in the works of other early church fathers.[2]

The Evangelists that were still Eminent at that Time

Among those that were celebrated at that time was Quadratus, who, report says, was renowned along with the daughters of Philip for his prophetical gifts. And there were many others besides these who were known in those days, and who occupied the first place among the successors of the apostles. And they also, being illustrious disciples of such great men, built up the foundations of the churches which had been laid by the apostles in every place, and preached the Gospel more and more widely and scattered the saving seeds of the kingdom of heaven far and near throughout the whole world. For indeed most of the disciples of that time, animated by the divine word with a more ardent love for philosophy, had already fulfilled the command of the Saviour, and had distributed their goods to the needy. Then starting out upon long journeys they performed the office of evangelists, being filled with the desire to preach Christ to those who had not yet heard the word of faith, and to deliver to them the divine Gospels. And when they had only laid the foundations of faith in foreign places, they appointed others as pastors, and entrusted them with the nurture of those that had recently been brought in, while they themselves went on again to other countries and nations, with the grace and the co-operation of God. For a great many wonderful works were done through them by the power of the divine Spirit, so that at the first hearing whole multitudes of men eagerly embraced the religion of the Creator of the universe. But since it is impossible for us to enumerate the names of all that became shepherds or evangelists in the churches throughout the world in the age immediately succeeding the apostles, we have recorded, as was fitting, the names of those only who have transmitted the apostolic doctrine to us in writings still extant.

Pantænus the Philosopher

About that time, Pantænus, a man highly distinguished for his learning, had charge of the school of the faithful in Alexandria. A school of sacred learning, which continues to our day, was established there in ancient times, and as we have been informed, was managed by men of great ability and zeal for divine things. Among these it is reported that Pantænus was at that time especially conspicuous, as he had been educated in the philosophical system of those called Stoics. They say that he displayed such zeal for the divine Word, that he was appointed as a herald of the Gospel of Christ to the nations in the East, and was sent as far as India. For indeed there were still many evangelists of the Word who sought earnestly to use their inspired zeal, after the examples of the apostles, for the increase and building up of the Divine Word. Pantænus was one of these, and is said to have gone to India. It is reported that among persons there who knew of Christ, he found the Gospel according to Matthew, which had anticipated his own arrival. For Bartholomew, one of the apostles, had preached to them, and left with them the writing of Matthew in the Hebrew language, which they had preserved till that time.

After many good deeds, Pantænus finally became the head of the school at Alexandria, and expounded the treasures of divine doctrine both orally and in writing.

6

A History of the English Church and People[3]   Bede

Introduction

Bede's classic work, *A History of the English Church and People,* is unique. There is nothing comparable to it in any other country. It is a detailed account which begins with the arrival of Gaius Julius Caesar in Britain and concludes with events of which Bede himself had personal knowledge. Though he was a prolific writer, dealing in his work mostly with biblical themes, his history is the most famous of his works. The two are inseparable in the minds of people who know the name Bede. It received such early fame that King Ceolwulf of Northumbia asked to see it. When the king returned it, Bede made his final revisions of it, wrote a dedication of his work "To the Most Glorious King Ceolwulf," and returned it to the ruler in order that he might have his own personal copy made. His record of early mission work in England is a valuable contribution to the study of mission history.[4]

Bede was born around 673. At the age of seven, he was placed in a monastery under the care of Abbot Benedict. In 682 he was transferred to the monastery of Saint Paul at Jarrow where he remained the rest of his life. At the end of his famous history which he finished at the age of fifty-nine, he gives a list of his writings. It includes some twenty-four biblical studies, several in more than one book (seven books on the *Song of Songs,* for example), letters, several histories and biographies—some in verse, and a number of works on hymnody, poetry, and related themes. He became so venerated as a writer and teacher, even in his own time, that he came to be known as "the Venerable Bede," a designation which has remained with him until today.[5]

The holy Pope Gregory sends Augustine and other monks to preach to the English nation, and encourages them in a letter to persevere in their mission

In the year of our Lord 582, Maurice, fifty-fourth in succession from Augustus, became Emperor, and ruled for twenty-one years. In the tenth year of his reign, Gregory, an eminent scholar and administrator, was elected Pontiff of the apostolic Roman see, and ruled it for thirteen years, six months, and ten days. In the fourteenth year of this Emperor, and about the one hundred and fiftieth year after the coming of the English to Britain, Gregory was inspired by God to send his servant Augustine with several other God-fearing monks to preach the word of God to the English nation. Having undertaken this task in obedience to the Pope's command and progressed a short distance on their journey, they became afraid, and began to consider returning home. For they were appalled at the idea of going to a barbarous, fierce, and pagan nation, of whose very language they were ignorant. They unanimously agreed that this was the safest course, and sent back Augustine—who was to be consecrated bishop in the event of their being received by the English—so that he might humbly request the holy Gregory to recall them from so dangerous, arduous, and uncertain a journey. In reply, the Pope wrote them a letter of encouragement, urging them to proceed on their mission to preach God's word, and to trust themselves to his aid. This letter ran as follows:

'Gregory, Servant of the servants of God, to the servants of our Lord. My very dear sons, it is better never to undertake any high enterprise than to abandon it when once begun. So with the help of God you must carry out this holy task which you have begun. Do not be deterred by the troubles of the journey or by what men say. Be constant and zealous in carrying out this enterprise which, under God's guidance, you have undertaken: and be assured that the greater the labour, the greater will be the glory of your eternal reward. When Augustine your leader returns, whom We have appointed your abbot, obey him humbly in all things, remembering that whatever he directs you to do will always be to the good of your souls. May Almighty God protect you with His grace, and grant me to see the result of your labours in our heavenly home. And although my office prevents me from working at your side, yet because I long to do so, I hope to share in your joyful reward. God keep you safe, my dearest sons.

'Dated the twenty-third of July, in the fourteenth year of the reign of the most pious Emperor Maurice Tiberius Augustus, and the thirteenth year after his Consulship: the fourteenth indiction.

Pope Gregory writes commending them to the Bishop of Arles

The venerable Pontiff also wrote to Etherius, Archbishop of Arles, asking him to offer a kindly welcome to Augustine on his journey to Britain. This letter reads:

'To his most reverend and holy brother and fellow-bishop Etherius: Gregory, servant of the servants of God.

'Religious men should require no commendation to priests who exhibit the love that is pleasing to God; but since a suitable opportunity to write has arisen, We have written this letter to you, our brother, to certify that its bearer, God's servant Augustine, with his companions, of whose zeal we are assured, has been directed by us to proceed to save souls with the help of God. We therefore request Your Holiness to assist them with pastoral care, and to make speedy provision for their needs. And in order that you may assist them the more readily, we have particularly directed Augustine to give you full information about his mission, being sure that when you are acquainted with this, you will supply all their needs for the love of God. We also commend to your love the priest Candidus, our common son in Christ, whom we have transferred to a small patrimony in our church. God keep you safely, most reverend brother.

'Dated the twenty-third day of July, in the fourteenth year of the reign of the most pious Emperor Maurice Tiberius Augustus, and the thirteenth year after his Consulship: the fourteenth indiction.'

Augustine reaches Britain, and first preaches in the Isle of Thanet before King Ethelbert, who grants permission to preach in Kent

Reassured by the encouragement of the blessed father Gregory, Augustine and his fellow-servants of Christ resumed their work in the word of God, and arrived in Britain. At this time the most powerful king there was Ethelbert, who reigned in Kent and whose domains extended northwards to the river Humber, which forms the boundary between the north and south Angles. To the east of Kent lies the large island of Thanet, which by English reckoning is six hundred hides in extent; it is separated from the mainland by a waterway about three furlongs broad called the Wantsum, which joins the sea at either end and is fordable only in two places. It was here that God's servant Augustine landed with companions, who are said to have been forty in number. At the direction of blessed Pope Gregory, they had brought interpreters from among the Franks, and they sent these to Ethelbert, saying that they came from Rome bearing very glad news, which infallibly assured all who would receive it of eternal joy in heaven and an everlasting kingdom with the living and true God. On receiving this message, the king ordered them to remain in the island where they had landed, and gave directions that they were to be provided with all necessaries until he should decide what action to take. For he had already heard of the Christian religion, having a Christian wife of the Frankish royal house named Bertha, whom he had received from her parents on condition that she should have freedom to hold and practise her faith unhindered with Bishop Liudhard, whom they had sent as her helper in the faith.

After some days, the king came to the island and, sitting down in the open air, summoned Augustine and his companions to an audience. But he took precautions that they should not approach him in a house; for he held an ancient superstition that, if they were practisers of magical arts, they might have opportunity to deceive and master him. But the monks were endowed with power from God, not from the Devil, and approached the king carrying a silver cross as their standard and the likeness of our Lord and Saviour painted on a board. First of all they offered prayer to God, singing a litany for the eternal salvation both of themselves and of those to whom and for whose sake they had come. And when, at the king's command, they had sat down and preached the word of life to the king and his court, the king said: 'Your words and promises are fair indeed; but they are new and uncertain, and I cannot accept them and abandon the age-old beliefs that I have held together with the whole English nation. But since you have travelled far, and I can see that you are sincere in your desire to impart to us what you believe to be true and excellent, we will not harm you. We will receive you hospitably and take care to supply you with all that you need; nor will we forbid you to preach and win any people you can to your religion.' The king then granted them a dwelling in the city of Canterbury, which was the chief city of all his realm, and in accordance with his promise he allowed them provisions and did not withdraw their freedom to preach. Tradition says that as they approached the city, bearing the holy cross and the likeness of our great King and Lord Jesus Christ as was their custom, they sang in unison this litany: 'We pray Thee, O Lord, in all Thy mercy, that Thy wrath and anger may be turned away from this city and from Thy holy house, for we are sinners. Alleluia.

The life and doctrine of the primitive Church are followed in Kent: Augustine establishes his episcopal see in the king's city

As soon as they had occupied the house given to them they began to emulate the life of the apostles and the primitive Church. They were constantly at prayer; they fasted and kept vigils; they preached the word of life to whomsoever they could. They regarded worldly things as of little importance, and accepted only the necessities of life from those they taught. They practised what they preached, and were willing to endure any hardship, and even to die for the truth which they proclaimed. Before long a number of heathen, admiring the simplicity of their holy lives and the comfort of their heavenly message, believed and were baptized. On the east side of the city stood an old church, built in honour of Saint Martin during the Roman occupation of Britain, where the Christian queen of whom I have spoken went to pray. Here they first assembled to sing the psalms, to pray, to say Mass, to preach, and to baptize, until the king's own conversion to the Faith gave them greater freedom to preach and to build and restore churches everywhere.

At length the king himself, among others, edified by the pure lives of these holy men and their gladdening promises, the truth of which they confirmed by many miracles, believed and was baptized. Thenceforward great numbers gathered each day to hear the word of God, forsaking their heathen rites and entering the unity of Christ's holy Church as believers. While the King was pleased at their faith and conversion, it is said that he would not compel anyone to accept Christianity; for he had learned from his instructors and guides to salvation that the service of Christ must be accepted freely and not under compulsion. Nevertheless, he showed greater favour to believers, because they were fellow-citizens of the kingdom of heaven. And it was not long before he granted his teachers in his capital of Canterbury a place of residence appropriate to their station, and gave them possessions of various kinds to supply their wants.

7

The Expansion of Christianity: the First Three Centuries [6]
Adolf Harnack

Introduction

We move from the ancient histories to the modern histories. Adolf Harnack epitomizes the careful scholarship of the modern historian. His collection of ancient data and his organization and interpretation of it paved the way for the work of later mission historians. It is not difficult to see in Latourette some of the influence of Harnack. The only limitation of Harnack's work is that it includes only the study of the first three centuries. His two massive volumes constitute a well-organized and exhaustive catalog of original documents relating to the expansion of Christianity in the early period and also a careful interpretation of them. It has become the standard work on the subject for that period.

(Karl Gustav) Adolf von Harnack (1851-1930) was a native of Estonia. He taught at Leipzig, Giessen, and Marburg. In 1888 he became professor of church history at the University of Berlin where he gained an international reputation as a New Testament scholar and early church historian. He remained at Berlin until 1921 during which time he also served as head of the Prussian State Library. He was the founder of the Evangelical Social Congress and was its president from 1903 to 1912. He was a voluminous writer, and a number of his works have been translated into English. Perhaps his most controversial work was, *What Is Chris-*

tianity? Harnack was regarded as the leading historian of his generation.[7]

Results

Do the materials thus amassed permit of any conclusions being drawn from them with reference to the statistics of Christianity? Can we get any idea, even approximately, of what was the number of Christians at the period when Constantine ventured to take the extraordinary step of recognizing the religion of the church and of granting privileges to the church itself?

Definite estimates are, of course, out of the question. It is highly precarious to essay any estimate of how large was the population in the separate provinces of the empire and throughout the empire as a whole about the beginning of the fourth century, and how much harder, it may be urged, would it be to calculate, even approximately, the number of Christians? Despite all this, however, we need not abandon hope of some statistical enumeration. For a relative method of calculation promises to yield important results, if we are careful to distinguish one province from another.

. . . .

Instead of attempting to give actual percentages, I shall aim at furnishing four categories or classes of provinces and districts: (1) Those in which Christianity numbered nearly one half of the population and represented the most widely spread or even the standard religion, by the opening of the fourth century; (2) those in which Christianity formed a very material portion of the population, influencing the leading classes and the general culture of the people, and being capable of holding its own with other religions; (3) those in which Christianity was sparsely scattered; and (4) finally, those in which the spread of Christianity was extremely weak, or where it was hardly to be found at all.

The first of these categories includes (1) *the entire province of what constitutes our modern Asia Minor, with the exception of some out-of-the-way districts,* which were then, as they still are, of small account in point of civilization. The process of Christianizing went on apace in the west, northwest, and certain districts of the interior, at an earlier period than in the east, north-east, and south, the local conditions varying here and there; but by the opening of the fourth century the latter districts appear to have equalled the former, becoming almost entirely Christian. . . . In Phrygia, Bithynia, and Pontus there were districts which by this time were practically Christian all over; also there were now towns and villages which contained but few or no pagans. Furthermore, as the numerous chor-episcopi prove, the Lowlands far and wide had been extensively Christianized. Most probably the network of the episcopal organization throughout all the Asiatic provinces was almost complete by *circa* 300 A.D., and in these provinces the reaction under Julian was unable to make any headway. (2) It includes *that portion of Thrace which lay over against Bithynia, i.e.* Europe (so-called); and (3) *Armenia.* It baffles our powers of judgment to estimate the actual extent to which Christianity was diffused in this country; all we can say is that the Christian religion had by this time become the official religion, and that the royal household was Christian. Eusebius treats the country as a Christian land, and takes the war waged by Maximinus Daza against the Armenians as a religious conflict. (4) Finally, there is *Edessa,* a city which according to Eusebius was entirely Christian. I would not venture to group any other provinces under this category.

The second category includes (1) *Antioch and Coele-Syria*— not merely the maritime towns of Syria and the Greek cities, be it noted, for by this time Christianity must have also penetrated deep into the Syriac population. Also (2) *Cyprus* and (3) *Alexandria, together with Egypt and the Thebais.* The episcopal organization of Egypt as a whole, which commenced by the close of the second century, was substantially finished by the opening of the fourth century, when the new religion had also penetrated deep into the lower non-Hellenic classes, as is proved by the origin and extraordinary spread of monasticism in these circles after the close of the third century, no less than by the rise of the Coptic versions and the ecclesiastical dialect. (4) Then came *Rome, Lower Italy, and certain parts of Middle Italy.* In Rome itself the majority of the upper classes still held aloof, and the events of the next seventy years show that we must not over-estimate the Christianization of the city by the opening of the fourth century. On the other hand, it is a well-established fact that Christianity was widely represented among the upper and even the highest ranks of society. Thus Eusebius was able to describe how Maxentius began by assuming the mask of friendship towards the Christians (though, of course, he soon changed his tactics), "in order to flatter the people of Rome," while the subsequent elevation of the cross by Constantine within the capital itself met with no resistance. Furthermore, the large number of churches in Rome, and the way in which the city was divided up for ecclesiastical purposes, show how thoroughly it was interspersed with Christians. By 250 A.D. the number of Christians in Rome cannot well have been less than 30,000. Subsequently, by the beginning of the fourth century it was probably doubled, perhaps quadrupled. As for Lower Italy and the districts of Middle Italy which lay in the vicinity of Rome, the fact that sixty Italian bishops could be got together as early as 251 A.D.—bishops who resided in out-of-the-way districts—permits us to infer the existence of quite a considerable Christian population *circa* 300 A.D. This population would be denser wherever Greeks formed an appreciable percentage of the inhabitants, *i.e.* in the maritime towns of Lower Italy and Sicily, although the Latin-speaking population would still remain for the most part pagan. The fact that the Christian church of Rome was predominantly Greek till shortly before the middle of the third century, is proof positive that up till then the Christianizing of the Latin population in Middle and Lower Italy must have been still in an inchoate stage, although it certainly made rapid strides between 250 and 320. (5) *Africa proconsularis and Numidia.*—We may unhesitatingly reckon these provinces in the present category, since the facts already mentioned prove that the majority of these towns contained Christian communities by the opening of the fourth century, and that the whole country was divided over the Donatist controversy. One might even be disposed to add these provinces to those of the first category, were it not for the inscriptions, which warn us against over-estimating the amount of Christianity in individual towns during the third century. True, the inscriptions are no reliable guide even here. How much Christianity, nay, how much early Christianity even, may lie hid in them! Only, we are no longer able to lay hands on it. (6) *Spain.*—The canons of the synod of Elvira, together with the lists of that synod, justify us (though upon this point I am not quite certain of the facts) in including the Spanish provinces within this category, for these canons show the extent to which Spanish Christianity had become mixed up with local civilization by the year 300, and they also show how deeply it had penetrated all the relationships of life. (7) The overwhelming probability is—to judge from the situation as we find it in the fourth century—that certain (*i.e.* the maritime) parts of *Achaia, Thessaly, Macedonia, and the islands* are similarly to be reckoned in this category, as well as *the southern coast of Gaul.*

Our third category will embrace (1) *Palestine,* where some Greek towns like Caesarea had a considerable number of Christians, as well as one or two purely Christian localities. As a whole, however, the country offered a stout resistance to Christianity. (2) *Phoenicia,* where the Greek cities on the coast had Christian communities, while the interior, dominated by a powerful and hostile religion, continued to be but slightly affected by Christianity. (3) *Arabia,* where a Christian life of some kind unfolded itself amid the Greco-Latin cities with their peculiar civilization. (4) *Certain districts in Mesopotamia,* (5-12) *the interior of Achaia, of Macedonia, and of Thessaly,* with *Epirus, Dardania, Dalmatia, Mœsia,* and *Pannonia.* The two last-named large provinces adopted Christianity at a comparatively late period but it must have shot up rapidly once it entered them. (13) *The northern districts of Middle Italy and the eastern section of Upper Italy.* (14) and (15), Mauretania and Tripolitana.

Finally, our fourth category includes—apart from regions outside the empire such as Persia, India, and Scythia (though Western Persia at the opening of the fourth century may be included more accurately, perhaps, in our third category)—(1) *the towns of ancient Philistia;* (2) *the north and north-west coasts of the Black Sea;* (3) *the western section of Upper Italy*— Piedmont having no ecclesiastical organization even by the opening of the fourth century; (4) *Middle and Upper Gaul;* (5) *Belgica;* (6) *Germany;* and (7) *Rhoetia.* To get some idea of the sparseness of Christianity in Belgica, and consequently in Middle and Upper Gaul, as well as in Germany and Rhaetia, one has to recollect what has been already said upon the church of Treves, and also to compare the facts noted with regard to the church of Cologne. But let me at this point set a small problem in arithmetic. Treves was the most important city in all these provinces, and yet the sole church there certainly cannot have included more than from 500 to 1000 members, while an even smaller total is probably to be fixed. Now, if we assume that twelve bishops, at the very outside, may be counted in Middle and Northern Gaul, Germany, Belgica, and Rhaetia put together, and if we multiply this number by 500-700, adding also soldiers and some natives to our total, we get a membership of not more than 10,000 Christians for all these provinces. From which it follows that in a statistical account of the church for the opening of the fourth century, these provinces, together with the rest of those grouped under our fourth category, might be omitted altogether, without any serious loss.

The radical difference between the eastern and the western sections of the empire is particularly striking. Indeed, if one makes the use of Greek or Latin a principle of differentiation, the relative percentage of Christians in the former case becomes higher still. And the explanation is simple enough. While a Greek Christianity had been in existence since the apostolic age, any Latin Christianity worth mentioning dated probably from the reign of Marcus Aurelius. Since the days when the adherents of the Christian faith had got their name in Antioch, Christianity had ceased to be a Jewish body. Strictly speaking, it had never been such, for it was rooted in what was a counter-movement to the Jewish church, being Hellenistic from the outset. It never divested itself entirely of this Hellenism, neither on Latin nor on Syrian soil. At least, wherever it went, until the close of the second century, it tended to promote the Hellenizing movement, and even at a later period it retained a strongly-marked Hellenistic element which clung to it and urged it on. The transference of the empire's headquarters to the East at once preserved and accentuated the Greek character of the church even as an influence which told upon the western section of the empire—and that at a time when East and West already stood apart, and when a distinctive Latin Christianity accordingly began to shape itself with vigour. But it was the Hellenism of Asia Minor, not that of Egypt, which now took the lead, a Hellenism with elements and associations stretching as far back as the civilization of Persia. *And there lay also the headquarters of the Christian church at the opening of the fourth century.*

We cannot procure any rough and ready figures giving the total percentages of Christians for the eastern and the western sections of the empire; and even were such figures available, they would be valueless, for the aspect presented by the separate provinces or groups of provinces is far too varied. More weight attaches to such proofs as we have already led. From these we find that Asia Minor was the most Christian country (with Armenia and Edessa), that, in short, it was practically Christianized; that, in the second place, it is closely followed by Coele-Syria with Antioch, Egypt (and Alexandria), Rome (and Lower Italy), Africa proconsularis and Numidia, and lastly, the maritime districts of Southern Gaul—with regard to the strength of their Christian elements. The resultant picture tells its own tale to the historical expert. If Christianity in these *influential* provinces not merely existed, but existed in large numbers, and existed as a *power* (which, we have seen, was actually the case); if it had already become the dominant power in Asia Minor especially, and if it had already (as has been shown) made its way into the very heart of the army, then it is a matter of almost entire indifference how it fared in the other provinces, or how vigorous was the Christian element in these districts. Moreover, the church was international. Consequently, it was latent, so to speak, as a powerful force even in provinces that were but thinly Christianized. Behind the tiniest isolated church stood the church collective, and this, so far from being a fanciful idea, was a magnitude supremely real.

For a number of years previous to his famous and historical "flight" to Gaul, Constantine stayed at the court of Diocletian in Nicomedia. In one sense of the term, he was no longer a youth when he lived there. He kept his eyes open in a city or province in which he was confronted everywhere with the church, with her episcopate, and with her power over the minds of men. *His Asiatic impressions accompanied him to Gaul,* where they reappeared in the form of political considerations which led him to make his decisive resolve. His most serious opponent, Maximinus Daza, the Augustus of the East, was unteachable; but that very fact made him the most useful tutor Constantine could have had. For the career of Daza made Constantine see as clear as print what were the methods which could not, and therefore dare not, any longer be employed in dealing with Christianity.

It is idle to ask whether the church would have gained her victory even apart from Constantine. Some Constantine or other would have had to come upon the scene. Only, as one decade succeeded to another, it would be all the easier for anyone to be that Constantine. All over Asia Minor, at any rate, the victory of Christianity was achieved before ever Constantine did come on the scene, whilst it was assured throughout the countries mentioned in our second class. Enough to know these facts regarding the spread of Christianity! It required no special illumination and no celestial army-chaplain (to quote the saying of Lactantius about him) to have this brought to light, or to bring about what was already in existence. All that was needed was an acute and forceful statesman, and *one who at the same time had a vital interest in the religious situation.* Such a man was Constantine. He was gifted, inasmuch as he clearly recognized and firmly grasped what was inevitable. It was not by aid of anything artificial or arbitrary that he laid down the basal principles of his imperial state church; what he did was to let the leading provinces have the religion they desired. Whereupon other provinces had simply to follow suit.

Was there anything remarkable, it may be asked, in the rapidity with which the Christian religion came to extend itself? We have only, it is true, a small amount of parallel material relating to the other religions in the empire, which might serve us for the purposes of such a comparison; still, my reply to such a question would be in the affirmative. The facts of the case do justify the impression of the church-fathers in the fourth century, of men like Arnobius and Eusebius and Augustine—the impression that their faith had spread from generation to generation with inconceivable rapidity. Seventy years after the foundation of the very first Gentile Christian church in Syrian Antioch, Pliny wrote in the strongest terms about the spread of Christianity throughout remote Bithynia, a spread which in his view already threatened the stability of other cults throughout the province. Seventy years later still, the Paschal controversy reveals the existence of a Christian federation of churches, stretching from Lyons to Edessa, with its headquarters situated at Rome. Seventy years later, again, the emperor Decius declared he would sooner have a rival emperor in Rome than a Christian bishop [vol. i. pp. 351, 352]. And ere another seventy years had passed, the cross was sewn upon the Roman colours.

It has been our endeavour to decipher the reasons for this astonishing expansion. These reasons, on the one hand, were native to the very essence of the religion (as monotheism and as evangel). On the other hand, they lay in its versatility and amazing power of adaptation. But it baffles us to determine the relative amount of impetus exerted by each of the forces which characterized Christianity: to ascertain, *e.g.,* how much was due to its spiritual monotheism, to its preaching of Jesus Christ, to its hope of immortality, to its active charity and system of social aid, to its discipline and organization, to its syncretistic capacity and contour, or to the skill which it developed in the third century for surpassing the fascinations of any superstition whatsoever. Christianity was a religion which proclaimed the living God, for whom man was made. It also brought men life and knowledge, unity and multiplicity, the known and the unknown. Born of the spirit, it soon learnt to consecrate the earthly. To the simple it was simple; to the sublime, sublime. It was a universal religion, in the sense that it enjoined precepts binding upon all men, and also in the sense that it brought men what each individual specially craved. Christianity became a church, a church for the world, and thereby it secured the use of all possible means of authority, besides the sword itself. It continued to be exclusive, and yet it drew to itself any outside element that was of any value. By this sign it conquered; for on all human things on what was eternal and on what was transient alike, Christianity had set the cross.

8

Outline of a History of Protestant Missions from the Reformation to the Present Time [8]
Gustav Warneck

Introduction

Gustav Warneck's *Outline of a History of Protestant Missions from the Reformation to the Present Time* filled a vital need for a comprehensive work on Protestant missions up to that time (1892). In part I, after an introductory word on missions from biblical times to the Reformation, he deals with the four major periods of Protestantism: Reformation, Orthodoxy, Pietism, and Missions. He concludes with a history of missionary societies. In six chapters, part II gives a history of evangelical missions in the various parts of the world and concludes with an estimate of their results. This work went through ten printings and provided a wealth of material from which subsequent missiologists have drawn.

Gustav Warneck (1834-1910), was born in Naumburg, Germany. He was a pastor and Mission Inspector at Barmen before becoming a professor. In 1896 (1897) he assumed the first professorship of missions to be established in Europe (on the continent). This was at Halle, which had been a center for missions the century before. In 1874 he founded a mission journal for the scientific study of missions. For the same purpose he founded, in 1879, the Mission Conference of Saxony. In addition to his history, he wrote a five-volume systematic treatise on the science of missions. This earned him the reputation of being the founder of the Protestant science of missions.[9]

The Age of Pietism

35. It was in the age of Pietism that missions struck their first deep roots, and it is the spirit of Pietism which, after Rationalism had laid its hoar-frost on the first blossoming, again revived them, and has brought them to their present bloom. The various theological objections, by which the orthodox doctrine prevented the inception of missionary plans, began to die, and that even without their becoming the subject of active controversy; virtually, it was only round the theory as to the "call" that there was much debate. And this debate would have been more keen had it not been theologians of genuine university training whom the older Pietism—as distinguished from the Moravian church—appointed to missionary service. The vision of the religious condition of the world beyond Europe, to which the growing commerce of the world was ever giving truer adjustment, made the assumption of a universally diffused or previously diffused knowledge of Christianity ever more untenable, and so corrected the old expositions of Scripture and the old interpretation of history. But that which brought about the radical change lay in the nature of Pietism itself, which over against the dominant ecclesiastical doctrine exhibited the worth and power of a living, personal and practical Christianity. The energetic seeking of conversion, as well as a general zeal for fruitfulness in good works, begat an activity which, as soon as it was directed towards

the non-Christian world, could not but assume the tendency to seek the conquest of the world for Christ. It is true, indeed, that much narrow-mindedness clung to Pietism, and that this in many ways impaired the freshness and the popularity of its Christianity; but notwithstanding that narrowness, so soon as it allowed itself to be impregnated by missionary ideas, there came to it a width of horizon by which it excelled all its adversaries. While derided as "conventicle Christianity," it embraced the whole world with its loving thoughts, and these loving thoughts it translated into works of love, which sought to render help alike to the misery of the heathen and to that within Christendom. In spite of its "fleeing from the world" (Weltflucht), it became a world-conquering power. It is the parent, as of missions to the heathen, so also of all those saving agencies which have arisen within Christendom for the healing of religious, moral, and social evils, and which we are wont to call home-missions; a combination which was already typically exemplified in Aug. Herm. Francke. Let us now turn back to him.

36. The merit of Francke, in respect of missions to the heathen, does not consist in his having been the first in German Lutheran Christendom to express missionary ideas, or the first to translate these ideas into action. As we have seen, missionary voices were not wanting even in the seventeenth century, and the initiative to the beginning of the Danish-Halle mission came from King Frederick IV. But even before the Danish initiative, Francke had been no stranger to missionary ideas. True, the notable treatise, *Pharus missionis evangelicae,* discovered in the archives of the orphanage,—the full title of which reads: . . . . Lighthouse of evangelical missions, or advice concerning the propagation of the faith by means of conversion of the nations, chiefly of the Chinese; forerunner of a larger work to the most mighty King Frederick of Prussia, in which a demonstration of the truth, moving causes, the preparatories of conversion, the endeavour at an evangelical sending, necessary aids, as well as the mode of conversion and the conservation of the converts, are described in their first principles and submitted to the judgment of the Brandenburg Society, as well as to the serious consideration of all learned and pious men,—is not by Francke, as has recently been proved. Its author was a Hessian theologian, Dr. Conrad Mel, who has fallen into unmerited oblivion. But other works of Francke bordered closely on missions. Evidence of this is furnished

in the treatise published by Frick, and composed about Easter 1701, containing the magnificent "Project" of Aug. Herm. Francke for a "Seminarium universale," or the founding of a nursery (Pflanzgarten), in which a real improvement of all classes within and without Germany, in Europe and all other parts of the world, should be looked for. Certainly, in this "Project" Francke had principally in view the quickening of Christendom, but that he included also "foreign nations," and designated his institute as "Seminarium nationum," is ample testimony to his universal intention. Add to this the founding of the "Collegium orientale" (1702), and the endeavours directed, in connection with the ideas of the younger Ludolf, to the awakening of the Greek and Eastern churches, endeavours which had as consequence the sending of a great number of the scholars of Francke to Russia and Constantinople; and then, if account is taken of the suggestions offered by Leibnitz, it is evident that the issue of these creative thoughts in real foreign missionary efforts is, psychologically, completely mediated. Besides this universalism of intention, which distinguished Francke amongst his contemporaries, and the powerful personality of the man, who was as mighty in secret prayer as in practical action, as strong in faith as in tact, as narrow as a Pietist as he was wide-hearted as a Christian, there was in effect a threefold qualification which fitted him to be the leader of the new missionary life. First, next to Spener, he was the chief representative of the Pietist movement, which, notwithstanding all its one-sidednesses, first awakened within and beyond the Lutheran church the fresh spiritual life, which became the mother-womb of a true missionary vitality. Secondly, as the founder of the orphanage he enjoyed a reputation far beyond Germany, and exercised a vast influence upon the living Christians of his time. And thirdly, as a most gifted teacher, he knew how to make his orphanage a "Seminarium universale" for winning all kinds of workers into the service of the kingdom of God: not that he trained such workers in a school, but that in those who came in near contact with him he stirred a spirit of absolute devotion to divine service, such as he himself possessed in highest measure, and which made them ready to go anywhere where there was need of them. Thus it was quite natural that Francke appointed the missionaries of the Danish mission, that he was their adviser, and that he gathered behind them at home praying and giving missionary congregations. True, he did not succeed in making missions the actual business of congregations or of the church, for the "official" church declined the service. It was (and it remains still) only "ecclesiolae in ecclesia," which formed the missionary church at home. But there was this great advance, that from Francke's time onwards missions were no longer regarded merely as a duty of colonial governments, but as a concern of believing Christendom, that individual voluntaryism (freewillinghood) was involved in them, and that this voluntaryism was made active in furnishing means for their support. Without Francke the Danish mission would soon have gone to sleep again. In 1710 he also published the first regular mission reports. In short, Halle was the real centre of the Tranquebar mission. It was in the missionary atmosphere of Halle, too, that later the first missionary hymn originated, that of Bogatzky, "Wach auf, du Geist der ersten Zeugen," which gave to the missionary and reforming ideas of Francke expression in classic poetry. It is to be wondered at how a man overburdened with home work, and entirely dependent for the support of his institutions on the free-will offerings of Christian love, developed such energetic activity on behalf of foreign missions and so magnanimously collected for them. But he knew himself to be a debtor to both, Christians as well as non-Christians, and he thought highly of the faith working by love which multiplies itself the more the greater is the field of action which is assigned to it. In Francke there is personified the connection of rescue work at home with missions to the heathen,— a type of the fact that they who do the one leave not the other undone. Home and foreign missions have from the beginning been sisters who work reciprocally into one another's hands.

37. In Germany, still more strongly than in Denmark, orthodoxy opposed the young missionary enterprise, if for no other reason than that it was connected with Pietism, which orthodoxy so keenly combated. The most moderate criticism was that of B. E. Löscher, who in his *Unschuldige Nachrichten* (1708) declared himself not positively hostile, but only cool in the matter, and cautioned against countenancing it meanwhile. Most orthodox opponents, however, were much more vehement. By the Faculty of Wittenberg the missionaries in 1708 were plainly called "false prophets," because, notwithstanding their calling by a princely head, which ought to have broken that reproach, their regular call was not established; and the Hamburg preacher Neumeister, author of the noble hymn "Jesus nimmt die Sünder an," closed an

Ascensiontide sermon, in 1722, in which he declared that "the so-called missionaries are not necessary to-day," with the words—

" 'Go into all the world,' the Lord of old did say;
But now: 'Where God has placed thee, there He would have thee
   stay.' "

Owing to this cool, indeed hostile, attitude of orthodoxy, it was natural that the Pietist circles became the homes of the new missionary life, and moulded its form. If, consequently, certain pietistic narrownesses clung to that life, yet the neglect of the defenders of orthodoxy deprived them of all right to be harshly critical. Without doubt these narrownesses have not been without detriment in various ways to the missions of the present, but—and in face of the one-sided criticism of Pietism, which has become the fashion to-day, it is our duty to emphasise this—the blessing which the overruling providence of God has caused to rest on the missions of Pietism is much greater than this detriment. For the narrowness of Pietism was a safeguard against the mediaeval error of external conversions in masses; it led evangelical missions back to apostolic lines, and bred them to a healthy Christian development out of narrowness into breadth.

38. As to the history of the Danish Halle mission, to which we shall return in our survey of India, let it suffice to note here that from Francke's institutions there have been sent out, in the course of a century, about sixty missionaries, amongst whom, besides conspicuous men like Ziegenbalg, Fabricius, Jänecke, Gericke, Christian Friedrich Schwartz was distinguished as a star of the first magnitude. Amid various little strifes and ample distress, occasioned partly by the colonial authorities and partly by the confusions of war, this—if by no means ideal, yet on the whole solid and not unfruitful (about 15,000 Christians)—mission maintained itself, until, in the last quarter of the century and afterwards, Rationalism at home dug up its roots. Only when the universities, having fallen completely under the sway of this withering movement, ceased to furnish theologians, was the first trial made, in 1803, of a missionary who had not been a university student. Meanwhile a more living missionary interest had been awakened in England, and so the connection which had already for some time existed with friends of missions there, and especially the alliance with the Church Missionary Societies, saved the Tamul mission from ruin. Then later,

the Dresden-Leipsic Lutheran Missionary Society stepped into the old heritage of the fathers, after Halle had long ceased to be an active centre.

39. Along with the undertaking of the East Indian mission, the missionary college at Copenhagen turned its attention also to two northern mission fields, Lapland and Greenland. In the former, besides the faithful schoolmaster Isaac Olsen, it was notably the self-denying Thomas von Westen (who from 1716 to 1722 undertook three missionary journeys) and the Swede, Per Fjellström (who was active in literary labours), who sought the spiritual elevation of the still really heathen people. The impulse to the Greenland mission came from the ardent Norwegian, Hans Egede, who, after overcoming great difficulties, went himself and his family to Greenland in 1721, in connection with a mercantile company holding a charter from the King of Denmark. He returned, after fifteen years of abounding activity amid toil and suffering, in order to forward the education in Copenhagen of further missionaries for Greenland,—an effort, however, which led to no real result. Still, his work, which at first he handed over to his son Paul, was carried on from Denmark, though certainly with feeble energy. But even before the departure of Egede, German missionaries joined in the work. They were sent by a community which, from its origin onwards, has been most intimately associated with the history of missions: they were missionaries of the church of the Brethren. It was through this community that evangelical missions took their most decided step forwards.

40. But how came the little church of the Brethren to put its hand to missions to the heathen, and so to open a new chapter in the history of missions? In a manner which may be clearly recognised, it was the work of God. "He tied the threads, prepared the paths, chose and fitted the men, and then spake His Almighty word, 'Let it be.'"

First, as to the human instruments whom God prepared to carry on His work among the heathen, these were Nicolaus Ludwig, Count von Zinzendorf, and the Moravian Brethren, for whom he made ready a home in Herrnhut. Manifestly it was by the special leading of Divine providence that Count Zinzendorf, who was to become so eminent an instrument for the work of converting the heathen, came as a boy into Francke's institutions in Halle. He says himself later of that time: "The daily opportunity in Professor Francke's house of hearing edifying tidings of the kingdom of Christ, of speaking with witnesses from all lands, of making acquaintance with missionaries (especially Bartholomew Ziegenbalg), of seeing men who had been banished and imprisoned, as also the institutions then in their bloom, and the cheerfulness of the pious man himself in the work of the Lord, . . . mightily strengthened within me zeal for the things of the Lord." Under these influences the pious boy, when only fifteen years of age, formed with some like-minded comrades an "Order," whose chief rule ran thus: "Our unwearied labour shall go through the whole world, in order that we may win hearts for Him Who gave His life for our souls." With his friend Frederic von Wattewille in particular he made a compact "for the conversion of the heathen, and of such as no one else would go to, by instruments to whom God would direct them."

Already in early youth Zinzendorf was filled with burning love to the Person of the crucified Saviour, so that he could declare, "I have but one passion, and it is He, He only." And this man, aflame with glowing love for the Saviour, had a peculiar instinct for fellowship. His was not a nature quietly in-turned upon itself, but the craving of his heart was to form societies which were bound to the Lord Jesus. "I admit no Christianity without fellowship," he declared. Besides, Zinzendorf possessed quite a pre-eminent talent for organisation, which made him a blessed 'Ordinarius' [ruling bishop], who knew how to give to every society and to every work fitting order, form, and fashion.

41. But what could the best organiser with the most ardent love of the Saviour begin without instruments? With men of commonplace cast even a Zinzendorf could effect nothing. In order to establish an expansive missionary work among the heathen in that age, there was need of men of extraordinary faith and courage. "The storming column of the missionary host must be a chosen troop of daring energy and persistent endurance." God furnished to the Count that chosen troop. It consisted of a number of Moravian Brethren, who for the sake of their faith had been forced to leave their fatherland, and whom Count Zinzendorf, the grandson of a sire who likewise for the sake of his faith had been driven from Austria, had hospitably sheltered on his estate of Berthelsdorf. On the 17th of July 1722 the first tree at Hutberg, near Berthelsdorf, was felled, on which occasion Christian David the carpenter exclaimed prophetically, "Here hath the swallow found her house and the bird its nest, Thine altars, O Lord of Hosts." That was

the beginning of the church of the Brethren, which gradually attracted to itself at Herrnhut many especially of the ever-increasing numbers of settlers from Moravia, and which hid within itself the human material out of which the Spirit of God makes His witnesses: men of inflexible resolve, stern towards themselves, ready for every labour and privation, perfectly calm amid the greatest dangers, and burning with zeal to save souls.

As to their character, only some examples. When the first missionaries, David Nitzschmann, a carpenter, and Leonard Dober, a potter, went to the West Indies in 1732, their purpose, to convert the negro slaves, was declared in Copenhagen to be a foolish freak, and the directors of the Danish West India Company refused them a passage on their ships. That, however could not turn aside men with the courage of faith, who were certain of their Divine call. When the chief chamberlain, Von Pless, who was well disposed towards them, asked, "But how will you manage at St. Thomas?" Nitzschmann made answer, "We will work as slaves with the negroes." And when he rejoined, "You cannot do that; it will never be permitted," Nitzschmann averred, "Then I am willing to work as a carpenter at my trade." "Good, but what will the potter do?"—"I shall just pull him through along with me." "Verily then," said the chamberlain, "in that fashion you can go with one another through the whole world."

Of a great company of brethren and sisters who in 1734 were also sent to the West Indies, principally to St. Croix, ten died in the course of the year. When the startling news of this sore loss reached Herrnhut, there was indeed, in the first moment, deep depression because of the severe and unexpected blow. But it did not last for long: with the full joy of faith the congregation sang the verse which Zinzendorf composed on receipt of the tidings, and which has become so celebrated—

> "Ten were sown right far away,
>   As were they lost indeed,—
>   But o'er their beds stands, "These are they
>   Of Afric's race the seed."

In January 1739 the Count himself landed on St. Thomas, just when, without his knowing anything of it, the workers there had been cast into prison. Before landing he asked his two companions, "What shall

we do if the brethren are no longer here?"—"So be it; *we* are here,"
rang out the answer. Then he exclaimed, "Gens aeterna—these Moravians."

Nor did the other members of the church lag behind these Moravians.
In 1734, along with a comrade who was trained in theology, the physically frail Saxon tailor Gottlieb Israel was sent to St. Thomas, where
he laboured with rich blessing. When nearing the island the ship was
wrecked, and the faithless crew immediately abandoned it in the only
lifeboat. With some negroes, the two missionaries, who had been left
on the wreck, sought to save themselves on the rocks on which the
ship was shattered, with the view perchance of reaching land from
it. For long they found themselves in most perilous plight on the narrow
reef. At length Feder, the companion of Israel, tried to save himself
by passing over the stones between the reef and the land on to the
rocky shore. A piercing cry! Feder lies in the water, and the surge
throws him with full force against the rock; for an instant Israel looks
upon the death-blanched face of the brother, and—the sea has swallowed him. "And what didst thou then, when thou sawest thy brother
drowned before thine eyes?" was asked of him afterwards. "Then I
sang the verse—

> "'Where are ye, ye scholars of heavenly grace,
> Companions of the cross of our Lord?
> Your hallowed pathway where may we trace,
> Be it at home or abroad?
> Ye breakers of strongholds, where are ye found?
> Rocks and dens, and the wild waste ground,
> The isles of the heathen, the furious waves,—
> These are from of old your appointed graves.'"

"How was it with thee in thy soul?"—"I would have been the Lord's,
if I had died. The text for the day was quite clear to me: 'How the
morning star shines, full of grace and truth from the Lord.'"

When Johann Sörensen was asked if he was ready to go to Labrador,
he made answer: "Yes, to-morrow, if you give me only a pair of shoes."
And Drachart, before he entered that land of ice, exclaimed, "Strike
me dead, yea, strike me dead." Such stout-hearted, resolute, brave
warriors were needed for breaking open the way for missions. God
therefore called the Herrnhuters.

42. On the 10th of February 1728 a memorable "day of prayer and fellowship" was observed in Herrnhut. Amid praise and prayer and earnest discourse the Count sat amongst his "Brethren." "The love of Christ constraineth us," and "we cannot but speak the things which we have seen and heard," was the persuasion of all, and all felt a mighty impulse "to venture something real for God." Distant lands were named: Turkey and Morocco, Greenland and Lapland. "But it is quite impossible to reach them," objected the "Brethren." "The Lord can and will give grace and strength for that," rang out the answer of Zinzendorf, and his dauntless childlike trust so profoundly inspired all, that on the day following twenty-six unmarried Brethren joined together to prepare themselves in case the call of the Lord should come to them. Thus that "Brother-chamber" became a kind of missionary school, in which by all sorts of instruction men were fitted for future missionary service. There now lacked only the outward occasion, which should turn the missionary idea into missionary action. A special Divine dispensation furnished that occasion also.

In the year 1731, Count Zinzendorf journeyed to Copenhagen, to the coronation of his friend Christian VI. For many reasons he had long hesitated about undertaking this journey, but at last he declared confidently "that as a servant of his Lord he could not do as he would but must go," and he had ever clearer presentment "that by his journey God had secret purposes to serve, which in their own time would be made manifest." Among the circle of sincere confessors of the Lord Jesus who surrounded the Court, Zinzendorf had intercourse especially with the chief chamberlain, Von Pless, and with Count Laurwig, in whose service there was a negro, by name Anton, a native of the West Indian island of St. Thomas, belonging to the Danes. The three Brethren who accompanied Zinzendorf to Copenhagen came frequently in contact with this negro. Their testimony opened his heart, and he confided to them how, when sitting on the shore in St. Thomas, he had often looked for a revelation from above, and had prayed to God for light. In vivid colours he further depicted the wretched condition of the negro slaves there, and told that he had a sister and a brother who were longing for the knowledge of God. Of all this Zinzendorf naturally received minute information. His stay in Copenhagen led also to his becoming acquainted with two Greenlanders, who turned his eyes towards their fatherland, where for some years the Norwegian

Egede had been labouring as a missionary. The Count, however, was unwilling to do anything without the consent of the church, and on his return to Herrnhut he laid before them all the thoughts which stirred his heart in Copenhagen. Two days later a company of singing Brethren went past his house. Pointing to them, Zinzendorf exclaimed, "Amongst these there are messengers to the heathen, to St. Thomas, Greenland, and Lapland"; and so it actually proved. Among them were the first four who offered themselves as ready to go to the West Indies and to Greenland. Almost a whole year was spent in cool consideration of the whole matter; and then when, in respect of Dober, the lot gave answer: "Let the lad go, the Lord is with him," all deliberation was at an end, and Dober went with Nitzschmann to St. Thomas, and the two cousins Matthew and Christian Stach to Greenland.

43. That small beginning was followed immediately by a strong forward movement. Not only were ever larger bands sent to the West Indies, but in that first "Sturm und Drang" [storm and stress] period missions were begun also among the Samoyedes and the Lapps, in Persia and China, in Ceylon and the East Indies, in Constantinople and Wallachia, in Caucasus and Egypt,—which, it is true, had later to be given up; while the missions in the West Indies and Greenland, Surinam and South Africa, and others afterwards begun in America, Australia, and Asia, form until this day the blessed fields of the missionary labours of the "Brethren." There lay indeed in this first busy haste something of the restless temperament of the Count, which by his own confession inclined towards extravagances; and these numerous missions, undertaken in rapid succession, occasioned a wasteful dispersion of energies; still there was something heroic in the little community daring to set on foot such world-encircling enterprises. That a community now existed which addressed its whole energy to missions to the heathen, and so had become a city set upon a hill,—that is the permanent historical importance of the missionary work of Zinzendorf. In two decades the little church of the Brethren called more missions into life than did the whole of Protestantism in two centuries. When Zinzendorf passed away on the 9th of May 1760, he could exclaim on his deathbed, "Did you in the beginning really think that the Saviour would do so much as we now see with our eyes? Among the heathen my design only reached to first fruits; now there are thousands. What a mighty host already stands around the Lamb from our service!" Yea,

verily, as the inscription on his tombstone reads, "He was appointed to bring forth fruit, and fruit which remains." On his death one of his fellow-workers could say of him with truth, "The present time may or may not recognise it, but it will not be hidden from posterity that this man was a servant of Christ on whose heart lay day and night the salvation of the heathen, and that all ends of the earth might see the salvation of God." It was truth which the pious Count sang on the occasion of the world-renowned communion service on the 13th of August 1737—

> "Herrnhut shall not longer stand
> Than the works of Thine own hand
> Have free course therein,
> And love unite within,
> Till ready we, and willing, be
> To be spread out o'er the earth
> As a good salt for its health."

The church of the Brethren was a "salt of the earth," mainly in that it was *par excellence* a missionary church, and has remained so even after the death of Zinzendorf to this day.

44. The vast missionary energy of the church of the Brethren, numerically so insignificant (numbering to-day about 37,000 souls), is a unique fact in the history of the whole Christian church, and it is explained only by the fact that this church, notwithstanding all the weaknesses attaching to it, is the manifestation of a fellowship grounded in evangelical faith and rooted in the love of Christ, in which the dispositions of Mary and Martha are healthily blended into one. "Missions," writes Baron von Schrautenbach, "are characteristically the common affair,— so perfectly according to the genius of the community that, had they not existed, one could not conceive how they could not but day by day have arisen." Accordingly, the missionary enterprise is the work of the community as such. "The Unity of the Brethren and missions are indissolubly united. There will never be a Unity of Brethren without a mission to the heathen, nor a mission of the Brethren which is not the concern of the church as such." Without doubt the church of the Brethren "lives" to this day because of its missions. "It will be difficult to determine," says Schrautenbach again, "whether these missions have in later times borne more fruit within or without." "To

venture in faith,"—that from the beginning onwards made the little church so brave in action. Its watchword is spoken in the characteristic verse—

> "We will most gladly dare,
> While here we fare,
> Rest to forswear
>   That deed would miss.
> We would seek labour there
>   Where labour is;
> Nor of the work despair,
> But joy in care,
> And stones would bear
>   For the edifice."

There was no lack of those who offered themselves for missionary service even in the most dangerous fields. Differing from the Danish-Halle practice, missionaries who had not studied were sent out, and their humility and faithfulness gradually overcame the prejudice against the "unlearned laymen." At the first the expenses were comparatively small; the Brethren were not only accustomed to extreme simplicity and frugality, but had to earn their maintenance by the work of their hands. Debts were always quickly discharged, partly by the church, partly by outside friends and well-wishers. With patient self-denying love they interested themselves especially in the most miserable among the heathen "to whom no one else would go." Of mass-conversions— on this point in entire accord with the Pietists of Halle—they would on principle know nothing. "See you," Zinzendorf said to the missionaries "if you can win some souls to the Lamb"; and Spangenberg declared, "We are persuaded that our call is not to work anywhere for national conversions, that is, for the bringing of whole nations into the Christian church." This principle, as natural under the given condi tions as it was practically sound for missionary beginnings, became the cause of the lack of independence in mission-congregations, and of the neglect to train a native pastorate; defects which linger still to-day in the missions of the Brethren, although for a long time now efforts have been made to remedy them. In extenuation, however, we must keep in view that most of the objects of the missions of the Brethren stood on a low level of civilisation, and were formed of populations in part nationally disorganised and degraded. The instructions to missionaries were very simple, and the missionary methods were of a purely spiritual kind. The baptized were organised into congregations altogether after the model of those at home, and these were diligently visited on the part of the missionary directorate, which formed an integral part of the "Unitäts-Aeltestenkonferenz" [the governing board of the Moravian church].

Thus there arose within evangelical Christendom a missionary centre from which, without any ulterior ideas of colonial interest, and without any connection with political powers, but from purely religious motives, numerous heralds of the faith, men of self-sacrificing spirit, and blessed in their labour, went forth into three quarters of the globe,— a missionary centre which, as the living embodiment of a missionary church, summoned Protestanism to follow its example. But there was no following. Not only evangelical Germany, but Protestantism outside of Germany, remained cool and uninterested as regards missions. The reason for this did not lie only in the circumstance that Pietism, which had become the bearer of missions, was both in its Halle and in its Moravian complexion out of sympathy with church circles; there was a lack of spiritual life, and the age of the Enlightenment, which soon set in and brought all Christendom under the influence of a pedantic rationalism, had neither understanding nor inclination for missions. It was no longer the objections of the old orthodoxy which were brought forward in opposition to the duty of missions; but the discounting of the Christian faith, emptied of its mysteries, the indifference to the claim of Christianity to be in possession of the absolute truth, and the consequent form of tolerance, which would allow every one, Christian or non-Christian, to be saved after his own fashion,— these gave to the duty of missions the aspect of something superficial and arrogant. The more this tendency developed into the spirit of the age, not only did the antipathy of its adherents to every missionary effort become the greater, but just so much the more did this tendency fall like a mildew upon the missionary life actually existing. The church of the Brethren, indeed, was only washed round by the waves of the Enlightenment, not flooded by them, and held its missions above water,—one might truly say, its missions held it above water; on the other hand, the old Pietistic circles in the State churches were decomposed and paralysed by the Enlightenment,—until from South Ger-

many there came a rejuvenescence of the old Pietism, which, in association with the religious revival diffusing itself from England over the
Continent, brought forth, about the close of the century, a new missionary life.

Nevertheless, in what it did for missions, Germany, in the eighteenth
century, towered above all the other countries of evangelical Christendom. Missionary labourers like Francke, and especially Zinzendorf,
were nowhere else to be found. They were assuredly the "Fathers"
of evangelical missions to the heathen; the other forerunners of the
missions of the present were but as the fringe on the evening cloud.
On them and their work depends more or less directly almost all that
came to pass on a larger scale in the future for the extension of the
kingdom of God amongst the heathen.

45. In Holland the first zeal of the State missions decayed. They
had always been becoming more mechanical, and with the dawn of
the period of the Enlightenment, missionary duty to the colonies was
either forgotten or it was discharged in the most external fashion by
incompetent colonial clergymen. Most of the native Christian congregations went to decay from want of supervision. More and more countenance was given to Mohammedanism for political reasons, until this
tolerance towards Islam became almost tolerance towards evangelical
missions. Only in quite recent times has some change been introduced
into this perverted colonial policy.

46. In England also the eighteenth century presents no pleasant aspect. True, in 1701 there came to life "The Society for the Propagation
of the Gospel in Foreign Parts," designed in the first instance for the
British colonies in North America and the West Indies; but the slender
growth of the annual income, from £1535 in 1701 to £2608 in 1791,
shows that the society only dragged out a sickly existence. For the
actual converting of the heathen it made during that time only some
feeble endeavours amongst the Indians and negroes of America. More
was done by "The Society for Promoting Christian Knowledge."
Mainly through the zeal of Anton Wilhelm Boehme, a pupil of Francke,
who had settled in England and was appointed a court preacher there,
it was early induced to enter into union with the Danish-Halle mission,
and to support it with money. Afterwards it took some of the Danish-
Halle missionaries, Schwartz among them, entirely over into its service,
and in this way was instrumental to a transference of a portion of

the Danish-Halle mission-field into English hands. As the result of the circulation of the writings of Francke in England, this mission was in general rather popular; even at court contributions were gathered for it; and in a friendly private letter King George I. at least assured Ziegenbalg and Gründler of his interest in their work. In Edinburgh also there was formed in 1709 a "Society in Scotland for Propagating Christian Knowledge," which, however, did no mission work among the heathen beyond some measure of activity after 1740 in behalf of the North American Indians. Amongst the few missionaries sent out by its means, David Brainerd, in spite of the shortness of his work among the Delaware Indians, has a name distinguished in the history of missions. He died in 1747, only 29 years of age; but his biography, written by President Edwards, has exercised a great missionary influence: William Carey, Samuel Marsden, and Henry Martyn received decisive impulses from it. Lastly, the Rev. Dr. Doddridge (*d.* 1751) endeavoured to form a little missionary association in his congregation at Northampton and amongst his associates in office, and to train missionaries for the Indians, but his pupils left him from weakness of faith, and the interest in missions which he aroused seems scarcely to have gone beyond the bounds of his parish.

47. Certainly an active part in missions lay near enough to the English at this time, since their supremacy on the sea already surpassed that of all other European nations. In North and Central America, in Western Africa, and above all in the East Indies, a wide door to the heathen had in this way been opened to them. But beyond supporting the Indian and Danish-Halle missions, nothing was done by England for the extension of the kingdom of God among non-Christian peoples till towards the end of the eighteenth century. And why during that long time does the history of British missions remain almost a blank page?—Because there was lacking the spirit of faith which alone has power to write that page. "With the Restoration a deluge of satire was poured upon the Puritan régime. Court amusements, theatrical plays, and witticisms combined to make Christianity ridiculous, and the fashion of the day was to be a scoffer at religion. In that epoch England produced those 'free-thought' writings which have wrought so much harm in the world. Both parties in the Church kept aloof, but the anti-hierarchical party gradually lost the inward power which

it formerly had; in the history of that time it figures much more as only a political party, which allied itself to the Whigs. The Episcopal party, however, at the same time suffered a lapse of another kind. In order to counteract scoffers, recourse was had to the idea of exhibiting Christianity chiefly on the side on which it is open to the fewest objections, the side of its ethical teaching, and in order to commend it to the wise of this world the doctrines of faith were by degrees explained away. . . . In short, it was then that the system which is wont nowadays (1797) to be called 'Neology' was devised." How dark the night was which followed on that decline can best be perceived from the conditions which attended the breaking of the new day. The religious and moral decline of the Church of England was so great, that in 1726 Bishop Butler refused the election to the primacy because he thought it was too late to save the church. In the Preface to his celebrated *Analogy* he wrote: "It is come, I know not how, to be taken for granted by many persons, that Christianity is not so much as a subject of inquiry; but that it is now at length discovered to be fictitious. And accordingly they treat it as if, in the present age, this were an agreed point among all people of discernment." In the upper circles it excited laughter when the conversation happened upon religion. Blackstone, the celebrated advocate, had the fancy, at the beginning of the reign of George III., to go from church to church to hear all the preachers of repute. "I did not hear," he says, "a single sermon which had in it more Christianity than the writings of Cicero, and it was impossible for me to discover whether the preacher was a follower of Confucius, Mahomet, or Christ." The great majority of the clergymen, many of whom held several benefices at the same time—one actually 17—which they attended to through miserably paid vicars, "hunted, shot, farmed, swore, played, drank, but—seldom preached, and when they preached it was so badly that it was a comfort that they spoke to empty pews." The bishops led the way with the worst of examples: they were wholly worldly men. Archibishop Cornwallis gave such scandalous balls and plays in Lambeth Palace, that the king sent him a written command to stop them. At the same time there prevailed, especially in the upper classes, an immorality which stood in flagrant contrast to the beautiful moral sermons which had taken the place of the proclamation of the Gospel. Whoredom, adultery, gambling, swearing, drunkenness, Sabbath desecration passed for aristocratic passions. Among the Dissenters matters were not so bad, but even their communities lay in a spiritual sleep. "In the secure possession of the desired religious liberty they forgot the great living principles of their forefathers, as well as their own duty and responsibility."

48. With the religious and moral life in such a sunken condition, it was impossible, in spite of all colonial progress, that a missionary life could strike root. There must first come a religious revival to make the dead bones live, and this revival came,—one of the greatest and most permanent known in Christian church history. It did not come along the way of literature, which Butler and others had entered in defence of the calumniated faith, valuable as are the services which the writings of these men rendered; and it did not come through the labours of the worldly church officers, neither of the State church nor of the free church; these officers only repressed it. It came, as all great spiritual movements have ever come, through individual divinely endowed instruments, who—almost all clergymen of the State church— had experienced a personal quickening out of death into life, and then, as witnesses of this life in preaching of spiritual power, brought about the dawn of a new day. At the head of these men stand John Wesley (1703-1791) and George Whitefield (1714-1770). These two men, of kindred spirit though differently constituted, and at a later date severed from one another, were from their youth religiously inclined; they sincerely sought the truth, and led a morally earnest, almost ascetic, life; but they did not know the secret of the Gospel of redemption in the blood of Christ, of the salvation of the sinner by grace, and of justification by faith. These fundamental truths they knew not, although John Wesley founded among the students in Oxford in 1730 a society, nicknamed "the Holy Club," for the study of the Bible and for service among the poor and prisoners and destitute persons, which was joined amongst others by Whitefield. Wesley went in 1736 to Georgia in North America as preacher, and at the same time as missionary to the Indians, but did not accomplish much; here, however, he came into contact with members of the church of the Brethren, particularly with Spangenberg, and through them, especially through his intercourse with Bishop Böhler in London, whither he returned in 1738, and after he had in the same year visited Herrnhut, where he met with Zinzendorf, he found righteousness and peace in faith in the

crucified Christ, an experience to which Luther's Preface to his "Exposition of the Epistle to the Romans" materially contributed. In like manner Whitefield also owed his knowledge of evangelical truth substantially to German Pietism, as he testifies in his diaries that "through the reading of the writings of Aug. H. Francke the beam of a Divine light broke into his soul like a flash, and then for the first time he knew that he must become a quite different and new creature." Both these men, who were possessed of great popular eloquence, began now as itinerant preachers to proclaim through the whole land the forgotten evangelical foundation truths, with the convincing power of personal experience and burning indefatigable zeal, simply, and with stirring appeal to the heart. The churches being soon closed to them, they preached in the open air, almost daily, to thousands, and with great success, in spite of much derision and persecution.

But Wesley and Whitefield did not remain isolated witnesses; they were joined by a small number of men, chiefly from the Church of England, who had been led to a living faith, partly independently of them and partly through their influence. These men have not become so well known as the great initiators of the revival, but they have contributed greatly not only to its expansion, but to its purifying. And this movement, of which the Methodist denomination, forced into existence mainly by the opposition of the State church, is only an offshoot, was not confined to England alone; amid the storms and troubles which marked the history of the world towards the end of the century, this movement propagated itself upon the continent of Europe and in North America, bridging over all national and confessional boundaries, and forming societies in which pulsed the life of primitive love. No doubt this revival, much more than the German Pietist revival, bore a certain impress of the forcing process, and something of its methodist hue it has carried also into other lands; but what distinguished it was its striving after a personal apprehension of salvation, joy in the glad tidings of the Gospel, the warmth of its testimony, the cordiality of its brotherly love, zeal for the practical attestation of faith, and above all the impulse to save others after one had himself been saved.

In its beginnings this movement was not a missionary movement, but the new spiritual life which it brought forth was the soil in which a new missionary life took root.

9

A History of the Expansion of Christianity [10]
Kenneth Scott Latourette

Introduction

The seven-volume work by Kenneth Scott Latourette, *A History of the Expansion of Christianity,* has become the standard work on the history of Christian missions. Latourette's organization, interpretation, and documentation (30,000 references) of this work has made it the most sought after source in the field today. Volume I deals with *The First Five Hundred Years.* It traces the advance of Christianity from its obscure Palestinian beginning westward as far as Spain, northward as far as Ireland, southward as far as Ethiopia, and eastward as far as India. Volume II describes *The Thousand Years of Uncertainty.* It recounts the tragic losses to Islam in Palestine, Syria, Mesopotamia, Persia, Arabia, North Africa, Egypt, and the Iberian peninsula in the first wave of Muslim advance; and in Turkey and Central Asia in the second wave. However, it also accents the Christian advance farther into central and western Europe and Britain, into the new territories of Scandinavia, the Slavic lands, and even into China (though the Nestorian mission there was short-lived). Volume III, *Three Centuries of Advance,* chronicles the phenomenal advance of Roman Catholicism especially in the Americas but also in Asia. It also highlights the Protestant beginnings through the profound influence of European Pietism which experienced a revival in the latter part of the period. It further deals with the early stirrings in Britain and North America.

The next three volumes reveal the incredible story of Protestant missionary advance over the globe during *The Great Century* (Nineteenth). Volume IV deals with Europe and the United States, volume V with North

Africa and Asia, and volume VI with the Americas, Australia, and Africa. Of course, Latourette continues his account of Roman Catholicism and of the Orthodox Church in this predominately Protestant era. Volume VII, *Advance Through the Storm,* deals with the period between the two world wars, 1914-1944. Though some new territories were being conquered, the primary frontiers were not geographical. A whole new series of conflicting and challenging movements and issues became the new frontiers. Latourette's special approach in dealing with the reasons of both advance and decline and his interpretation of the effect of Christianity and the environment on each other, along with his invaluable summaries and extensive documentation, make this comprehensive and inclusive study a monumental work indeed.

Kenneth Scott Latourette was born in Oregon City, Oregon, in 1884. He was educated at McMinnville College, Oregon, and at Yale. He was ordained as a Baptist minister. After receiving his doctorate at Yale, he went to China to teach in the Yale-in-China program. When illness forced his return, he taught at colleges in Oregon and Ohio. In 1921, he became professor of missions and oriental history at Yale University, a post which he held until his retirement in 1953. A pioneer among American scholars in the study of East Asia, he wrote a number of definitive works on China and Japan. He then expanded his literary interests to global concerns. In addition to his classic study on the expansion of Christianity, he wrote a standard one-volume *History of Christianity* (1953). Just before he died in 1968, he completed another monumental work, a five-volume study of *Christianity in a Revolutionary Age: A History of Christianity in the Nineteenth and Twentieth Centuries.* This significant work which covers material up to the 1960s is a kind of sequel to his early seven volume masterpiece.[11]

Among Latourette's personal and public achievements were: president of the American Baptist Convention, member of the American Baptist Foreign Mission Society for twenty years, president of the American Society of Church History and the American Historical Association, president of the Far Eastern Association and the Japan International Christian University Foundation. He was active in the International YMCA and the International Missionary Council, and played a part in the drafting of the constitution of the World Council of Churches. He was one of the leading missionary statesmen of his day.[12]

The Great Century. By Way of Summary and Anticipation

The period to which we have devoted three volumes requires a summary. In the nineteenth century the geographic stream of Christianity so broadened that we have been compelled to allot as much space to its expansion as we did to its course in all the preceding eighteen centuries. This has required us to traverse practically all of the land surface of the globe. It has involved us in many countries and peoples. In spite of the fact that we have ruthlessly compressed the story, so multiform were the activities of Christianity and so wide its extension that we have been constrained to record great numbers of movements and names. To some readers these must have seemed very confusing. At times the chief trends may have appeared to be obscured by the many details. Before we move on to the fateful years which followed 1914 we must, therefore, pause for a moment for retrospect and for an attempt to disentangle from the masses of facts which we have poured upon our pages the main strands which have run through the decades. We shall then be in a position to view with a little more understanding the stormy era ushered in by the events of 1914 and be better prepared to cast our eyes back over the course of Christianity from the beginning. It is these two tasks which we have reserved for our final volume. As a preparation for that undertaking we must endeavour to see the period from A.D. 1800 to A.D. 1914 as a whole.

The nineteenth century confronted Christianity with problems which for variety and magnitude were unprecedented in the history of that faith. Again, as more than once before in its experience, Christianity faced the disintegration of a culture with which it had become intimately associated. In its first five centuries it had won the professed allegiance of the Græco-Roman world. The achievement had not been completed when that world fell to pieces. The decay had begun long before Christianity became prominent, but that faith proved powerless to arrest it. Moreover, the rise of the Crescent not only tore away much of the Mediterranean from the Cross but also handicapped the latter's spread in the East. Yet Christianity survived the collapse of the Roman Empire and provided the vehicle through which much of the civilization of the region governed by that realm was transmitted to future ages and to other peoples. Christianity entered potently into the creation of the culture of medieval Europe. Indeed, it helped to mould more phases of the Europe of the Middle Ages than it had of the Græco-Roman era. In spite of the obstacles presented by Islam, it expanded, although in minority enclaves, across the entire breadth of Asia. Then the structure of medieval Europe gave place to a new and different one which arose from it. The Crescent, borne by the Ottoman Turks, rose over the Cross in Asia Minor, Constantinople, and the Balkans. The Christian communities scattered across central and eastern Asia disappeared. In its chief remaining stronghold, western Europe, Christianity suffered from internal divisions and corrupt leadership. While Christianity was still at low ebb, European peoples began voyages, conquests, and settlements which carried them over much of the surface of the globe. Then great revivals in the form of Protestantism and the Catholic Reformation brought fresh access of life to the Christianity of western Europe. New movements made that Christianity more vigorous than it had yet been. So potent was it that missionaries accompanied or followed the explorers and settlers and in great areas preceded them and even went where they did not. Christianity was planted more widely than it had ever been and ameliorated the impact of European upon non-European peoples. In the second half of the eighteenth century Christianity was again threatened. The nations through which it had chiefly spread in the preceding three centuries, Spain and Portugal, were in decline. Rationalistic scepticism made sterile the faith of many. The French Revolution, in part anti-Christian, shook Europe. Western peoples were torn by wars, some of them worldwide in their dimensions. These changes were but a prelude to others which profoundly altered the entire life and thought of Western peoples. The scientific method was developed and applied to man and his physical environment. The Industrial Revolution came. Vast shifts and great increases of population were witnessed. Huge cities arose. Man's mental horizons expanded. Old political forms and social institutions disappeared or were altered almost beyond recognition. Many Western Europeans openly disowned Christianity and in several countries the Church was disestablished and ceased to be the official faith of the nation. European peoples poured into sparsely settled portions of the globe and gave rise to new nations. They mastered all the Americas, the islands of the Pacific, and Africa. They dominated most of Asia. Could Christianity persist in this new age? Would it not be at the most a more or less slowly vanishing remnant of an outgrown and discredited order? There were many, among them some of the most intelligent and vocal spokesmen of the fresh movements, who were certain that this would be its fate. Indeed, they declared that the mortal illness had set in and that the death throes could already be discerned.

Once again Christianity proved its capacity to survive the demise of a culture which it had helped to shape and of which it appeared to be an integral part. Not only did it continue but, as in western Europe after the fall of the Roman Empire, it went on to enhanced power. Although its significance was not then appreciated, the revival had commenced in the fore part of the eighteenth century, before the break-down of the old order had more than begun. It gathered momentum as the decades passed. Through it Christianity accompanied and here and there pioneered in the expansion of European peoples. Never had the faith won adherents among so many peoples and in so many countries. Never had it exerted so wide an influence upon the human race. Measured by geographic extent and the effect upon mankind as a whole, the nineteenth century was the greatest century thus far in the history of Christianity. That extension and that effect mounted as the century wore on. They were growing when, in 1914, world-shattering events ushered in a new period.

Some features of the nineteenth century favoured the spread of Christianity. The era was one of comparative peace. No wars of the magnitude of those which preceded 1815 and of those which began in 1914 disturbed mankind. Western peoples were accumulating wealth

PAX ROMANA

and were multiplying in numbers and in power. Technically they were still embraced within Christendom and their faith came to non-European peoples with the prestige of their dazzling might. Some of their wealth, although only a small fraction of it, was devoted to the financing of Christian missions. Improved means of communication facilitated the travel of missionaries and contacts between the younger churches and the parent churches of the Occident. The disintegration of non-European cultures under the impact of the Occident lessened resistance to Christianity. In some instances the collapse of the old orders made for a wistful and even eager acceptance of the Christian faith as a source of certainty and guidance in a crumbling world.

Although several exterior circumstances facilitated it, the nineteenth century expansion of Christianity would not have occurred had the faith not displayed striking inward vitality. That vitality expressed itself in part through the revivals which began in the eighteenth and in part through others which came in the nineteenth century.

These were in both Roman Catholicism and what for lack of a better name is called collectively, although inaccurately, Protestantism. They were particularly marked in Protestantism. Indeed, in some respects the nineteenth century was pre-eminently the Protestant century. In both numbers and influence Protestantism grew relatively much more rapidly than did any other major division of Christianity. The main current of the Christian stream seemed now to be flowing through it.

The reasons for the forging to the fore of Protestantism were not simple nor were all of them clear. They were associated with the leadership of the predominantly Protestant Great Britain in the industrial revolution and with the outstanding place of the British Isles and the United States, both more Protestant than Roman Catholic, in the expansion of European peoples in the nineteenth century. Just as between the fifteenth and the nineteenth century the expansion of Europe and of Christianity had been chiefly through Spain and Portugal, Roman Catholic by faith, so now it was powers in which Protestanism was the characteristic religion which were in the ascendant. How far the Portuguese and the Spaniards on the one hand, and the Anglo-Saxons, British and American, on the other, owed their leadership to the particular form of Christianity which they espoused is not clear. That in each instance their faith had some share in their hegemony appears probable. That in the earlier period Roman Catholicism and in the latter period Protestantism profited by the association is certain. Both the vigour and the power of these peoples contributed to the extension of the forms of the faith with which they were so intimately bound.

In several ways the spread of Christianity in the nineteenth century was by processes which differed strikingly from those of any previous period. In spite of the intimate connexion with the expansion of European, ostensibly Christian peoples, there was less direction and active assistance from the state than in any era since the beginning of the fourth century. The extension was chiefly by voluntary organizations supported by the gifts of private individuals. More of these bodies came into being than in any previous century. Never before had Christianity or any other religion had so many individuals giving full time to the propagation of their faith. Never had so many hundreds of thousands contributed voluntarily of their means to assist the spread of Christianity or of any other religion. In general, higher standards were maintained by both Protestants and Roman Catholics for the instruction and baptism of converts from non-Christian religions than had been customary since the first three centuries. To this generalization there were many exceptions, but the trend was decidedly in that direction. This was partly because of a similar tendency in Europe and America. By tradition, Christianity had been the group religion of western and northern European peoples. It had been accepted through mass movements, as have been most religions, and it continued as part of the group heritage. Yet this was not in full accord with the initial genius of Christianity. While it had social implications, the life into which the Christian Gospel led could be entered upon only by individual decision and faith. In the nineteenth century the climate of opinion was increasingly against the automatic identity of membership in the community and the Church. This was partly from revolt against the Church and partly from the greater emphasis by the churches upon the standards for membership. Since the higher requirements were insisted upon by the more earnest elements in the churches, and since it was from these elements that the missionaries and their supporters were chiefly drawn, it was to be expected that the prerequisites for baptism of non-Christians would be fairly exacting.

Thanks to the several favouring circumstances, in the course of the nineteenth century Christianity was diffused across most of the land surface of the globe.

In eastern Europe the Greek Orthodox Church made advances at the expense of paganism and Islam. Here and there in many countries of Europe there were conversions from the Jews. Yet there occurred no mass movement of Jews towards Christianity. In the vast shifts of population in western Europe which accompanied the rise of industrialism and the growth of great cities, thousands lost the close touch with the Church which had traditionally been that of their ancestors. A large proportion of the labourers in the factories drifted away from their hereditary faith. However, in many areas the churches followed the migrations to the cities. New parishes were created and church buildings erected. Fresh methods were devised to meet the novel conditions. In England particularly the labour movement and the co-operatives for the purchase and sale of the necessities of life for the labourers and the middle classes had much of their impulse from the Christian faith, especially through the nonconformist bodies.

In the United States the period opened with less than one-tenth of the population counted as members of churches. During the century Christianity was confronted with a vast westward migration of population, with an almost equally great influx from Europe, with the Indians and the Negroes, exploited non-Christian minorities, and with the progressive industrialization of the land. It met these problems with a high degree of success. The church membership rose from less than one-tenth to more than two-fifths of the total population. The gains were all along the line. Progress was registered in the older settled portions of the country, in winning an increasing proportion of the westward moving population, in holding to their hereditary faith very large sections of the immigration from Europe, and in bringing to baptism about the same proportion of Negroes and Indians as of the whites.

In Canada an even higher proportion of the population acknowledged a relationship with the churches than in the United States, and that in the face of settlement in the West, of fresh immigration from across the Atlantic, of widely scattered Indian tribes, and of Eskimos. Practically all the sparse population of Greenland became Christians. In the West Indies great advances were made among the Negroes who constituted the large majority of the inhabitants of most of the islands under British, Danish, and Dutch rule.

In Latin America the fore part of the nineteenth century witnessed discouraging reverses. During the throes of the struggle for independence and in the subsequent political developments, the Church suffered severely. The successful struggle of the American-born whites to free themselves from the domination of the European-born cost it a large proportion of its higher clergy and its missionaries. The efforts of the new governments to obtain the kind of control over the Church which had been exercised by the Spanish and Portuguese crowns and the reluctance of Spain to acknowledge the new political status brought Rome much embarrassment and retarded the adjustment to the new order. The suspicion and enmity of anti-clericals in high office wrought restrictions on the Church. As a survivor of the colonial era, the Church seemed to many of the progressive obscurantist and the last bulwark of an outmoded and oppressive regime. Many of the missions to the non-Christian Indians fell into ruin and in some sections the quality of the clergy declined. However, the actual numerical losses were slight. In the latter part of the century here and there the morale of the Church began to show improvement. Moreover, Protestantism entered, partly by immigration and partly by active missions to non-Protestants. It made some gains among non-Christian Indians, but its converts were mostly from nominal Roman Catholics. The Eastern churches were represented by small groups of immigrants.

In Australia and New Zealand new nations, predominantly of British stock, came into being. In them the churches were strong and held the professed allegiance of the overwhelming majority of the population. In the islands of the Pacific, very numerous but most of them small, Christianity made rapid progress. In some of them practically the entire population became Christian. In the larger islands conversion was retarded. As in Australia and New Zealand, the Christianity thus planted was chiefly Protestant and secondarily Roman Catholic.

In the great congeries of islands known as the East Indies, the larger part of them brought under Dutch rule, Christianity achieved striking gains, but amongst the animistic rather than the Moslem or Hindu population. Until 1914 the advance was made mainly by Protestant rather than Roman Catholic agencies.

The Philippines, since the sixteenth century the major outpost of Christianity in the western Pacific, continued to be overwhelmingly Roman Catholic. In the nineteenth century that branch of the faith gained slowly among the animistic folk in the mountains but was unable to make an impression upon the Moros, Moslem Malays in the southern islands. After the American occupation, in 1898, Protestantism entered and won adherents, chiefly from the Roman Catholics. A large nationalistic schism tore away hundreds of thousands from the Roman Catholics into an independent church. The Roman Catholics began a reorganization of their forces.

In Madagascar notable accessions came to Christianity, both Protestant and Roman Catholic, chiefly from the dominant Hòva but also from some of the other tribes. In several of the island groups between Madagascar and India or which fringed Africa Christianity was either planted for the first time or was reinforced.

In South Africa a new nation arose, governed by a British and Dutch minority, within the British Empire. The white population was, for the most part, professedly Christian. Active missions, mostly Protestant, won large numbers of the blacks. In all the other political entities into which Africa south of the Sahara was carved by European states before 1914, Christianity, both Roman Catholic and Protestant, had a rapid spread, particularly in the generation immediately preceding 1914.

Roman Catholic and Protestant missionaries were numerous and active on the northern shores of Africa and in western Asia. Since, however, the region was overwhelmingly Moslem, few converts were made. On the northern coast of Africa, chiefly in Algeria and Tunisia, Christian communities arose, but by immigration from Europe. Elsewhere in the traditional strongholds of Islam Christian missionaries found their fields predominantly among the Christian minorities which persisted from pre-Moslem days.

In India a striking growth of Christianity was witnessed. It was facilitated by the British conquest, but it came primarily in consequence of the revivals in the Christianity of the Occident. The majority of the missionaries were not British. Roman Catholic missionaries were mostly from the continent of Europe and a large proportion of the Protestant emissaries were from that continent and the United States. Yet the British led in the Protestant enterprise and had a part, even though small, in the Roman Catholic undertaking. In 1914 Christianity was strong, as it had been in 1800, in the Portuguese enclaves and the South. It had also made extensive gains in other parts of the land, notably in the South. The ancient communities of Syrian or St. Thomas Christians persisted, but in so far as they increased they did so almost entirely by an excess of births over deaths. They gained very few converts. The great advances were made by the Roman Catholics and the Protestants. These were mainly from among the depressed classes and the primitive hill tribes.

In 1914 Ceylon had a larger percentage of Christians than did any other land in Asia except Siberia, some portions of western Asia, and, if they be included in the Asiatic world, the Philippines. The Christians of Ceylon were chiefly the fruits of the Portuguese occupation. To them were added some by nineteenth century Roman Catholic and Protestant missions. In Burma the gains were mainly among the Karens and somewhat more by Protestants than by Roman Catholics. In Siam, because of the nearly solidly Buddhist character of the population, the numerical advances, whether by Roman Catholics or by Protestants, were not so striking as in some of the neighbouring lands. In British Malaya there were accessions from Chinese and Indian immigrants. In the portions of Indo-China which by 1914 had come under French control, Roman Catholic Christianity, dating from pre-nineteenth century times, enjoyed a prosperous growth, and that in spite of persecution in the first three-quarters of the century and of the anti-clerical bias of much of the later French administration.

In the vast Chinese Empire Christianity made progress, but at unequal rates in the various sections. Its accessions were mostly in the two decades immediately preceding 1914. They were chiefly in the provinces along the coast and the lower reaches of the Yangtze River, the areas most affected by the impact of the Occident. They were least numerous in the regions farthest from the sea, Tibet, Sinkiang, and Mongolia. Yet no province or outlying dependency was without them. Numerically Roman Catholicism was much stronger than Protestantism, for it had been in the land much longer. However, proportionately Protestantism was growing more rapidly.

In Japan the missionary activity which had been forcibly suspended early in the seventeenth century could not be renewed until past the middle of the nineteenth century. When it was resumed, the discovery was made that Christianity had not been entirely extirpated by the rigours of persistent persecution, but had merely been driven into hiding and had been somewhat reduced in strength. Through the adherence of many of these Christians, Roman Catholicism had an initial high rate of accessions. The Russian Orthodox Church was represented, chiefly through the leadership of a great missionary. However, the major advance was by Protestants, predominantly through missionaries from the United States, and mainly from the intellectual and professional classes most affected by Western learning.

In Korea Roman Catholic Christianity arrived late in the eighteenth century. In spite of recurring persecution of great severity it gained an enduring foothold. The suspension of persecution and the partial conformation to Western cultural patterns which followed the treaties of the 1880's were accompanied by a marked extension of the Christian communities. Protestantism, as in Japan propagated mainly from the United States, prospered more than did Roman Catholicism.

In the huge but thinly settled portions of Asia occupied by Russia, Christianity made notable gains through migration from Europe. It was mostly Orthodox, but there were Roman Catholic and Protestant minorities. There were also Orthodox missions among the animistic aborigines.

This rapid and compact summary will at least serve to show how widely Christianity had been disseminated in the nineteenth century. Nothing to equal it had previously been seen in the history of the faith. Nothing remotely approaching it could be recorded of any other religion at any time in the human scene.

We must note, however, that Christianity did not displace rival cults over as wide areas as it had in some earlier stages of its spread. In this respect it had no achievement comparable to its elimination of the historic faiths of the Mediterranean world in its first five centuries or to its destruction of its rivals in western Europe in what we have termed "the thousand years of uncertainty." Nor did it deal such shattering blows to non-Christian religions for so many millions as it had between A.D. 1500 and A.D. 1800 in Mexico, much of the west coast of South America, and the Philippines. Among non-European peoples its major gains were from animistic or near-animistic folk and against some of the near-primitive types of faith. Here and there, as in some of the islands of the Pacific, it eradicated the antecedent cults. Against the major high religions of Asia, however, it made only slight advances. This may have been in part because of the brevity of the time in which it had to operate. In most of Asia it did not get well under way until the second half of the century. The twentieth and twenty-first centuries might conceivably tell a different story. Yet down to A.D. 1914 the major non-Christian systems of Asia and even of animistic

Africa were either substantially intact or had only begun to disintegrate.

More important even than geographic spread is the question of the effect which Christianity had upon its varied environments.

This is much more difficult to determine than the rather obvious fact of the world-wide extension of the faith. Some questions, of extreme importance, can probably not be answered beyond cavil. How far, for instance, if at all, was Christianity responsible for the origin of the scientific method, the closely related development of nineteenth century industry, and the associated renewed expansion of Western peoples which were outstanding features of the period? That by the discipline which it gave the western European mind through the scholasticism which its theology inspired in the Middle Ages and by the faith to which it contributed in the orderliness, dependability, and rationality of the universe Christianity was one of the sources of the scientific approach seems not only possible but probable. Yet he would be rash who would venture the assertion that it was the essential source. That at times Christian missionaries, most notably David Livingstone, were pioneers in nineteenth century exploration by Europeans is clear. That their Christian faith constituted their driving and sustaining motive seems also incontrovertible. That but for them the geographic discoveries would not soon have been made would be a most dubious generalization. That it was the daring faith bred in the European spirit by Christianity which inspired even seemingly irreligious individuals reared in the milieu of which it was an ingredient to climb unscaled mountains, to search for the North and South Poles, and to embark upon vast industrial undertakings and the building of huge empires is an interesting hypothesis. That it is indubitable truth only the ignorant or the rashly dogmatic would confidently assert. Similarly the situation is too complex to deny or to affirm that Christianity was either a waning or a growing force in the culture of the Occident. Plausible cases can be made for both contentions.

However, although there are many unresolved and probably unresolvable uncertainties, in some phases of culture potent Christian influences can be clearly established.

One of the most obvious of these was the emergence of Christian churches in areas where they had not existed at the dawn of the nineteenth century. This was seen especially in large portions of North America, in New Zealand and much of Australia, in many of the islands of the Pacific, in vast reaches in Africa, and in many sections of India, the Chinese Empire, Japan, Korea, and Siberia.

Another of the well authenticated effects of Christianity was, as in all ages, the transformation to be seen in individual character. In a very large proportion, perhaps in most of its converts, Christianity worked a moral and spiritual change. In some lives, usually the small minority, this was revolutionary. There were those who found satisfaction after a long and agonizing spiritual quest. Others won emancipation from a crippling habit. Some were released from hate. Many were absolved from the fear of the surrounding spirit world. To a few choice souls the Christian faith meant not so much a revolution as an enrichment of insights obtained through nurture in other religions. To some with a keen social conscience the Christian faith brought courage to face apparently impossible odds in fighting entrenched evils or in seeking to build wholesome order in an age of destructive change. To millions who were not fresh converts, but who had behind them generations of Christian heritage, Christianity was also an important formative factor. It entered into the moral and spiritual ideals in which they were nurtured. In a real sense each, no matter what his ancestry, had on his own account to begin the Christian life. For many this was through the processes of prolonged nurture. For others it was by soul-shaking struggles. To all who were genuinely Christian, there were crises along the way brought by decisions which had to be reached, burdens which could not well be avoided, illness, or other misfortune, in the meeting of which the resources of the faith were of major importance.

In the realm of the intellect and of education Christianity made outstanding contributions. Christian missionaries reduced more languages to writing than had been given that expression in all the previous history of the race. For the tongues of the majority of mankind means of writing already existed, but the speech of many millions had not been provided with these facilities until that was done by Christian missionaries of the nineteenth century. These previously illiterate languages, although spoken by only the minority of the race, were more numerous than those which had heretofore been rendered literate. The prime purpose of missionaries in this achievement was the spread and maintenance of the Christian faith. Portions or all of the Bible were translated by nineteenth century missionaries into more languages than had ever any other one book. Missionaries were not content with issuing religious literature. They also put into one or another non-European language much material from the Occident which was not strictly in the field of religion but which they hoped would prove useful to the peoples among whom they laboured. Such were the treatises on international law and the large medical literature prepared for the Chinese.

Never before had any other set of agencies pioneered in education for as many different peoples as did the Christian missions of the nineteenth century. Even Christianity itself, which already had behind it a notable record in education, in this respect surpassed its previous history. This was true of schools of all grades, from the elementary through the university. Christianity stimulated on the one hand the spread among the masses of the rudiments of education and on the other the most advanced training and research, with the pushing forward of the borders of human knowledge into the hitherto unknown. This was seen especially on the geographic frontiers of the advance of western European peoples. As scattered illustrations of these generalizations one remembers the scores of colleges and universities planted by the churches on the westward-moving frontier of white settlement in the United States and Canada; the part of Christian home missionaries in bringing into being inclusive tax-supported public education in some of the newer of the United States; the achievement of Roman Catholics in the United States in the creation of church-controlled systems of education from primary grades through the universities; the fact that in 1914 the large majority of the universities of the United States which were outstanding in their advanced research, although largely or entirely independent of ecclesiastical control, owed their inception to one or another of the churches or to a religious movement; the commanding position held by Oxford and Cambridge, ecclesiastical foundations, in higher education in the British Empire; and the fashion in which Christian missionaries led the way in the creation of schools of Western types in many non-Occidental lands, from some of the smaller islands of the Pacific to the huge continent of Africa and to the ancient lands of northern Africa and of western, southern, and eastern Asia.

From Christianity issued impulses which contributed to the fight against some of the chronic ills which have afflicted mankind. In country after country and among people after people Christian missionaries were pioneers in modern Occidental medicine and surgery. This was notably true in China, where the medical profession of the twentieth century owed its origin and the early stages of its development almost entirely to Protestant missions. The world-wide nursing profession of the nineteenth and twentieth centuries had one of its main sources in the institution of Kaiserswerth inaugurated by a Christian pastor in the attempt to meet the needs of an obscure parish. Missionaries later introduced it into region after region. Both in Occidental and non-Occidental lands, care for the blind, the insane, and the lepers owed much to devoted Christians. Hundreds of hospitals, large and small, in all the continents and in many of the islands of the sea were indebted to the churches for their inception. In China Christians fought the opium traffic and helped some of its victims to emancipation. Negro slavery, the largest scale exploitation of members of one race by another in the annals of mankind, was abolished through movements which had as their chief creators men and women whose consciences were made tender and whose resolution was given persistence and confidence by their Christian faith. On many fronts earnest Christians, numbers of them missionaries, fought the mistreatment of other races by their fellow-Occidentals. They sought, not without success, to ease the shock of the impact of Western culture upon non-Western peoples and to assist the latter to a wholesome adjustment to the impinging culture of the Occident. Christian idealism contributed to the benevolent objectives and programmes of British, Dutch, and American imperialism of the latter part of the period—as it had modified Spanish and Portuguese colonial laws and policies in the sixteenth, seventeenth, and eighteenth centuries. The efforts to curb war which displayed their chief strength in Great Britain and the United States usually were due at the outset to devout men and women who drew their convictions from their Christian faith.

The basic structure of Western civilization was not revolutionized. It was still marked by extreme nationalism and materialism and from time to time was disturbed by wars. It was far from conforming to Christian patterns. Yet Christianity was modifying it both in the Occident and in its outreach in other portions of the globe. By a strange contradiction, some of the chronic ills of mankind, notably slavery and war, attained their acme in the nineteenth and twentieth centuries among peoples which had been long subjected to Christian influences, yet the most vigorous movements which mankind had ever witnessed to free the world of these evils had their rise and development among these very peoples and to a great degree stemmed from Christianity. Whether the culture of the Occident was more or less shaped by Christianity than it had been two centuries earlier is impossible to determine. Christianity was potent within it as it had been since the nominal conversion of western Europe. Not in the centuries which Europeans termed the Middle Ages and when Western peoples numbered only a few millions and were an inconsiderable factor in the life of the race as a whole could Western civilization be properly termed Christian. Now in the day when Europeans had multiplied and had mastered most of the world it could still not accurately be given the appellation of Christian. Yet in both ages Christianity was an appreciable force within the Occident, modifying even though not fully informing every phase of life.

Not only was Western civilization not made over to conform fully to Christian standards. It was also true that in 1914 no non-European people could properly be designated as Christian. In the Philippines and a few of the smaller islands of the Pacific the majority of the population called themselves by that name. Their collective life bore the marks of Christianity, but no phase attained even approximately to Christian standards. In the major non-European peoples those calling themselves Christian were only a small percentage of the total population.

It was clear that Christianity, while powerful in human affairs, was as yet far from remaking mankind into the image of its ideal. Some of the states of the Occident were officially Christian. Several subscribed to Christian principles in their laws, morals, and social institutions. At least one large government, however, had frankly severed a Christian connexion of long standing and in others the drift was in that direction. Professing Christians were more numerous and more widely spread than ever before. Their faith was having a greater effect upon mankind as a whole than in any former period. Yet the trend was towards the situation in the first three centuries in the Græco-Roman world, when Christians were self-conscious minorities, in the world but not fully of it. This was in part due to the nature of Christianity. The goal set forth in the New Testament could probably never be fully attained "within history." Judged by the standards of Jesus and the early Apostles no individual could hope to be perfect this side of the grave.

However, there was that in the Christian faith which forbade Christians ever to rest content short of its high calling. In it, too, was that which encouraged them to strive to attain the exacting goal. They were assured that if not within history, then beyond it, they were to be "filled unto all the fulness of God." They could not be satisfied to leave the world about them to destruction. They might believe that the full realization of the Christian hope by any human society was impossible. Yet they were commanded to love their neighbours. That meant that they must seek to relieve the myriad wants of those about them. Moreover, one of the obligations laid upon them in the New Testament was to teach all nations to observe all that their Lord had commanded them, an injunction which made a duty the attempt to bring all mankind to the standards of the Sermon on the Mount. This was to be their objective and in the endeavour to attain it they were promised the companionship of an unseen all-powerful Presence. With these qualities in its very nature, Christianity, if it were not to deny its genius, must continue to be a leaven in the affairs of men. It was still young. Presumably it had only begun its course. The nineteen centuries during which it had been present were only a small fraction of the total history of the race. If one could judge by its past record, Christianity would continue to spread. In general, it came to the year 1914 on an ascending curve. It was now for the first time almost world-wide in its representation. Much of that was the achievement of the preceding few decades. Christianity was gaining momentum.

In what for the present may seem an anticlimax, we must pause to say something of the effect of the nineteenth century environment upon Christianity. Clearly the Christianity of 1914 was not identical with that of 1800. This was partly because of inner developments within the faith itself, partly because of changes brought by expansion, and partly because of the temper of the times. It is not easy to disentangle the various factors which issued in the modifications, but some of the alterations are obvious.

The main strains of Christianity which were present in 1800 continued. However, by 1914 what is usually called Protestantism was, in relation to the others, much stronger than at the beginning of the nineteenth century. Indeed, the term Protestantism had become more than ever a misnomer. What was embraced under that designation had never been merely a reaction against Roman Catholicism. It had, rather, been a series of fresh movements which the structure of Latin Christianity had not proved flexible enough to retain. These movements had now been so long separated from the parent stock that they could less than ever be deemed a protest. They were positive affirmations with their own ecclesiastical structures and their characteristic forms of religious experience and expression. The fresh awakenings within Protestantism in the eighteenth and nineteenth centuries were making that wing of Christianity ever more distinct from Roman Catholicism and increasingly an independent set of movements. Protestantism preserved many features of historic Christianity. By clinging to the Bible even more emphatically than did Roman Catholics and the Eastern churches it conserved much of the primitive spirit of the faith. Anglicanism and some phases of Lutheranism held to much of what had been developed by the church of the West in pre-Reformation times. Yet what had come out of the Roman Church at the time of the Reformation was clearly not a waning series of schisms. More and more the main stream of vitality in the Christian movement seemed to be flowing through it. This trend was strengthened by the nineteenth century spread of Christianity. Relatively Protestantism had a greater extension than any other form of the faith. It was ceasing to be so largely what it had been at the outset, a Teutonic expression of the transmitted Latin Christianity. It was becoming world-wide. In the largest of the new nations which arose out of the nineteenth century migrations of European peoples, the United States, Protestantism was dominant. In some of the others, Australia, New Zealand, the Union of South Africa, and, to a somewhat less degree, Canada, it was in the majority. In the traditionally Roman Catholic areas of Latin America and the Philippines it was winning growing minorities. In non-European lands it was making proportionately more rapid gains than was Roman Catholicism. In India, Ceylon, Indo-China, China, and some parts of Africa it was numerically not so strong as Roman Catholicism, but in Japan, Korea, the Netherlands Indies, and several sections of Africa Protestants outnumbered Roman Catholics, and in India and China they were having a greater effect upon the country as a whole. Such major social reforms as the anti-slavery, temperance, and peace movements issued more from Protestant than from Roman Catholic Christianity. In developing educational systems Protestantism was the more potent.

In some of its phases Protestantism was partly conforming to its environment. It was, in general, more inclined to adjust itself to the intellectual currents of the day than were the other main types of Christianity. Although by tradition fissiparous, it was beginning to come together in various co-operative enterprises. These were especially marked on the new geographic frontiers. In the United States, Canada, China, Japan, and India where many forms of Protestantism existed side by side, the trend was towards interpenetration of one variety by another and towards working together in common tasks. Through Protestantism a distinct kind of Christianity was already beginning to emerge in the United States. Here and there were indications of similar trends in Japan, China, and India.

The Roman Catholic Church also showed the effects of the nineteenth century environment. This was in part in a refusal to conform to such tendencies in its *milieu* as civil marriage, secularized education, and the application of some forms of historical method to the Bible and to its own history. It rejected its own "modernists." It was not as subservient to the state as it had been in the preceding three centuries. It affirmed the infallibility of the Pope. That pontiff had far more effective administrative power in the whole of his communion than he had enjoyed for several centuries. The Roman Catholic Church was spreading rapidly, but as a more and more highly co-ordinated body under a centralized authority.

Of the Eastern churches the strongest was that of Russia. The Russian Orthodox Church responded less to the spirit of the times than did either Protestantism or Roman Catholicism. It did not move out of Russia to any great extent. It remained in the position to which Peter the Great had reduced it, ancillary to the power of the Tsar and an instrument for enforcing Tsarist autocracy and assimilating non-Russian peoples to Russian culture.

In many ways 1914 marked no sudden break in the stream of Christian history. Numbers of the movements which had been gathering headway before that year persisted. After 1914 Christianity was still expanding, chiefly by conversions from non-European peoples. It became more nearly evenly distributed over the earth's surface than ever before. Through the development of indigenous leadership it also became more deeply rooted among non-European peoples. It continued to have profound effects, some of them of increasing magnitude, particularly upon non-European cultures in Africa, India, China, and Japan. What we have loosely but with confessed inaccuracy termed Protestantism more and more drew together through various phases of what came to be called the Ecumenical movement and reached out towards all branches of non-Roman Catholic Christianity. It even approached Roman Catholics, although very tentatively, in an attempt at reciprocal understanding and fellowship.

However, after 1914 the advances made by Christianity were accomplished in the face of a succession of storms. As never before, wars and revolutions shook the entire fabric of human life. Civilization the world around was in a stage of violent transition. To the spread of Christianity in that period of man's history, still incomplete, we turn in our next and final volume.

Notes

1. Eusebius, "The Evangelists that were still Eminent at that Time" and "Pantaenus the Philosopher," in Arthur Cushman McGiffert, trans. and ed., *The Church History of Eusebius*. Vol. I, *A Select Library of Nicene and Post-Nicene Fathers of the Christian Church*, second series (Grand Rapids: William B. Eerdmans Publishing Company, 1952), pp. 169, 224-225. Used by permission.

2. Hugh Jackson Lawlor and John Ernest Leonard Oulton, trans. and eds., *Eusebius, Bishop of Caesarea*, Vol. II (London: S.P.C.K., 1954), pp. 1-2, 7.

3. Chapters 23-26 from Bede: *A History of the English Church and People*, trans. Leo Sherley-Price (Penguin Classics, rev. ed., 1968), pp. 66-71. © Leo Sherley-Price, 1955, 1968. Reprinted by permission of Penguin Books Ltd.

4. C. J. Stranks, *The Venerable Bede* (London: S.P.C.K., 1955), p. 19.

5. Ibid., pp. 5-8, 18; Bede, *A History of the English Church and People*, pp. 336-338.

6. Adolf Harnack, "Results," *The Expansion of Christianity in the First Three Centuries*, Vol. II, James Moffat, trans. and ed. (New York: G. P. Putnam's Sons, 1905), pp. 452-453, 456-468.

7. Raymond W. Albright, "(Karl Gustav) Adolf Harnack," *Twentieth Century Encyclopedia*, p. 492.

8. Gustav Warneck, "The Age of Pietism," *Outline of a History of Protestant Missions from the Reformation to the Present Time* (New York: Fleming H. Revell Company, 1902), pp. 53-73.

9. W. Holsten, "Gustav Warneck," *Concise Dictionary*, pp. 643-644.

10. Chapter 10 (pp. 440-456) from *A History of the Expansion of Christianity*, Volume 6 "The Great Century in Northern Africa and Asia, 1800-1914" by Kenneth Scott Latourette. Copyright 1944 by Harper & Row, Publishers, Inc. By permission of the publishers.

11. Charles W. Forman, "Kenneth Scott Latourette," *Concise Dictionary*, pp. 336-337.

12. Ibid.

III

Missionary Biographies

General Introduction

Some of the best sources of mission history and one of the richest legacies of the missionary enterprise are the many missionary biographies which the movement has produced. It will be impossible to present even portions of most of the more significant ones. The ones included here can only be representative. In the journals and letters to follow, we shall gain glimpses into the lives of some of the other great stars of the missionary galaxy. All of this, however, will reveal only part of the illustrious company.

Just from the great century, the number of biographies is almost endless. Some of the more notable ones are: *The Lives of Robert and Mary Moffat* by John S. Moffat (Africa); *Memoirs of the Life and Labors of Robert Morrison* by E. Morrison (China); *Memoirs of the Life of the Rev. John Williams* by E. Prout (South Sea Islands); *The Life, Letters and Journals of the Rev. and Hon. Peter Parker M.D.* by G. B. Stevens (China); *Life of John Geddie, D.D.* by G. Patterson (New Hebrides); *Verbeck of Japan* by W. E. Griffis. The following selections will represent both early and later biographies.

10

Life of St. Martin [1]
Sulpitius Severus

Introduction

Martin was born in the town of Sabania in the province of Pannonia, Central Europe probably in 316. His father was a military officer and forced his son to follow in his steps, though as a child of ten, when he ran

117

away from home and took refuge in a church, he was possessed with the idea of being a monk. Even as a soldier, he lived like a monk. In time he was able to free himself from the military and pursue his ambition to be a monk. He became so famous for his piety and compassion that he was virtually conscripted to become a bishop. Even after he became bishop of Tours, however, he maintained the simple and rigorous lifestyle of a monk. He died in 397. Until recent times, Martin was to France what Patrick has been to Ireland. The following excerpts from his biography will reveal the forces that shaped his life and the nature of his work as a missionary-bishop.[2]

Sulpitius Severus (360?-410?) was a contemporary of Martin and was one of his greatest admirers and defenders. He seemed to sense the greatness of Martin in an unusual way. To write Martin's life became an obsession with him. He says: "I panted, I burned to write his life" (chapter XXV). He was so awed by Martin that his reverence for him was almost unreal. In chapter XXV he tells of his visit to Martin. Martin welcomed him "with amazing humility and loving kindness." He was overwhelmed when Martin stooped to wash his feet. He said: "I had not the courage to resist . . . I was so subdued by his authority that it would have seemed a sacrilege to prevent him from doing his will." He was enthralled by the manner and speech of Martin: "And in the words, the conversation of Martin, what gravity! What dignity! How penetrating, strong, prompt, easy were his answers to questions about the Gospels." Because Martin's austere manner offended some, Severus was his chief defender. He wrote numerous letters defending him and wrote a number of dialogues on his miracles.[3]

Christ appears to St. Martin

Accordingly, at a certain period, when he had nothing except his arms and his simple military dress, in the middle of winter, a winter which had shown itself more severe than ordinary, so that the extreme cold was proving fatal to many, he happened to meet at the gate of the city of Amiens a poor man destitute of clothing. He was entreating those that passed by to have compassion upon him, but all passed the wretched man without notice, when Martin, that man full of God, recognized that a being to whom others showed no pity, was, in that respect, left to him. Yet, what should he do? He had nothing except the cloak in which he was clad, for he had already parted with the rest of his garments for similar purposes. Taking, therefore, his sword with which he was girt, he divided his cloak into two equal parts, and gave one part to the poor man, while he again clothed himself with the remainder. Upon this, some of the by-standers laughed, because he was now an unsightly object, and stood out as but partly dressed. Many, however, who were of sounder understanding, groaned deeply because they themselves had done nothing similar. They especially felt this, because, being possessed of more than Martin, they could have clothed the poor man without reducing themselves to nakedness. In the following night, when Martin had resigned himself to sleep, he had a vision of Christ arrayed in that part of his cloak with which he had clothed the poor man. He contemplated the Lord with the greatest attention, and was told to own as his the robe which he had given. Ere long, he heard Jesus saying with a clear voice to the multitude of angels standing round—"Martin, who is still but a catechumen, clothed me with this robe." The Lord, truly mindful of his own words (who had said when on earth—"Inasmuch as ye have done these things to one of the least of these, ye have done them unto me"), declared that he himself had been clothed in that poor man; and to confirm the testimony he bore to so good a deed, he condescended to show him himself in that very dress which the poor man had received. After this vision the sainted man was not puffed up with human glory, but, acknowledging the goodness of God in what had been done, and being now of the age of twenty years, he hastened to receive baptism. He did not, however, all at once, retire from military service, yielding to the entreaties of his tribune, whom he admitted to be his familiar tent-companion. For the tribune promised that, after the period of his office had expired, he too would retire from the world. Martin, kept back by the expectation of this event, continued, although but in name, to act the part of a soldier, for nearly two years after he had received baptism.

High Esteem in which Martin was held

Nearly about the same time, Martin was called upon to undertake the episcopate of the church at Tours; but when he could not easily be drawn forth from his monastery, a certain Ruricius, one of the citizens, pretending that his wife was ill, and casting himself down at his knees, prevailed on him to go forth. Multitudes of the citizens having previously been posted by the road on which he traveled, he is thus under a kind of guard escorted to the city. An incredible number of people not only from that town, but also from the neighboring cities, had, in a wonderful manner, assembled to give their votes. There was but one wish among all, there were the same prayers, and there was the same fixed opinion to the effect that Martin was most worthy of the episcopate, and that the church would be happy with such a priest. A few persons, however, and among these some of the bishops, who had been summoned to appoint a chief priest, were impiously offering resistance, asserting forsooth that Martin's person was contemptible, that he was unworthy of the episcopate, that he was a man despicable in countenance, that his clothing was mean, and his hair disgusting. This madness of theirs was ridiculed by the people of sounder judgment, inasmuch as such objectors only proclaimed the illustrious character of the man, while they sought to slander him. Nor truly was it allowed them to do anything else, than what the people, following the Divine will, desired to be accomplished. Among the bishops, however, who had been present, a certain one of the name Defensor is said to have specially offered opposition; and on this account it was observed that he was at the time severely censured in the reading from the prophets. For when it so happened that the reader, whose duty it was to read in public that day, being blocked out by the people, failed to appear, the officials falling into confusion, while they waited for him who never came, one of those standing by, laying hold of the Psalter, seized upon the first verse which presented itself to him. Now, the Psalm ran thus: "Out of the mouth of babes and sucklings thou hast perfected praise because of thine enemies, that thou mightest destroy the enemy and the avenger." On these words being read, a shout was raised by the people, and the opposite party were confounded. It was believed that this Psalm had been chosen by Divine ordination, that Defensor might hear a testimony to his own work, because the praise of the Lord was perfected out of the mouth of babes and sucklings in the case of Martin, while the enemy was at the same time both pointed out and destroyed.

Martin as Bishop of Tours

And now having entered on the episcopal office, it is beyond my power fully to set forth how Martin distinguished himself in the discharge of its duties. For he remained with the utmost constancy, the same as he had been before. There was the same humility in his heart, and the same homeliness in his garments. Full alike of dignity and courtesy, he kept up the position of a bishop properly, yet in such a way as not to lay aside the objects and virtues of a monk.

. . . .

Martin escapes from a Falling Pine-tree

Again, when in a certain village he had demolished a very ancient temple, and had set about cutting down a pine-tree, which stood close to the temple, the chief priest of that place, and a crowd of other heathens began to oppose him. And these people, though, under the influence of the Lord, they had been quiet while the temple was being overthrown, could not patiently allow the tree to be cut down. Martin carefully instructed them that there was nothing sacred in the trunk of a tree, and urged them rather to honor God whom he himself served. He added that there was a moral necessity why that tree should be cut down, because it had been dedicated to a demon. Then one of them who was bolder than the others says, "If you have any trust in thy God, whom you say you worship, we ourselves will cut down this tree, and be it your part to receive it when falling; for if, as you declare, your Lord is with you, you will escape all injury." Then Martin, courageously trusting in the Lord, promises that he would do what had been asked. Upon this, all that crowd of heathen agreed to the condition named; for they held the loss of their tree a small matter, if only they got the enemy of their religion buried beneath its fall. Accordingly, since that pine-tree was hanging over in one direction, so that there was no doubt to what side it would fall on being cut, Martin, having been bound, is, in accordance with the decision of these pagans, placed in that spot where, as no one doubted, the tree was about to fall. They began, therefore, to cut down their own tree, with great glee and joyfulness, while there was at some distance a great multitude of wondering spectators. And now the pine-tree began to totter, and to threaten its own ruin by falling. The monks at a distance grew pale, and, terrified by the danger ever coming nearer, had lost all hope and confidence, expecting only the death of Martin. But he, trusting in the Lord, and waiting courageously, when now the falling pine had uttered its expiring crash, while it was now falling, while it was just rushing upon him, simply holding up his hand against it, he put in its way the sign of salvation. Then, indeed, after the manner of a spinning-top (one might have thought it driven back), it swept round to the opposite side, to such a degree that it almost crushed the rustics, who had taken their places there in what was deemed a safe spot. Then truly, a shout being raised to heaven, the heathen were amazed by the miracle, while the monks wept for joy; and the name of Christ was in common extolled by all. The well-known result was that on that day salvation came to that region. For there was hardly one of that immense multitude of heathens who did not express a desire for the imposition of hands, and abandoning his impious errors, made a profession of faith in the Lord Jesus. Certainly, before the times of Martin, very few, nay, almost none, in those regions had received the name of Christ; but through his virtues and example that name has prevailed to such an extent, that now there is no place thereabouts which is not filled either with very crowded churches or monasteries. For wherever he destroyed heathen temples, there he used immediately to build either churches or monasteries.

11

Raymund Lull, First Missionary to the Moslems [4]
Samuel M. Zwemer

Introduction

Raymund (Ramón) Lull was born in Palma, the capital of Majorca in 1235. He inherited a large estate from his father who had received it as a gift for his part in the defeat of the Saracens. Raymund grew up as a page in the royal courts and lived a very profligate life as a youth. This style of life was changed, however, as a result of five visions which compelled him to a life of devotion and service to Christ. Because of his earlier contacts with Muslims, he developed an interest in them and was determined to Christianize them not by the sword but by persuasion. He was first connected with monastic life, giving himself to fasting and prayer. During this time he was often in a state of ecstasy experiencing visions. He was greatly tempted to become a monastic recluse. In his famous work, *The Tree of Love,* the Lover (Lull) meets a pilgrim in the forest. The Lover complains of the evil in the world and expresses the desire to live as a hermit among nature. The pilgrim rebukes him for his selfish retreat and tells him that his place is in the world, not out of it. He is to live as a missionary preacher and by this service bring honor to the Beloved (Christ). This was Lull's literary way of expressing his call to be a missionary.[5]

He, therefore, turned from his monastic life, learned Arabic (which he later taught), and made numerous missionary journeys into Moslem countries, returning occasionally to Europe, especially Paris.[6] His devotional life was expressed through his literary works: *The Art of Contemplation, The Book of Love and the Beloved,* and *The Tree of Love.* His work among the Moslems was attended with success but also with grave conflict. Samuel Zwemer's final chapter tells the story of Lull's last missionary journey and his martyrdom.

Samuel Marinus Zwemer (1867-1952) was born in Michigan, the son of Dutch immigrants. After completing college and seminary studies, he went with a group of pioneer missionaries to Arabia in 1890. Later their work was adopted by the Reformed Church of America. He was an especially effective missionary to the Muslims. In 1911 he began a scholarly journal, *The Moslem World,* which he edited for thirty-six years. From 1929 to 1937, he was professor of missions and history of religions at Princeton Seminary. He authored or jointly authored some fifty books. Some of his better known works are: *Arabia, the Cradle of Islam* (1900), *The Muslim Christ* (1912), and *The Cross Above the Crescent* (1943). He identified deeply with Lull, the first missionary to the Muslims.[7]

His Last Missionary Journey and His Martyrdom

. . . .

The scholastics of the Middle Ages taught that there were five methods of acquiring knowledge—observation, reading, listening, conversation, and meditation. But they left out the most important method, namely, that by suffering. Lull's philosophy had taught him much, but it was in the school of suffering that he grew into a saint. Love, not learning, is the key to his character. The philosopher was absorbed in the missionary. The last scene of Lull's checkered life is not at Rome nor Paris nor Naples in the midst of his pupils, but in Africa, on the very shores from which he was twice banished.

At the council of Vienne Lull had rejoiced to see some portion of the labors of his life brought to fruition. When the deliberations of the council were over and the battle for instruction in Oriental languages in the universities of Europe had been won, it might have been thought that he would have been willing to enjoy the rest he had so well deserved. Raymund Lull was now seventy-nine years old, and the last few years of his life must have told heavily even on so strong a frame and so brave a spirit as he possessed. His pupils and friends naturally desired that he should end his days in the peaceful pursuit of learning and the comfort of companionship.

Such, however, was not Lull's wish. His ambition was to die as a missionary and not as a teacher of philosophy. Even his favorite "Ars Major" had to give way to that *ars maxima* expressed in Lull's own motto, "He that lives by the life can not die."

This language reminds one of Paul's Second Epistle to Timothy, where the Apostle tells us that he too was now "already being offered, and that the time of his departure was at hand." In Lull's "Contemplations" we read: "As the needle naturally turns to the north when it is touched by the magnet, so is it fitting, O Lord, that Thy servant should turn to love and praise and serve Thee; seeing that out of love to him Thou wast willing to endure such grievous pangs and sufferings." And again: "Men are wont to die, O Lord, from old age, the failure of natural warmth and excess of cold; but thus, if it be Thy will, Thy servant would not wish to die; he would prefer to die in the glow of love, even as Thou wast willing to die for him."

Other passages in Lull's writings of this period . . . show that he longed for the crown of martyrdom. If we consider the age in which Lull lived and the race from which he sprang, this is not surprising. Even before the thirteenth century, thousands of Christians died as martyrs to the faith in Spain; many of them cruelly tortured by the Moors for blaspheming Mohammed.

Among the Franciscan order a mania for martyrdom prevailed. Every friar who was sent to a foreign shore craved to win the heavenly palm and wear the purple passion-flower. The spirit of the Crusades was in possession of the Church and its leaders, even after the sevenfold failure of its attempts to win by the sword. Bernard of Clairvaux wrote to the Templars: "The soldier of Christ is safe when he slays, safer when he dies. When he slays it profits Christ; when he dies it profits himself."

Much earlier than the end of the Middle Ages the doctrines of martyrdom had taken hold of the Church. Stories of the early martyrs were the popular literature to fan the flame of enthusiasm. A martyr's death was supposed, on the authority of many Scripture passages, to cancel all sins of the past life, to supply the place of baptism, and to secure admittance at once to Paradise without a sojourn in Purgatory.

One has only to read Dante, the graphic painter of society in the Middle Ages, to see this illustrated. Above all, it was taught that martyrs had the beatific vision of the Savior (even as did St. Stephen), and that their dying prayers were sure of hastening the coming of Christ's kingdom.

But the violent passions so prevalent and the universal hatred of Jews and infidels made men forget that "not the *blood* but the cause makes the martyr."

Raymund Lull was ahead of his age in his aims and in his methods, but he was not and could not be altogether uninfluenced by his environment. The spirit of chivalry was not yet dead in the knight who forty-eight years before had seen a vision of the Crucified and had been knighted by the pierced hands for a spiritual crusade.

. . . .

The dangers and difficulties that made Lull shrink back from his journey at Genoa in 1291 only urged him forward to North Africa once more in 1314. His love had not grown cold, but burned the brighter "with the failure of natural warmth and the weakness of old age." He longed not only for the martyr's crown, but also once more to see his little band of believers. Animated by these sentiments, he crossed over to Bugia on August 14, and for nearly a whole year labored secretly among a little circle of converts, whom on his previous visits he had won over to the Christian faith.

Both to these converts, and to any others who had boldness to come and join them in religious conversation, Lull continued to expatiate on the one theme of which he never seemed to tire, the inherent superiority of Christianity to Islam. He saw that the real strength of Islam is not in the second clause of its all too brief creed, but in its first clause. The Mohammedan conception of the unity and the attributes of God is a great half-truth. Their whole philosophy of religion finds its pivot in their wrong idea of absolute monism in the Deity. We do not find Lull wasting arguments to disprove Mohammed's mission, but presenting facts to show that Mohammed's conception of God was deficient and untrue. If for nothing else he deserves the honor, yet this great principle of apologetics in the controversy with Islam, as first stated by Lull, marks him the great missionary to Moslems.

"If Moslems," he argued, "according to their law affirm that God loved man because He created him, endowed him with noble faculties, and pours His benefits upon him, then the Christians according to their law affirm the same. But inasmuch as the Christians believe more than this, and affirm that God so loved man that He was willing to become man, to endure poverty, ignominy, torture, and death for his sake, which the Jews and Saracens do not teach concerning Him; therefore is the religion of the Christians, which thus reveals a Love beyond all other love, superior to that of those which reveals it only in an inferior degree." Islam is a loveless religion. Raymund Lull believed and proved that Love could conquer it. The Koran denies the Incarnation, and so remains ignorant of the true character not only of the Godhead, but of God (Matt. xi. 27).

At the time when Lull visited Bugia and was imprisoned, the Moslems were already replying to his treatises and were winning converts from among Christians. He says: "The Saracens write books for the destruction of Christianity; I have myself seen such when I was in prison. . . . For one Saracen who becomes a Christian, ten Christians and more become Mohammedans. It becomes those who are in power to consider what the end will be of such a state of things. God will not be mocked."

Lull did not think, apparently, that lack of speedy results was an argument for abandoning the work of preaching to Moslems the unsearchable riches of Christ.

. . . .

For over ten months the aged missionary dwelt in hiding, talking and praying with his converts and trying to influence those who were not yet persuaded. His one weapon was the argument of God's love in Christ, and his "shield of faith" was that of medieval art which so aptly symbolizes the doctrine of the Holy Trinity.

. . . .

Of the length, breadth, depth, and height of the love of Christ, all Lull's devotional writings are full.

At length, weary of seclusion, and longing for martyrdom, he came forth into the open market and presented himself to the people as the same man whom they had once expelled from their town. It was Elijah showing himself to a mob of Ahabs! Lull stood before them and threatened them with divine wrath if they still persisted in their errors. He pleaded with love, but spoke plainly the whole truth. The consequences can be easily anticipated. Filled with fanatic fury at his boldness, and unable to reply to his arguments, the populace seized him, and dragged him out of the town; there by the command, or at least the connivance, of the king, he was stoned on the 30th of June, 1315.

Whether Raymund Lull died on that day or whether, still alive, he was rescued by a few of his friends, is disputed by his biographers. According to the latter idea his friends carried the wounded saint to the beach and he was conveyed in a vessel to Majorca, his birthplace, only to die ere he reached Palma. According to other accounts, which seem to me to carry more authority, Lull did not survive the stoning by the mob, but died, like Stephen, outside the city. Also in this case, devout men carried Lull to his burial and brought the body to Palma, Majorca, where it was laid to rest in the church of San Francisco.

An elaborate tomb was afterward built in this church as a memorial to Lull. Its date is uncertain, but it is probably of the fourteenth century. Above the elaborately carved panels of marble are the shields or coat-of-arms of Raymund Lull; on either side are brackets of metal work to hold candles. The upper horizontal panel shows Lull in repose, in the garb of a Franciscan, with a rosary on his girdle, and his hands in the attitude of prayer.

May we not believe that this was his attitude when the angry mob caught up stones, and crash followed crash against the body of the aged missionary? Perhaps not only the manner of his death but his last prayer was like that of Stephen the first martyr.

It was the teaching of the medieval Church that there are three kinds of martyrdom: The first both in will and in deed, which is the highest; the second, in will but not in deed; the third, in deed but not in will. St. Stephen and the whole army of those who were martyred by fire or sword for their testimony are examples of the first kind of martyrdom. St. John the Evangelist and others like him who died in exile or old age as witnesses to the truth but without violence, are examples of the second kind. The Holy Innocents, slain by Herod, are an example of the third kind. Lull verily was a martyr in will and in deed. Not only at Bugia, when he fell asleep, but for all the years of his long life after his conversion, he was a witness to the Truth, ever ready "to fill up that which is behind of the afflictions of Christ" in his flesh "for His body's sake which is the Church."

To be stoned to death while preaching the love of Christ to Moslems—that was the fitting end for such a life. "Lull," says Noble, "was the greatest of medieval missionaries, perhaps the grandest of all missionaries from Paul to Carey and Livingstone. His career suggests those of Jonah the prophet, Paul the missionary, and Stephen the martyr. Tho his death was virtually self-murder, its heinousness is lessened by his homesickness for heaven, his longing to be with Christ, and the sublimity of his character and career."

12

Henry Martyn: Confessor of the Faith [8]
Constance E. Padwick

Introduction

Henry Martyn (1781-1812) was born at Truro, Cornwall, the United Kingdom, and received an excellent education at Cambridge. He was ordained in 1805 and left the same year for India as a chaplain of the East India Company. In Calcutta he came under the influence of Carey and his fellow missionaries. Their work in translation inspired him to a similar career. However, he was more scientifically trained for his work as a linguist than the self-taught Carey. Carey had worked in Sanskrit and the related languages of the Hindu world. Martyn decided to work in Arabic, Persian, and Urdu (Hindustani), the three major languages of the Muslim world. So accurate was his work that all subsequent translations in Urdu have been based upon it.[9]

Martyn divided his labors between his scholarly translation work and itineration as an evangelist. His health was poor, and he died of tuberculosis at the early age of thirty-one. Besides being recognized for his remarkable translation work, Martyn's early death made him a missionary hero, and he became a source of inspiration for the missionaries who followed him in the great century. A man of deep devotion, he left behind a journal which was published by John Sargent in 1819.[10] The following selection from his biography describes in a moving manner Martyn's "last journey."

Henry Martyn's biographer, Constance Evelyn Padwick (1886-1968), belongs in that long line of missionaries to the Muslim world which began with Lull. She was born in West Thorrey, Sussex, England. She began her missionary career in 1916 in Egypt, and in 1937 went to Palestine where she served until 1947. Her last decade of service to the Muslim world was in the Sudan and in Turkey. Like the pioneers before—Lull, Martyn, Zwemer—she left her mark by what she wrote as much as by what she did.[11]

Besides her biographies of Martyn (first written in 1922) and *Temple Gairdner of Cairo* (1929), she was a significant contributor to the Central Literature Committee for Muslims in the 1930s. She also produced school texts in basic Arabic while serving in the Nuba Mountains of the Sudan. Perhaps her most definitive literary work was her study, *Muslim Devotions* (1961). This volume, which was prepared for the non-Muslim Western reader, was the result of twenty years of friendly dialogues with Muslims, careful investigation of the Muslim faith and practice from the Middle East to Southeast Asia, and the author's own creative insight into the Muslim world. It has made a significant contribution to the difficult task of dialogue between Christians and Muslims.[12]

The Traveler

. . . .

In that yet medieval Persia, the aspiring poet or man of letters still laid his book before the Shah on his throne of marble spread with cloth of gold. Fateh Ali Shab, ruler of Persia, over-lord of Georgia and Kurdistan, was not only the statesman who received and balanced the claims of embassies from George III, from Napoleon, from the

Tzar Alexander and from the Governor General Wellesley. He was, as he sat blazing with jewels before a prostrate court, the fountain of taste and the judge of letters for his kingdom. It needed but a pronouncement of praise in his hollow rolling voice, and the fortunes of a volume were made.

Henry Martyn, seeing through Persian eyes, determined to gain for the New Testament the respect yielded to a book approved at court.

As his translation work drew to a close, he set scribes preparing two volumes of exquisite penmanship for the Shah and for his heir, Prince Abbas Mirza, "the wisest of the princes." The scribes began work in November, 1811. They brought him the finished volumes in May, 1812, three months after the translator's work was done. Lingering in Shiraz and waiting for their manuscript, he "beguiled the tediousness of the day" by an absorbing study of the Psalms in Hebrew, and a translation of the Psalter into Persian. It enthralled him so that he "hardly perceived" the passing of the days. "I have long had it in contemplation," he wrote to Lydia [his fiancée]. "I have often attempted the 84th Psalm, endeared to me on many accounts, but have not yet succeeded. The glorious 16th Psalm I hope I have mastered."

When the scribes brought in their fair copies, Martyn wrapped up the costly manuscripts uncorrected. He had none like-minded whom he could put in charge of the precious volumes, and he was determined to lay the books himself in the royal hands, correcting them as he traveled. For he knew that he was a sick man. He must race disease if he desired to see the Book on its way. A long dispute with a Sufi doctor would leave him still with a raw pit of pain where his breath came and went.

He had copies ready for the press. Four were sent by his direction to India that his friends at Serampore might print his translation.[13] Other copies he carried with him on his wanderings, intending, if he lived, to pass them on to some press in the west, perhaps at his own University of Cambridge. He spent his last hours at Shiraz with his fellow-translator in giving instructions for the care and delivery of the Book in case of his own death.

That done, a little before the closing of the gates at sunset on May 11, 1812, he left Shiraz and joined a caravan outside the walls, starting that night to ride across the great Persian plateau from south to north.

He was riding as servant of the Book to Tabriz where Sir Gore

Ouseley lived; for he could only be introduced into the jeweled presence of the Shah by the ambassador who represented his nation.

The air of the uplands was cool enough for day traveling, and the diary is full of notes on the face of the countryside.

. . . .

At night they shuddered in open caravan-serais that seemed to let in wind and rain alike. Martyn after a day's ride drew out of its wrappings the precious volume prepared for the Prince, and sat late into the night in some leaky-hovel, poring over the correction of his scribe's exquisite Persian lettering.

After twelve days of riding they came across the poppy fields to Isfahan, a city of domes and minarets and pigeon towers, seen from far across the plain. Martyn had for companion in the caravan another Englishman traveling also to Tabriz to join Sir Gore Ouseley's suite. Consequently they were lodged as foreigners of mark in one of the palaces of the Shah. Here they paused a week and there was time for Martyn to seek out, according to his wont, his fellow Christians of those parts. He called first on "the Italian missionary, a native of Aleppo, but educated at Rome. He spoke Latin very sprightly." Then to Julfa to visit the Armenians, of whose ancient and desolate Church he was always a lover, and with whom he spent many hours.

On the first night of June, the caravan left Isfahan, its plane trees and its fountains, its niggardly merchants and its dreams of bygone glory. "Soon after midnight we mounted our horses. It was a mild moonlight night and a nightingale filled the whole valley with his notes. Our way was along lanes, a murmuring rivulet accompanied us till it was lost in a lake."

At daylight they rode out of these enchanted scenes on to the great plain of Kashan where fat melons grow in bare sand, and far away against the blue stands up a snowy mountain wall, the northern barrier of the Persian land.

After eight days they came to Teheran, the half-ambitious, half-squalid city of modern royalty, behind walls of unbaked clay. They reached those walls two hours before sunrise, and all the twelve gates were shut.

"I spread my bed upon the high road, and slept till the gates were open; then entered the city and took up my abode." Here, at the Persian capital, was the favorite palace of the great Shah, with a marble bath where his ladies might play, and a picture gallery for which, when Martyn came, an artist was painting from memory a likeness of Sir John Malcolm, the magnificent ambassador whom Persia could not forget.

Here came the first hitch in Martyn's plans. No muleteers could be found at the moment willing to travel to Tabriz, where lay the British ambassador who would introduce him and his book into the royal presence. It meant delay. And Martyn in 1812 could not brook delay. While life was yet in him he must press on with the Book. He held letters of introduction to the Shah's Vizier. Better than lose the time he could not spare, should he not travel alone to the Shah's summer camping ground, a night's journey outside the city, and ask the Prime Minister himself to bring him to the royal presence?

He ventured. He rode out of Teheran alone with his servant, and found the Vizier lying ill on the veranda of the Shah's tent of audience. Only that many colored tent curtain hung between Martyn and his goal. The Vizier had two royal secretaries by his couch.

They took very little notice, not rising when I sat down, as their custom is to all who sit with them; nor offering me a water-pipe. The two secretaries on learning my object in coming, began a conversation with me on religion and metaphysics which lasted two hours. The premier asked how many languages I understood; whether I spoke French; where I was educated; whether I understood astronomy and geography, and then observed to the others that I spoke good Persian. As they were well-educated gentlemanly men, the discussion was temperate.

But Martyn had to betake himself to the caravanserai that night, no nearer to the jeweled figure in the audience tent, fed with words and offered no courteous hospitality. He had not come with the pomp that impresses such diplomats, and the Vizier had no intention of becoming sponsor for a lonely stranger.

Martyn spent the evening on the roof of the inn, sharing the mat of a poor traveling merchant who supposed that the western powers yet paid tribute to Mohammedan masters for permission to live.

Three days later he attended the Vizier's levee bearing the precious Book. All eyes were turned on the solitary Frank. In that court where verbal swordmanship was the art of arts, a discussion was inevitable, but Martyn knew that an angry discussion would ruin his chance of seeing the face of the Shah.

He could not prevent the very clash that he dreaded. "There was a most intemperate and clamorous controversy kept up for an hour or two; eight or ten on one side and myself on the other." He came unfriended; the Vizier encouraged the attack, and the veneer of polish was broken through as they set upon him.

Their vulgarity in interrupting me in the middle of a speech; their utter ignorance of the nature of an argument; their impudent assertions about the law and the gospel, neither of which they had ever seen in their lives, moved my indignation a little.

His indignation, but not his fear. This Martyn seems to have forgotten how to fear. The Vizier who had at first set them by the ears came up at last to the angry group, stilled the hubbub and put to Martyn before them all a crucial question. He challenged the stranger to recite the Moslem creed. "Say God is God and Mohammed is the Prophet of God."

It was an electric moment, the whole court at attention.

I said, "God is God" but added, instead of "Mahomet is the prophet of God," "and Jesus is the Son of God."

They all rose up as if they would have torn me in pieces, snarling out one of the classic fighting cries of the Moslem world, "He is neither begotten nor begets." "What will you say when your tongue is burnt out for this blasphemy?"

He held them in silence.

My book which I had brought expecting to present it to the king lay before Mirza Shufi, the Vizier. As they all rose up after him to go, some to the king and some away, I was afraid they would trample on the book; so I went in among them to take it up, and wrapped it in a towel before them; while they looked at it and me with supreme contempt.

I walked away alone to my tent to pass the rest of the day in heat and dirt.

A message followed him from the Vizier refusing to present him to the Shah and referring him to his own ambassador.

"Disappointed of my object in coming to the camp," he says, "I lost no time in leaving it." He found again his English fellow-traveler who had secured muleteers and now set off for Tabriz, traveling for the first nine days along a road where the Shah himself was soon to pass on his way to Sultanieh [Sultaniyeh]. The north wind from the Caspian blew over the mountains, and even at midday in June the air was cool. The fresh tang of the breeze carried Martyn home; he fancied himself trudging the roads near Cambridge with a friend at his side, or following a path by the Cornish shore with one beloved companion. "While passing over the plain, mostly on foot, I had them all in my mind, and bore them all in my heart in prayer."

The shadows of the royal progress lay on all the villages.

All along the road where the king is expected, the people are patiently waiting, as for some dreadful disaster: plague, pestilence or famine are nothing to the misery of being subject to the violence and extortion of this rabble soldiery.

When they had passed the Shah's camping ground at Sultanieh they came into a new world, a country that has been a meeting place of the races of mankind. The speech around them began to change from Persian to Turkish, and the caravanserais were the halting place of men whose mules or camels followed the trade routes of the ancient world from East to West.

We found large bales of cotton brought by merchants from Teheran, intended for Turkey. There were also two Tartar merchants, natives of Astrachan, who had brought iron and tea for sale. They wished to know whether we wanted tea of Cathay.

Here in outlandish parts, the two Englishmen fell sick.

June 25, 1812. After a restless night rose so ill with fever, that I could not go on. My companion, Mr. Canning, was nearly in the same state. We touched nothing all day.

After another night of fever, Martyn was for dragging on, but Mr. Canning was not well enough to start. They had before them a stage of eight or ten hours without a house on the way and they had been unable to eat for two days and were suffering from headache and consant giddiness. No doubt it was wiser to delay, but it added anxiety as to whether their supplies could hold out as far as Tabriz. They were becoming desperately short of money.

Next day the servants were down with fever too, and Martyn's head was "tortured with shocking pains." He put it down to exposure to the sun which had great power even though the wind blew cold.

June 29 was a day of acute pain. "I was almost frantic."

"I endeavoured," he says, his Christianity in 1812 anticipating later teachings, "to keep in mind all that was friendly; a friendly Lord presiding; and nothing exercising me but what would show itself at last friendly."

The fever passed for that time, leaving him "half dead" but determined to take the road. When they told him at midnight that his horse was ready he "seemed about to sink into a long fainting fit and almost wished it. . . . I set out more dead than alive."

Next day, shivering or burning by turns and almost lightheaded, he reached the outer bulwarks of the mountains that guard Persia on the north, "a most natural boundary it is." The face of the land began to be broken up with very rocky foothills where camels graze on scrubby bushes. His horse threaded his way for him through the boulders, for Martyn in high fever could not make his brain obey him, but traveled bewildered through the past, wandering in "happy scenes in India or England." They lost him once; for riding on ahead he had come to a bridge, and scarce knowing what he did, left his horse and crept under the shadow of the arch, where he sat with two camel-drivers, happy to be still and cool. The caravan passed over the bridge without the sick man's observation, and his fellow-traveler, coming back to search for him, found at first only a grazing horse and feared the worst.

So they passed poor hill villages and came out to the pure clean air, the lovely natural pastures and the churlish shepherds of Azerbaijan. By some miracle Martyn in "fever which nearly deprived me of reason" still sat his horse.

At last, as the dawn of July 7 shone coldly on the Blue Mosque and the Citadel, he reached the gate of Tabriz, and "feebly asked for a man to show me the way to the ambassador's." He had been two months on the road when Sir Gore Ouseley and his lady received him at the point of death.

They did all that they could. The violence of the fever they could not allay for another fortnight, but they "administered bark" and tended him as if he were a son. As he lay there under their kind hands, the sick man knew that he had no more strength to travel, as he had longed, to Damascus, to Baghdad, and into the heart of Arabia to search for ancient versions and perfect the Arabic New Testament. His task seemed dropping from his hands. Sir Gore Ouseley told him that he was too ill to see the Shah or the Prince, and doubtless dreaded another collision between Martyn and the mullahs of the court. But he comforted his guest with the promise that he would give every possible eclat to the Book by presenting it himself. The good ambassador did more. He had extra copies made for high officials of open mind, who might speak well of the Book to the potentate. When at length the New Testament reached the royal hands, the Shah was graciousness itself.

In truth [said the royal letter of thanks to the ambassador] through the learned and unremitted exertions of the Reverend Henry Martyn it has been translated in a style most befitting sacred books, that is in an easy and simple diction. . . . The whole of the New Testament is completed in a most excellent manner, a source of pleasure to our enlightened and august mind.
If it please the most merciful God we shall command the Select Servants who are admitted to our presence, to read to us the above-mentioned book from the beginning to the end.

Sir Gore Ouseley did yet more. He carried a copy with him to St. Petersburg, and there, at the instigation of a Russian prince, the Bible Society printed the Persian Book, with the British ambassador as volunteer proofreader. Sir Gore Ouseley's Russian edition came into the world in the year of Waterloo, while the sister edition in Calcutta was still struggling through the press.
So Martyn's task passed into other hands, and he lying sick almost to death in a mansion of Tabriz saw nothing more within his strength in the East. The ambassador had handed him a letter; at last, after more than eighteen months, a letter from Lydia. To her and to Cornwall the sick man turned. Would strength be granted him to reach her? Might he not carry home the New Testament, to be printed perhaps in his own Cambridge? If he could only reach Lydia, surely he would be well enough with her to start for more service in the East.

Made an extraordinary effort and, as a Tartar was going off instantly to Constantinople, wrote letters to Mr. Grant for permission to come to England, and to Mr. Simeon and Lydia informing them of it.

We have both those letters written by the hand of a man who tells his correspondent that he has not the strength to search his papers for the last home letters.

"I have applied for leave to come to England on furlough; a measure you will disapprove," so he tells Simeon, his feverish brain remembering the relentless standards of work in the Cambridge parish and the brisk upright figure of the leader who never spared himself. "But you would not were you to see the pitiable condition to which I am reduced." A Henry Martyn's plea against some fancied charge of idleness must have been hard reading to his friend. Then the old passion seizes the sick man, and the pen flies in his feverish hand as he turns to the beloved work and warns Simeon about some publication mooted in Cambridge for Moslem readers. Let it not go to press until it has been approved by men who know the East and know eastern ways of seeing, imagining and reasoning. He tells of the last treatise he had written in Shiraz and, with a rare note of satisfaction in any work of his own, records his hope that "there is not a single Europeanism in the whole of it."

But I am exhausted; pray for me, beloved brother, and believe that I am, as long as life and recollection last, yours affectionately,

H. MARTYN.

To Lydia, lest she should dwell on his sickness, he writes of his spiritual solace; "The love of God never appeared more clear, more sweet, more strong." Then, lest she should build on his coming, he adds, "I must faithfully tell you that the probability of my reaching England alive is but small."

The Tartar courier galloped off with the letters and the sick man lay back exhausted. Nothing was left him to do, but to gather strength for the homeward journey.

A month later, "a mere skeleton" after two months of fever, he sat up in a chair and wrote his will "with a strong hand."

August 21-31. Making preparations for my journey to Constantinople, a route recommended to me by Sir Gore as safer, and one in which he could give me letters of recommendation to two Turkish governors.

Sir Gore also procured an order for Martyn to use the Government post-horses as far as Erivan. But Martyn had seen the hardships that the levies of royal underlings brought upon the peasants. "These post-horses I was told were nothing else than the beasts the prince's servants levy on every village. I determined not to use them."

Before setting out he wrote a last letter to Lydia, a letter to be read and re-read on her knees where his portrait hung beneath a print of the Crucifixion in a room that looked out across the shimmer of Mount's Bay.

In three days, I intend setting my horse's head towards Constantinople, distant above thirteen hundred miles. . . . Soon we shall have occasion for pen and ink no more; but I trust I shall shortly see thee face to face.

Belive me to be yours ever, most faithfully and affectionately,

H. Martyn.

On September 2, 1812, he set out with a little party of guides and servants, while the ambassador and his lady, having done all they could to help him, measured with doubtful eyes the strength of the haggard convalescent against fifteen hundred miles of hardship.

At sunset we left the western gate of Tabriz behind us. The plain towards the west and south-west stretches away to an immense distance bounded by mountains so remote as to appear from their soft blue to blend with the skies.

He "ambled on" with the keen sense of the convalescent for the beauty and freedom of the outside world, gazing at "the distant hills with gratitude and joy." His way through Azerbaijan and Armenia always tending westward was the "Royal Road" of ancient Persia along which the service of the Great King passed from Susa to the west. It was marked at each twentieth or twenty-fifth mile by a post-station built of mud bricks, such as went to the building of Babylon the great. Here men and beasts fared much alike as to lodging.

In cities where Martyn had letters of introduction he might hire a room from a citizen. "I was led from street to street till at last I was lodged in a wash-house belonging to a great man, a corner of which was cleared out for me."

A room secured, at the end of the day's hard riding there were the perennial discomforts of such travel: mosquitoes and lice, "the smell of the stable so strong that I was quite unwell," and the incessant crowding and chatter of people who could not or would not understand his desire to rest alone. It was always Martyn too who must be the one to wake at midnight, rouse his party and stand urgent over them as they dawdled round the baggage sleepy and loath to start.

The traveling was hard even for a hale man. He crossed the Araxes [Aras]; he left great Ararat upon his left ("so may I, safe in Christ, outride the storm of life and land at last on one of the everlasting hills," he prayed, thinking of Noah); he passed through a rich land of streams where a precious trunk full of books was dropped and soaked, and he had a midnight fire built to dry them. He spent nights in rooms built over or beside the family stable for the sake of the warmth from the beasts in winter, but now in September overpowering in heat and stench; and he rode on, "thinking of a Hebrew letter," and so "perceiving little of the tediousness of the way. . . . All day on the 15th and 16th Psalms and gained some light on the difficulties."

So meditating on his songs of degrees, he came to Erivan, and laid the ambassador's letter before a provincial governor to whom his distant overlord, the Shah, seemed but a shadowy personage.

I was summoned to his presence. He at first took no notice of me, but continued reading his Koran. After a compliment or two, he resumed his devotions. The next ceremony was to exchange a rich shawl dress for a still richer pelisse on pretence of its being cold. The next display was to call for his physician, who after respectfully feeling his pulse stood on one side.

Having sufficiently impressed the thin, sick traveler with his greatness, he called a secretary to pick up from the floor the letter of the British ambassador, and to read it in his august ears. The letter interested him and he grew languidly attentive, but his hopes were set on some grapes and melons cooling before him in a marble fountain, and he sent the saint away, not knowing that he had met a man of God.

On September 12, Martyn left his servants waiting for fresh horses, and rode alone to visit his brothers the Armenian monks at Etchmiazin [Echmiadzin], the mother-city of their church.

The wayworn figure rode into "a large court with monks, cowled and gowned, moving about. On seeing my Armenian letters they brought me at once to the Patriarch's lodge where I found two bishops at breakfast." He struck up at once a friendship with a young monk of his own age named Serope, "bold, authoriative and very able," and full of reforming plans for his Church, "but then he is not spiritual." They talked all day. "When the bell rang for vespers, we went together to the great Church."

Next day Martyn waited on the Patriarch, who received him on a throne, surrounded by standing monks. "I told the Patriarch that I was so happy in being here that I could almost be willing to be a monk with them."

When the young monk who welcomed Martyn had become a silvery-bearded bishop he told a European traveler his impressions of that visit. "He described Martyn to me as being of a very delicate frame, thin, and not quite of the middle stature, a beardless youth, with a countenance beaming with so much benignity as to bespeak an errand of Divine love. Of the affairs of the world he seemed to be so ignorant that Serope was obliged to manage for him respecting his traveling arrangements and money matters. A Tartar was employed to take him to Tokat. He (Serope) was greatly surprised, he said, that Martyn was so eminent a Christian; 'since (said he) all the English I have hitherto met with not only make no profession of religion, but live seemingly in contempt of it.'"

Serope took Martyn in hand, changed most of his traveling kit, and bought him a sword against the Kurdish robbers.

So he left them with new baggage and a new train, "a trusty servant from the monastery" carrying his money.

On September 19 they passed from the Persian province of Erivan to the neighbor province of Kars, and so left the domains of the Shah for those of the Sultan of Turkey.

Troubles began.

The headman of the village paid me a visit. He was a young Mussulman and took care of all my Mussulman attendants; but he left my Armenians and me where he found us. I was rather uncomfortably lodged, my room being a thoroughfare for horses, cows, buffaloes and sheep. Almost all the village came to look at me.

Each day there were alarms of Kurdish robbers. Martyn's escort met even poor companies of peasants with suspicion and with pieces cocked, and every traveling party was passed with furtive glances and hands lingering on weapons. Each trifling incident of the way revealed that one of the company, the Tartar guide named Hassan, was a man with the nature of that soldiery which could plait a crown of thorns for a scourged prisoner.

The Tartar began to show his nature by flogging the baggage-horse with his long whip; but one of the poor beasts presently fell with his load.

Or again:

In this room I should have been very much to my satisfaction had not the Tartar taken part of the same bench. It was evident that the Tartar was the great man here: he took the best place for himself; a dinner of four or five dishes was laid before him. When I asked for eggs they brought me rotten ones.

With a stern vigorous master Hassan might have done good service. With a sick man he showed himself a brute.

September 24. A long and sultry march over many a hill and vale. Two hours from the last stage is a hot spring: the water fills a pool having four porches. The porches instantly reminded me of Bethesda's pool. In them all the party undressed and bathed. The Tartar to enjoy himself more perfectly had his calean [water pipe] to smoke while up to his chin in water.

Kars was left behind, then Erzerum, but fever was winning the race.

September 29. We moved to a village where I was attacked with fever and ague.

October 1. We were out from seven in the morning till eight at night. After sitting a little by the fire I was near fainting from sickness. I learned that the plague was raging at Constantinople and thousands dying every day. The inhabitants of Tocat were flying from their town from the same cause.

October 2. Some hours before day I sent to tell the Tartar I was ready, but Hassan was for once riveted to his bed. However, at eight, having got strong horses, he set off at a great rate. He made us gallop as fast as the horses would go to Chifflik, where we arrived at sunset. I was lodged at my request in the stables of the post-house. As soon as it began to grow a little cold the ague came on, then the fever.

In the night Hassan sent to summon me away, but I was quite unable to move. Finding me still in bed at the dawn he began to storm furiously at my detaining him so long; but I quietly let him spend his ire, ate my breakfast and set out at eight. He seemed determined to make up for the delay, for we flew over hill and dale to Sherean [Sheheran], where we changed horses. From thence we travelled all the rest of the day and all night. It rained. The ague came on. There was a village at hand but Hassan had no mercy. At one in the morning we found two men under a wain with a good fire; I dried my lower extremities, allayed the fever by drinking a good deal of water and went on. The night was pitchy dark so that I could not see the road under my horse's feet. We arrived at the munzil at break of day. Hassan was in great fear of being arrested here; the governor of the city had vowed to make an example of him for riding to death a horse belonging to a man of this place.

. . . .

October 5. The merciless Hassan hurried me off. The munzil, however, not being distant I reached it without much difficulty. I was pretty well lodged and felt tolerably well till a little after sunset, when the ague came on with a violence I had never before experienced; I felt as if in a palsy, my teeth chattering and my whole frame violently shaken.

Two Persians came to visit him as he lay shivering.

These Persians appear quite brotherly after the Turks. While they pitied me, Hassan sat in perfect indifference, ruminating on the further delay this was likely to occasion. The cold fit after continuing two or three hours was followed by a fever, which lasted the whole night.
October 6. No horses being to be had, I had an unexpected repose. I sat in the orchard, and thought with sweet comfort and peace of my God; in solitude my Company, my Friend and Comforter. Oh, when shall time give place to eternity! When shall appear the new heaven and new earth wherein dwelleth righteousness! There shall in no wise enter in anything that defileth: none of that wickedness which has made men worse than wild beasts shall be seen or heard of any more.

There was no later entry in the journal; but he had not come yet to the end of that impossible ride. Day after day they dragged him on, waking him out of feverish sleep.

. . . .

On October 14, 1812, Martyn bade his Armenian servant Sergius make a list of his papers and carry them for him to Constantinople.

They had ridden him to death, but there is no story of that deathbed. We know that he came at the last "a young man, wanting still the years of Christ," to Tokat under its weird pile of castellated hill, a city of the coppermerchants, but then grim with plague. We know too that in fever his mind was always moving among friends in India or in England.

So he came to Tokat, and the mule-bells in the narrow streets jingled in dying ears. Or were they sheep-bells? sheep bells on the moors?

They probably laid him down to die amid the babel of an eastern kahn. . . . That everlasting smell of the stable! Why could not the General find a better place for service than the riding school? But then the Lord was born in a stable. A man could worship there. . . . But that raging voice! If only the tormenting flood of words might cease! Was it Sabat or the Tartar? Sons of thunder, both of them. Sons of thunder He called them, yes, and loved them too.

Why that never ending clatter on the cobbles? Little hurrying feet of donkeys. And people too. Surely so many people were never seen in Truro Street before, and all so beautiful. There was Corrie, what a friend he was! and Sally with Cousin Emma, and Sargent and Dr. Cardew (but no matter; the lesson was ready to show up)—and Lydia. Of course she would come at last. How her face was shining like a star. How all the faces shone with the light of God. . . . Was that an Armenian priest standing at prayer? Simeon had surely come at last with the Bread and Wine. How sweet his voice grew, like the music in King's Chapel! "We praise Thee, we bless Thee, we worship Thee, we glorify Thee, we give thanks to Thee for Thy great glory."

"For Thou only art holy; Thou only art the Lord; Thou only, O Christ. . . ."

Some weeks later an Armenian named Sergius, hot from travel, carried a bundle of papers into the house of Mr. Isaac Morier at Constantinople, and said that they came from his master who had died on October 16, 1812, at Tokat, where the Armenian clergy gave him Christian burial.

13

Ann of Ava [14]
Ethel Daniels Hubbard

Introduction

Constance Padwick not only stands in the long line of missionaries to the Muslim world; she stands also in the long line of women who have been an essential part of the world missionary enterprise. From Priscilla of the apostolic era, to Leoba of the period of the great Anglo-Saxon missionaries to Germany,[15] to the time of the modern mission movement, women have been indispensible in the expansion of the Christian faith. Since the great century, women have been particularly significant in the cause of missions. The single women, illustrated by Constance Padwick, have been invaluable in their contribution. The remarkable careers of Mary Slessor of Africa and Amy Carmichael of India are good examples. The wives of missionaries, outstanding in their own right, add to that illustrious company of women. Anne Luther Bagby of Brazil is but one example among many. After significant service while raising her children, all of whom became missionaries (the ones who lived to adulthood), she launched a new career which was nothing short of phenomenal. Her service spanned sixty-one years of mission work in Brazil (1881-1942).[16]

One of the most notable of these women was Ann Hasseltine Judson, the first wife of Adoniram Judson. She and her husband were among the first American couples to become missionaries at the beginning of the modern mission movement. They sailed for India in 1812, and arrived in Burma where they began their work in 1813. They were an extremely devoted couple and made a marvelous team. As strong a personality as Adoniram was, he did not overshadow her. An example of her intelligence and ingenuity may be illustrated from the fact that from Siamese (Thai) captives in Rangoon, she was able to acquire enough of their language to translate into Thai a catechism and one of the Gospels. She is most remembered, however, for her heroic loyalty to her husband while he was a prisoner. It was an excruciating ordeal; and the irony of it all was that shortly after his release, while they were making plans for a new start, Ann died suddenly.[17] Part of the prison ordeal is recounted in the following chapter from Ethel Daniels Hubbard's graphic story of Ann Hasseltine Judson.

Hubbard also wrote another moving missionary biography, *The Moffats* (1917). This story of Robert and Mary Moffat, pioneers in Africa and the parents of the wife of the famous David Livingstone, reads like a novel. The final scene of the last chapter, "Reveille," is one of the most moving accounts in all the literature of missionary biography. It is the author's imaginary reflection of what must have filled the mind and heart of the aged Moffat, the lone surviver of that remarkable two-generation missionary family, as he stood in Westminster Abbey watching the awesome procession which brought and placed the remains of his famous son-in-law to rest among the great of England.[18]

Prisoners in a Heathen Village

. . . .

One day in May, 1825, a cart of the usual variety bumped and thumped with the usual violence along the hot, dusty highway leading from Ava to Amarapoora. Under its shabby cover sat a motley group of travelers—two little Burmese girls, a Bengali servant, and an American woman with a baby in her arms. From Ava, in the early morning, the little party had set forth, conveyed for a few miles in a covered boat on the "little river," and then transferred to the stuffy, jolting cart for the remaining two miles.

At Amarapoora, their expected destination, a disappointment fell upon the band of travelers. The object of their journey was not yet attained, for lo, the prisoners who had yesterday been removed by stealth from the death prison at Ava were not to be found at Amarapoora. Only two hours before they had been sent on their way to a village four miles beyond.

Mrs. Judson, the leader of this little search party, or relief expedition, gave orders to proceed, but their cartman stolidly refused to go farther. Under the scorching sun of midday she bartered and cajoled for an hour, until another cartman agreed to convey them to Aungbinle, the miserable goal of their journey. Throughout that day of travel Mrs. Judson held the baby Maria in her arms, with no relaxation of tired muscles and nerves.

In the late afternoon, the village of Aungbinle was reached and the prison, the central place of interest, sought with haste. It was an old, tumble-down building in the last stages of dilapidation. Some workmen were on the top trying to manufacture a roof of leaves. While their abode was thus being prepared, the prisoners huddled together under a low projection outside, chained two and two and nearly dead with the immense discomfort of the journey.

There Mrs. Judson found her husband, a ghost of his former self, even his prison self. He gathered strength to say, "Why have you come? I hoped you would not follow, for you cannot live here."

Darkness was falling and Mrs. Judson had no shelter for the night. Might she put up a little bamboo house near the prison, she asked the jailer?

"No," he answered, "it is not customary."

Would he then find her a place where she might spend the night? He led her to his own house, which consisted of two small rooms, one of which he placed at her disposal.

It was a poor little place, half filled with grain and accumulated dirt, yet it harbored Mrs. Judson and her children not for one night only but for a long succession of nights and days. Some half-boiled water stayed her thirst and hunger that first night, when upon a mat spread over the grain she and her baby dropped in utter exhaustion.

In the morning she listened to the mournful tale her husband had to tell of the march of the prisoners from Ava to Aungbinle. Scarcely had she left the prison yard at Ava two days ago—so the story ran— when a jailer rushed in, seized Mr. Judson by the arm, stripped off his clothing, except shirt and pantaloons, tore off his fetters, tied a rope around his waist and dragged him to the courthouse, where he found the other foreign prisoners already assembled in a disconsolate group.

As soon as he arrived they were tied together two by two and the ropes given like reins into the hands of slaves who were to be their drivers. The *lamine-woon,* the officer in charge, mounted his horse and gave orders for the procession to start.

It was then eleven o'clock in the day, in the month of May, one of the hottest months of the year. Hats and shoes had been seized by the jailers, so there was no protection from the direct rays of the sun above nor the sunbaked earth beneath. They had proceeded about half a mile when Mr. Judson's feet became blistered and his fevered body so exhausted that, as they crossed the "little river," he would gladly have thrown himself into its cool waters and escaped his misery forever. But quickly he dispelled the thought as cowardice unworthy a Christian man. *They had still eight miles to travel!*

Before long the prisoners' bare feet became entirely destitute of skin. Every step was like treading upon burning coals, yet their brutal keepers goaded them on without mercy. When about half way they stopped for water, and Mr. Judson piteously begged the *lamine-woon* to allow him to ride his horse a mile or two as it seemed as if he could not take another step. A scathing, contemptuous look was the only reply he received.

He then asked Captain Laird, with whom he was tied, and who was a robust man, if he might lean upon his shoulder as he walked. Captain Laird consented, and so long as his strength lasted, supported his fellow traveler as they toiled along together.

Just as the limit of endurance was reached, a Bengali servant of Mr. Gouger's joined the ranks, and perceiving Mr. Judson's agony, tore off his Indian headdress made of cloth and gave half to his master and half to Mr. Judson. It was the work of a few seconds to wrap the cloth around the bruised feet and resume the march that must not be halted for sick or wounded prisoners.

The Bengali then walked by Mr. Judson's side and almost carried him the rest of the way. Had it not been for his timely help Mr. Judson would probably have met the fate of their Greek fellow prisoner who fell by the way, was beaten and dragged until his drivers were themselves weary, then carried in a cart to Amarapoora, where he died an hour after his arrival.

At Amarapoora the *lamine-woon* reluctantly decided to encamp for the night, realizing that his prisoners would perish on the way if forced to go on to Aungbinle that day. An old shed was secured for their resting-place, but what mockery of the word it was when none of the necessities were provided to ease their dreadful fatigue.

Moved by feminine curiosity, the wife of the *lamine-woon* came to look upon the foreign prisoners, and something more than curiosity stirred within her at the sight. She went away and ordered fruit, sugar, and tamarinds for their supper, and rice for their breakfast, which was the only food supply granted for famished men on their journey.

In the morning no member of the battered regiment was able to walk, and carts were furnished for their transfer to Aungbinle. As they neared the journey's end, they spent their small residue of strength surmising the fate that was to befall them.

Upon sight of the dilapidated prison they concluded with one accord that they were to be burned to death, just as the rumor circulated at Ava had predicted. They were endeavoring to fortify their souls for this awful doom when a band of workmen appeared and began repairing the prison. It was about this time that Mrs. Judson came to the end of her toilsome journey in the prison yard at Aungbinle.

Life in this uncivilized inland village marked a new stage in the suffering career of Mrs. Judson. It was now a fight for mere existence, for the bare necessities that hold body and soul together. The village boasted no market for food supplies and scarcely a roof to cover the homeless stranger. With her husband chained in the prison, her three-months-old baby dependent upon her for the very breath of life, two Burmese children clamoring for food and raiment, and a forlorn little heathen village as a background, PROBLEM would hardly spell Mrs. Judson's predicament.

The first of the new series of tragic adventures befell the Judson family the next day after their arrival in Aungbinle. Smallpox entered their household and fastened itself upon Mary Hasseltine, one of the Burmese girls whom they had adopted. Child though she was, Mary had been Mrs. Judson's only helper in the care of the baby Maria. Now the overtaxed mother must divide her time between the sick child at home and the sick husband in prison, who was still suffering from fever and his sorely-mangled feet.

From dawn to dark Mrs. Judson went from the house to the prison, from the prison to the house, back and forth, the baby borne always in her arms. Though she contracted a mild form of smallpox herself, she still continued her round of ministrations, serving not only her own family, but the entire community as well, since every child, young and old, who had never had smallpox was brought to her for vaccination! She had experimented upon the jailer's children with such success that her fame spread through the village. The foreign lady evidently possessed some charm whereby to ward off or lighten disease.

Gradually her patients recovered and the prisoners were established in more comfortable condition than in the death prison at Ava, being bound with one pair of fetters in lieu of three and five. But for Mrs. Judson the limit of physical endurance was reached. She had spent her strength for others' needs until there was none left to her credit and a miserable tropical disease took possession of her worn body. She became so weak that she could barely crawl to the prison. Yet in this pitiable condition she set forth in a Burmese cart to go to Ava in quest of medicines and food.

Upon reaching the deserted house on the river bank she was stricken with such a desperate attack that death seemed the only possible outcome, and to die near her husband's prison in Aungbinle was the one remaining desire in life. By taking small doses of laudanum at intervals she succeeded in quelling the disease to such an extent that, though unable to stand, she made the return journey by boat on the river and by cart through the mud to Aungbinle.

In sickness, home becomes the one charmed spot on earth, but what a home-coming was this! The end of the journey measured the end of endurance. The last vestige of strength vanished and her tremendous power of will was overthrown by the violence of the disease. The Bengali cook, who had been left in charge, came out to help his mistress, but at sight of her he burst into tears, so changed and emaciated had she become in the few days' absence. She stumbled into the little crowded room and dropped upon the mat, where she lay for two months, helpless with pain and weakness.

During Mrs. Judson's sickness the Bengali cook came valiantly to the rescue of the afflicted family. Day after day he provided and cooked the food, sometimes walking long distances for fuel and water, oftentimes delaying his own meal until nighttime that his patients' needs might be first supplied. He forgot caste and wages in his anxiety to serve the foreigners whom he loved. To this Hindu servant the Judson family owed the preservation of their lives during those weeks of dire want and misery.

Upon the youngest of their number fell the sharp edge of their misfortunes. Because of her mother's sickness the baby Maria was deprived of her natural food supply and no milk could be obtained in the village. Night after night the sick mother was compelled to listen to the wails of her child who was crying for food, and there was none to give! By sending presents to the jailers Mrs. Judson won permission for her husband to carry the baby through the village begging a few drops of nourishment from those Burmese mothers who had young children.

Afterwards, in narrating her experiences to the home people in America, Mrs. Judson wrote:

I now began to think the very afflictions of Job had come upon me. When in health, I could bear the various trials and vicissitudes through which I was called to pass. But to be confined with sickness and unable to assist those who were so dear to me, when in distress, was almost too much for me to bear, and had it not been for the consolations of religion, and an assured conviction that every additional trial was ordered by infinite love and mercy, I must have sunk under my accumulated sufferings.

To the stricken band of prisoners there came one day a faint gleam of hope. The *pakan-woon* had been convicted of high treason to the empire and promptly executed. Now this *pakan-woon* was the Burmese officer who boldly aspired to take Bandoola's place after his defeat and death. He made fair promises of large pay to the soldiers and guaranties of victory over the British army, so that the King was dazzled by his easygoing assurance and committed all power into his hands.

He was the bitter enemy of foreigners and it was during his highhanded reign that the foreign prisoners were removed from Ava to Aungbinle. They now learned for a certainty that he had sent them to the remote village for the express purpose of slaughtering them there and of coming himself to witness the gruesome spectacle. Frequently the news had spread through the prison of his expected arrival, but for what devilish intent no one had suspected. His death brought extension of life and hope to the war captives at Aungbinle.

It was not until six months had been lived out in the country prison and its environs that hope of escape definitely entered the Judson household. One day in November, 1825, a courier came to their door bearing a message from Mrs. Judson's loyal friend, the Governor, in Ava. Last night, so the letter read, an edict was issued in the royal palace for Mr. Judson's release from prison. The news was corroborated later in the day by an offical order repealing the prison sentence.

With a joyful heart Mrs. Judson made preparations for departure in the early morning, when, lo, her plans were frustrated by the dastardly conduct of the jailers, who insisted that Mrs. Judson's name was not mentioned in the official document, therefore they could not permit her to leave the place.

"But I was not sent here as a prisoner," she protested. "You have no authority over me."

But no, she could not go, and the villagers should not be allowed to provide a cart for her conveyance. At this juncture Mr. Judson was removed from the prison to the jailers' house, where, by threats and persuasions added to gifts of provisions, they agreed to let Mrs. Judson depart with her husband.

It was noon the next day when the Judson family, accompanied by an official guard, left Aungbinle to return to Ava. At Amarapoora on the way Mr. Judson was detained for examination, and forwarded thence to the courthouse at Ava. With her little bodyguard of children Mrs. Judson pursued her own course and reached the house on the river bank at dusk.

In the morning she went in search of her husband and to her dismay found him again in prison, though not the death prison. She hastened to her old friend, the Governor, and besought an explanation. He informed her that Mr. Judson had been appointed interpreter for the Burman army in its negotiations with the British and that he was to go straightway to the army camp at Maloun.

Accordingly, on the morrow Mrs. Judson bade her husband farewell, while he embarked on the crude little river craft for the passage to Maloun. Upon arrival at camp, he was compelled to enter at once upon his task as interpreter, without so much as an hour to recuperate his lost energy. His stay in camp lasted six weeks and entailed sufferings equal to his prison experience, with the difference that chains were subtracted and hard work added.

Meantime Mrs. Judson drew a breath of relief, supposing that the value of her husband's services as interpreter would insure him kind treatment in the Burmese camp. Ignorance of his actual situation was a mercy, for there was no room in her life at this time for the added burden of anxiety.

Day by day her power of resistance grew less until she fell prey to that horrible disease, spotted fever. On the very day when she first recognized its fatal symptoms, a Burmese woman came to the door and volunteered her services as nurse for Maria. This incident was a direct expression of God's watchful care, because repeatedly she had sought to find a nurse for the baby and failed. Now in her exigency the help came without solicitation.

Once given entrance, the fever ran its course with violence. At the outset Mrs. Judson measured her weakness against its virulence and concluded it must be a losing fight. As the disease developed she tried to think how she could provide for little Maria in the event of her death and decided to commit her to the care of a Portuguese woman. As her mind was grappling with this painful question, reason failed, and trials and tribulations were swept into a whirl of delirium.

At this crucial moment Dr. Price was released from prison and hastened to her bedside. Had the doctor's coming been delayed a few hours she would probably have passed beyond human aid. In fact, the Burmese neighbors, in their childish curiosity, had already crowded into the house to look wonderingly upon the solemn spectacle of death.

"She is dead," they said in awe-stricken tones, "and if the king of angels should come in here he could not save her."

Yet Dr. Price bent all his energies to the task of restoring the life that was being given in vicarious sacrifice for the Burmese people, though they did not know it. Vigorous measures were prescribed; her head was shaved and blisters applied to head and feet; the Bengali servant was ordered to press upon her the nourishment she had refused for days. As consciousness gradually returned, after days of delirium, her first realization was of this faithful servant standing by her bedside urging her to take a little wine and water.

By microscopic degrees, health, or its semblance, came again to the life shattered by anxiety, privation, and disease. One day during the slow convalescence, while she was still too weak to stand upon her feet, a message was brought to the sick room that left a panic of joy and fear in its train. Mr. Judson had been sent back to Ava and was under detention at the courthouse. What was to be his fate the messenger could not say!

During the night Mr. Judson had entered the city and had traversed the very street that passed his own door! A feeble little light glimmered within telling him the house was not unoccupied. But what unknown and fearful events might have taken place in those six weeks of absence! Oh, for one look behind that closed door!

He begged, bribed, cajoled, and threatened the jailers who constituted his guard, but to no avail. They pleaded the official command to deliver their prisoner without delay at the courthouse, which command they dared not disobey.

Consequently, Mr. Judson finished the night in an outbuilding near the courthouse, speculating anxiously as to his probable fate. On the river journey to Maloun he had chanced to see the official communication that accompanied him to Ava, "We have no further use for Yoodthan," the message read. "We therefore return him to the golden city." What new task would the "golden city" exact of its foreign captive before the price of liberty should be fully paid?

On the morrow Mr. Judson was summoned before the court session and hurriedly examined. Not one of his acquaintances was present at court that morning to identify him and explain the curt message forwarded from Maloun.

"From what place was he sent to Maloun?" inquired the presiding officer.

"From Aungbinle," was the reply.

"Let him then be returned thither," was the careless verdict.

The case was thus summarily disposed of, and the plaintiff dispatched to an out-of-the-way shed, serving as temporary prison, to await removal to Aungbinle. In these obscure quarters he spent a restless, tantalizing day. Here he was in the same city with his wife and child, separated only by a few minutes' distance, yet powerless to go to them or to hear one word of intelligence concering them. Tantalus, parched with thirst and standing forever in the water he could not reach, was in no worse predicament.

Toward night Moung Ing came to his relief, having searched in vain for him throughout the day. At intervals this faithful Burmese had returned to the house to report his fruitless quest to the waiting wife. For her, too, the day had been almost insupportable. The "last straw" had been Moung Ing's discovery that her husband was ordered back to Aungbinle. She could scarcely breathe after the shock of these tidings.

If ever in her life Mrs. Judson felt the potency of prayer it was on that dreadful day. "I could not rise from the couch," she afterwards wrote. "I could make no efforts to secure my husband; I could only plead with that great and powerful Being who has said, 'Call upon me in the day of trouble, and I will hear, and thou shalt glorify me,' and who made me at this time feel so powerfully this promise that I became quite composed, feeling assured that my prayers would be answered."

It was in this desperate situation that Mrs. Judson resolved to appeal once again to the Governor, who had so many times befriended them.

"Entreat him," she instructed Moung Ing, "to make one more effort for the release of Mr. Judson, and to prevent his being sent to the country prison," where, she thought wistfully, "I cannot follow and he must needs suffer much."

For the last time the friendly Governor came to the relief of the foreign lady who had so fully captured his homage. He sent a petition to the high court of the empire, offered himself as security for Mr. Judson, and won his release.

Early the next morning Mr. Judson was summoned to the Governor's house, there to receive the prize that is beyond rubies, his freedom. With a step more rapid, a heart more hopeful, than for two years past, he hurried through the streets of Ava to his own home.

The door of his house stood open as he approached, and, unobserved by any one, he entered. There, crouching in the ashes before a pan of coals sat a grimy, half-clothed Burmese woman, holding in her arms a puny, puny baby so covered with dirt that never for a moment did Mr. Judson dream it could be his own child.

He crossed the threshold into the next room, where, lying across the foot of the bed, as if she had fallen there, was the figure of a woman. Her face was white, her features drawn and sharp, and her whole form shrunken and emaciated. Her brown curls had been cut off and an old cotton cap covered her head.

Everything in the room spoke of neglect and ignorance in keeping with the face of the Burmese nurse who held the baby before the fire. In these squalid surroundings lay the beautiful, high-spirited woman who for fourteen years had never once "counted her life dear unto herself" if only she might follow the companion of her heart in his high path of service for God and man. "In journeyings often, in perils in the city, in perils in the wilderness, in perils in the sea, in perils among false brethren; in labor and travail, in watchings often, in hunger and thirst, in fastings often, in cold and nakedness; besides those things that are without"—daily anxiety for the little struggling Burmese church—thus ran the course of their Christlike sacrifice.

It may have been a tear that glanced her cheek, or a breath that came too near, or the sense of a dear, familiar presence more palpable than touch, for Ann Judson stirred uneasily in her sleep and opened her brown eyes—to look into her husband's face.

Notes

1. From chapters 3, 9, 10, and 13 of the *Life of St. Martin,* Alexander Robers, trans. and ed. *The Works of Sulpitius Severus,* Vol. XI, *A Select Library of Nicene and Post-Nicene Fathers of the Christian Church,* second series (Grand Rapids: William B. Eerdmans, 1955), pp. 5, 8, 10. Used by permission.

2. Ibid., pp. 1, 2, 16; Mary Caroline Watt, St. Martin of Tours (London: Sands and Co., 1928), pp. 9-33.

3. Ibid., pp. xiv-xix, 51-52.

4. Samuel M. Zwemer, "His Last Missionary Journey and His Martydom," *Raymund Lull: First Missionary to the Moslems* (New York: Funk and Wagnalls Company, 1902), pp. 132-146.

5. Ramon Lull, *The Book of the Lover and the Beloved,* E. Allison Peers, trans. and ed. (London: Society for Promoting Christian Knowledge, 1928), pp. 2-11; Lull, *The Tree of Love,* E. Allison Peer, trans. and ed. (London: Society for Promoting Christian Knowledge, 1926), pp. 13-14, 99-100.

6. Lull, *The Book of the Lover and the Beloved,* pp. 4-11.

7. Charles W. Foreman, "Samuel Marinus Zwemer," *Concise Dictionary,* pp. 681-682.

8. "The Traveler" from *Henry Martyn: Confessor of Faith* by Constance E. Padwick. Copyright 1950. Moody Press, Moody Bible Institute of Chicago. Used by permission.

9. John Sargent, A Memoir of Rev. Henry Martyn, B. D. (New York: American Tract Society); Stephen Neill, "Henry Martyn," *Concise Dictionary,* p. 372.

10. Ibid.

11. Kenneth Cragg, "Constance Evelyn Padwick," *Concise Dictionary,* p. 465.

12. Ibid.

13. The manuscript arrived safely, but not till 1814. It was published at Calcutta in 1816. Martyn's friend Mirza Seid Ali was actually sent for from Shiraz that he might see it through the press. When he came, he told the Calcutta group that he had with him the translation of the Psalms that had been the solace of Martyn's last months at Shiraz. Martyn no doubt regarded this as an uncompleted task. He had taken no steps to preserve it for the Church. But it formed the nucleus of the beautiful Persian Old Testament published in 1846 in Edinburgh and presented to the Shah in 1848.

14. Ethel Daniels Hubbard, "Prisoners in a Heathen Village," *Ann of Ava* (New York: Friendship Press, 1941), pp. 149-164. Used by permission.

15. Rudolf of Fulda, "The Life of St. Leoba," Talbot, pp. 205-226.

16. Helen Bagby Harrison, *The Bagbys of Brazil* (Nashville: Broadman Press, 1954); E. C. Routh, "Ann Luther Bagby," *Encyclopedia of Southern Baptists,* Vol. I (Nashville: Broadman Press, 1958), p. 103. See also R. Rierce Beaver, *All Loves Excelling: American Protestant Women in World Mission* (Grand Rapids: William B. Eerdmans Publishing Co., 1968).

17. Latourette, *The Great Century in Northern Africa and Asia,* Vol. VI, pp. 229, 243; Paul D. Clasper, "Adoniram Judson," *Concise Dictionary,* pp. 314-315. See also part V, 23.

18. Ethel Daniels Hubbard, *The Moffats* (New York: Friendship Press, New Edition, 1944), pp. 162-164.

IV

Missionary Journals and Diaries

General Introduction

No type of missionary literature has had a greater influence on the Christian world than the journals and diaries of the great missionaries. David Brainerd's journal strongly influenced Carey and Henry Martyn, and Martyn's journal in turn made a continuing impact for the missionary cause in the early part of the great century. The following journals and diaries are representative of the accounts of the "journeys of the soul" which have been produced through the Christian centuries. Though they cover a wide historical range, there are common strains of Christian devotion and missionary zeal in them all. What a debt the Christian world owes to these missionaries who took the time to keep these records and who were open and candid enough to share the pain and struggle and the joy and victory of their missionary pilgrimages!

14

"Confession" [1]
Patrick

Introduction

Patrick, the pioneer missionary to Ireland, belongs to that company of great missionaries which began with the apostle Paul. The latest calculations places his birth at 389 and his death at 461, though one tradition has him living to around the age of 120. He was a native of Britain, the son of a deacon and grandson of a presbyter. At the age of sixteen he was carried into slavery in Ireland. Later, when he was back in Britain, he had a vision and a call to return to Ireland as a missionary. It appears that he was opposed in this effort by his own countryman. He did find his way to Ireland, however, and amid difficulties was able to achieve considerable success in his evangelistic labors.[2]

Although Patrick was limited in his education, he came in time to be widely recognized and highly regarded. Many stories of miracles performed by his hand came to be circulated. Despite his limited learning, a number of literary works are attributed to him. His best known is "Confession," which is more of personal autobiography than a journal. It is not a confession in the normal sense of the term. Another work by Patrick has come to be known as "The Letter." In addition, he wrote a hymn known as "The Lorica of St. Patrick." Also a collection of sayings bears his name. His "Confession," though somewhat disjointed, reflects a profound knowledge of the Scriptures. In fact, a significant number of his autobiographical lines are expressed through a kind of biblical paraphrase. A life of Patrick was written by Muirchu around 700 or a little before. An earlier work by Bishop Tirechan, dated between 664 and 668, though not a formal biography, contains valuable data of a biographical and historical nature.[3]

Confession

1. I, Patrick the sinner, am the most illiterate and the least of all the faithful, and contemptible in the eyes of very many.

My father was Calpurnius, a deacon, one of the sons of Potitus, a presbyter, who belonged to the village of Banavem Taberniæ. Now he had a small farm hard by, where I was taken captive.

I was then about sixteen years of age. I knew not the true God; and I went into captivity to Ireland with many thousands of persons, according to our deserts, because we departed away from God, and kept not his commandments, and were not obedient to our priests, who used to admonish us for our salvation. And the Lord *poured upon us the fury of his anger,*[4] and scattered us amongst many heathen, even *unto the ends of the earth,* where now my littleness may be seen amongst men of another nation.

2. And there the Lord *opened the understanding* of my unbelief that, even though late, I might call my faults to remembrance, and that I might *turn with all my heart* to the Lord my God, who *regarded* my *low estate,* and pitied the youth of my ignorance, and kept me before I knew him, and before I had discernment or could distinguish between good and evil, and protected me and comforted me as a father does his son.

3. Wherefore then I cannot keep silence—nor would it be fitting— concerning such great benefits and such great grace as the Lord hath vouchsafed to bestow on me in the land of my captivity; because this is what we can render unto him, namely, that after we have been chastened, and have come to the knowledge of God, we shall exalt and *praise his wondrous works* before *every nation which is under the whole heaven.*

. . . .

9. On this account I had long since thought of writing; but I hesitated until now; for I feared lest I should fall under the censure of men's tongues, and because I have not studied as have others, who in the most approved fashion have drunk in both law and the Holy Scriptures alike, and have never changed their speech from their infancy, but rather have been always rendering it more perfect.

. . . .

12. Whence I who was at first illiterate, an exile, unlearned verily, who know not how to provide for the future—but this I do know most surely, that *before I was afflicted* I was like a stone lying in the deep mire; and *he that is mighty* came, and in his mercy lifted me up, and verily raised me aloft and placed me on the top of the wall. And therefore I ought to cry aloud that I may also *render somewhat to the Lord* for his benefits which are so great both here and in eternity, the value of which the mind of men cannot estimate.

13. Wherefore then be ye astonied, *ye that fear God, both small and great,* and ye clever sirs, ye rhetoricians, hear therefore and search it

out. Who was it that called up me, fool though I be, out of the midst of those who seem to be wise and skilled in the law, and *powerful in word* and in everything? And me, moreover, the abhorred of this world, did he inspire beyond others—if such I were—only that *with reverence and godly fear* and *unblameably* I should faithfully be of service to the nation to whom the love of Christ conveyed me, and presented me, as long as I live, if I should be worthy; in fine, that I should with humility and in truth diligently do them service.

14. And so it is proper that according to *the rule of faith* in the Trinity, I should define doctrine, and make known the gift of God and *everlasting consolation, without being held back* by danger, and spread everywhere the name of God without fear, confidently; so that even *after my decease* I may leave a legacy to my brethren and sons whom I baptized in the Lord, many thousands of persons.

. . . .

23. And again, after a few years, I was in Britain with my kindred, who received me as a son, and in good faith besought me that at all events now, after the great tribulations which I had undergone, I would not depart from them anywhither.

And there verily *I saw in the night visions* a man whose name was Victoricus coming as it were from Ireland with countless letters. And he gave me one of them, and I read the beginning of the letter, which was entitled, "The Voice of the Irish"; and while I was reading aloud the beginning of the letter, I thought that at that very moment I heard the voice of them who lived beside the Wood of Foclut which is nigh unto the western sea. And thus they cried, as with one mouth, "We beseech thee, holy youth, to come and walk among us once more."

And I was exceedingly *broken in heart,* and could read no further. And so I awoke. Thanks be to God, that after very many years the Lord granted to them according to their cry.

24. And another night whether within me or beside me, *I cannot tell, God knoweth,* in most admirable words which I heard and could not understand, except that at the end of the prayer he thus affirmed, "He who *laid down his life for thee,* he it is who speaketh in thee." And so I awoke, rejoicing.

25. And another time I saw him praying within me, and I was as it were within my body; and I heard [One praying] over me, that is,

over *the inner man;* and there he was praying mightily with groanings. And meanwhile I was astonied, and was marvelling and thinking who it could be that was praying within me; but at the end of the prayer he affirmed that he was the Spirit. And so I awoke, and I remembered how the Apostle saith, *The Spirit helpeth the infirmities of our prayer, for we know not what we should pray for as we ought; but the Spirit himself maketh intercession for us with groanings which cannot be uttered, which cannot be expressed in words.* And again, *The Lord our Advocate maketh intercession for us.*

. . . .

30. Therefore *I thank him who hath enabled me* in all things, because he did not hinder me from the journey on which I had resolved, and from my labour which I had learnt from Christ my Lord; but rather *I felt in myself* no little *virtue proceeding from him,* and my *faith has been approved in the sight of God and of men.*

. . . .

36. Whence came to me this wisdom, which was not in me, I who neither *knew the number of my days,* nor cared for God? Whence afterwards came to me that gift so great, so salutary, the knowledge and love of God, but only that I might part with fatherland and kindred?

37. And many gifts were proffered me with weeping and tears. And I displeased them, and also, against my wish, not a few of my elders; but, God being my guide, in no way did I consent or yield to them. It was not any grace in me, but God who overcometh in me; and he withstood them all, so that I came to the heathen Irish to preach the Gospel, and to endure insults from unbelievers, so as to *hear the reproach of my going abroad,* and [endure] many persecutions *even unto bonds,* and that I should give up my free condition for the profit of others. And if I should be worthy, I am ready [to give] even *my* life *for his name's sake* unhesitatingly and very gladly; and there I desire to spend it even unto death, if the Lord would grant it to me.

38. Because I am a debtor exceedingly to God, who granted me such great grace that many peoples through me should be regenerated to God and afterwards confirmed, and that clergy should everywhere be ordained for them for a people newly come to belief, which the Lord took *from the ends of the earth,* as he had in times past promised through his prophets: *The Gentiles shall come unto thee from the ends of the earth, and shall say, As our fathers have got for themselves false idols, and there*

is no profit in them. And again, *I have set thee to be a light of the Gentiles, that thou shouldest be for salvation unto the ends of the earth.*

39. And there I wish to *wait for his promise* who verily never disappoints. As he promises in the Gospel, *They shall come from the east and west and from the south and from the north, and shall sit down with Abraham and Isaac and Jacob;* as we believe that believers will come from all parts of the world.

40. For that reason therefore, we ought to fish well and diligently, as the Lord forewarns and teaches, saying, *Come ye after me, and I will make you to become fishers of men.* And again he saith through the prophets, *Behold I send fishers and many hunters, saith God,* and so forth.

Wherefore then, it was exceedingly necessary that we should spread our nets so that a *great multitude* and a throng should be taken for God, and that everywhere there should be clergy to baptize and exhort a people poor and needy, as the Lord in the Gospel warns and teaches, saying, *Go ye therefore now and teach all nations, baptizing them in the name of the Father, and of the Son, and of the Holy Ghost: teaching them to observe all things whatsoever I have commanded you: and, lo, I am with you alway, even unto the end of the world.* And again he saith, *Go ye therefore into all the world, and preach the Gospel to every creature. He that believeth and is baptized shall be saved; but he that believeth not shall be damned.* And again, *This Gospel of the kingdom shall be preached in all the world for a witness unto all nations: and then shall the end come.*

And in like manner the Lord, foreshewing by the prophet, saith, *And it shall come to pass in the last days, saith the Lord, I will pour out of my Spirit upon all flesh: and your sons and your daughters shall prophesy, and your young men shall see visions, and your old men shall dream dreams: and on my servants and on my handmaidens I will pour out in those days of my Spirit; and they shall prophesy.* And Hosea saith, *I will call them my people, which were not my people; and her one that hath obtained mercy which had not obtained mercy. And it shall come to pass, that in the place where it was said, Ye are not my people; there shall they be called the children of the living God.*

41. Wherefore then in Ireland they who never had the knowledge of God, but until now only worshipped idols and abominations—how has there been lately *prepared a people* of the Lord, and they are called children of God?

. . . .

15

The Journal of Matthew Ricci [5]
Matthew Ricci

Introduction

Matthew Ricci (1552-1610) was born in Macerata, Italy, of an aristocratic family. He had the best of early education, and in 1571 he entered the Society of Jesus in Rome where he studied philosophy and theology. He also studied mathematics under Christopher Clavius, regarded as perhaps the greatest mathematician of his time. Ricci was one of the most learned men of his day, and he used his learning in gaining an entree' to China. He began his missionary career in 1583 and labored there until his death.[6]

Ricci was the prototype of the great Jesuit missionaries to China. He mastered Mandarin, the language of royalty and the scholars, and was careful in studying and understanding the culture and customs of the Chinese. He learned their classics and was sympathetic toward the veneration which the scholars had for Confucius and the other Chinese philosophers and religious leaders. Though he was unapologetically Christian and always identified himself as a priest, he adopted the dress of the Chinese scholars. Because of his learning and affability, he became an official member of that distinguished and honored circle. He amazed the Chinese with his knowledge of science and mathematics. He further astounded them with his world map, for the Chinese scholars of the time believed China to be the center of the world, surrounded only by barbarians. Among his literary accomplishments was a Chinese translation of Euclid. At the time of his death, he was the emperor's official astronomer and mathematician.[7]

Ricci's best known theological work was *The True Knowledge of God* (1603). His greatest distinction is that he was the leader of a company of missionaries who established the first permanent Christian work in China. He left behind a detailed journal of his life and work as a missionary in the "Celestial Empire," which was assembled, and rewritten in Latin by his friend and colleague, Trigault. This is the reason the valuable work bears more the format of a chronicle than a journal.[8]

Progress in Nankin

Let us now turn our attention to the residence in the Royal City of Nankin. There were two priests in residence there; Father Lazzaro Cattaneo, who was recalled from Nancian, and Father Giovanni Roccia. Father Cattaneo managed well and increased the harvest. He won the friendship of the Magistrates and made many converts. Among them were Martin, the son of the first convert, Paul, his wife and all the rest of the family. From Nankin Father Lazzaro returned to Macao, because of ill health, and his Father Assistant, who took over the post and was zealous in following the same lines of development, made more than a hundred converts, within the first two years of his sojourn. It was during this time that Paul, the leading convert of Nankin, died at the age of seventy-four; a man whose extraordinary zeal for the spread of Christianity gave promise of a high award in heaven. From the time he became a Christian, due to his intense devotion, he often expressed a wish to live on for a few years more, so that he might teach others, by his example and his authority, to follow in his footsteps. Like the pious matrons in Xaucea, he built a beautiful chapel in his home, so his women folks could attend Mass, and next to it added another room, as a reception room for converts. The chapel was just completed when the Lord called him, overcome as he was by old age, but his sickness could not prevent him from being present at the first Mass celebrated in his chapel. Several times in his last illness he insisted upon making a general confession. Paul was the first one to be baptized in that city, and also the first one to profit by the sacrament of penance, and he died peacefully and contented.

Martin, the son of Paul, was as gallant as his father. He was the first one in this city who dared to omit certain funeral rites, forbidden by the Church, and to conduct a strictly Christian funeral, despite the criticism it evoked, and his example was followed by many others. There was no lack of objectors who found fault with what he did, each in his own way. Before his father's funeral and against the counsel of those advising him to the contrary, he did a very courageous thing, considering the circumstances in which it was done. It has already been noted that after a death, the Chinese sometimes keep the corpse in the house for a long time before burial. Departing from this custom and facing numerous protests, Martin was the first one to make a public declaration of his father's faith and at the same time of his own. He posted a sign in a public place, where everyone could read it, stating that his father had repudiated the worship of idols and embraced the Christian faith, also, that in his last will and testament he forbad the presence at his funeral of all ministers of the idol worshipping sect and of all or any of their rites or ceremonies. This sign, as it stated, was to attest that he belonged to the same faith as his father, and that he was hereby fulfilling his father's last wish and command. The venerable old man was buried from the Mission House, with full Christian burial ceremonies. This was the first time the converts ever saw a Christian funeral and they found in it a great source of consolation.

. . . .

We come now to what we consider to be an extraordinary conversion to an infant Church. There was an old man of seventy-eight, living in the neighborhood of the Mission Residence. He was Chief of the Military Prefects, before his retirement, after which his position and his properties were transferred to his oldest son. His interest in Christianity was awakened by his servants, and it was not long before he became a convert. When the time came to do away with the household idols, his son entered a vehement protest, asserting that the father had constituted him head of the family, and that he wanted to regulate family affairs according to his own way of thinking. The dissension was long drawn out, but the intensity of the faith of the parent and the grace of God finally conquered. With renewed ardor and with his son present, the old gentleman called two of his convert servants, summoned one of the Fathers, and told them to take every one of the miserable household gods over to the Mission House and burn them. This caused the son to become very angry, but he dared not use force, for fear of his father. Instead, he poured out his indignation on the servants, who left the house bearing a double burden of idols and of contumely. The old man accompanied them to the Mission House, where he witnessed the burning of the idols, and was then baptized with an increase of satisfaction, corresponding to the growing desire with which he had sought it. Later on, the son set aside his animosity and was reconciled with the Fathers, but he was not interested in seeking a way to salvation.

There was another man, named Ciu, who fell sick some time after he had been baptized, and realizing that his life was in danger, he asked to confess his post-baptismal faults, and to fortify his departure with the holy Eucharist. He, too, left orders that he should be buried with Christian ceremonies, and his wife, to whom he committed this request, followed his example by adopting his faith and by sharing it with the rest of her family. Such examples as these had a very salutary effect on all the converts.

The number of Christians was also increasing in the nearby villages. A chapel was erected in the home of one of the more distinguished converts, and his wife, who became the sole custodian, kept it in excellent order. At times the Fathers went there to celebrate Mass and to instruct converts, who were so well cared for at this house that there was scarcely ever an absentee. In addition to her care for the neophytes, this lady also extended her charity to the Fathers, as her namesake, Martha, of the Gospel, did to the Lord.

It was during the second year of Father Cattaneo's sojourn here that something of real importance happened. Paul, the most prominent luminary of this Church, whose death we have just recorded, became a disciple of Christ, at the Mission House. He was one of those men from whom great things are to be expected, and Heaven had ordained that he should ornament this infant church. Born in the City of Scianhai, about eight days journey from Nankin, in the Province of Nankin, he was a distinguished intellectual, admirably endowed, and naturally inclined to good. What he had been especially looking for, as a member of the sect of the literati, was something about which they are particularly reticent, namely, definite knowledge about the next life and about the immortality of the soul. There is no sect whatever, among the Chinese that utterly rejects this immortality. He had heard much about celestial glory and happiness in the weird hallucination of the idol worshippers, but his active mind could repose in nothing but the truth. In 1597 he gained first place in the examinations for the degree of Licentiate at Pekin, an honor which carried the very highest prestige. In his quest for the Doctorate he was not so fortunate and he counted his failure as a special grace of God, asserting that this was the cause of his salvation. He had only one son and his great fear was that with that son the family might come to an end, an eventuality which the Chinese, somewhat unreasonably, look upon as a catastrophe. With the acquisition of the faith came good fortune; two grandsons and success in his examination for the Doctorate. This examination took place four years after he became a licentiate, but in it he was the victim of an unfortunate incident. By an oversight he was admitted to the examination as number three hundred and one, whereas the law limited the number to three hundred, and so his paper was rejected. With that, not wishing to face the humiliation of returning to his own people, he withdrew to the Province of Canton. It was here at Xaucea that he first became acquainted with the Fathers, in a conversation with Father Cattaneo, who was living at that Mission at the time, and it was here also that he first made a reverence to a crucifix.

Paul met Father Ricci in Nankin in the year 1600, and spoke to him about the Christian religion, of which he had heard something, previously. This was only a transient meeting, as Paul was in a hurry to get back to his home, and at that time he probably heard no more than that the God in whom Christians believe, is the first principle of all things. It seems, however, as if God had reserved this man to himself for enlightenment. The mystery of the Most Holy Trinity was, in a way, represented to him in a dream. He saw three chapels in a temple. In the first he saw the figure of a person, whom someone present called God the Father. In the second he saw another figure, wearing a royal crown, whom he heard called, God the Son, and he heard a voice telling him to bow down in reverence before these forms. In the third chapel he saw nothing and made no obeisance. It may be that God did not wish to represent the Holy Spirit to a pagan, by the form of a dove, to which we are accustomed, in order not to offend one who was still a pagan, because the Chinese, no matter what sect they may belong to, never pay reverence to any deity unless that deity be represented in human form. Later on, when the doctrine of the Church, relative to the Holy Trinity, was being explained to him at Nankin, he remembered this dream, but said nothing about it, because on another occasion he had heard from one of the Fathers that we should not believe in dreams. Again, a long time afterwards in Pekin, he heard Father Matthew say that in the past God revealed many things to his servants, in dreams. Then he asked the Father if it were permitted to place credence in some dreams, and with considerable exaltation, he narrated the dream just mentioned.

To return to his conversion, in the year 1603 he returned to Nankin on a business trip and went to visit Father Giovanni Roccia. He bowed before the statue of the Blessed Virgin, as he entered the house, and on first hearing of some of the principles of Christianity, he immediately decided to embrace the Catholic faith. During that whole day and up to nightfall, he remained in peaceful contemplation of the principal articles of Christian belief. He took home a compendium of Christian Doctrine and also a manuscript copy of Father Ricci's Catechism; the text of an edition which had not as yet been published. He was so pleased with these two books that he stayed up the whole night reading them, and before he returned on the following day, he had memorized the entire Compendium of Christian Doctrine. He asked Father Roccia to explain certain passages to him, as soon as possible, because he had to return home before the end of the year, and he wanted to be baptized before going. In order to find out whether or not he really was serious about this, the Father told him that he would have to come for instruction, once a day and every day for a week, to which he replied, "Not only once, I shall come twice a day," which he did, and always arriving very promptly. If Father happened to be away when he arrived, he took his lesson from one of the Brothers, or from a house student. He was baptized the day he left for home, and from there he sent back two letters, in which he manifested very clearly how deeply he had imbibed the Doctrines of the Christian law.

Several months later, he came back to Nankin, to review the course he had taken, and he went straight to the Mission House, lest it might appear that he had visited someone else first. This time he stayed with the Fathers for two weeks, much to the joy of his hosts and to the benefit of the domestic servants. He attended the sacrifice of the

Mass every day and he was continually making inquiries, for fear, as it seemed, that he might miss some point or other of Christian doctrine. He found a great consolation in going to confession whenever he returned to pay a visit, and especialy so, on his way back to Pekin, to retake the examination for the Doctorate. Once he came really rejoicing and, as it were, bringing in the sheaves. He had persuaded two of the class of the literati and several friends from his district, to put aside their idol worship. He taught them their prayers, and not long afterwards they became Christians, all being baptized on the same day.

. . . .

16

David Brainerd's Journal[9]

Introduction

David Brainerd (1718-1747) was born in Haddam, Connecticut. His father died when he was nine, and his mother died five years later. He was befriended by the great Jonathan Edwards, to whose daughter Jerusha he was later engaged to be married. Shortly before he entered Yale at the age of twenty-one, he had a conversion experience. He was expelled from Yale in 1742 for attending services of the Separatists and for making uncomplimentary remarks about the college minister. Although he later apologized, he was never permitted to reenter. In 1743, he began his work with the Indians under the sponsorship of the Society for Promoting Christian Knowledge. He was ordained in 1744, and soon after this he began his famous work among the Indians of New Jersey. In three short years after his ordination, he died of tuberculosis at the early age of twenty-nine. He kept a diary of his life and work, however, and almost immediately upon its publication, it captured the hearts of the Protestant world.

For over a century it was one of the most popular documents in evangelical circles. Its influence has been enormous. It had a singular influence upon such missionary giants as William Carey and Henry Martyn.[10]

Brainerd was deeply mystical, and his piety often expressed itself in a strongly emotional way. In his journal he describes the joys and frustrations both of his mission work and of his own personal spiritual pilgrimage. Like the Psalms, the very openness and candor with which he describes his experiences won for him a profound place in the hearts of Christians and especially young missionaries. That the diary of a missionary, which describes the soul and work of that missionary during so brief a period, should make such an impact, is one of the most astounding facts in all the history of the missionary enterprise.

The Rise and Progress of a Remarkable Work of Grace

. . . .

CROSSWEEKSUNG, IN NEW JERSEY, AUGUST, 1745.

August 3. I visited the Indians in these parts in June last, and tarried with them some considerable time, preaching almost daily; at which season God was pleased to pour upon them a spirit of awakening and concern for their souls, and surprisingly to engage their attention to divine truths. I now found them serious, and a number of them under deep concern for an interest in Christ. Their convictions of their sinful and perishing state having, in my absence from them, been much promoted by the labors and endeavors of the Rev. Mr. William Tennent, to whom I had advised them to apply for direction, and whose house they frequented much while I was gone. I preached to them this day with some view to Revelation 22:17, "And whosoever will, let him take the water of life freely," though I could not pretend to handle the subject methodically among them.

The Lord, I am persuaded, enabled me, in a manner somewhat uncommon, to set before them the Lord Jesus Christ as a kind and compassionate Saviour, inviting distressed and perishing sinners to accept everlasting mercy. And a surprising concern soon became apparent among them. There were about twenty adult persons together (many of the Indians at remote places not having as yet had time to come since my return hither), and not above two that I could see with dry eyes. Some were much concerned, and discovered vehement longings of soul after Christ, to save them from the misery they felt and feared.

Lord's Day, August 4. Being invited by a neighboring minister to assist in the administration of the Lord's Supper, I complied with his request, and took the Indians along with me; not only those that were together the day before, but many more that were coming to hear me; so that there were near fifty in all, old and young. They attended the several discourses of the day, and some of them that could understand English, were much affected, and all seemed to have their concern in some measure raised.

Now a change in their manners began to appear very visible. In the evening when they came to sup together, they would not taste a morsel till they had sent to me to come and ask a blessing on their food; at which time sundry of them wept, especially when I minded them how they had in times past eaten their feasts in honor to devils, and neglected to thank God for them.

August 5. After a sermon had been preached by another minister, I preached, and concluded the public work of the solemnity from John 7:37, "In the last day . . ." In my discourse addressed the Indians in particular, who sat by themselves in a part of the house; at which time one or two of them were struck with deep concern, as they afterwards told me, who had been little affected before; others had their concern increased to a considerable degree. In the evening (the greater part of them being at the house where I lodged) I discoursed to them, and found them universally engaged about their souls' concern, inquiring, "What they should do to be saved?" And all their conversation among themselves turned upon religious matters, in which they were much assisted by my interpreter, who was with them day and night.

This day there was one woman, who had been much concerned for her soul ever since she first heard me preach in June last, who obtained comfort, I trust, solid and well grounded. She seemed to be filled with love to Christ, at the same time behaved humbly and tenderly, and appeared afraid of nothing so much as of grieving and offending Him whom her soul loved.

August 6. In the morning I discoursed to the Indians at the house where we lodged. Many of them were then much affected and appeared surprisingly tender, so that a few words about their souls' concerns would cause the tears to flow freely, and produce many sobs and groans.

In the afternoon, they being returned to the place where I had usually preached among them, I again discoursed to them there. There were about fifty-five persons in all, about forty that were capable of attending divine service with understanding. I insisted upon I John 4:10, "Herein is love." They seemed eager of hearing; but there appeared nothing very remarkable, except their attention, till near the close of my discourse. Then divine truths were attended with a surprising influence, and produced a great concern among them. There were scarce three in forty that could refrain from tears and bitter cries.

They all, as one, seemed in an agony of soul to obtain an interest in Christ; and the more I discoursed of the love and compassion of God in sending His Son to suffer for the sins of men; and the more I invited them to come and partake of His love, the more their distress was aggravated, because they felt themselves unable to come. It was surprising to see how their hearts seemed to be pierced with the tender and melting invitations of the gospel, when there was not a word of terror spoken to them.

There were this day two persons that obtained relief and comfort, which (when I came to discourse with them particularly) appeared solid, rational, and scriptural. After I had inquired into the grounds of their comfort and said many things I thought proper to them, I asked them what they wanted God to do further for them. They replied, "They wanted Christ should wipe their hearts, quite clean." Surprising were now the doings of the Lord, that I can say no less of this day (and I need say no more of it) than that the arm of the Lord was powerfully and marvelously revealed in it.

August 7. Preached to the Indians from Isaiah 53:3-10. There was a remarkable influence attending the Word, and great concern in the assembly; but scarce equal to what appeared the day before, that is, not quite so universal. However, most were much affected, and many in great distress for their souls; and some few could neither go nor stand, but lay flat on the ground, as if pierced at heart, crying incessantly for mercy. Several were newly awakened, and it was remarkable that as fast as they came from remote places round about the Spirit of

God seemed to seize them with concern for their souls.

After public service was concluded, I found two persons more that had newly met with comfort, of whom I had good hopes; and a third that I could not but entertain some hopes of, whose case did not appear so clear as the others; so that there were now six in all that had got some relief from their spiritual distresses, and five whose experience appeared very clear and satisfactory. And it is worthy of remark, that those who obtained comfort first were in general deeply affected with concern for their souls when I preached to them in June last.

August 8. In the afternoon I preached to the Indians; their number was now about sixty-five persons, men, women, and children. I discoursed from Luke 14:16-23 and was favored with uncommon freedom in my discourse. There was much visible concern among them while I was discoursing publicly; but afterwards when I spoke to one and another more particularly, whom I perceived under much concern, the power of God seemed to descend upon the assembly "like a rushing mighty wind," and with an astonishing energy bore down all before it.

I stood amazed at the influence that seized the audience almost universally, and could compare it no nothing more aptly than the irresistible force of a mighty torrent, or swelling deluge, that with its insupportable weight and pressure bears down and sweeps before it whatever is in its way. Almost all persons of all ages were bowed down with concern together, and scarce one was able to withstand the shock of this surprising operation. Old men and women, who had been drunken wretches for many years, and some little children, not more than six or seven years of age, appeared in distress for their souls, as well as persons of middle age. And it was apparent these children (some of them at least) were not merely frightened with seeing the general concern; but were made sensible of their danger, the badness of their hearts, and their misery without Christ, as some of them expressed it.

The most stubborn hearts were now obliged to bow. A principal man among the Indians, who before was most secure and self-righteous and thought his state good because he knew more than the generality of the Indians had formerly done, and who with a great degree of confidence the day before, told me, "he had been a Christian more than ten years," was now brought under solemn concern for his soul, and wept bitterly. Another man advanced in years, who had been a murderer, a powwow (or conjurer) and a notorious drunkard, was likewise brought now to cry for mercy with many tears, and to complain much that he could be no more concerned when he saw his danger so very great.

They were almost universally praying and crying for mercy, in every part of the house, and many out of doors, and numbers could neither go nor stand. Their concern was so great, each one for himself, that none seemed to take any notice of those about them, but each prayed freely for himself. And, I am to think, they were to their own apprehension as much retired as if they had been, individually, by themselves in the thickest desert; or, I believe rather, that they thought nothing about any but themselves, and their own states, and so were everyone praying apart, although all together.

It seemed to me there was now an exact fulfillment of that prophecy, Zechariah 12:10,11,12; for there was now "a great mourning, like the mourning of Hadadrimmon"; and each seemed to "mourn apart." Methought this had a near resemblance to the day of God's power, mentioned in Joshua 10:14. I must say I never saw any day like it in all respects. It was a day wherein I am persuaded the Lord did much to destroy the kingdom of darkness among this people today.

This concern in general was most rational and just. Those who had been awakened any considerable time complained more especially of the badness of their hearts. Those newly awakened, of the badness of their lives and actions past; all were afraid of the anger of God and of everlasting misery as the desert of their sins. Some of the white people who came out of curiosity to "hear what this babbler would say" to the poor ignorant Indians were much awakened, and some appeared to be wounded with a view of their perishing state.

Those who had lately obtained relief were filled with comfort at this season. They appeared calm and composed, and seemed to rejoice in Christ Jesus. Some of them took their distressed friends by the hand, telling them of the goodness of Christ and the comfort that is to be enjoyed in Him, and thence invited them to come and give up their hearts to Him. I could observe some of them, in the most honest and unaffected manner (without any design of being taken notice of) lifting up their eyes to heaven as if crying for mercy, while they saw the distress of the poor souls around them.

There was one remarkable instance of awakening this day that I cannot but take particular notice of here. A young Indian woman, who, I believe, never knew before she had a soul nor ever thought of any such thing, hearing that there was something strange among the Indians, came to see what was the matter. In her way to the Indians she called at my lodgings, and when I told her I designed presently to preach to the Indians, laughed, and seemed to mock; but went however to them.

I had not proceeded far in my public discourse, before she felt effectually that she had a soul. Before I had concluded my discourse, she was so convinced of her sin and misery and so distressed with concern for her soul's salvation that she seemed like one pierced through with a dart, and cried out incessantly. She could neither go nor stand, nor sit on her seat without being held up. After public service was over, she lay flat on the ground praying earnestly, and would take no notice of, nor give any answer to any that spoke to her. I hearkened to know what she said, and perceived the burden of her prayer to be, *Guttummaukalummeh wechaumeh kmeleh Ndah,* that is, "Have mercy on me, and help me to give You my heart." Thus she continued praying incessantly for many hours together. This was indeed a surprising day of God's power and seemed enough to convince an atheist of the truth, importance and power of God's Word.

August 9. Spent almost the whole day with the Indians, the former part of it in discoursing to many of them privately, especially to some who had lately received comfort, endeavoring to inquire into the grounds of it, as well as to give them some proper instructions, cautions, and directions.

In the afternoon discoursed to them publicly. They were now present about seventy persons, old and young. I opened and applied the Parable of the Sower, Matthew 13. Was enabled to discourse with much plainness, and found afterwards that this discourse was very instructive to them. There were many tears among them while I was discoursing publicly, but no considerable cry. Yet some were much affected with a few words spoken from Matthew 11:28, "Come unto me, all ye that labor," with which I concluded my discourse. But while I was discoursing near night to two or three of the awakened persons, a divine influence seemed to attend what was spoken to them in a powerful manner, causing the persons to cry out in anguish of soul, although

I spoke not a word of terror. On the contrary, I set before them the fullness and all-sufficiency of Christ's merits and His willingness to save all that came to Him, and thereupon pressed them to come without delay.

The cry of these was soon heard by others, who, though scattered before, immediately gathered round. I then proceeded in the same strain of gospel invitation, till they all, except two or three, melted into tears and cries and seemed in the greatest distress to find and secure an interest in the great Redeemer. Some who had but little more than a ruffle made in their passions the day before, seemed now to be deeply affected and wounded at heart. The concern in general appeared near as prevalent as it was the day before. There was indeed a very great mourning among them, and yet everyone seemed to mourn apart. For so great was their concern, that almost everyone was praying and crying for himself, as if none had been near. *Guttummaukalummeh, guttummauka-lummeh,* that is, "Have mercy upon me, have mercy upon me," was the common cry.

It was very affecting to see the poor Indians, who the other day were hallooing and yelling in their idolatrous feasts and drunken frolics, now crying to God with such importunity for an interest in His dear Son! Found two or three persons, who, I had reason to hope, had taken comfort upon good grounds since the evening before. These, with others that had obtained comfort, were together and seemed to rejoice much that God was carrying on His work with such power upon others.

August 10. Rode to the Indians and began to discourse more privately to those who had obtained comfort and satisfaction, endeavoring to instruct, direct, caution and comfort them. But others being eager of hearing every word that related to spiritual concerns, soon came together one after another. When I had discoursed to the young converts more than half an hour, they seemed much melted with divine things and earnestly desirous to be with Christ. I told them of the godly soul's perfect purity and full enjoyment of Christ immediately upon its separation from the body, and that it would be forever inconceivably more happy than they had ever been for any short space of time when Christ seemed near to them, in prayer or other duties.

That I might make way for speaking of the resurrection of the body, and thence of the complete blessedness of the man, I said, "But perhaps some of you will say, I love my body as well as my soul, and I cannot bear to think that my body should lie dead, if my soul is happy." To which they all cheerfully replied, *Muttoh, muttoh* (before I had opportunity to prosecute what I designed respecting the resurrection), "No, no." They did not regard their bodies, if their souls might be but with Christ. Then they appeared willing to be absent from the body, that they might be present with the Lord.

When I had spent some time with these, I turned to the other Indians and spoke to them from Luke 19:10, "For the Son of man is come to seek . . ." I had not discoursed long before their concern rose to a great degree, and the house was filled with cries and groans. When I insisted on the compassion and care of the Lord Jesus Christ for those that were lost, who thought themselves undone and could find no way of escape, this melted them down the more and aggravated their distress that they could not find and come to so kind a Saviour.

Sundry persons, who before had been but slightly awakened, were now deeply wounded with a sense of their sin and misery. One man in particular, who was never before awakened, was now made to feel that "the word of the Lord was quick and powerful, sharper than any two-edged sword." He seemed to be pierced at heart with distress, and his concern appeared most rational and scriptural; for he said that all the wickedness of his past life was brought fresh to his remembrance, and he saw all the vile actions he had done formerly as if done but yesterday.

Found one that had newly received comfort, after pressing distress from day to day. Could not but rejoice and admire divine goodness in what appeared this day. There seems to be some good done by every discourse; some newly awakened every day, and some comforted. It was refreshing to observe the conduct of those that had obtained comfort, while others were distressed with fear and concern; that is, lifting up their hearts to God for them.

Lord's Day, August 11. Discoursed in the forenoon from the Parable of the Prodigal Son, Luke 15. Observed no such remarkable effect of the Word upon the assembly as in days past. There were numbers of careless spectators of the white people, some Quakers, and others. In the afternoon I discoursed upon a part of Peter's sermon, Acts 2, and at the close of my discourse to the Indians made an address to the white people. Divine truths seemed then to be attended with power both to English and Indians. Several of the white heathen were awakened and could not longer be idle spectators, but found they had souls to save or lose as well as the Indians; a great concern spread through the whole assembly. This also appeared to be a day of God's power, especially towards the conclusion of it, although the influence attending the Word seemed scarce so powerful now as in some days past.

The number of the Indians, old and young, was now upwards of seventy. One or two were newly awakened this day, who never had appeared to be moved with concern for their souls before. Those who had obtained relief and comfort, and had given hopeful evidences of having passed a saving change, appeared humble and devout and behaved in an agreeable and Christian-like manner. I was refreshed to see the tenderness of conscience manifest in some of them, one instance of which I cannot but notice. Perceiving one of them very sorrowful in the morning, I inquired into the cause of her sorrow. I found the difficulty was that she had been angry with her child the evening before and was now exercised with fears lest her anger had been inordinate and sinful. This so grieved her that she waked and began to sob before daylight, and continued weeping for several hours together.

. . . .

August 16. Spent a considerable time in conversing privately with sundry of the Indians. Found one that had got relief and comfort, after pressing concern, and could not but hope, when I came to discourse particularly with her, that her comfort was of the right kind. In the afternoon, I preached to them from John 6:26-34. Toward the close of my discourse, divine truths were attended with considerable power upon the audience, and more especially after public service was over, when I particularly addressed sundry distressed persons.

There was a great concern for their souls spread pretty generally among them. Especially there were two persons newly awakened to a sense of their sin and misery, one of whom was lately come, and the other had all along been very attentive, and desirous of being awakened, but could never before have any lively view of her perishing state. But now her concern and spiritual distress was such that, I thought, I had never seen any more pressing.

Sundry old men were also in distress for their souls so that they could not refrain from weeping and crying aloud, and their bitter groans were the most convincing, as well as affecting evidence of the reality and depth of their inward anguish. God is powerfully at work among them! True and genuine convictions of sin are daily promoted in many instances, and some are newly awakened from time to time, although some few, who felt a commotion in their passions in days past, seem now to discover that their hearts were never duly affected.

I never saw the work of God appear so independent of means as at this time. I discoursed to the people, and spoke what, I suppose, had a proper tendency to promote convictions. But God's manner of working upon them appeared so entirely supernatural and above means that I could scarce believe He used me as an instrument, or what I spake as means of carrying on His work. It seemed, as I thought, to have no connection with, nor dependence upon means in any respect. Although I could not but continue to use the means which I thought proper for the promotion of the work, yet God seemed, as I apprehended, to work entirely without them. I seemed to do nothing, and indeed to have nothing to do, but to "stand still and see the salvation of God." I found myself obliged and delighted to say, "Not unto us," not unto instruments and means, "but to thy name be glory." God appeared to work entirely alone, and I saw no room to attribute any part of this work to any created arm.

August 17. Spent much time in private conferences with the Indians. Found one who had newly obtained relief and comfort, after a long season of spiritual trouble and distress—he having been one of my hearers at the Forks of Delaware for more than a year, and now followed me here under deep concern for his soul—and had abundant reason to hope that his comfort was well grounded and truly divine. Afterwards discoursed publicly from Acts 8:29-39, and took occasion to treat concerning baptism, in order to their being instructed and prepared to partake of that ordinance. They were yet hungry and thirsty for the Word of God, and appeared unwearied in their attendance upon it.

Lord's Day, August 18. Preached in the forenoon to an assembly of white people, made up of Presbyterians, Baptists, and Quakers. Afterwards preached to the Indians from John 6:35-40. There was considerable concern visible among them, though not equal to what has frequently appeared of late.

August 19. Preached from Isaiah 55:1, "Ho, every one that thirsteth." Divine truths were attended with power upon those who had received comfort, and others also. The former were sweetly melted and refreshed with divine invitations, the latter much concerned for their souls, that they might obtain an interest in these glorious gospel-provisions that were set before them. There were numbers of poor impotent souls that waited at the pool for healing, and the Angel seemed, as at other times of late, to trouble the waters so that there was yet a most desirable and comfortable prospect of the spiritual recovery of diseased, perishing sinners.

August 24. Spent the forenoon in discoursing to some of the Indians, in order to their receiving the ordinance of baptism. When I had opened the nature of the ordinance, the obligations attending it, the duty of devoting ourselves to God in it, and the privilege of being in covenant with Him, sundry of them seemed to be filled with love to God, and delighted with the thoughts of giving up themselves to Him in that solemn and public manner, melted and refreshed with the hopes of enjoying the blessed Redeemer.

Afterwards I discoursed publicly from I Thessalonians 4:13-17, "But I would not have you be ignorant." There was a solemn attention and some visible concern and affection in the time of public service, which was afterwards increased by some further exhortation given them to come to Christ and give up their hearts to Him, that they might be fitted to "ascend up and meet him in the air," when He shall "descend with a shout, and the voice of the archangel."

There were several Indians newly come, who thought their state good and themselves happy because they had sometimes lived with the white people under gospel-light, had learned to read, were civil; although they appeared utter strangers to their own hearts and altogether unacquainted with the power of religion, as well as with the doctrines of grace. With those I discoursed particularly after public worship and was surprised to see their self-righteous disposition, their strong attachment to the covenant of works for salvation, and the high value they put upon their supposed attainments. Yet after much discourse, one appeared in a measure convinced that "by the deeds of the law no flesh living can be justified," and wept bitterly, inquiring what he must do to be saved!

This was very comfortable to others who had gained some experimental acquaintance with their own hearts. For before they were grieved with the conversation and conduct of these newcomers, who boasted of their knowledge, and thought well of themselves, but evidently discovered to those that had any experience of divine truths that they knew nothing of their own hearts.

Lord's Day, August 25. Preached in the forenoon from Luke 15:3-7. There being a multitude of white people present, I made an address to them at the close of my discourse to the Indians. But I could not so much as keep them orderly; for scores of them kept walking and gazing about, and behaved more indecently than any Indians I ever addressed. A view of their abusive conduct so sunk my spirits that I could scarce go on with my work.

In the afternoon discoursed from Revelation 3:20, at which time the Indians behaved seriously, though many others were vain. Afterwards baptized twenty-five persons of the Indians, fifteen adults and ten children. Most of the adults I have comfortable reason to hope are renewed persons; and there was not one of them but what I entertained some hopes of in that respect, though the case of two or three of them appeared more doubtful.

After the crowd of spectators was gone, I called the baptized persons together and discoursed to them in particular, at the same time inviting others to attend. I minded them of the solemn obligations they were now under to live to God, warned them of the evil and dreadful consequences of careless living, especially after this public profession of Christianity; gave them directions for their future conduct, and encouraged them to watchfulness and devotion by setting before them the comfort and happy conclusion of a religious life.

This was a desirable and sweet season indeed! Their hearts were engaged and cheerful in duty, and they rejoiced that they had in a public and solemn manner dedicated themselves to God. Love seemed to reign among them! They took each other by the hand with tenderness and affection, as if their hearts were knit together, while I was discoursing to them. All their deportment toward each other was such that a serious spectator might justly be excited to cry out with admiration, "Behold how they love one another"! Sundry of the other Indians, at seeing and hearing these things, were much affected and wept bitterly, longing to be partakers of the same joy and comfort that these discovered by their very countenances as well as conduct.

August 26. Preached to my people from John 6:51-55. After I had discoursed some time, I addressed those in particular who entertained hopes that they were "passed from death to life." Opened to them the persevering nature of those consolations Christ gives His people, and which I trusted He had bestowed upon some in that assembly; showed them that such have already the "beginnings of eternal life" (v. 54), and that their heaven shall speedily be completed.

I no sooner began to discourse in this strain but the dear Christians in the congregation began to be melted with affection to, and desire of the enjoyment of Christ and of a state of perfect purity. They wept affectionately and yet joyfully, and their tears and sobs discovered brokenness of heart, and yet were attended with real comfort and sweetness. This was a tender, affectionate, humble, delightful melting, and appeared to be the genuine effect of a Spirit of adoption, and very far from the Spirit of bondage that they not long since labored under. The influence seemed to spread from these through the whole assembly, and there quickly appeared a wonderful concern among them. Many who had not yet found Christ as an all-sufficient Saviour were surprisingly engaged in seeking after Him. It was indeed a lovely and very desirable assembly. Their number was now about ninety-five persons, old and young, and almost all affected either with joy in Christ Jesus, or with utmost concern to obtain an interest in Him.

Being fully convinced it was now my duty to take a journey far back to the Indians on Susquehannah River (it being now a proper season of the year to find them generally at home), after having spent some hours in public and private discourses with my people, I told them that I must now leave them for the present, and go to their brethren far remote and preach to them. I told them I wanted the Spirit of God should go with me, without whom nothing could be done to any good purpose among the Indians—as they themselves had opportunity to see by the barrenness of our meetings at times, when there was much pains taken to affect and awaken sinners yet to little or no purpose. I asked them if they could not be willing to spend the remainder of the day in prayer for me that God would go with me and succeed my endeavors for the conversion of those poor souls. They cheerfully complied with the motion, and soon after I left them (it being then about an hour and half before sunset) they began, and continued praying all night till break of day, or very near, never mistrusting, they tell me, till they went out and viewed the stars, and saw the morning star a considerable height, that it was later than common bedtime. Thus eager and unwearied were they in their devotions! A remarkable night it was, attended, as my interpreter tells me, with a powerful influence upon those who were yet under concern, as well as those that had received comfort.

There were, I trust, this day two distressed souls brought to the enjoyment of solid comfort in Him, in whom the weary find rest. It was likewise remarkable that this day an old Indian, who has all his days been an obstinate idolater, was brought to give up his rattles (which they use for music in their idolatrous feasts and dances) to the other Indians, who quickly destroyed them. This without any attempt of mine in the affair, I having said nothing to him about it; so that it seemed it was nothing but just the power of God's Word, without any particular application to this sin, that produced this effect. Thus God has begun, thus he has hitherto surprisingly carried on a work of grace amongst these Indians. May the glory be ascribed to Him, who is the sole Author of it!

17

David Livingstone's Journal[11]

Introduction

David Livingstone (1813-1873) is one of the best known names of history. Yet this physician, explorer, geographer, ethnographer, and folk hero was first and foremost a missionary. He was born of a poor family in Scotland and as a youth worked for thirteen years in a cotton mill in his hometown of Blantyre. He managed to receive an education, however, and under the influence of an independent religious community in Hamilton, he made a decision to become a missionary. He received a medical degree from Glasgow University in 1840 and the next year went as a medical missionary to Africa under the London Missionary Society.[12]

In Africa, Livingstone joined himself to the mission settlement of the pioneer Robert Moffat. Here he married the Moffat's daughter, Mary. His first journey, exploring the possibilities for mission work in different areas, gave him an appetite for missionary travel and exploration. On one of his early journeys, he became the first non-African to see Lake Ngami (1849). He soon became obsessed with the idea of exploring Africa and opening it up for civilization and Christianity. It soon became apparent that he could not carry his family with him on these long and dangerous journeys, and he decided to send his wife and children back to Britain. Livingstone was a man of deep tenderness, and this was a great sacrifice for him and his family. His love for his family, however, took second place to his passion to explore Africa and open it to the gospel.[13]

Livingstone was fascinated by the great Zambesi River, which he first beheld in 1851 and regarded as "God's highway into the interior." He spent sixteen years in Africa before he returned to Britain. When he did return, his fame preceded him. The report of his travels and discoveries had made him a national hero. He returned to Africa with the rank of consul and led an official expedition further into the interior. However, he was still a missionary, and his explorations opened the door for the work of the Church of Scotland and other mission work. In those days he came in close contact with the slave traffic for which he developed a deep contempt and against which he fought all his life.[14]

Later Livingstone was able to pursue his mission independently, largely due to the success of his two works: *Missionary Travels* (1857) and *Zambesi Narrative* (1865). He was convinced that the quickest way to end the loathsome slave trading was to open Africa for other forms of trading and commerce. On his ventures he was alone with African companions. When he was not heard from for a long period of time while exploring the interior, concern for his health and safety led to the famous expedition of Henry Morton Stanley to find Livingstone. As the traveling correspondent of the *New York Herald,* Stanley's mission was amply funded. The purpose of the mission was to find Livingstone, and if he were alive, to bring back a full report of his activities, and if he were dead, to bring back his bones. The meeting of Stanley and Livingstone is one of the best known accounts of history. The words of Stanley upon meeting Livingstone—"Dr. Livingstone, I presume"—are among the best known lines in the English language.[15]

Stanley could not persuade Livingstone to return with him. Twenty months later Livingstone died, on his knees, in the posture of prayer. The story of the end of his life is one of the most remarkable in history. His companions removed his heart and viscera and buried them beneath a large mvula tree, and on the trunk of the tree was deeply carved the name *Livingstone.* The body was embalmed with raw salt and wrapped in calico, bark, and sailcloth. His attendants mounted it on a pole, and a procession of sixty men started on a dangerous journey of fifteen hundred miles which lasted eight months, to carry the beloved remains of Livingstone to the East Coast where a ship was waiting to carry him to Britain. He was buried with England's great in Westminster Abbey (near the entrance), some dozen days within a year of the time of his death. Largely through his efforts and inspiration, within a month after his death the slave market of Africa was officially closed.[16]

He needs no epitaph to guard a name
Which men shall prize while worthy work is known;
He lived and died for good—be that his fame:
Let marble crumble: this is LIVING-STONE[17]

Livingstone's journal reveals the passion which compelled him on his mission. It also provides a number of insights into his character, personality, and above all, his Christian devotion. The following section on his famous meeting with Stanley reveals, among other things, his humanity in his reaction to the theft of his vital goods, his gratitude for the coming of Stanley, and his deep devotion to the Christ who was the supreme motivation of his unusual life. The entry on his next to the last birthday was a "Birthday prayer: My Jesus, my king, my life, my all. Once more I dedicate my whole self to Thee. Accept me and grant, O gracious Father, that ere this year is gone, I may finish my task. In Jesus' name I ask it. Amen, so let it be. David Livingstone."

Unexpected Relief—H. M. Stanley Arrives

23rd October 1871. (Rombola.) At dawn, off to Ujiji. Welcomed by Arabs, particularly by Moenyeghere. I was now reduced to a skeleton. With food available, however, I hoped that rest would soon restore me, but in the evening my people came and told me that Shereef had sold off all my goods, and Moenyeghere confirmed it by saying: 'We protested, but he did not leave a single yard of calico out of three thousand or a single string of beads out of 700 lb.' This was distressing. I had made up my mind, if I could not get people at Ujiji, to wait till men could come from the coast, but to wait in beggary was what I never contemplated, and I now felt miserable.

Shereef was evidently a moral idiot, for he came without shame to shake hands with me, and when I refused, assumed an air of displeasure as having been badly treated, and afterwards came with his 'good luck' salutation twice a day; and on leaving said: 'I am going to pray,' till I told him that if I were an Arab his hands and both ears would be cut off for thieving, and I wanted no salutations from him. In my distress it was annoying to see Shereef's slaves passing from the market with all the good things that my goods had bought.

24th October. My property had been sold to Shereef's friends at nominal prices. Syed bin Majid, a good man, proposed that they should be returned, and the ivory taken from Shereef, but they would not return stolen property, though they knew it to be stolen. But one morning Syed bin Majid said to me: 'Let me, I pray you, sell some ivory and give you goods.' But I said: 'Not now, but by and by.' I had still some barter goods left, which I had deposited with Mohammed bin Saleh.

But when my spirits were at their lowest ebb, the Good Samaritan was close at hand, for one morning Susi came running at the top of his speed and gasped out: 'An Englishman. I see him,' and darted off to meet him. An American flag at the head of the caravan told the nationality of the stranger. Bales of goods, baths of tin, huge kettles, cooking pots, tents, etc., made me think: 'This must be a luxurious traveller, and not one at his wits' end like me.

28th October. It was Henry Morton Stanley, the travelling correspondent of the *New York Herald,* sent by James Gordon Bennett, Jr, at the expense of £4,000, to obtain accurate information about Dr Livingstone, and, if dead, to bring home my bones.

The news that he had to tell me, who had been two whole years without any tidings from Europe, made my whole frame thrill. The terrible fate that had befallen France, the telegraphic cables successfully laid in the Atlantic, the election of General Grant, the death of the good Lord Clarendon, my constant friend, the proof that Her Majesty's Government had not forgotten me by voting £1,000 for supplies, and many other points of interest, revived emotions that had remained dormant in Manyuema, appetite returned, instead of the spare tasteless two meals a day, I fed four times daily, and in a week began to feel strong.

I am not a demonstrative man, as cold indeed as we islanders are reputed to be, but this disinterested kindness of Mr Bennett, so nobly carried out by Mr H. M. Stanley, was simply overwhelming. I do feel extremely grateful, and at the same time I am a little ashamed at not being more worthy of the generosity. Mr Stanley has done his part with untiring energy and good judgment, in the teeth of very serious obstacles.

. . . .

20th and 21st November. Passed a very crowded population, the men calling on us to land and be fleeced and insulted. They threw stones, and one, apparently slung, alighted close to the canoe.

We came on until after dark, and landed under a cliff to rest and cook; but a crowd came and made inquiries. They told us to sleep and to-morrow friendship would be made. We put our luggage on board, and set a watch on the cliff. A number of men came along cowering behind rocks, which then aroused suspicion, and we slipped off quietly. They called after us, as men baulked of their prey.

We went on five hours and slept, and then this morning came on to Magala, where the people are civil. The lake narrows here to about ten miles, as the western mountains come towards the eastern range that is about north-north-west magnetic.

24th November. To point Kizuka in Mukamba's country. A Molongwana asserted most positively, that all the water in Tanganyika flowed into the River Lusizé, and then on to Ukerewé of Mtéza. Nothing could be more clear than his statements.

25th November. We came in about two hours to some villages on a high bank, where Mukamba is living. The chief, a good-looking young man, came and welcomed us. Our friend of yesterday declared, as positively as before, that the waters of the Lusizé flowed *into* Tanganyika, and not the way he said yesterday. I have not the slightest doubt that the Tanganyika discharges somewhere, though we may not be able to find it. Lusizé goes to, or comes from, Luanda and Karagwé. This is hopeful, but I suspend judgment.

28th November. This afternoon Luhinga, the superior of Mukamba, came, and showed himself very intelligent. He named eighteen rivers, four of which enter Tanganyika; all come into, but none leave, the lake.

. . . .

The Parting with H. M. Stanley
1st January 1872. Prayer: May the Almighty help me to finish my work this year for Christ's sake.

. . . .

27th January. On across long land waves, and the only bamboos east of Mpokwa Rill, to breakfast. In going on, a swarm of bees attacked a donkey Mr Stanley bought for me, and instead of galloping off as the other did, the fool of a beast rolled down and over and over. I did the same, and then ran and dashed into a bush, like an ostrich pursued; and then, whisking a bush round my head. They gave me a sore head and face before I got rid of the angry insects. I never saw men attacked before. The donkey was completely knocked up by the stings on his face, head, and lips, and died two days after in consequence.

Unyanyembé was reached on 18th February.

By the arrival of the fast Ramadan on 14th November, and a nautical almanac, I discovered that I was twenty-one days too fast in my reckoning.

Mr Stanley used some very strong arguments in favour of my going home, recruiting my strength, getting artificial teeth, and then returning to finish my work, but my judgment said: 'All your friends will wish you to make a complete work of the exploration of the Nile before you retire.' My daughter Agnes says: 'Much as I wish you to come home, I would rather have you finish your work to your own satisfaction, than return merely to gratify me.' Rightly and nobly said, my darling Nannie. Vanity whispers pretty loudly: 'She is a chip off the old block.' My blessing on her and all the rest.

I propose to go from Unyanyembé to Fipa, then round the south end of Tanganyika, Tambeté, or Mbeté, then across the Chambesi, round the south of Lake Bangweulu, and due west to the ancient fountains, leaving the underground excavations till after visiting Katanga. This route will serve to certify that no other sources of the Nile can come from the south without being seen by me. No one will cut me out after this exploration has been accomplished, and may the good Lord of all help me to show myself His stout-hearted servant, an honour to my children, and, perhaps, to my country and race.

. . . .

20th February. To my great joy I found four flannel shirts from Agnes, and I was delighted to find two pairs of fine English boots from my friend Waller. Heavy rain. I am glad to be in shelter.

14th March. Mr Stanley leaves. Our march extended from 26th December 1871 to 18th February 1872, fifty-four days. This was three hundred miles.

I commit to his care my journal, sealed with five seals. The impressions on them are made by an American gold coin, anna and half-anna, and a cake of paint with royal arms. Positively not to be opened.

Tedious waiting for Reinforcements

19th March. Birthday prayer: My Jesus, my king, my life, my all. Once more I dedicate my whole self to Thee. Accept me and grant, O gracious Father, that ere this year is gone, I may finish my task. In Jesus' name I ask it. Amen, so let it be. David Livingstone.

. . . .

The origin of the primitive faith, in Africans and others, seems always to have been a divine influence on their dark minds, which has proved persistent in all ages. One portion of primitive belief—the continued existence of departed spirits—seems to have no connection whatever with dreams, or, as we should say, with 'ghost-seeing,' for great agony is felt in prospect of bodily mutilations, or burning of the body after death, as they are believed to render return to one's native land impossible. They feel that they would thus lose the power of doing good to those once loved, and evil to those who deserve their revenge.

11th May. A serpent of dark olive colour was found dead at my door this morning, probably killed by a cat. Puss approaches very closely, and strikes her claws into the head with a blow as quick as lightning, then holds the head down with both paws, heedless of the wriggling mass of coils behind it. Then she bites the neck and leaves it, looking with interest at the disfigured head, as if she knew that therein had lain the hidden power of mischief.

13th May. He will keep His work, the gracious One—full of grace and truth. He said: 'Him that cometh unto Me I shall in no wise cast out.' He *will* keep His word. Then I can come humbly and present my petition, and it will be all right. Doubt here is inadmissible, surely. D. L.

21st May. I wish I had some of the assurance possessed by others, but I am oppressed by the apprehension that it may, after all, turn out that I have been following the Congo, and who would risk being put into a cannibal pot and converted into a black man for it?

23rd May. A family of ten whidah-birds *(Vidua purpurea)* come to the pomegranate-trees in our yard. The eight young ones, full-fledged, are fed by the dam as young pigeons are. The food is brought up from the crop, without the bowing and bending of the pigeon. They chirrup briskly for food. The dam gives most, while the red-breasted cock gives to one or two and then knocks the rest away.

25th to 27th May. Two whidah-birds, after their nest has been destroyed several times, now try again in another pomegranate-tree in the yard. They put back their eggs, as they have power to do, and build again.

Another pair of the kind (in which the cock is red-breasted) have ten chickens, and also rebuild afresh. The cock bird feeds all the brood. Each little one puts his head on one side as he inserts his bill, chirruping briskly, and bothering him. The young ones lift up a feather, as a child would a doll, and invite others to do the same in play. So, too, with another pair. The cock skips from side to side, with a feather in his bill, and the hen is pleased. Nature is full of enjoyment.

Cock whidah died in the night. The brood came and chirruped to it for food, and tried to make it feed them, as if not knowing death! A wagtail dam refused a young caterpillar, till it had been killed— she ran away from it, but then gave in when ready to be swallowed. The first smile of an infant, with its toothless gums, is one of the pleasantest sights in nature. It is innocence claiming kinship, and asking to be loved in its helplessness.

31st May. In reference to this Nile source I have been kept in perpetual doubt and perplexity. I know too much to be positive. Great Lualaba may turn out to be the Congo or Nile, or a shorter river after all. The fountains flowing north and south seem to favour its being the Nile; great westing is in favour of the Congo. It would be comfortable to be positive like Baker. How soothing to be positive.

13th to 15th June. On 22nd June Stanley will be a hundred days gone. He must be in London now. Sangara, one of Stanley's men, reports that my caravan (the expected porters) is at Ugogo. Lewalé doubts him. Nothing can be believed in this land, unless it is in black and white, and but little even then. The most circumstantial details are often mere figments of the brain. The half one hears may be safely called false, and the other half doubtful, or not proven.

19th June. Whidahs though full-fledged still, gladly take food from their dam, putting down the breast to the ground and cocking up the bill, and chirruping in the most engaging manner they know. She still gives them a little, but administers friendly shoves-off too. They all pick up feathers and grass, and hop from side to side of their mates as if saying: 'Come, let us play at making little houses.

The wagtail has shaken her young off, and has a new nest. She warbles prettily, very much like a canary. The young whidah-birds crouch closely together at night for heat. They look like a woolly ball on a branch. By day they engage in pairing and coaxing each other. They come to the same twig every night. Like children, they try and lift heavy weights of feathers above their strength.

24th June. The medical education has led me to a continual tendency to suspend judgment. What a state of blessedness it would have been if I had possessed the dead certainty of the homoeopathic persuasion, and as soon as I had found Bangweulu, Moero, and Kamolondo flowing down the great central valley, bellowed out: 'Hurrah! Eureka!' and gone home in the honest belief that I had settled it. Instead, I am not even now 'cock-sure' that I am not following down what may, after all, be the Congo.

Livingstone's son, Oswell, with a British Search-party

27th June. Received a letter from Oswell, dated Bagamoio, 14th May, which awakened thankfulness and deep sorrow.

. . . .

29th June. Received a packet containing one letter, one *Pall Mall Gazette,* one *Overland Mail,* and four *Punches.* Provision has been made for my daughter by Her Majesty's Government of £300, but I do not understand the matter clearly.

3rd July. Received a note from Oswell, written in April last, containing the sad intelligence of Sir Roderick (Murchison's) departure from amongst us. Alas! Alas! This is the only time in my life that I ever felt inclined to use the word, and it bespeaks a sore heart. The best friend I ever had, true, warm, and abiding—he loved me more than I deserved. He looks down on me still. I must feel resigned to the loss by the Divine Will, but still I regret and mourn.

Wearisome waiting this, and yet the men cannot be here before the middle or end of this month. I have been sorely let and hindered on this journey, but it may be all for the best.

5th July. Weary! Weary!

21st July. Some philosophizing is curious. It represents our Maker as forming the machine of the universe, setting it a-going, and able to do nothing more outside certain of his laws. He, as it were, laid the egg of the whole and, like an ostrich, left it to be hatched by the sun. We can control laws, but He cannot! A fire set to this house would consume it, but we can throw on water and consume the fire. We control the elements, fire and water. Is He debarred from doing the same, and more, who has infinite wisdom and knowledge? He is surely greater than His laws. Civilization is only what has been done with natural laws.

30th July. Weary waiting this, and the best time for travelling passes unused. High winds from the east every day bring cold, and to the thinly clad Arabs fever.

What is the atonement of Christ? It is Himself. It is the inherent and everlasting mercy of God made apparent to human eyes and ears. The everlasting love was disclosed by our Lord's life and death. It showed that God forgives because He loves to forgive. He works by smiles if possible; if not, by frowns. Pain is only a means of enforcing love. If we speak of strength, lo! He is strong. The Almighty. The Over Power. The Mind of the Universe. The heart thrills at the idea of His greatness.

Notes

1. Patrick, "Confession," in *St. Patrick: His Writings and Life,* Newport J. D. White, ed. (New York: The Macmillan Company, 1920), pp. 31-45. Copyright held by the Society for Promoting Christian Knowledge.

2. Ibid., pp. 1-51.

3. Ibid., pp. 54-109.

4. As far as possible, in the quotations from the Bible, which are printed in italics, the rendering of the English Version of 1611 has been followed, except in O. T. Apocrypha, in which the Douay Version of 1609 has been used.

5. Matthew Ricci, "Progress in Nankin," in *China in the Sixteenth Century: The Journals of Matthew Ricci: 1583-1610,* Louis J. Gallagher, S. J., trans. and ed. (New York: Random House, 1953), pp. 426-432.

6. Ibid.; Sister M. Juliana, M. M., "Matthew Ricci," *Concise Dictionary,* pp. 525-526.

7. Ibid.

8. Ibid.; Gallagher, pp. xi-xv.

9. David Brainerd, "The Rise and Progress of a Remarkable Grace" from *Life and Diary of David Brainerd* by Jonathan Edwards. Copyright 1949. Moody Press, Moody Bible Institute of Chicago, pp. 213-229. Used by permission.

10. Ibid., pp. 43-54; J. Leslie Dunstan, "David Brainerd," *Concise Dictionary,* pp. 67-68.

11. David Livingstone, "Unexpected Relief—H. M. Stanley Arrives," *Livingstone's Travels,* James I. Macnair, ed. (New York: The Macmillan Company, 1954), pp. 368-379. Copyright held by J. M. Dent and Son, Ltd.

12. Cecil Northcutt, "David Livingstone," *Concise Dictionary,* pp. 354-355.

13. Ibid.

14. Ibid.

15. Ibid.

16. George Seaver, *David Livingstone: His Life and Letters* (New York: Harper and Brothers Publishers, 1957), pp. 627-628; Cecil Northcutt, *David Livingstone: His Triumph, Decline and Fall* (Philadelphia: The Westminster Press, 1973).

17. *Punch* on the burial of David Livingstone in Westminster Abbey, April 18, 1874.

V

Missionary Letters

General Introduction

The missionary letters, along with the journals, provide an invaluable source of information concerning missionaries, their labors, and the context and nature of their work. They also provide insight into the personalities of those who have made the mission movement. How much poorer we would be without the letters of these men and women, and what a debt we owe to those who possessed enough sense of history to preserve these valuable pieces of missionary memorabilia. The following selections of letters written by or to great missionary personalities over the Christian centuries reflect a variety of concerns: accommodation in communication, praise to God for victory, prayer request for the conversion of a people, loneliness, complaints to an authority over mistreatment of natives, anxious waiting to enter a new field, sorrow in the loss of a loved one, hope in the midst of loneliness, a history-making challenge to a supporting constituency.

18

From Origen to Gregory Thaumaturgus[1]

Introduction

Origen's letter to Gregory Thaumaturgus was one of the first Christian documents to deal with the indigenous principle and the problem of contextualization in mission methodology. Origen, the great Alexandrian philosopher-theologian who had been Gregory's teacher, in a letter written around 230, admonishes him to make full use of his knowledge of philosophy, the arts, and the sciences in understanding and communicating the Christian message. He illustrates from the Old Testament how the Hebrew people made use of Egyptian materials in the service of God. He warns against the wrong use of these items, however, and suggests to his protege' that he use wisdom and discretion in determining what aspects and how much of the culture he should use as a preparation for the gospel. Even though Origen recognizes that Gregory is qualified to be either a finished Roman lawyer or Greek philosopher, he challenges him to pursue the study of the Scriptures and to use all his gifts and background studies to enhance his understanding of the Christian faith in preparation for a larger and more meaningful vocation. Origen's advice not only confirmed Gregory in his search for truth through Christianity, but it led to his becoming a Christian evangelist and later a bishop. Moreover, the principles of contextualization which Origen applied to Gregory, Gregory doubtless in turn applied later in his own unusually effective work as a missionary-bishop.

Gregory was born of a prominent heathen family in Neocaesarea, Pontus, probably around 200. In the year 240 he became bishop of his native city. Actually, in his early ministry in Neocaesarea, he was more of a pastoral missionary, for there were very few Christians there at the beginning of his work. He was immediately successful, and his fame soon spread far. He early acquired the name Thaumaturgus which means "wonder-worker." He was a man of unusual personal charisma, and the multitudes flocked to him.[2]

Gregory fathered the first mass-movement in Christian history. Through his ministry and influence Pontus was almost totally Christianized. It is said that when he became bishop of Pontus there were only seventeen Christians there; but when he died after thirty years, there were only seventeen pagans. Gregory of Nyssa celebrated Thaumaturgus' life in his work, "Life and

Eulogy." Thaumaturgus himself wrote a number of significant works on biblical, theological, and practical themes. His debt to and love for Origen, his mentor, are expressed in his famous, "The Oration and Panegyric Addressed to Origen." [3]

A Letter from Origen to Gregory

1. GREETING in God, my most excellent sir, and venerable son Gregory, from Origen. A natural readiness of comprehension, as you well know, may, if practice be added, contribute somewhat to the contingent end, if I may so call it, of that which any one wishes to practise. Thus, your natural good parts might make of you a finished Roman lawyer or a Greek philosopher, so to speak, of one of the schools in high reputation. But I am anxious that you should devote all the strength of your natural good parts to Christianity for your end; and in order to this, I wish to ask you to extract from the philosophy of the Greeks what may serve as a course of study or a preparation for Christianity, and from geometry and astronomy what will serve to explain the sacred Scriptures, in order that all that the sons of the philosophers are wont to say about geometry and music, grammar, rhetoric, and astronomy, as fellow-helpers to philosophy, we may say about philosophy itself, in relation to Christianity.

2. Perhaps something of this kind is shadowed forth in what is written in Exodus from the mouth of God, that the children of Israel were commanded to ask from their neighbours, and those who dwelt with them, vessels of silver and gold, and raiment, in order that, by spoiling the Egyptians, they might have material for the preparation of the things which pertained to the service of God. For from the things which the children of Israel took from the Egyptians the vessels in the holy of holies were made,—the ark with its lid, and the cherubim, and the mercyseat, and the golden coffer, where was the manna, the angels' bread. These things were probably made from the best of the Egyptian gold. An inferior kind would be used for the solid golden candlestick near the inner veil, and its branches, and the golden table on which were the pieces of shewbread, and the golden censer between them. And if there was a third and fourth quality of gold, from it

would be made the holy vessels; and the other things would be made of Egyptian silver. For when the children of Israel dwelt in Egypt, they gained this from their dwelling there, that they had no lack of such precious material for the utensils of the service of God. And of the Egyptian raiment were probably made all those things which, as the Scripture mentions, needed sewed and embroidered work, sewed with the wisdom of God, the one to the other, that the veils might be made, and the inner and the outer courts. And why should I go on, in this untimely digression, to set forth how useful to the children of Israel were the things brought from Egypt, which the Egyptians had not put to a proper use, but which the Hebrews, guided by the wisdom of God, used for God's service? Now the sacred Scripture is wont to represent as an evil the going down from the land of the children of Israel into Egypt, indicating that certain persons get harm from sojourning among the Egyptians, that is to say, from meddling with the knowledge of this world, after they have subscribed to the law of God, and the Israelitish service of Him. Ader [4] at least, the Idumaean, so long as he was in the land of Israel, and had not tasted the bread of the Egyptians, made no idols. It was when he fled from the wise Solomon, and went down into Egypt, as it were flying from the wisdom of God, and was made a kinsman of Pharaoh by marrying his wife's sister, and begetting a child, who was brought up with the children of Pharaoh, that he did this. Wherefore, although he did return to the land of Israel, he returned only to divide the people of God, and to make them say to the golden calf, "These be thy gods, O Israel, which brought thee up from the land of Egypt." And I may tell you from my experience, that not many take from Egypt only the useful, and go away and use it for the service of God; while Ader the Idumaean has many brethren. These are they who, from their Greek studies, produce heretical notions, and set them up, like the golden calf, in Bethel, which signifies "God's house." In these words also there seems to me an indication that they have set up their own imaginations in the Scriptures, where the word of God dwells, which is called in a figure Bethel. The other figure, the word says, was set up in Dan. Now the borders of Dan are the most extreme, and nearest the borders of the Gentiles, as is clear from what is written in Joshua, the son of Nun. Now some of the devices of these brethren of Ader, as we call them, are also very near the borders of the Gentiles.

3. Do you then, my son, diligently apply yourself to the reading of the sacred Scriptures. Apply yourself, I say. For we who read the things of God need much appreciation, lest we should say or think anything too rashly about them. And applying yourself thus to the study of the things of God, with faithful prejudgments such as are well pleasing to God, knock at its locked door, and it will be opened to you by the porter, of whom Jesus says, "To him the porter opens." And applying yourself thus to the divine study, seek aright, and with unwavering trust in God, the meaning of the holy Scriptures, which so many have missed. Be not satisfied with knocking and seeking; for prayer is of all things indispensable to the knowledge of the things of God. For to this the Saviour exhorted, and said not only, "Knock, and it shall be opened to you; and seek, and ye shall find," but also, "Ask, and it shall be given unto you." My fatherly love to you has made me thus bold; but whether my boldness be good, God will know, and His Christ, and all partakers of the Spirit of God and the Spirit of Christ. May you also be a partaker, and be ever increasing your inheritance, that you may say not only, "We are become partakers of Christ," but also partakers of God.

19

Gregory the Great to Augustine of Canterbury [5]

Introduction

Gregory I, called the great, was born in Rome of a wealthy family, members of the nobility, probably around 540. His father was a Roman senator, but he died when Gregory was small. After this his mother entered cloistral life, and Gregory was reared in that deep religious atmosphere, which had a profound influence upon him. He received an excellent education in Roman classical and religious studies. However, he did not know Greek, and that world of learning seemed closed to him. Emperor Justin II made him prefect of the city, but he renounced it for monastic life. Inheriting his father's wealth, he built six cloisters in Sicily and turned his own home in Rome into a monastery (St. Andrew's) which he entered himself in 575. Because of his unusual gifts he was persuaded by Benedict I to leave the monastery and return to the public service of the church. He later served as a religious diplomat to Constantinople. Gregory soon became recognized for his strong leadership ability, and in 590 he became bishop of Rome.[6]

Gregory was an outstanding administrator. He strengthened the bishopric of Rome and laid the foundation for its influence through the Middle Ages. Although he did not care for philosophy and the arts, he led in liturgical reform and introduced the style of singing which is known as the Gregorian chant. One of his greatest accomplishments was his sponsorship of mission work. He established missions in Sicily, Sardinia, and Lombardy. His best known sponsorship was the mission to Britain. Gregory's writings, *The Book of Pastoral Rule* and his many epistles, had significant influence upon the succeeding centuries. Though many of his views were narrow, his missionary vision was unlimited.[7]

Gregory's sponsorship of Augustine and his missionary companions was one of the most significant developments in mission history. Augustine was a monk in the monastery of St. Andrew's in Rome which Gregory had founded and where he had also lived as a monk. Augustine's strong personality and obvious gifts impressed Gregory, and he commissioned him to lead a band of missionaries to Britain. Christianity had gone much earlier to Britain as is evidence from the life of Patrick and others, but it had never made an impact upon the nation.[8]

Augustine's mission was accomplished with great difficulty. He finally landed in England with his companions in 597. He went first to the more favorable kingdom of Kent, ruled by Ethelbert, who was married to the Christian Frankish princess, Bertha. When she married the English king, her own private bishop, Luidard, had accompanied her. This gave Augustine an entreé. The most significant development, however, was the conversion of Ethelbert himself. Though he did not force his subjects to become Christians, his influence was enormous. The influence of the king, the leadership of Augustine, and the sponsorship, encouragement (personal and professional), and reinforcements of Gregory made the perfect combination.[9]

For the first time Christianity flourished in England. It was reported that Augustine received ten thousand converts for baptism on one Christmas day alone. Ethelbert permitted Augustine to establish his headquarters in his political capital, Canterbury, where the king's wife had already established her place of Christian worship under Luidard. In time this city became recognized as the Christian center of England. In 601 Augustine, the apostle to the English nation, was made Archbishop of Canterbury, the leading Christian office in Britain until this day. He died in 604.[10]

To Augustine, Bishop of the Angli

Gregory to Augustine, &c.

Glory to God in the highest, and on earth peace to men of good will (Luke ii. 14); because a grain of wheat, falling into the earth, has died, that it might not reign in heaven alone; even He by whose death we live, by whose weakness we are made strong, by whose suffering we are rescued from suffering, through whose love we seek in Britain for brethren whom we knew not, by whose gift we find those whom without knowing them we sought. But who can describe what great joy sprung up here in the hearts of all the faithful, for that the nation of the Angli through the operation of the grace of Almighty God and the labour of thy Fraternity has cast away the darkness of error, and been suffused with the light of holy faith; that with most sound mind it now tramples on the idols which it formerly crouched before in insane fear; that it falls down with pure heart before Almighty God; that it is restrained by the rules of holy preaching from the lapses of wrong doing; that it bows down in heart to divine precepts, that in understanding it may be exalted; that it humbles itself even to the earth in prayer, lest in mind and soul it should lie upon the earth. Whose is this work but His who says, *My Father worketh hitherto, and I work* (John v. 17)? who, to shew that He converts the world, not by men's wisdom, but by His own power, chose unlettered men as His preachers whom He sent into the world? And He does the same even now, having deigned to work mighty works in the nation of the Angli through weak men. But in this heavenly gift, dearest brother, there is ground, along with great joy, for most serious fear. For I know that Almighty God has displayed great miracles through thy Love in the nation which He has willed to be chosen. Wherefore thou must needs rejoice with fear for this same heavenly gift, and tremble in rejoicing:—rejoice, that is, because the souls of the Angli are drawn by outward miracles to inward grace; but tremble, lest among the signs that are done the infirm mind lift itself up to presumption about itself, and from being exalted in honour outwardly, fall inwardly through vain glory. For we ought to remember how, when the disciples returned with joy from preaching, and said to their heavenly Master, *Lord, in thy name even the devils are subject unto us* (Luke x. 17), they straightway heard, *In this rejoice not; but rather rejoice because your names are written in heaven* (Ib. v. 20). For they had set their minds on private and temporal gladness, when they rejoiced in the miracles. But they are recalled from private to common, from temporal to eternal gladness, when it is said to them, *In this rejoice ye, because your names are written in heaven.* For not all the elect work miracles; and yet the names of all of them are kept enrolled in heaven. For to the disciples of the Truth there should not be joy, save for that good which they have in common with all, and in which they have no end to their gladness.

It remains, therefore, dearest brother, that in the midst of the things which through the operation of God thou doest outwardly, thou shouldest ever nicely judge thyself within, and nicely understand both what thou art thyself and how great is the grace in the midst of that same nation for the conversion of which thou hast received even the gift of doing signs. And if at any time thou shouldest remember having offended against our Creator, whether in tongue or in deed, ever recall these things to thy memory, that memory of guilt may keep down the rising glory of the heart. And whatsoever thou mayest receive, or hast received, in the way of doing signs, regard these powers as not granted to thyself, but to those for whose salvation they have been conferred upon thee.

Further, there occurs to my mind, while I think on these things, what took place with one servant of God, even one eminently chosen. Certainly Moses, when he led God's people out of Egypt, as thy Fraternity knows, wrought wonderful miracles. Fasting forty days and nights in Mount Sina, he received the tables of the Law; among lightnings and thunders, while all the people trembled, he was attached to the service of Almighty God, being alone with Him even in familiar colloquy (Exod. xxx., xxxi.); he opened a way through the Red Sea; he had a pillar of a cloud to lead him on his journey; to the people when an hungered he gave manna from heaven; flesh to those who longed for it he supplied in the wilderness by a miracle, even unto overmuch satiety (Exod. xiii., xiv., xvi.). But, when in a time of drought they had come to the rock, he was distrustful, and doubted being able to draw water from the same, which still at the Lord's command he opened without fail in copious streams. But how many and great miracles after these he did during eight and thirty years in the desert who can count or search out (Exod. xvii.; Num. xx.)? As often as a doubtful matter had troubled his mind, he resorted to the tabernacle, and enquired of the Lord in secret, and was forthwith taught concerning it, God speaking to him (Exod. xxxiii. *seq.*). When the Lord was wrath with the people, he appeased Him by the intervention of his prayer; those who rose in pride and dissented in discord he engulphed in the jaws of the gaping earth; he bore down his enemies with victories, and shewed signs to his own people. But, when the land of promise had at length been reached, he was called into the mountain, and heard of the fault which he had committed eight and thirty years before, as I have said, in that he had doubted about drawing water from the rock. And for this reason he was told that he might not enter the land of promise (Num. xxvii.). Herein it is for us to consider how formidable is the judgment of Almighty God, who did so many signs through that servant of His whose fault He still bare in remembrance for so long a time.

Wherefore, dearest brother, if we find that even he whom we know to have been especially chosen by Almighty God died for a fault after so many signs, with what fear ought we to tremble, who do not yet know whether we are chosen?

But what should I say of the miracles of the reprobate, when thy Fraternity well knows what the Truth says in the Gospel; *Many shall come in that day saying to me, Lord in thy name we have prophesied, and in thy name have cast out devils, and in thy name have done many wonderful works. But I will say unto them, I know not who ye are: depart from me all ye workers of iniquity* (Matth. vii. 22; Luke xiii. 27)? The mind, then, should be much kept down in the midst of signs and miracles, lest haply one seek therein one's own glory, and exult in private joy for one's own exaltation. For through signs gains of souls should be sought, and His glory by whose power these very signs are done. But there is one sign that the Lord has given us for which we may exceedingly rejoice, and acknowledge the glory of election in ourselves, seeing that He says, *In this shall it be known that ye are my disciples, if ye have love one to another* (John xiii. 35). Which sign the prophet demanded, when he said. *Make with me, Lord, a sign for good, that they which hate me may see it, and be confounded* (Ps. lxxxv. 17).

These things I say, because I desire to abase the mind of my hearer in humility. But let thy very humility have its confidence. For I, a sinner, maintain a most certain hope that through the grace of our Almighty Creator and Redeemer, our God and Lord Jesus Christ, thy sins are already remitted, and thou art chosen for this purpose, that those of others may be remitted through thee. Nor will you have sorrow for any guilt in the future, while you strive to cause joy in heaven for the conversion of many. Truly the same our Maker and Redeemer, speaking of the repentance of men, says, *Verily I say unto you there will be joy in heaven over one sinner that repenteth, more than over ninety and nine just persons, which need no repentance* (Luke xv. 7). And if for one penitent there is great joy in heaven, of what kind may we believe the joy to be for so large a people, converted from its error, which, coming to faith, has condemned by penitence the evil things it did. In this joy, then, of heaven and the angels let us repeat the very words of the angels with which we began: let us say therefore, let us all say, *Glory to God in the highest, and on earth peace to men of good will.*

20

Letters of Boniface [11]

Introduction

Boniface (675-754?), "the Apostle to Germany," was born Winfrid of a prosperous Anglo-Saxon family of the lower nobility in Exeter, England. He was a precocious child and was placed at an early age in a monastery where he received a good education in the Scriptures and the church fathers as well as the classics. He was ordained at around the age of thirty and was then placed in charge of an abbey school. He soon became dissatisfied with this cloistered life, however, and was attracted to the new movement of missionary work on the Continent. In time he became one of the most effective of the Anglo-Saxon missionaries to the Continent at that time. He became a bishop in 722 at which time he was given the name Boniface. In 744 he founded the monastery at Fulda which became a famous center for missionary outreach. Later he became Archbishop of Mainz. However, despite his high office, he was always a missionary at heart. On one of his journeys, he and fifty-three of his companions were killed by an angry pagan mob. The letters of Boniface reflect a wide range of interests, but the most conspicuous aspect of them is what they reveal of the missionary-bishop's compassion for the German people and his burning desire for their conversion to Christianity.[12]

Boniface requests the prayers of Abbot Aldherius for himself and for the German idolaters [732-754]

To his reverend brother, Abbot Aldherius, Boniface, humble servant of the servants of God, sends greeting in Christ.

From the depths of my heart I beg your gracious love to bear me in mind in your holy prayers and I urge you to implore for me our merciful God, who is the author of our wanderings, that He will hold our frail vessel in His guiding and protecting hand, preserve it from the waves of the German tempests, and bring it safely to the peaceful shore of the heavenly Jerusalem. Salute all our dear brethren in God in your holy community with our kiss of love and devotion. We commend ourselves to your prayers, so that, living or dying, we may be one with you in loving communion. And to make stronger this bond between us, we shall strive to deserve the affection of your brotherly love so far as lies within our power.

We beg you also to intercede for the peoples of the Germanic race who are given over to the worship of idols, beseeching our Lord, who gave His own blood for the salvation of the whole world and who desires that all men shall be saved and shall come to a knowledge of the truth, that He may bring them to acknowledge their Creator and lead them into the bosom of Mother Church.

. . . .

We earnestly pray that Your Blessedness may be well and prosperous in Christ.

Boniface calls upon all Anglo-Saxons to pray for the conversion of the Saxons [c. 738]

To all his reverend fellow bishops, to all those clothed with the grace of priesthood, deacons, canons, clerks, abbots, and abbesses set over the true flock of Christ, monks living in humble submission to God, virgins consecrated by vows to God, and all consecrated handmaids of Christ—and, in general, to all God-fearing catholics of the stock and race of the Angles, Boniface named also Winfred, born of that same race, German legate of the Church Universal, servant of the Apostolic See and called Archbishop for no merit of his own, sends greetings of humble communion and unfeigned love in Christ.

We earnestly beseech your brotherly goodness to be mindful of us, who are worth so little, in your prayers that we may be delivered from the snare of Satan the huntsman and from wicked and cruel men, that the word of God may make its way and be glorified. We beseech you to obtain through your holy prayers, that our Lord and

God Jesus Christ, "who will have all men to be saved, and to come unto the knowledge of God," may turn the hearts of the pagan Saxons to the catholic faith, that they may free themselves from the snares of the devil in which they are bound and may be gathered among the children of Mother Church.

. . . .

May the Omnipotent Creator always keep the unity and communion of your affection in power and progress in Christ.

21

Letter of Bartholomew de Las Casas to Philip II of Spain [13]

Introduction

Bartholomew de Las Casas (1474–1566) represents the highest expression of both the civilization and the Christianity which the Spanish brought to the New World. The first part of his career was as a typical Colonial priest. After some dozen years, however, he underwent a dramatic spiritual renewal. Immediately after this he entered an untiring campaign against the mistreatment of the indigenous peoples, a cause which was to occupy him throughout his long and fruitful life. The letter which follows reflects this concern which became an obsession with Las Casas. He became Bishop of Chiapas in Mexico and was appointed Protector General of the Indians. A high point in his fight for the rights of the natives came in a celebrated debate with the scholastic theologian Juan Gines de Sepulveda in 1550-51. Sepulveda held the view that the Indians were among the races whom Aristotle taught were destined for slavery. Las Casas returned to Spain and spent twenty years working on behalf of the Indians and their rights. One of his significant accomplishments was the introduction of legislation which did away with the cruel *encomiendo* system which kept the natives as virtual slaves in their own land.[14]

In his frantic effort to relieve the situation with the Indians, Las Casas, being a pragmatic man as well as an idealist, made a tragic mistake which he later acknowledged and deeply regretted. He agreed, as a compromise, to the introduction of Africans into Latin America to do the labor which the Indians had done. However, it became only another form of slavery, to the chagrin and sadness of Las Casas. He should not be condemned for this tragic blunder, however, for he almost single-handedly turned the tide of a cruel system which in time was to be totally destroyed. He was not only a great missionary but he deserves as well to be regarded as one of the greatest champions of human rights in history. He paved the way for the coming of the famous missionary padres who left their mark on the Americas from South America to California, and he was the forerunner of the great human rights leaders who changed the course of history.[15]

Letter to Philip II

. . . .

VERY HIGH AND VERY POTENT LORD: I received two letters simultaneously from Your Highness: the date of the last was April 1st and accompanying it was the Royal cedula concerning the passage from Hispaniola to Honduras for the monks whom Your Highness is sending to those provinces. For all of which I kiss your Royal hands and for your kindness in granting that the bulls should be sent so promptly as to reach me in time to serve at my consecration, which, by divine grace, took place here in San Pablo on Passion Sunday as I already wrote Your Highness the day after. I trust to God our Lord that this dignity, to which, by divine Providence, our lord and sovereign the Emperor has elevated me, despite my unworthiness and inability to support it, may prove a sufficient instrument for better fulfilling my old desires to do the will of God, of which God has deigned to make use in those countries. It is His will that His Holy Faith should be preached and that the beings he has created and redeemed should know Him and that His predestined ones should be saved and His Majesty and Your Highness receive great services.

. . . .

In this city and throughout Andalusia there is a large number of Indians held unjustly as slaves; and when the licentiate Gregorio Lopez was here by order of His Majesty, they kept many Indians imprisoned after the order was given for their release, some being hidden and others taken into the country and elsewhere. I have even been told by a man who knows—to clear his conscience—that there was a great deal of bribery and corruption among wicked people, who used three or four or ten ducats to outrage God, stealing the liberty of the Indians and thus leaving many in perpetual slavery: they also hid the truth by threatening the Indians who showed themselves and by other means, such as withholding facts from the licentiate Gregorio Lopez which he could not divine, but which should have been told him. The only remedy for such injustices, according to the officials of this house who are very good people as far as I can see and who have consciences, is that Your Highness should order to be proclaimed throughout Andalusia that all those who have Indians must bring or send them to this house within a certain time, otherwise they shall all be considered as free; adding other penalties for non-compliance. According to the provision made by His Majesty, there should be an immediate settlement of the pretensions of those who allege a title by purchase, which allows them to hold an Indian as a slave until it is ascertained from whom he was first acquired; for they stole them all and sold them when they arrived here. Any such Indian should not remain in their possession but should be placed where he could earn enough to clothe himself and save sufficient to return to his country—because they subject him to a thousand oppressions and cruelties. I have seen things of that sort daily since my arrival. San Pablo is crowded with Indians who think that I can take them or can relieve their captivity and the torments they suffer. And their masters, discovering this by their absence, promptly beat them and put them in irons, even those whom the licentiate Gregorio Lopez left neither in slavery nor free. Not to prolong this letter, I do not relate many other things to Your Highness.

I likewise beg Your Highness to order some relief that is final and not indefinite, for the men who were thus left neither slaves nor free: because I do not know what relief it can be considered, to leave them neither free nor slaves until they die; for meanwhile, they are daily treated worse and worse by those who call them slaves and dogs, because they consider that the licentiate Gregorio Lopez approved of their captivity, etc., tying their hands the more tightly. I have seen what I state ever since I came here. Your Highness would both laugh at and abominate the spice dealers of this city, who barter spices for Indians and for gold (as it is they who mostly own them), and their fierceness in making war on the Indians, that makes them to seem like dummy lions, painted. What I wish Your Highness would do to protect all such Indians as are left neither slaves nor freemen and all who are bound in any way, would be to oblige their owners to exhibit a receipt of the sale: because it is clear to every one, save to those whose perceptions God has allowed to be weakened by their malice, audacity, and ambition, that there has never been a war in all the Indies for which there was any real authority given by His Majesty or by his royal predecessors. The royal instructions on this point have never been heeded, as I have seen and on my conscience affirm, and as all those violaters admit. Consequently, as there was never just cause, it follows that all the wars were unjust and that no Indians could have been justly enslaved: all the more so since the Spaniards attacked them in time of peace and captured millions of them. This being the real truth, Your Highness should order that all such owners be obliged to prove the title of him who sold any such Indian, and so on back till the first one who stole or treacherously captured him is unearthed. In the meantime the Indians should be taken from them and placed as above indicated, all of which should be done within a limited time, so that the legal proceedings would not last eternally; and when they are finished the said Indian should be declared free.

But what I would take on my conscience and would answer for to God on my deathbed is, that Your Highness should proclaim throughout this kingdom that all the Indians here must be free—because in truth they are just as free as I am. In this Casa de Contractacion, outside its judges and officials such as the treasurer, accountant, and agents, who seem to me to be those I have mentioned above, and some few minor officials, I see there little zeal or kindness for the Indians, and I observe such disinclination to accomplish anything in their favour, that however small may be the pendulum, they work it with as much effort as though it were a tower they had to move.

Truly I think Your Highness must order everything to be done gratis and willingly;—or if not, then pay somebody who will do it. There is very great need here for somebody to help these poor Indians, being as they are, in great want and more than miserable, because they do not know how to ask for justice. They have been so intimidated and thrust down in to the very abyss, that they dare not complain. I do not find a single man who will take pity on them: but on the contrary, every one persecutes, terrorizes, and despises them. And I am sure God will execute justice and exact vengeance for all this. It would be well if Your Highness would order a salary to be paid some man who would act as their lawyer in the House, commanding all necessary authority to be attached to his office, and that the officials should help him in it. If it is necessary to consult His Majesty for this, do not let these poor wretches suffer for want of protection as they have always done. There is a porter in this House, a good man who, according to what I have seen and the officials told me, has repeatedly taken pity on them, and I beseech Your Highness to grant me and all the Indians the favour of ordering him to be appointed as protector of all the Indians in this Kingdom and of their affairs in this House, authorising him to report all the happenings of any importance to Your Highness and to the Royal Council of the Indies. Let this power be given to Diego Collantes, porter of the said House; and to ensure his using it the more faithfully until Your Highness pleases to grant him a salary, I will pay him twenty decats yearly, so that he may do his duty in the said office. The truth is, that although he is a good man, the position needs a man with much more authority but for the present he would suffice. Juan de la Quadra, who was secretary to the licentiate Gregorio Lopez while he was here, spoke to me about these matters. He seems to me an honest, upright person and one who feels deeply the crimes committed in this city against the Indians. He is writing to Your Highness on the subject and I beseech Your Highness to order some remedy provided for the actual necessities. He informs me that he is writing in the sense of what I said above.

The licentiate Bartolomé Ortiz did not bring his Indians to be registered within the period intimated to him and says that he protested against the sentence before this Royal Council, also with regard to other Indians whom he held as slaves despite the fact that they were free. Amongst these was an Indian woman who was beyond question free, and had been declared free by Gregorio Lopez, who left orders for her to be sent at the licentiate's expense to the Island of Cuba from whence he brought her. Ortiz also appealed from this decision. As I asked that she might now be given the letter and order of Your Highness permitting her to return with this fleet, Ortiz presented a statement showing that his case was at present in appeal before this Royal Council.

I beseech Your Highness not to permit these appeals and delays in cases which are favourable to the liberty of the Indians and of everybody in the world, because there will be no end to them nor will a single Indian ever obtain his liberty. I beg that Your Highness will order this Indian woman and others to be liberated and allowed to return to their country.

It is indeed a great weight on my conscience to leave the Indians in this country, because, as they only mix with servants and other unmanageable and vicious persons and see the taverns full of loose people, without order or restraint, and other public places full of bad examples, it must happen that they, being human, will follow the example of their companions. In their own country, on the contrary, they live much better than here, even if there are not so many Christians. I beseech Your Highness to issue such orders that not one man of them may remain here.

It would also be well if Your Highness ordered an explanation of the proclamation that you commanded to be published throughout all the Indies, prohibiting the officials of India House from receiving Indians into this kingdom: also instructions as to what they must do to forbid this traffic, under penalty of death, to ship captains and sailors, so that no one would dare to bring an Indian, nor allow one to be brought here. Let them know that they are forewarned in such cases. Seville 20th April 1544. Your humble servant who kisses Your Royal hands.

> FRAY BARTHOLOMEW DE LAS CASAS,
> *Bishop of Chiapa.*

To-night the following occurred—an Indian came to me complaining that notwithstanding his certificate of freedom, given him by Gregorio Lopez, his owner kept him in slavery and treated him worse than a slave, sending him out with a donkey to carry and sell water. He showed me his certificate of freedom, in the presence of ten or twelve monks. I told him to go to-day to the Casa de Contractacion so that its officials might correct the abuse, and I sent a servant with him to show him the building—because if his master found out, he would keep him until he called in the officials. Finally his owner discovered him and took the letter and tore it up. He said "bring chains and put them on this dog." The Indian escaped through a window and they cried after him, "Thief, thief," so that somebody down below came and beat him, and stabbed him in the jaw. He managed to reach a place where some of my servants were, and they are trying to cure him: but he is dying. One of my servants went to the assistant to tell him what had happened, but the latter answered that he was not astonished that people killed the Indians, because they stole and did much harm. I beg Your Highness to note how destitute they are of any pity. With judges so cruelly unjust and tyrannical, Your Highness may imagine what sort of things happen over there [in the colonies] with the Spaniards against the Indians, when they dare do these things in Seville where, the other day a judge ordered an Indian to be stabbed to death.

FRAY BARTHOLOMEW DE LAS CASAS,
Bishop.

22

Letters of Francis Xavier Awaiting Entry into China[16]

Introduction

Francis Xavier (1506-1552), generally recognized as one of the greatest of all the Christian missionaries, was born in Basque country. When he was around twenty-seven, he joined with the famous Ignatius Loyola and became one of the six founding members of the Society of Jesus. A vital part of the Roman Catholic Counter Reformation which came in the wake of the Protestant Reformation, he was founder of the Jesuit missionary movement. In 1542 he was sent to India both as a missionary of the church and as an ambassador of Portugal. He landed first on the island of Goa, a Portuguese colony. Here he ministered tirelessly. He also concerned himself with reform and pled with the Portuguese crown to take measures requiring the colonial leaders to assume leadership in the work of Christian missions. Xavier then moved to the mainland of India where he first worked with the large Tamil tribe. Next he moved farther in his labors beyond India to neighboring Malacca (modern Eastern Indonesia).[17]

In 1549 Xavier made his way to Japan. He and his companions were surprised to find the high civilization which existed in Japan at that time. His three brief years in Japan made an immense impact. He left Japan out of a desire to revisit Goa and then to make an effort to enter the great, forbidden China. He died at the prime age of forty-six on the lonely island of Chang-Chuen-Shan (Sancian) off the coast of China waiting in vain for passage to that forbidden land. His letters to his colleague, Father Perez of Malacca, and to his benefactor, Diogo Pereira, reveal the auguish he felt at that time. The account of this lonely vigil reads like a great romantic epic, like the literary masterpieces that have recounted those hopeless waits for some good news from across the sea. Although Xavier was very much a child of his age, his insatiable thirst to claim more and more territory for the Christian faith (as he understood and loved it) has made him one of the greatest examples of the unconquerable missionary spirit in all the annals of the movement. In one incredible decade he traveled over ten thousand miles, much of it on foot, from the sweltering heat of the tropics to the bitter cold of Japan. When death claimed him he was still dreaming the impossible dream for the cause which was his life and his breath.[18]

Letter to Father Perez of Malacca

By the mercy and goodness of God our Lord I and all those who came on the ship of Diogo Pereira arrived safely at this port of Sancian, where we found many other ships belonging to merchants. Sancian is thirty leagues from Canton and numerous merchants from the latter place come here to do business with the Portuguese. I tried hard to persuade one of them to take me to Canton, but [at first] they all begged to be excused, saying that their lives and fortunes would be put in jeopardy if the governor of Canton discovered my presence. Nothing I could offer would induce them to give me a passage on one of their ships. By the good pleasure of God our Lord, however, an honourable citizen of Canton eventually agreed to take me for two hundred *cruzados* in a little junk manned only by his sons and servants, so that the governor might not come to hear from mariners that it was a merchant who smuggled me in. More than that, he volunteered to keep me hidden in his house for three or four days, after which he would escort me before dawn, with my books and other little properties, to a gate of the city whence I could at once proceed to the governor's palace to tell him that we had come in order to make our way to the court of the King of China and to show him the letter of the Lord Bishop to His Highness. . . . According to other Chinamen this course involves two risks, first, that the man taking us, when paid his money, may cast us adrift on some desert island or dump us in the sea to make himself safe against discovery by the governor, and secondly, that, even if we reached Canton and appeared before the governor, he might order us to be tortured or consigned to a dungeon . . . , since the King of China had so stringently forbidden foreigners entrance into his territories without his express written permission. But there are other perils much greater than those two, which the Chinese would not understand and which would take too long to recount, though I cannot refrain from telling you something of them. The danger of all dangers would be to lose trust and confidence in the mercy of God for whose love and service we came to manifest the law of Jesus Christ, His Son, our Redeemer and Lord, as He well knows. . . . To distrust Him would be a far more terrible thing than any physical evil which all the enemies of God put together could inflict on us, for without God's permission neither the devils nor their human ministers could hinder us in the slightest degree. . . . We are therefore determined to make our way into China at all costs, and I hope in God that the upshot of our journey will be the increase of our holy faith, however much the devil and his ministers may persecute us. If God is for us who can overthrow us? When the *Santa Cruz* leaves here for Malacca I hope it will bring you news of how we were received in Canton and of what the governor did to us. . . . Alvaro Ferreira and Antonio the Chinaman have been sick all the time, but just now, by the mercy of God, are feeling better. Antonio will not do as an interpreter for he has forgotten how to speak Chinese, but a certain Pero Lopez, captured in battle by Antonio de Lopez Bobadilha, who can read and write Portuguese and knows Chinese sufficiently well, has offered himself with much good will to be my companion. May God reward him in this life and the next. . . . When I came to Sancian we made a little chapel where I said Mass daily until I went down with fever. I was ill for a fortnight, but now by the mercy of God am all right again. There is plenty to do here, what with confessions, care of the sick, and the task of making peace between persons at loggerheads with one another. I do not know that there is anything more to tell you except that we are absolutely determined to go to China. All the Chinese merchants I have seen here appear to be honourable men. . . . Either because they consider that we have some law written in our books superior to their own laws, or because they are lovers of novelties, they all make a show of great pleasure at our going to their country though none of them will take the risk of helping us on our way. . . .

Letter to Diogo Pereira

I am watching every day for the return of the merchant who has agreed for twenty *picos* of pepper to convey me to Canton. . . . If men knew as well as God does about my journey, they would see that it is all your doing, for you are paying all the expenses. Your manager, Tomas Escander, has carried out your instructions to the letter and given me everything I required. May God our Lord requite you for all your immense charity to me. My Chinaman is known to

Manuel de Chaves and gave him refuge in his house in Canton for several days after his escape from prison, and that fact renews my hope every day that he will come for me. Manuel will write to tell you about my going and how I was received in Canton. If it should happen by God's permission that the merchant does not come for me and I am precluded this year from going to China, I know not what I shall do, whether to return to India or to sail to Siam, with hopes of being allowed to join the annual embassy of the King of Siam to China. If it is to India I go, it will be with no hope of anything being done in the matter of China while Alvaro da Ataíde da Gama holds sway, unless God provides otherwise. What I feel on this score I forbear to say. . . . Manuel de Chaves will let you know if I go to Siam in the junk which Diogo Vaz de Aragão bought out here . . . so that by some means or other you may get a letter through to me telling me what you have decided to do this year. Whether you come in the [Siamese] embassy or not, we might meet in Ke-moi or some other port, but God grant that it may be inside China. . . . But if we do not see each other again in this life, may the merciful God bring us together in the glory of Paradise, where we shall see each other always and for ever. Your true and affectionate good friend, Francisco.

23

From Adoniram Judson to His Mother-in-Law
on the Death of His Wife [19]

Introduction

Adoniram Judson (1788-1850), one of the leaders of the modern mission movement, was born in Malden, Massachusetts. As a seminary student, he was caught up in the enthusiasm for missions which was developing in New England at that time. He was strongly influenced by Carey and other pioneer missionaries and especially by the famous sermon by Claudius Buchanan, "The Star in the East." Though a visit to England had resulted in his alignment with the London Missionary Society, upon returning to America he persuaded the newly formed American Board of Commissioners for Foreign Missions to appoint him.[20]

In 1812, Judson married Ann Hasseltine whose inspiring story has already been recounted briefly (see part III, 14). The same year they sailed for India. Convinced that he would have to defend himself doctrinally against the staunch Baptist Carey, he studied the New Testament teaching on baptism on the ship en route to India and became himself a convinced Baptist. Luther Rice, though on a separate ship, had a similar experience. They were baptized in Calcutta by William Ward, one of the famous "Serampore trio." Feeling that they could no longer receive funds from the Congregationalist American Board, it was decided that Judson would remain and Rice would return to America and try to rally the unorganized Baptists to the support of Judson. As a result there was formed in 1814 the Triennial Convention, the parent body of the major white Baptist organizations in the United States.[21]

After a series of difficulties in locating a place of service, the Judsons settled in Rangoon, Burma, on July 13, 1813. Judson was an accomplished linguist, and in time he translated the Bible into Burmese and prepared a large dictionary. Both documents are in use today in Burma, a testimony to Judson's skill as a linguist. This was only the basis for his work, however. Public preaching and dialogue with Buddhists were his major methods of mission work. He resisted becoming a teacher for which he had excellent gifts. He chose rather the role of an itinerant evangelist.[22]

After serious problems in Rangoon, the Judsons moved to Ava, the capital. Here Judson was imprisoned. This was a deeply traumatic experience for the young missionary couple and their small child. Judson was released at the end of the Anglo-Burmese war and served as an interpreter for the peace negotiations. After this they moved to Amherst and then to Moulmein. It was here that Ann died and Judson passed through a period of deep depression. The following letter to his mother-in-law reveals the depth of his grief in the passing of his beloved Ann. Though discouraged, Judson did not despair. He continued his evangelistic and literary work, resisting the temptation to join his colleague George Dana Boardman in the new responsive work among the animistic hill tribesmen of Karen, choosing rather the more difficult work among the Buddhists in the strategic urban centers.[23]

In 1834 Judson married Sarah Boardman, the widow of his colleague who worked among the Karens. Sarah died in 1845, and Judson decided after thirty-two years of missionary labor, to return home. While in America, though he arrived at the time of the division of the Northern and Southern Baptists over slavery and issues of methodology, he was still able to enhance greatly the mission cause among the Baptists. While on furlough he married Emily Chubbock (Fanny Forester was her pen name). Judson and his new wife returned to work in Rangoon and Moulmein. He died five years later on a sea voyage taken in an effort to regain his health.[24]

Judson's famous words, "the future is as bright as the promises of God," constitute a kind of text for his courageous life amid such discouraging odds, especially in the earlier years of his missionary effort. Both his ideas and his example strongly influenced the direction of missions in the great century. Judson and his colleagues succeeded in developing what has continued until today as one of the strongest Christian communities in Asia. He was deeply loved in both Asia and America and remains today one of the sublime figures of mission history.

To Mrs. Hasseltine, of Bradford, Mass.

AVA, December 7, 1826.

DEAR MOTHER HASSELTINE: This letter, though intended for the whole family, I address particularly to you; for it is a mother's heart that will be most deeply interested in its melancholy details. I propose to give you, at different times, some account of my great, irreparable loss, of which you will have heard before receiving this letter.

I left your daughter, my beloved wife, at Amherst, the 5th of July last, in good health, comfortably situated, happy in being out of the reach of our savage oppressors, and animated in prospect of a field of missionary labor opening under the auspices of British protection. It affords me some comfort that she not only consented to my leaving her, for the purpose of joining the present embassy to Ava, but uniformly gave her advice in favor of the measure, whenever I hesitated concerning my duty. Accordingly I left her. On the 5th of July I saw her for the last time. Our parting was much less painful than many others had been. We had been preserved through so many trials and vicissitudes, that a separation of three or four months, attended with no hazards to either party, seemed a light thing. We parted, therefore, with cheerful hearts, confident of a speedy reunion, and indulging fond anticipations of future years of domestic happiness. After my return to Rangoon, and subsequent arrival at Ava, I received several letters from her, written in her usual style, and exhibiting no subject of regret or apprehension, except the declining health of our little daughter, Maria. Her last was dated the 14th of September. She says, "I have this day moved into the new house, and, for the first time since we were broken up at Ava, feel myself at home. The house is large and convenient, and if you were here I should feel quite happy. The native population is increasing very fast, and things wear rather a favorable aspect. Moung Ing's school has commenced with ten scholars, and more are expected. Poor little Maria is still feeble. I sometimes hope she is getting better; then again she declines to her former weakness. When I ask her where papa is, she always starts up, and points towards the sea. The servants behave very well, and I have no trouble about anything, excepting you and Maria. Pray take care of yourself, particularly as it regards the intermittent fever at Ava. May God preserve and bless you, and restore you in safety to your new and old home, is the prayer of your affectionate Ann."

On the 3d of October, Captain F., civil superintendent of Amherst, writes, "Mrs. Judson is extremely well." Why she did not write herself by the same opportunity, I know not. On the 18th, the same gentleman writes, "I can hardly think it right to tell you that Mrs. Judson has had an attack of fever, as before this reaches you she will, I sincerely trust, be quite well, as it has not been so severe as to reduce her. This was occasioned by too close attendance on the child. However, her cares have been rewarded in a most extraordinary manner, as the poor babe at one time was so reduced that no rational hope could be entertained of its recovery; but at present a most favorable change has taken place, and she has improved wonderfully. Mrs. Judson had no fever last night, so that the intermission is now complete." The tenor of this letter was such as to make my mind quite easy, both as it regarded the mother and the child. My next communication was a letter with a black seal, handed me by a person, saying he was sorry to have to inform me of the death of the child. I know not whether this was a mistake on his part, or kindly intended to prepare my mind for the real intelligence. I went into my room, and opened the letter with feelings of gratitude and joy, that at any rate the mother was spared. It was from Mr. B., assistant superintendent of Amherst, dated the 26th of October, and began thus:—

MY DEAR SIR: To one who has suffered so much, and with such exemplary fortitude, there needs but little preface to tell a tale of distress. It were cruel indeed to torture you with doubt and suspense. To sum up the unhappy tidings in a few words, *Mrs. Judson is no more.*

At intervals I got through with the dreadful letter, and proceed to give you the substance as indelibly engraven on my heart:—

Early in the month she was attacked with a most violent fever. From the first she felt a strong presentiment that she should not recover, and on the 24th, about eight in the evening, she expired. Dr. R. was quite assiduous in his attentions, both as a friend and physician. Captain F. procured her the services of a European woman from the 45th regiment; and be assured all was done that could be done to comfort her in her sufferings, and to smooth the passage to the grave. We all deeply feel the loss of this excellent lady, whose shortness of residence among us was yet sufficiently long to impress us with a deep sense of her worth and virtues. It was not until about the 20th that Dr. R. began seriously to suspect danger. Before that period the fever had abated at intervals; but its last approach baffled all medical skill. On the morning of the 23d, Mrs. Judson spoke the last time. The disease had then completed its conquest, and from that time up to the moment of dissolution, she lay nearly motionless, and apparently quite insensible. Yesterday morning I assisted in the last melancholy office of putting her mortal remains in the coffin, and in the evening her funeral was attended by all the European officers now resident here. We have buried her near the spot where she first landed, and I have put up a small, rude fence around the grave, to protect it from incautious intrusions. Your little girl, Maria, is much better. Mrs. W. has taken charge of her, and I hope she will continue to thrive under her care.

Two days later, Captain Fenwick writes thus to a friend in Rangoon:—

I trust that you will be able to find means to inform our friend of the dreadful loss he has suffered. Mrs. Judson had slight attacks of fever from the 8th or 9th instant, but we had no reason to apprehend the fatal result. I saw her on the 18th, and at that time she was free from fever, scarcely, if at all, reduced. I was obliged to go up the country on a sudden business, and did not hear of her danger until my return on the 24th, on which day she breathed her last, at 8 P.M. I shall not attempt to give you an account of the gloom which the death of this most amiable woman has thrown over our small society. You, who were so well acquainted with her, must feel her loss more deeply; but we had just known her long enough to value her acquaintance as a blessing in this remote corner. I dread the effect it will have on poor Judson. I am sure you will take care that this mournful intelligence may be opened to him as carefully as possible.

The only other communication on this subject, that has reached me, is the following line from Sir Archibald Campbell to the envoy: "Poor Judson will be dreadfully distressed at the loss of his good and amiable wife. She died the other day at Amherst, of remittent fever, eighteen days ill."

You perceive that I have no account whatever of the state of her mind, in view of death and eternity, or of her wishes concerning her darling babe, whom she loved most intensely. I hope to glean some information on these points from the physician who attended her, and the native converts who must have been occasionally present.

I will not trouble you, my dear mother, with an account of my own private feelings—the bitter, heart-rending anguish, which for some days would admit of no mitigation, and the comfort which the gospel subsequently afforded—the gospel of Jesus Christ, which brings life and immortality to light. Blessed assurance,—and let us apply it afresh to our hearts,—that, while I am writing and you perusing these lines, her spirit is resting and rejoicing in the heavenly paradise,—

"Where glories shine, and pleasures roll
That charm, delight, transport the soul;
And every panting wish shall be
Possessed of boundless bliss in thee."

And there, my dear mother, we also shall soon be, uniting and participating in the felicities of heaven with her for whom we now mourn. "Amen. Even so, come, Lord Jesus."

AMHERST, FEBRUARY 4, 1827.

Amid the desolation that death has made, I take up my pen once more to address the mother of my beloved Ann. I am sitting in the house she built, in the room where she breathed her last, and at a window from which I see the tree that stands at the head of her grave, and the top of the "small rude fence" which they have put up "to protect it from incautious intrusion."

Mr. and Mrs. Wade are living in the house, having arrived here about a month after Ann's death; and Mrs. Wade has taken charge of my poor motherless Maria. I was unable to get any accounts of the child at Rangoon; and it was only on my arriving here, the 24th ultimo, that I learned she was still alive. Mr. Wade met me at the landing-place, and as I passed on to the house, one and another of the native Christians came out, and when they saw me they began to weep. At length we reached the house; and I almost expected to see my love coming out to meet me, as usual. But no; I saw only in the arms of Mrs. Wade a poor little puny child, who could not recognize her weeping father, and from whose infant mind had long been erased all recollection of the mother who loved her so much.

She turned away from me in alarm, and I, obliged to seek comfort elsewhere, found my way to the grave. But who ever obtained comfort there? Thence I went to the house, in which I left her, and looked at the spot where we last knelt in prayer, and where we exchanged the parting kiss.

The doctor who attended her has removed to another station, and the only information I can obtain is such as the native Christians are able to communicate.

It seems that her head was much affected during her last days, and she said but little. She sometimes complained thus: "The teacher is long in coming; and the new missionaries are long in coming; I must die alone, and leave my little one; but as it is the will of God, I acquiesce in his will. I am not afraid of death, but I am afraid I shall not be able to bear these pains. Tell the teacher that the disease was most violent, and I could not write; tell him how I suffered and died; tell him that you see; and take care of the house and things until he returns." When she was unable to notice anything else, she would still call the child to her, and charge the nurse to be kind to it, and indulge it in every thing, until its father shall return. The last day or two, she lay almost senseless and motionless, on one side, her head reclining on her arm, her eyes closed; and at eight in the evening, with one exclamation of distress in the Burman language, she ceased to breathe.

February 7. I have been on a visit to the physician who attended her in her illness. He has the character of a kind, attentive, and skilful practitioner; and his communications to me have been rather consoling. I am now convinced that every thing possible was done, and that, had I been present myself, I could not have essentially contributed to avert the fatal termination of the disease. The doctor was with her twice a day, and frequently spent the greater part of the night by her side. He says that, from the first attack of the fever she was persuaded she should not recover; but that her mind was uniformly tranquil and happy in the prospect of death. She only expressed occasional regret at leaving her child, and the native Christian schools, before her husband, or another missionary family, could arrive. The last two days she was free from pain. On her attention being roused by reiterated questions, she replied, "I feel quite well, only very weak." These were her last words.

The doctor is decidedly of opinion that the fatal termination of the fever is not to be ascribed to the localities of the new settlement, but chiefly to the weakness of her constitution, occasioned by the severe privations and long-protracted sufferings she endured at Ava. O, with what meekness, and patience, and magnanimity, and Christian fortitude, she bore those sufferings! And can I wish they had been less? Can I sacrilegiously wish to rob her crown of a single gem? Much she saw and suffered of the evil of this evil world, and eminently was she qualified to relish and enjoy the pure and holy rest into which she has entered. True, she has been taken from a sphere in which she was singularly qualified, by her natural disposition, her winning manners, her devoted zeal, and her perfect acquaintance with the language, to be extensively serviceable to the cause of Christ; true, she has been torn from her husband's bleeding heart, and from her darling babe; but infinite wisdom and love have presided, as ever, in this most afflicting dispensation. Faith decides that it is all right, and the decision of faith eternity will soon confirm.

I have only time to add—for I am writing in great haste, with very short notice of the present opportunity of sending to Bengal—that poor little Maria, though very feeble, is, I hope, recovering from her long illness. She began indeed to recover, while under the care of the lady who kindly took charge of her, at her mother's death; but when, after Mr. Wade's arrival, she was brought back to this house, she seemed to think that she had returned to her former home, and had found in Mrs. Wade her own mother. And certainly the most tender, affectionate care is not wanting to confirm her in this idea.

> I remain, my dear mother,
>   Yours, in the deepest sorrow,
>
>   A. JUDSON, JR.

24

Letter from Hudson Taylor to a Close Friend [25]

Introduction

James Hudson Taylor (1832-1905), was one of the towering figures of the second half of the great century. He was born in Barnsley, Yorkshire, England. At the age of seventeen he had a dramatic conversion experience which was followed by a strong sense of mission call to China, a country which at that time was closed except for treaty ports. He cut short his medical studies and went to China under the Chinese Evangelization Society, arriving in Shanghai in 1854. He soon severed this connection because of lack of support. In 1858 he married Maria Dyer, in Ningpo, and two years later returned to England to complete his medical studies.[26]

In 1865 Taylor founded the China Inland Mission, the prototype of the interdenominational "faith" mission. Besides his medical work and linguistic work (he translated the New Testament into the Ningpo dialect), Taylor became known for his strong ideas about mission work. He wearied of the competition between missions in the port cities and developed a plan to man all the inland provinces as quickly as possible. He followed indigenous principles, adopting the national dress and customs as much as possible.[27]

Taylor was a man of profound spirituality. He had a deepening spiritual experience after he had served for a number of years in China. Besides being the great charismatic leader around which the missionaries of China rallied, he was a recognized spiritual leader internationally. He was a strong supporter of Keswick and other spiritual movements. Taylor traveled extensively in China, Europe, and North America. Although he did not believe in appealing directly for funds, he did believe in placing the mission cause before the sending churches. So powerful was his influence as a recruiter of missionaries that in 1895 the China Inland Mission had 641 missionaries, about one half of the total Protestant force in China at that time.[28]

Although Taylor was a model of spirituality, he also was a man of deep humanness. He could be as lonely as any other missionary, despite the vast spiritual resources from which he was able to draw. The following letter to his friend, a Mr. Berger, reflects this loneliness. Yet it is also an example of the strong faith which

compelled Taylor and which sustained him and gave
him a sense of victory in the face of loneliness. So
popular was Taylor both as a missionary hero and a
model of spirituality that his biography, written by
his son and daughter-in-law, went through ten editions
in the decade and a half after its first printing.[29] The
China Inland Mission continues its influence today as
the Overseas Missionary Fellowship.[30]

To Mr. Berger, August 14

It is Sunday evening. I am writing from Mr. White's bungalow.
The cool air, the mellow, autumnal beauty of the scene, the magnificent
Yangtze—with Silver Island, beautifully wooded, reposing, as it were,
on its bosom—combine to make one feel as if it were a vision of
dreamland rather than actual reality. And my feelings accord. But a
few months ago my home was full, now so silent and lonely—Samuel,
Noel, my precious wife, with Jesus; the elder children far, far away,
and even little T'ien-pao in Yang-chow. Often, of late years, has duty
called me from my loved ones, but I have returned, and so warm
has been the welcome! Now I am alone. Can it be that there is no
return from this journey, no home-gathering to look forward to! Is it
real, and not a sorrowful dream, that those dearest to me lie beneath
the cold sod? Ah, it is indeed true! But not more so, than that there
is a home-coming awaiting me which no parting shall break into, no
tears mar. . . . Love gave the blow that for a little while makes the
desert more dreary, but heaven more home-like. "I go to prepare a
place for you": and is not our part of the preparation the peopling it
with those we love?

And the same loving Hand that makes heaven more home-like is
the while loosening the ties that bind us to this world, thus helping
our earth-cleaving spirits to sit looser, awaiting our own summons,
whether personally to be "present with the Lord," or at "the glorious
appearing of our great God and Saviour." "Even so, come, Lord Jesus,"
come quickly! But if He tarry—if for the rescue, the salvation of some
still scattered upon the mountains He can wait the full joy of having
all His loved ones gathered to Himself—surely we, too, should be

content, nay, thankful, a little longer to bear the cross and unfurl the banner of salvation. Poor China, how great her need! Let us seek to occupy a little longer.

I have been very ill since I last wrote to you, through a severe attack of dysentery. My strength does not return rapidly. I feel like a little child. . . . But with the weakness of a child I have *the rest of a child.* I know my Father reigns: this meets all questions of every kind. I have heard to-day that war has broken out in Europe, between France and Prussia; that it is rumoured that England joins the former and Russia the latter. If so fearful doings may be expected; but, "the Lord reigneth."

25

From Lottie Moon to Southern Baptist Women [31]

Introduction

Charlotte Diggs Moon (1840-1912), one of the leading single women missionaries of the modern mission movement and a forerunner of the modern missionary stateswoman, was born in Viewmont, Virginia, in 1840. She was one of the 0 1t educated women of her day and taught in Kentucky and Georgia before becoming a missionary. She was appointed a missionary to China in 1873 by the Foreign Mission Board of the Southern Baptist Convention. In addition to filling traditional male roles as a missionary, she was an avid student of contemporary missions.[32]

The most significant role she performed, however, was as a missionary stateswoman. She bombarded her home constituency, especially the women, with letters of challenge concerning mission commitment. Deeply challenged by the effective Woman's Board of Missions of the Methodist Episcopal Church of the South, she wrote to Southern Baptist women, shaming and challenging them in light of the example of the Methodist women. Impressed by the special mission offering which the Methodist women received at Christmas-time, Miss Moon wrote an open letter to Southern Baptist women which was published in the *Foreign Mission Journal*. Her letter of September 15, 1887, appeared in the December issue of the *Journal*. She continued to write, pleading for reinforcements for the work in China. In May of 1888 the Woman's Missionary Union was organized, in Richmond, Virginia. Later that year, H. A. Tupper, the executive of the Foreign Mission Board, challenged the new WMU to raise enough money in the churches to send out two new missionaries to China. The goal was $2,000.00, and the women raised over $3,000.00.[33]

This special Christmas offering later was named after Lottie Moon. The Week of Prayer and Lottie Moon Christmas Offering for Foreign Missions has become an institution in the life of the largest Protestant community in the United States and the largest Baptist constituency in the world. The pattern of a week of prayer and a Christmas offering for world missions has been adopted in virtually all of the some ninety countries where Southern Baptists have mission work today. The name Lottie Moon has become a household word among the Baptist families in this family of Baptists around the world. From the modest $3,315.26 given at Christmas in 1888, the offering at Christmas in 1977 was $31,938,553.04.[34] This Lottie Moon Christmas offering is matched annually by just under one half of the budget of the Southern Baptist Convention to constitute the largest mission contribution by any one Protestant group in the United States.[35]

It is significant and worthy of special note that the inspiration for and architect of this movement was a woman, a single missionary who labored lovingly among the Chinese for forty years. Though deeply loved by the Chinese who called her "the Heavenly Book Visitor," she experienced the awesome loneliness of which other great missionaries often wrote. She spent fourteen years on the field before taking her first furlough. During the devastating famine in China around 1912, Miss Moon was discovered actually to be in a state of starvation herself. She gave all she had and left herself nothing to eat because the Chinese she had loved had none. Just before Christmas, a nurse, Cynthia Miller, started back to the United States with the frail Miss Moon. Death came before they embarked on the high seas, while the ship was docked in the Bay of Kobe, Japan. The time of her homegoing was symbolic—for her a kind of coronation. It happened at that beloved season which she had caused a whole people to associate with missions. Lottie Moon died on Christmas Eve.[36]

Letter from Lottie Moon to Southern Baptist Women

In a former letter I called attention to the work of Southern Methodist Women, endeavoring to use it as an incentive to stir up the women of our Southern Baptist churches to greater zeal in the cause of missions. I have lately been reading the minutes of the ninth annual meeting of the Woman's Board of Missions, M. E. South, and find that in the year ending in June, they raised over sixty-six thousand dollars. Their work in China alone involved the expenditure of more than thirty-four thousand dollars, besides which they have missions in Mexico, Brazil, and the Indian Territory. They have nine workers in China, with four more under appointment. I notice that when a candidate is appointed, straightway some conference society pledges her support in whole or in part.

. . . .

The efficient officers of this Methodist Woman's organization do their work without pay. Travelling and office expenses are allowed the President of the Board of Missions. This money is to be used at her discretion in visiting conference societies that are not able to pay her expenses. Office expenses alone are allowed the Corresponding Secretary and her assistant, and also the Treasurer. A sum is appropriated for publications, postage, and mite boxes. The expenses for all purposes are less than seventeen hundred dollars. In a word, Southern Methodist women, in one year, have contributed to missions, clear of all expenses, nearly sixty-five thousand dollars! Doesn't this put us Baptist women to shame? For one, I confess I am heartily ashamed.

I am convinced that one of the chief reasons our Southern Baptist women do so little is the lack of organization. Why should we not learn from the noble Methodist women, and instead of the paltry offerings we make, do something that will prove that we are really in earnest in claiming to be followers of him who "though he was rich for our sake became poor?" How do these Methodist women raise so much money? By prayer and self-denial. Note the resolution "unanimously approved" by the meeting above:

"Resolved, that this Board recommend to the Woman's Missionary Society to observe the week preceding Christmas as a week of prayer and self-denial. In preparation for this,

"Resolved, that we agree to pray every evening for six months, dating from June 25, 1887, for the outpouring of the Holy Spirit on the Woman's Missionary Society and its work at home and in the foreign fields." Its "work at home," be it noted, is to arouse an interest and collect money for the foreign field, as also the Indian Territory.

Need it be said why the week before Christmas is chosen? Is not "the festive season, when families and friends exchange gifts in memory of the Gift laid on the altar of the world for the redemption of the human race, the most appropriate time to consecrate a portion from abounding riches and scant poverty to send forth the good tidings of great joy to all the earth?"

In seeking organization we do not need to adopt plans and methods unsuitable to the views, or repugnant to the tastes of our brethren. What we want is not power, but simply combination in order to elicit the largest possible giving. Power of appointment and of disbursing funds should be left, as heretofore, in the hands of the Foreign Mission Board. . . .

Some years ago the Methodist Mission in China had run down to the lowest water-mark; the rising of the tide seems to have begun with the enlisting of the women of the church in the cause of missions. The previously unexampled increase in missionary zeal and activity in Northern Presbyterian churches is attributed to the same reason—the thorough awakening of the women of the church upon the subject of missions. In like manner, until the women of our Southern Baptist churches are thoroughly aroused, we shall continue to go on in our present "hand to mouth" system. We shall continue to see mission stations so poorly manned that the missionaries break down from overwork, loneliness, and isolation; we shall continue to see promising fields unattended and old stations languishing; and we shall continue to see other denominations no richer and no better educated than ours, outstripping us in the race. I wonder how many of us really believe that "it is more blessed to give than to receive?" A woman who accepts that statement of our Lord Jesus Christ as a fact and not as "impractical idealism," will make giving a principle of her life. She will lay aside sacredly not less than one tenth of her income or her earnings as the Lord's money, which she would no more dare to touch for personal use than she would to steal. How many there are among our women, alas! alas! who imagine that because "Jesus paid it all," they need pay nothing, forgetting that the prime object of their salvation was that they should follow in the footsteps of Jesus Christ in bringing back a lost world to God, and so aid in bringing the answer to the petition our Lord taught his disciples: "Thy kingdom come."

Notes

1. "A Letter from Origen to Gregory," in A. Cleveland Coxe, ed. *Fathers of the Third Century,* Vol. IV, *The Ante-Nicene Fathers* (Grand Rapids: William B. Eerdmans Publishing Company, 1951), pp. 393-394. Used by permission.

2. Ibid., pp. 3-6; N. Bonwetsch, "Gregory Thaumaturgus," *The New Schaff-Herzog Encyclopedia of Religious Knowledge,* Samuel Macauley Jackson, ed. (New York: Funk and Wagnalls Company, 1909), pp. 73-74; John Foster, After the Apostles (London: S.C.M. Press, Ltd. 1951), pp. 10, 106-110.

3. Ibid.

4. Origen evidently confounds Hadad the Edomite, of 1 Kings xi.14, with Jeroboam.

5. "To Augustine, Bishop of the Angli," *Selected Epistles of Gregory the Great, Bishop of Rome,* Vol. XIII, James Barmby, trans. and ed., *A Select Library of Nicene and Post-Nicene Fathers of the Christian Church,* second series (Grand Rapids: William B. Eerdmans Publishing Company, 1956), pp. 55-56. Used by permission.

6. James Barmby, *The Book of Pastoral Rule and Selected Epistles of Gregory the Great, Bishop of Rome,* Vol. XII, *A Select Library,* pp. vi-xxx; Wilhelm Walther, "Gregory I, the Great," *The New Schaff-Herzog Encyclopedia,* Vol. V, pp. 55-58.

7. Ibid.

8. Latourette, Vol. II, pp. 63-64; see part II, 6.

9. Ibid., pp. 64-69.

10. Ibid.

11. Letter XXIX (38) "Boniface requests the Prayers of Abbot Aldherius for himself and for the German idolators" and Letter XXXVI (46) "Boniface calls upon all Anglo-Saxons to pray for the conversion of the Saxons" in *The Letters of Saint Boniface*, Ephraim Emerton, trans. and ed. (New York: Columbia University Press, 1940), pp. 66-67, 74-75. Used by permission.

12. Ibid., pp. 3-20; Talbot, pp. 24-62; S. Hilpisch and C. M. Aherne, "St. Boniface," *New Catholic Encyclopedia*, II (New York: McGraw-Hill Book Company, 1967), pp. 665-668.

13. From Bartholomew de Las Casas to Philip II of Spain in *Bartholomew de Las Casas: His Life, Apostolate and Writings*, Francis Augustus MacNutt (Cleveland: The Arthur H. Clark Company, 1909), pp. 222-231.

14. Ibid.; Stephen Neill, "Bartholomew de Las Casas," *Concise Dictionary*, pp. 334-335.

15. Ibid.

16. Selections from *Saint Francis Xavier* by James Brodrick, S. J., pp. 514-518. Copyright 1952 by Pellegrini & Cudahy, (now a division of Farrar, Straus & Giroux, Inc.) Reprinted with the permission of Farrar, Straus & Giroux, Inc. World rights held by Burns, Oates, and Washbourne, Ltd., London.

17. Ibid., pp. 494-526; Stephen Neill, "Francis Xavier," *Concise Dictionary*, pp. 669-670.

18. Ibid.

19. Adoniram Judson, "To Mrs. Hasseltine of Bradford, Mass. Ava, December 7, 1826," *A Memoir of the Life and Labors of the Rev. Adoniram Judson, D.D.*, Vol. I, Francis Wayland (New York: Sheldon and Company, Publishers, 1866), pp. 417-423.

20. Ibid., pp. 11-92; Courtney Anderson, *To the Golden Shore* (Boston: Little, Brown, and Company, 1956), pp. 3-121; Paul Clasper, "Adoniram Judson," *Concise Dictionary*, p. 314.

21. Clasper; Raymond A. Parker, "Triennial Convention," *Encyclopedia of Southern Baptists*, Vol. II, pp. 1427-1428; Wayland, pp. 93-127.

22. Clasper; Wayland, pp. 128-325.

23. Clasper; Wayland, pp. 325-544.

24. Clasper, p. 315; Courtney Anderson, pp. 413-505.

25. Hudson Taylor, "To Mr. Berger, August 14," in *Hudson Taylor and the China Inland Mission*, Dr. and Mrs. Howard Taylor (London: The China Inland Mission, 1943), p. 201. Used by permission of the Overseas Missionary Fellowship.

26. Ibid.; John Pollock, "James Hudson Taylor," *Concise Dictionary*, pp. 586-588.

27. Ibid., p. 587.

28. Ibid.

29. Ibid.; See Dr. and Mrs. Howard Taylor, p. iv.

30. John Pollock, "China Inland Mission," *Concise Dictionary*, p. 106.

31. From Lottie Moon to Southern Baptist Women, Tungchow, China, September 15, 1887, *Foreign Mission Journal* (Richmond, Virginia, Dec. 1887), p. 2.

32. Una Roberts Lawrence, *Lottie Moon* (Nashville: Sunday School Board of the Southern Baptist Convention, 1927), pp. 13-180; E. C. Routh, "Lottie (Charlotte) Moon," *Encyclopedia of Southern Baptists*, Vol. II, p. 923.

33. Lawrence, pp. 148-247; Baker James Cauthen and others, *Advance: A History of Southern*

Baptist Foreign Missions (Nashville: Broadman Press, 1970), pp. 29-30; R. Pierce Beaver, *All Loves Excelling,* pp. 99-102.

34. Ibid.; "Missions Update," *The Commission* (Richmond, Virginia, July, 1978), p. 39.

35. Edward R. Dayton, ed., *Mission Handbook: North American Protestant Ministries Overseas* (Monrovia, CA: Missions Advanced Research and Communication Center, 1976), p. 52.

36. Lawrence, pp. 248-317; Routh, "Lottie (Charlotte) Moon."

VI

Missionary Theory and Practice

General Introduction

Behind all mission endeavor is a conscious or unconscious methodology. From the early church fathers to contemporary missiologists, there has been a concern for the *how* of missions and the philosophical basis of that *how*. From almost every significant missionary personality in every age of the Christian movement, we have gained insight into mission theory and practice. These insights have come from every type of literary medium through which the mission cause has been conveyed through the centuries: histories, biographies, memoirs, journals, letters, tracts, sermons, minutes of mission meetings, theologies, philosophies, formal treaties on strategy, and even poems, hymns, and other literary art forms. Even though there were earlier attempts at mission theory (especially by Roman Catholic theologians), the self-conscious, systematic development of formal mission methodology was to await the arrival of the great strategists of the nineteenth and twentieth centuries. Many notable personalities have played significant roles in this regard, but the following four men have been perhaps the most influential and the most celebrated, certainly in the Protestant world.

26

"On Steps Towards Helping a Native Church to Become Self-Supporting, Self-Governing and Self-Extending" [1]
Henry Venn

Introduction

In the year 1796—the very time when the modern mission movement was getting its start—two men were

243

born: one destined to be the greatest European missionary statesman and strategist of his century and the
other destined to be the greatest American missionary
statesman and strategist of his century. The former
was Henry Venn and the latter, Rufus Anderson.

Henry Venn (1796-1873) was born in England to a
long line of Anglican clergymen. His father was the
rector of Clapham, and his grandfather (his namesake)
the author of the widely acclaimed *The Compleate Duty
of Man* (1763), whose memoir the younger Henry completed and edited. Venn was a complex person, both
a man of his age and a missionary strategist far ahead
of his time. Some of his limitations stemmed from
his acceptance of the British colonial power structure
and his assumption of the superiority of the white
man.[2]

Nevertheless, Venn was a man of enormous insight,
laying the groundwork upon which all mission strategists of the future would build. He and his American
counterpart, Rufus Anderson, were the architects of
the main influential principle of missionary strategy
to emerge from the great century: the indigenous principle. He and Anderson coined almost identical phrases
which have become the classic expressions of indigen-
ity (the "three-selves" of mission strategy): "self-support, self-government, self-extension." Anderson used
the term "self-propagation." Venn used these designa-
tions in a letter in 1867, and Anderson used them in
a book published in 1869. To what extent these men
collaborated, we are not sure (communication across
continents was not as easy then as it is today). Venn
reviewed Anderson's book in the *Church Missionary Intelligencer* in 1869, the year the book was published and
two years after he had used similar phrases to express
the same concept.[3]

Venn was chief secretary of the influential Church
Missionary Society from 1841 to 1872. During this
time he was the undisputed dean of missionary strate-

gists in Europe (British and Continental). His writings were almost legion. He wrote books (a life of Francis Xavier), reviews, prefaces, sermons, pamphlets, articles, definitive letters, and many papers on misson strategy. Max Warren has classifed 128 separate works, some of which exist in several parts. Included in this list are minutes which are conceded to be principally if not exclusively the work of Venn. This significant collection constitutes some of the most definitive and influential material ever produced on mission philosophy, and is invaluable as historical data in determining the evolution of Protestant mission philosophy.[4]

On Steps Towards Helping a Native Church to Become Self-Supporting, Self-Governing and Self-Extending

. . . .

7. Under the new system, a Church Council will be formed, the three native Ministers being members of it. The Corresponding Committee will appoint a Chairman, either a Missionary, or the Secretary of the Corresponding Committee, or one of the Native Ministers when their number increases. The Chairman will appoint two other members of the Church Council, of any race or position. The lay members of the Congregation will appoint three more. The Council is to be appointed periodically, annually, probably, at first, so that members may be changed as they are found suitable or unsuitable, and the balance of European and native influence may be adjusted from time to time.

8. The Council will meet periodically, say once a month, or every fortnight, "to consult upon the interests of the Native Church, and for the general superintendence of its affairs." The reports of the subordinate agents, as well as of the Native Pastors, will be presented to the Council. A Native Church Fund having been constituted, the Society's grant will be remitted monthly to the Council as a grant in aid of the Native Church Fund. If the Native Church Fund increases, the Council will decide what new agency shall be instituted.

9. In all these arrangements no change is made in the direct Mission work. All preaching and school superintendence will go on as before.

The European Missionaries will have their districts, exterior to the Native Pastoral Districts and in such Missionary districts no change whatever will take place. The only changes will be in the superintendence and payment of the Native Pastors and their work. The responsibility of this superintendence will no longer rest upon the Missionaries and Corresponding Committee, but upon the Bishop and ecclesiastical authorities, as in the case of all new churches erected in the diocese. The Society will still maintain its influence by its aid to the Native Church Fund and by its representatives in the Council.

10. (ii). Another misapprehension has arisen, the Parent Committee fears, in the notion that the *new system draws an absolute line between ministering to the Native Christians, and ministering to the heathen,* cutting off the latter department wholly from the Native Church Agency, and assigning it to the Missionary Society. Far otherwise. The whole organisation is founded upon the three principles—self-support, self-government, and self-extension. Self-extension implies missionary action and missionary success.

11. The Missionary aspect of the Native Church is prominently put forward in the Minutes on Native Church organisation. One of the principal objects of the Christian companies, into which it is suggested that the converts should form themselves, is to concert and adopt plans for bringing their countrymen into the Christian Church. The Native Fund, also, will be available, after providing for the Pastor and church expenses, for the support of Scripture-readers and for Catechists among the heathen. Hence the limits of each Native Pastorate should include a portion of the heathen population, more or less, according to the zeal of the Native congregation. Fostered by the European Mission, which works side by side, and which keeps up the true standard of aggressive Christianity, the Native Church may ultimately become the more efficient Missionary Agency, as of old, when from the Church of Thessalonica, "sounded forth the word of the Lord, not only in Macedonia and Achaia, but also in every place, their faith to Godward was spread abroad."

12. (iii) A third misapprehension the Parent Committee would desire to notice. It is alleged that the *system is so complicated and artificial, that it will not be perpetuated in the Native Church,* after the agency of a foreign Mission is withdrawn and the Native Church is left to itself.

13. The Parent Committee fully admit that the system they are endeavouring to establish supposes far more zeal, spiritual life, and activity in the Native Church than are usually seen in the quiet working of a Church in a Christian land; and they fear that there is great danger of a Native Christian Church, even in the midst of heathenism, settling down in complacency with the Christian ministrations which it enjoys, without attempting to exercise any aggressive influence upon surrounding heathenism. It would not be difficult, alas! to point out such instances, even in the present early period of missionary labours. This experience and sense of danger urge the Parent Committee to prepare the Churches which their Missionaries gather out from among the heathen, to become centres of aggressive action, spreading light and life to all around. This they believe to be in accordance with the primitive and Apostolic standard.

14. The idea of assimilating a mission Church to a parish or congregation in an established Christian Community is likely to mislead, if applied to countries only partially evangelized; and yet it may be observed that the elements of the proposed new system have always been resorted to, even in the settled Christian Communities, in seasons of awakened Christian zeal and life. The meeting together of earnest Christians in small companies, conferences of clergy and laity on questions touching the advancement of true religion, a craving for synodical action in the Church,—these are universally the features of spiritual life; and the scheme proposed by the Committee is only an attempt to bring these principles into operation in the Mission Churches of the Society.

15. (iv) There is only one other misapprehension which the Committee will notice. It has been objected, that *in the new system the European element is too prominent,* and, in fact, depresses the Native: and that an European Chairman, with a veto, and the appointment of two members of the Church Council, will give the Council more the character of an European than a Native institution. But it will be seen that the printed regulations do not require an European Chairman, or even a single European member of the Council. Though, in the first instance, and while the tentative and transition stage lasts, it may be advisable to give a preponderating influence to European Missionaries, yet as the Native Councillors become efficient, and as the native contributions

enlarge, and the Society's grant in aid is diminished, the European element will be gradually withdrawn, until the Native Church becomes wholly free and independent.

16. Having thus endeavoured to remove some of the objections which have been alleged against the proposed new system for the organization of Native Churches in the Missions, the Parent Committee would point to the probable effect of a *Native Institution* for spreading Christianity, such as the action of the Native Church Council will exhibit, upon the heathen at large. Even now, many heathen subscribe to Christian schools and to the erection of Christian churches; it may be anticipated, therefore, that to the Native Church Fund, administered by Native Councillors, contributions will flow from that large and increasing class of the heathen who respect without embracing Christianity. The Eurasian Community, as well as the European, will feel a special interest in helping forward an indigenous movement.

17. But above all, the system is calculated to give confidence and self-reliance to the Native Christians, and to quicken their zeal and liberality. In Calcutta, one self-supporting Native congregation, originating with the Free-Church Missions, has existed three or four years, independent of missionary Societies. It prints and publishes an annual Report; and Missionaries in various parts of North India have spoken of the encouragement which this single instance of a self-supporting and self-governing Native Christian Institution has given to the Native converts of other denominations. At Agra, a Native Church Council was lately established, and a Native Christian of some wealth was elected a Councillor. He had hitherto been a retiring member of the Christian Church, but now, feeling an official responsibility, he urged the Council to undertake the erection of a new church, subscribed liberally and collected subscriptions for it; having, as he said, long hoped that Missionaries would one day build a church in that part of the city. These are specimens of the advantages which will be gained to the cause of Christianity, when the Native Church shall assume before the people the aspect of a national and not a foreign institution.

18. The Parent Committee have sufficiently pointed out in their printed Minutes on Church organization, that some change of the present system is required, in order to relieve overworked Missionaries from the position of Pastors, secular agents and paymasters, and to

set them free for the general direction of evangelistic work. For as long as Mission mainly depends upon its Missionaries, their hands are soon filled; and the work is also checked by the limited resources of the Missionary Society. But the proposed system, if it succeeds, has the power of expansion to any extent. Self-extension has no external limits.

19. The Parent Committee, in thus urging upon their Corresponding Committee, and upon their Missionaries, the system which appears to them most adapted to sustain and enlarge the Native Churches in the midst of heathenism, are not going beyond their province. While they earnestly anticipate the time when these Native Churches will become independent of all Missionary influences, it is their duty to prepare them for this independence before they relinquish their connexion with them. They have had a lamentable warning in the Mission in the West Indies against too hasty a withdrawal from a Mission field. They have had great encouragement in their attempts to organize a Church while still in their care by the experience in West Africa. They regard it, therefore, as a very solemn obligation resting upon every Missionary Society to train up their infant Churches "in the way they should go." But at the same time they are ready to submit their plans for correction to friends on the spot, and to consider of any other plans which may claim a fairer prospect of success . . .

27

Foreign Missions: Their Relations and Claims [5]
Rufus Anderson

Introduction

Rufus Anderson (1796-1880) was the chief architect of American mission methodology of the nineteenth century. Almost all American mission agencies adopted his aims, though implementation of them was more difficult. As a missionary statesman, he was unexcelled in the United States; and his influence, both as theoretician and administrator, was profound. Anderson, early in his career, had planned to go to India; but he was offered the assistant secretaryship of the American Board of Commissioners for Foreign Missions in 1826. He became the administrative head of the board six years later and served until 1866.[6]

He and Venn gave definitive expression to the indigenous principle which had been pioneered on the field by such missionary greats as Matthew Ricci. The "three-selves" format became the standard expression of the indigenous principle. This was articulated most clearly by Anderson in chapter VII, "Principles and Methods of Modern Missions," of his widely acclaimed book, *Foreign Missions: Their Relations and Claims,* published in 1869. We have already observed the influence of Anderson and Venn upon each other. They corresponded with each other and no doubt compared notes. Just how careful a student each was of the other is not certain, though their ideas were strikingly similar. Each appeared with his ideas almost simultaneously without the opportunity, in light of the communication limitation of the time, for one clearly to have been the mentor or disciple of the other.

Like Venn, Anderson produced voluminous documents on mission philosophy. He also wrote a number of mission histories. Most of his writings relating to theory and methodology are in the form of tracts. R. Pierce Beaver has developed a helpful classification of Anderson's works. He wrote some seventeen histories; twenty-one items directly on mission principles, methods, and problems; four documents of instructions to missionaries; twenty-three pieces of mission administration, information, and promotion; six deputation reports; and some eight personal and miscellaneous items. In addition to these seventy-odd documents are numerous unsigned articles written by Anderson in the *Missionary Herald* both during the ten-year period he served as editor and afterward.[7] Outstanding missionary statesmen and strategists, such as Robert E. Speer, were strongly influenced by Anderson and incorporated his basic principles into their writings.[8]

Principles and Methods of Modern Missions

I am now prepared to state, in a concise but positive form, what I believe to be the true and proper nature of a mission among the heathen. The mission of the Apostle Paul, as set forth in the fourth chapter, embraced the following things:—

1. The aim of the apostle was to save the souls of men.

2. The means he employed for this purpose were spiritual; namely, the gospel of Christ.

3. The power on which he relied to give efficacy to these means, was divine; namely, the promised aid of the Holy Spirit.

4. His success was chiefly in the middle and poorer classes,—the Christian influence ascending from thence.

5. When he had formed local churches, he did not hesitate to ordain presbyters over them, the best he could find; and then to throw upon the churches, thus officered, the responsibilities of self-government, self-support, and self-propagation. His "presbyters in every church," whatever their number and other duties, had doubtless the pastoral care of the churches.

Prominent, then, among the visible agencies in foreign missions, if we follow the great apostle, are LOCAL CHURCHES. I call them by no denominational name. They may be churches governed by popular vote, or by elders they have themselves chosen for the purpose. They are local bodies of associated Christians. The first duty of a missionary is to gather such a church. That will serve as a nucleus—and it is the only possible nucleus, a school not being one—of a permanent congregation. A missionary, by means of properly located, well organized, well trained churches, may extend his influence over a large territory. In such a country as India, or China, his direct influence may reach even scores of thousands.

I find nothing in the history of the mission of the Apostle Paul, which seems to me decisive, as to the manner in which these multiplied mission churches should be brought into social relations to each other,

and would cheerfully leave that to the good sense and piety of missionaries on the ground.

I now inquire, What should be the nature of the mission church?
It should be composed only of hopeful converts; and should have, as
soon as possible, a native pastor, and of the same race, who has been
trained cheerfully to take the oversight of what will generally be a
small, poor, ignorant people, and mingle with them familiarly and
sympathetically. And by a native pastor, I mean one recognized as
having the pastoral care of a local church, with the right to administer
the ordinances of baptism and the Lord's Supper.

This necessity of a native pastor to the healthful and complete development of a self-reliant, effective native church, is a discovery of recent
date. I cannot say, nor is it important to know, by whom this fundamental truth or law in missions was first declared. Like many discoveries
in science, it very probably was reached by a number of persons, at
nearly the same time, and as the result of a common experience.

As soon as the mission church has a native pastor, the responsibilities
of self-government should be devolved upon it. Mistakes, perplexities,
and sometimes scandals, there will be; but it is often thus that useful
experience is gained, even in churches here at home. The salary of
the native pastor should be based on the Christianized ideas of living
acquired by his people; and the church should become self-supporting
at the earliest possible day. It should also be self-propagating from
the very first. Such churches, and only such, are the life, strength,
and glory of missions.

A foreign missionary should not be the pastor of a native church.
His business is to plant churches, in well-chosen parts of his field,
committing them as soon as possible to the care of native pastors;
himself sustaining a common relation to all, as their ecclesiastical father
and adviser; having, in some sense, like the apostle, the daily care of
the churches. He might stand thus related to a score of churches, and
even more, however they were related to each other; and when he is
old, might be able to say, through the abounding grace of God, "Though
ye have ten thousand instructors in Christ, yet have ye not many
fathers; for in Christ Jesus I have begotten you all through the gospel." [9]

Self-evident as this idea of a mission church may seem on its announcement, it is not yet adopted in all Protestant missions, and until
of late, has seemed to gain ground very slowly. Its universal adoption,

however, cannot be far distant, and will add immensely both to the economy and the power of missions.

It is upon this view of the nature and relations of native churches, that we build our missionary system.

Education, schools, the press, and whatever else goes to make up the working system, are held in strict subordination to the planting and building up of effective working churches. But though held strictly in such subordination, we see in it the utmost latitude for the exercise of a wise discretion in the conduct of missions. The governing object to be always aimed at, is self-reliant, effective churches,—churches that are purely native. Whatever missionaries believe to be most directly conducive to this end, comes within the scope of their privilege and duty; of course, under reasonable restrictions growing out of their fundamental relations. The use of schools and the press comes under the question, how far they are subservient to the great end, namely, the rapid and perfect development of churches.

We thus perceive the place which education must hold in missions. Without education, it is not possible for mission churches to be in any proper sense self-governed; nor, without it, will they be self-supported, and much less self-propagating. For the church-members there must be common schools. This results from the degraded mental condition of the heathen world, as compared with the field of the apostolic missions. Scarcely a ray of light reaches it from sun, moon, or stars in the intellectual and moral firmament. Mind is vacant, crushed, unthinking, enslaved to animal instincts and passions; earthly, sensual, terribly debased. The common school, therefore, is a necessity among the degraded heathen, to help elevate the converts, and make the village church an effective agency. And the church-members, as far as may be, should be educated within the bounds of their own villages; and in such manner that a large number of them will abide with their people, and help to support their native pastor and schools, and make their Christian village a power in the land. At first, these schools must be sustained by the mission; but it is better for them, not long afterwards, to be sustained by the parents.

The native preachers and pastors come, almost of course, from the same depths of mental degradation; and since they must be enabled to stand alone and firmly in the gospel ministry, and be competent spiritual guides to others, they should of course have a higher training.

What this shall be, what it shall include and exclude, must depend on circumstances too various for general rules. But one thing is clear. Our army, liberated from the thralldom of pagan slavery, must be well officered in order to fight bravely.

The printing-press in missions is mainly for the schools and for the church-members, to whom, indeed, books are indispensable. Experience tends to the result of having missions cease to own printing establishments as soon as the needful printing can be secured from presses owned by others.

Wherein, then, do our modern missions differ from those of the apostolic age? They differ in several particulars.

1. Modern missionaries are sent forth and supported by churches in their native lands; by churches, too, of long standing and experience; and, so far at least as this country and Great Britain are concerned, by churches existing and operating in the midst of freedom and high religious intelligence. In this modern missions have certainly a great advantage over the primitive missions.

2. They have not the personal presence and active agency of apostles; but they have the four Gospels, the Acts of the Apostles, and their Letters of Instruction, all written under the guidance of inspiration; and the press, to multiply copies of these documents by thousands. A portion of the modern Evangelical Church, indeed, is coming into the practice of putting their missionaries under the control of missionary bishops, and regards these as successors of the apostles. But they evidently are not apostles, since they lack the "signs, and wonders, and mighty deeds," which St. Paul, in his Second Epistle to the Corinthians, declares to be the needful "signs of an apostle."

3. The pastorate in modern missions differs from that of the apostolic age, in that it ordinarily has but one pastor for each church; whereas the New Testament always uses the plural in speaking of the pastorate in the churches planted by the Apostle Paul. "They ordained presbyters in every church"; being influenced in this, perhaps (as has already said), by the usage of the Jewish synagogue. This practice seems to have been lost, with the very idea of the apostolic church, in the great decline of the Early and Middle Ages; and when that idea was recovered, as it was at the Reformation, and put in practice, the usage of having but one pastor in each church was adopted by all evangelical denominations, as being more conformed to the demands of the age. And this is now the general usage in all the evangelical churches;

and it has thence been transferred to the mission churches among the heathen. The apostolic principle is retained, but the form is changed. I speak only of the pastorate, in which the evangelical denominations agree; leaving entirely untouched the points concerning which the evangelical denominations differ.

Such is the simple structure of our foreign missions, as the combined result of experience, and of the apostolic example; in all which the grand object is to plant and multiply self-reliant, efficient churches, composed wholly of native converts, each church complete in itself, with pastors of the same race with the people. And when the unevangelized world shall be dotted over with such churches, so that all men have it within their power to learn what they must do to be saved, then may we expect the promised advent of the Spirit, and the conversion of the world.

It might be deemed an omission in my description of the missionary work, should I not advert to a series of efforts made in the cities of India, and more especially in Calcutta, to gain access for the gospel to the higher classes by means of English schools. In these schools a large number of high-caste Hindus have received a liberal Christian education, through the medium of the English language and literature. The result of the experiment is regarded as very hopeful by those who are making it. And there is certainly a development among the higher class of Hindus in Calcutta, and in some other of the India cities, that is worthy of attentive consideration. But the results of the experiments are not yet sufficiently developed to occupy a prominent place in a description of the fundamental nature of the missionary work.

I close with a few general remarks.

1. The foreign missionary, the home missionary, and the pastor have each substantially the same object. It is to plant churches, and make them shine as lights in the world. Our leading sentiment is as really applicable to home missionaries, as it is to foreign missionaries. The labors of the home missionary have a direct reference to the forming of self-governed, self-supported churches, and such churches are proofs of his success. The home missionary becomes then a pastor, or gives place to one sustaining that relation.

2. The great simplification in the use of means, and relying more on those which are spiritual, is a principal reason why a given amount of funds now sustains a more extended working mission than it for-

merly did. The grand object and means are the same; but the working process, becoming more spiritual, bears more effectively on the heart and conscience.

3. The proper test of success in missions, is not the progress of civilization, but the evidence of a religious life.

4. The gospel is applicable equally to all false religions. Generically considered, there can be but two religions: the one looking for salvation by *grace;* the other, by *works.* The principle of evil in all unbelieving men, is the same. The refuges of lies in Popery, in Judaism, in Mohammedanism, in Brahminism, Buddhism, and every form of paganism, are wonderfully alike. There is one disease, and one remedy. Before the gospel, the unbelieving world stands an undistinguished mass of rebellious sinners; unwilling that God should reign over them, unwilling to be saved except by their own works, and averse to all real holiness of heart and life. There is power in the doctrine of the cross, through grace, to overcome this. The doctrine of the cross—as will more clearly appear when we come to the evidences of success in missions—is the grand instrument of conquest. Not one of the great superstitions of the world could hold a governing place in the human soul, after the conviction has once been thoroughly produced, that there is salvation only in Christ. Be it what it may, the man, thus convinced, would flee from it, as he would from a falling building in the rockings of an earthquake.

28

Planting and Development of Missionary Churches [10]
John L. Nevius

Introduction

John Livingstone Nevius (1829-1893), one of the most revolutionary missionary strategists of his generation, went as a missionary to China under the American Presybyterian Board in 1856. He became deeply disenchanted with the current mission methods which he observed in the areas of the Yangtze Valley and Shantung where he served. His most articulate objection was to the payment of the native evangelists by the missions and to the paternalism and counterproductivity which he was convinced it fostered. He seems to have had little success in persuading others in China to adopt his method. However, a visit to Korea in 1890 provided for him an open door to explore the soundness of his theory. The Presbyterians adopted his plan, and some mission specialists are convinced that this has been the most significant contributing factor to the singular success of the Presbyterian work in Korea, which has developed the most effective urban-based Christian witness in Asia in modern times.[11]

Nevius built upon the "three-selves" concept of Venn and Anderson, but he took sharp exception to the practice of hiring nationals with mission funds, which was advocated even by Rufus Anderson despite his "self-support" concept.[12] This was Nevius' most significant contribution to the history of mission methodology, and his policy has been widely adopted by mission agencies since his day. He added to his strongly indigenous concept two other vital elements: thorough and systematic Bible study and missionary itineration. These were not new ideas, but Nevius gave them a new dimension by projecting them into the context of a more radically indigenous idea of planting and developing missionary churches. The following section from his classic volume accents his reaction to the "old system" and paves the way for his positive "new system" which he feels is the true New Testament pattern.[13] This work has gone through numerous editions and the current edition enjoys widespread appeal and use.

The Old System Criticised

Introductory

A request from the Editor of the "Chinese Recorder" to prepare for publication some account of the character and results of our country work in Shan-tung, and private letters from various sources asking for information on the same general subject, have furnished evidence that such information may be of service, more especially to young missionaries.

The interest which has been taken in our work in central Shan-tung by missionaries in other provinces is due no doubt to the fact that we have to some extent adopted new principles and methods. It is too early to determine what the final issue of this new departure will be, but perhaps not too soon to derive some important lessons from present facts and experiences and results so far as developed.

Old System vs. the New

1. The adoption of the new plan having beer the result in many cases of difficulties and discouragements in connection with the previous one, our present position will be best understood by considering the two systems, which may for the sake of convenience be called the Old and the New, in their relation to each other. In the following pages we will present the reasons which have led to the disuse of the former, the adoption of the latter, and the manner in which the transition has been made.

2. I think it may be stated that forty years ago, missionaries in China, with few if any exceptions, followed the Old Method. The change of view has not been sudden but gradual and always in the same direction, producing a continually widening and more irreconcilable breach between the two systems. There is now a prevailing disposition in our part of the field, at least among the missionaries of the American Presbyterian, the English Baptist, and the American Baptist Missions, to follow the New Plan, which may still, however, be regarded as in a formative and tentative stage of development.

3. These two systems may be distinguished in general by the former depending largely on paid native agency, while the latter deprecates and seeks to minimize such agency. Perhaps an equally correct and more generally acceptable statement of the difference would be, that, while both alike seek ultimately the establishment of independent, self-reliant, and aggressive native churches, the Old System strives by the use of foreign funds to foster and stimulate the growth of the native churches in the first stage of their development, and then gradually to discontinue the use of such funds; while those who adopt

the New System think that the desired object may be best attained by applying principles of independence and self-reliance from the beginning. The difference between these two theories may be more clearly seen in their outward practical working. The Old uses freely, and as far as practicable, the more advanced and intelligent of the native church members in the capacity of paid *colporteurs*, Bible agents, evangelists, or heads of stations; while the New proceeds on the assumption that the persons employed in these various capacities would be more useful in the end by being left in their original homes and employments.

4. The relative advantages of these systems may be determined by two tests—adaptability to the end in view, and Scripture authority. Some missionaries regard the principles and practices adopted by the Apostles in early times and recorded in the Scriptures as inapplicable to our changed circumstances in China in this nineteenth century. Leaving the consideration of this question for the present, it will no doubt be acknowledged by all, that any plan which will bear the application of the two tests of adaptability and Scripture authority, has a much stronger claim upon our regard and acceptance than a plan which can only claim the sanction of one test.

As a matter of fact the change of views of not a few of the older missionaries in China is due, not to theoretical, but practical considerations. The Old System has been gradually discarded because it did not work, or because it worked evil. In my own case I can say that every change in opinion was brought about by a long and painful experience; and conclusions arrived at have been only a confirmation of what I regard as the teachings of the Bible. The same conclusions might have been reached with an immense economy of time and labor by simply following the authoritative guide which God has given us. If the New System be indeed sanctioned by Scripture authority as well as by the tests of practical adaptability and use, an exchange or reversal in the application of the names New and Old would be more in accordance with fact.

Spirit and Attitude in this Discussion

1. In stating what I regard as serious objections to previous methods, I may come in conflict with the opinions of my brethren. I desire, however, to write, not in the spirit of a critic, much less of a censor, but as one earnestly desirous of knowing the truth. I have in former

years to a considerable extent believed in and worked upon the Old System, and what I have to say by way of strictures on it may be considered as a confession of personal error, rather than of fault-finding with others. Foreigners who have come to China to devote themselves to business or diplomacy have made their mistakes; it is not strange, but rather to be expected, that we should make ours. Let us acknowledge them and profit by them.

2. I am aware that it is possible to state facts in such a way that the impression given will be a false one, and the conclusions arrived at misleading. It will be my earnest endeavor in the ensuing papers, not only to give facts and honest conclusions therefrom, but to present them in such a way that the impression given will be, if not always an agreeable one, yet strictly true and just.

3. I wish further to disclaim all assumption of ability to speak authoritatively on this subject, as though I had myself reached its final solution. The effect of long experience in mission work has been in my case to deepen a sense of incompetency, and to excite wonder in remembering the inconsiderate rashness and self-dependence of a quarter of a century ago. Still, though we may not feel competent to give advice, we may at least give a word of warning. Though we may not have learned what to do in certain cases and under certain circumstances, is it not much to have learned what not to do, and to tread cautiously where we do not know the way, and to regard with hesitation and suspicion any preconceived opinion which we know to be of doubtful expediency, especially if it is unauthorized by Scripture teaching and example?

4. I gladly recognize the fact that the use of other methods, depending to a greater or less extent on paid agents, has in many cases been followed with most happy results; and that to a certain extent tried and proved native agents must be employed. I do not wish to make invidious comparisons, much less to decide where the happy mean in using a paid agency lies.

5. Let us bear in mind that the best methods cannot do away with the difficulties in our work which comes from the world, the flesh, and the devil, but bad methods may multiply and intensify them. For unavoidable difficulties we are not responsible; for those which arise from disregard of the teachings of Scripture and experience we are.

6. Let us also remember that while in undertaking the momentous task committed to us, we should by the study of the Scriptures, prayer for divine guidance, and comparison of our varied views and experiences, seek to know what is the best method of work; still, the best method without the presence of our Master and the Spirit of all Truth will be unavailing. A bad method may be so bad as to make it unreasonable to expect God's blessing in connection with it; a right and Scriptural method, if we trust in it, as our principal ground of hope, might be followed for a lifetime without any good results.

With this much by way of introduction, I now propose to consider some objections to the Old Method.

Old Method a Natural One

1. It is only natural that missionaries should at first seek and employ many native agents. They are anxious for immediate results, and home societies and the home churches are as impatient to hear of results as missionaries are to report them. No communications from the field seem so indicative of progress, and are so calculated to call forth commendation and generous contributions as the announcement that native laborers have been obtained, and are preaching the gospel. While the missionary himself is for months or years debarred from evangelistic work by his ignorance of the language, a native agency stands waiting his employ. His circumstances and his wishes add strong emphasis to the oft-repeated truism, "China must be evangelized by the Chinese." So urgent seems the necessity to obtain native assistants, that if such as he would like are not forthcoming, he is glad to avail himself in connection with some specially interesting inquirer, even before he is baptized, "What a capital assistant that man may make."

2. While the circumstances of the missionary furnish the strongest motives to induce him to multiply native agents as fast as possible, the circumstances of the natives naturally and very strongly lead to the same result. The dense population of this country, and the sharp struggle for existence which it necessitates, have developed in the Chinaman a singular aptitude for finding and using ways and means for making a living. The comparatively expensive mode of life, as a rule absolutely necessary for foreigners, in order to live in China with any reasonable hope of health and usefulness, naturally suggests the idea to the native that so intimate a relation as that which subsists between

a teacher and his disciples will in this case undoubtedly prove a profitable one. The Famine Relief work in the northern provinces left the impression that foreigners have money in abundance, and are very ready to give it to those in need; and there are many about us now as much in need as some who received aid during the famine. It is not strange, but only human, that natives under these circumstances should see their opportunity and make the most of it.

3. With these strong motives in the minds of the missionaries and natives conspiring to the same result, it is not without excuse that we should have fallen into what I now believe is a serious mistake, utterly unaware of the danger and injury to the mission cause which ten, twenty or thirty years of experience have disclosed. In this opinion I am not alone; and it is a significant fact that those who hold it, are for the most part persons who have had a long experience on mission ground. To some, these lessons have come too late to be of much service to them individually, but they will be none the less useful to those who are willing to profit by the experiences of others.

4. I fully recognize the fact that the employment and pay of native laborers is, under suitable circumstances, legitimate and desirable, as much so as the employment and pay of foreigners. Here, however, the important questions arise, who shall be employed, and when and how shall they be employed? These questions will come up for consideration in the course of this series of articles.

Objections to the Old Method

The following are some of the objections to what we have agreed to call the "Old System":

1. Making paid agents of new converts affects injuriously the stations with which they are connected.

A well-informed and influential man, perhaps the leading spirit in a new station, is one who can be ill-spared. His removal may be most disastrous to the station, and he himself may never find elsewhere such an opportunity for doing good. I have in mind four persons who about twenty-eight years ago gave great promise of usefulness in their homes in connection with our out-stations in Ning-po. While working with their hands in their several callings they bore testimony to the truth wherever they went, and were exciting great interest in their own neighborhoods. It was not long, however, before these men were employed, one by one mission, another by another, and the interest in Christianity in and about their homes ceased. It is to be hoped that they did some good in the positions which they afterward occupied, but I have not been able to learn of any of them, that his after career was a specially useful one. I refer to these cases not as unusual and exceptional. I could add many others from Chê-chiang and Shantung, and I doubt not that similar instances will occur to the minds of most missionaries who read this paper.

The injury to a station in these cases does not consist simply in the loss of the man's influence for good; positive evil is introduced. Envy, jealousy and dissatisfaction with their lot are very apt to be excited in the minds of those who are left. Others think that they also should be employed, if not as preachers, as servants, or in some other capacity. It would be a less serious matter if this feeling could be confined to the station where it originates, but unfortunately it extends to other places and there produces the same injurious effects. The religious interest which passed like a wave over the neighborhood, gives place to another wave of excitement, and the topics of conversation are now place and pay. The man employed has lost very much the character he bore as a disinterested worker for the spiritual good of others, and is now likely to be regarded by many as a kind of employ-agent who ought to use his influence to get them places.

2. Making a paid agent of a new convert often proves an injury to him personally.

He is placed in a position unfavorable to the development of a strong, healthy, Christian character. Some of these men, originally farmers, shopkeepers, pedlers or laborers in the fields, find themselves advanced to a position for which they are by previous habits and training unsuited. The long gown and the affected scholarly air are not becoming to them, and they naturally lose the respect of their neighbors and their influence over them. Men who were self-reliant and aggressive in their original positions, now perform their routine labors in a formal and perfunctory manner. Some, on the other hand, are puffed up with pride and self-conceit, and become arrogant and offensive. Here again I am not theorizing, but speaking from experience, and could multiply cases—as I presume most missionaries could—of deterioration of character in both directions above indicated.

No doubt the employment of some of these men has been followed by good results, but it is still a question whether they might not have accomplished more had they been left where they were found. Some of them have proved most unsatisfactory to their employers, but are retained in their places from year to year, because it seems an injustice to send them back to a mode of life for which they have become unfitted. Others have been dismissed from service, and returned to their homes disappointed and aggrieved; while not a few when they have been dropped as employees have dropped their Christianity, brought reproach upon the cause of Christ, become the enemies of the Church, and given evidence that they were only hirelings—never fit to be enrolled either as preachers or as church members.

3. The Old System makes it difficult to judge between the true and false, whether as preachers or as church members.

That the Chinese are adepts in dissembling, no one who has been long in China will deny. The fact that not a few who were earnest preachers have fallen away when they have ceased to be employed has already been referred to. How many others there are now in employ whose professions are suspended on their pay no one can tell. The Chinese are close analysts of character, and know how to adapt themselves to circumstances and individuals. They are less apt to deceive their own people than foreigners, and less apt to deceive others than those by whom they are employed. The desire that the native preacher may prove a true man biases the judgment. Doubtless the man employed is often self-deceived.

I have had a considerable number of intelligent, and to all appearances sincere Christians, connected with my stations, who fell back and left the Church when they found they were not to be employed. These and a still larger number of inquirers, who learned during the time of their probation that there was very little hope of getting place and pay and fell back before they were baptized, would in all probability, if their desire for employment had been gratified, be found to-day in the Church, sustaining perhaps a fair reputation as preachers or evangelists.

What lesson are we to learn from these facts and experiences? Is it not this, that so long as a free use is made of new converts as paid preachers, we deprive ourselves of one of the most effective means of separating the chaff from the wheat, and of assuring ourselves that the men we are employing are what we hope they are, and that we are not building, or vainly attempting to build, on a bad foundation.

4. The Employment System tends to excite a mercenary spirit, and to increase the number of mercenary Christians.

Of course we fully admit that many paid agents are sincere, earnest men and that they bring into the Church sincere and earnest believers, some perhaps who would not otherwise be reached. We are here simply pointing out an evil influence and tendency which are connected with one system and avoided by the other. A man will sometimes be found who will listen to a native preacher, apparently much interested, but knowing and caring very little about what is said. When he finds an opportunity, he obtains from the preacher, directly or indirectly, a knowledge of what pay he gets and how he obtained his position. This man perhaps becomes a diligent student of the Scriptures and passes an excellent examination as a candidate for baptism; but he is interested in Christianity only as a means to an end. When this mercenary spirit enters a church, it has a wonderful self-propagating power and follows the universal law of propagating after its kind. The mercenary preacher, whether paid or hoping to be paid, as naturally draws to himself others of like affinities as a magnet attracts iron filings.

In one of the districts of this province there seemed a few years since to be an unusual religious awakening. The interest spread from town to town, the number of inquirers was large, and hundreds of apparently sincere believers were gathered into the Church. It was afterward found that the movement was due largely to mercenary motives of different kinds, both in the propagating agents, and in those who were influenced by them. That district now seems to be struck with a blight. The larger part of those who were received are now excommunicated or under discipline; a very unfavorable impression has been made upon the people generally, and persons sincerely interested in the truth are kept back from seeking a connection with the Church by the unworthy examples of its members. In this district, Shiu-kuang, there is little hope of anything being accomplished until after the pruning process has been carried still farther, and we can make a new and better beginning. It is much easier to get unworthy members into the Church than it is to get them out of it, and very little good can be accomplished while they hang upon it as an incubus.

5. The Employment System tends to stop the voluntary work of unpaid agents.

The question naturally arises in the mind of the new convert, "If other persons are paid for preaching why should not I be?" Under the influence of jealousy and discontent it is easy to go a step farther and say, "If the missionary is so blind or so unjust as not to see or acknowledge my claims to be employed as others are, I will leave the work of spreading Christianity to those who are paid for it." This again is not an imaginary case but a common experience. It is evident that the two systems are mutually antagonistic, and whenever an attempt is made to carry them on together, the voluntary system labors under almost insurmountable difficulties. This is a serious objection to the Old System, that it stands in the way of the other, and makes the success of it well-nigh impossible.

6. The Old System tends to lower the character and lessen the influence of the missionary enterprise, both in the eyes of foreigners and natives.

The opprobrious epithet, "Rice Christians," has gained almost universal currency in the East, as expressive of the foreigners' estimate of the actual results of missionary work. This unfavorable judgment, formed by those who are supposed, as eye-witnesses, to have good grounds for it, finds its way to Christian nations in the West, who support missions, and prejudices the missionary cause in the opinion of those who would otherwise be its sympathetic supporters. It is a serious question how far missionaries are to blame for this. While we resent as false the sweeping generalization which would include all Christians in China, or the larger part of them, in this category, it is worse than useless to ignore the readiness of large classes of Chinamen to become "Rice Christians," and the difficulty of determining who do, and who do not, belong to this class. We must also admit the fact, that not a few of those who have found their way into the Church have proved, after years of trial, to be only "Rice Christians." The idea of getting rid of such altogether is undoubtedly a fallacious one. They have been connected with the Church, and probably will be, in all lands and in every age. Still, as this reproach has resulted largely from the fact that hitherto a considerable proportion of native Christians have "eaten the missionary's rice," one effective way for removing the reproach is obvious.

The injurious effects of the paid-agent system on the mass of the Chinese population outside of the Church, are perhaps still greater.

The general opinion of the Chinaman as to the motive of one of his countrymen in propagating a foreign religion, is that it is a mercenary one. When he learns that the native preacher is in fact paid by foreigners, he is confirmed in his judgment. What the motive is which actuates the foreign missionary, a motive so strong that he is willing to waste life and money in what seems a fruitless enterprise, he is left to imagine. The most common explanation is that it is a covert scheme for buying adherents with a view to political movements inimical to the state. Of course it is supposed that no loyal native will have anything to do with such a movement. If the Chinaman is told that this enterprise is prompted by disinterested motives, and intended for the good of his people, he is incredulous. Simple professions and protestations have little weight with him, in comparison with his own interpretation of facts. Observing that in some of our stations only those who are employed and paid remain firm in their adherence to the foreigner, while not a few of the others fall back, his opinion is still further confirmed; and he looks on with quiet complacency and rallies his unsuccessful neighbors on their having fallen behind their competitors in their scramble for money. Here again I am not imagining what may happen in the future, but am stating what has actually occurred. The result is that many well-disposed Chinamen of the better classes, who might be brought under Christian influences, are repelled, and those who actually find their way into the Church are composed largely of two opposite classes—those whose honest convictions are so strong that they outweigh and overcome all obstacles, and unworthy persons to whom that feature in mission work which we are controverting is its chief attraction.

Now we readily admit that whatever course we may take, the Chinese in general will still regard us as foreign emissaries, our religion as a feint and our converts as mercenaries. What we deprecate is, gratuitously furnishing what will be regarded as conclusive evidence that these unfavorable opinions are well founded. Our enemies are sufficiently formidable without our giving them an unnecessary advantage. The obstacles which oppose us are sufficiently appalling without our adding to them and in this way postponing the time of final success.

The above are some of the principal objections which may be urged against the paid-agent scheme. We will next consider what we regard as a better and more Scriptural way.

29

Missionary Methods: St. Paul's or Ours?[14]
Roland Allen

Introduction

Roland Allen (1868-1947) is currently the most influential deceased mission writer whose career began in the last century. A native of England, he was educated at Oxford and was ordained an Anglican priest in 1892. He went as a missionary to China in 1895 under the Society for the Propagation of the Gospel in Foreign Parts. Health reasons forced him to return to England in 1904. He was a parish priest until 1907 when he resigned over a doctrinal controversy. He served as a chaplain in World War I. In 1920 he began a fruitful career as a consultant to numerous missions on an international scale. He advised churches and mission agencies in Canada, India, and numerous African countries. He settled in Kenya in 1931 where he remained for the rest of his life.[15]

Allen wrote his definitive study, *Missionary Methods: St. Paul's or Ours?* in 1912 and *The Spontaneous Expansion of the Church* in 1927. Both have become mission classics and are very much in demand today. They have gone through a number of reprintings and editions. He wrote a number of other works. His *Ministry of the Spirit* is another standard work which is popular today. Allen had a deep love for the Bible and believed profoundly in the leadership of the Holy Spirit. He called the missionary enterprise back to its biblical roots with respect to both theology and methodology which he saw as inextricably intertwined. An example of the revolutionary implication of his radical biblical stance was his challenge of an exclusively professional and paid class of clergy. He first enunciated this in *Missionary*

Methods: St. Paul's or Ours? and he gave his life to developing these principles of biblical mission strategy.

Introductory

In little more than ten years St. Paul established the Church in four provinces of the Empire, Galatia, Macedonia, Achaia and Asia. Before A.D. 47 there were no Churches in these provinces; in A.D. 57 St. Paul could speak as if his work there was done, and could plan extensive tours into the far West without anxiety lest the Churches which he had founded might perish in his absence for want of his guidance and support.

The work of the Apostle during these ten years can therefore be treated as a unity. Whatever assistance he may have received from the preaching of others, it is unquestioned that the establishment of the Churches in these provinces was really his work. In the pages of the New Testament he, and he alone, stands forth as their founder. And the work which he did was really a completed work. So far as the foundation of the Churches is concerned, it is perfectly clear that the writer of the Acts intends to represent St. Paul's work as complete. The Churches were really established. Whatever disasters fell upon them in later years, whatever failure there was, whatever ruin, that failure was not due to any insufficiency or lack of care and completeness in the Apostle's teaching or organization. When he left them he left them because his work was fully accomplished.

This is truly an astonishing fact. That Churches should be founded so rapidly, so securely, seems to us to-day, accustomed to the difficulties, the uncertainties, the failures, the disastrous relapses of our own missionary work, almost incredible. Many missionaries in later days have received a larger number of converts than St. Paul; many have preached over a wider area than he; but none have so established Churches. We have long forgotton that such things could be. We have long accustomed ourselves to accept it as an axiom of missionary work that converts in a new country must be submitted to a very long probation and training, extending over generations, before they can be expected to be able to stand alone. To-day if a man ventures to suggest that there may be something in the methods by which St. Paul attained such wonderful results worthy of our careful attention, and perhaps of our imitation, he is in danger of being accused of revolutionary tendencies.

Yet this is manifestly not as it should be. It is impossible but that the account so carefully given by St. Luke of the planting of the Churches in the Four Provinces should have something more than a mere archaeological and historical interest. Like the rest of the Holy Scriptures it was "written for our learning." It was certainly meant to be something more than the romantic history of an exceptional man, doing exceptional things under exceptional circumstances—a story from which ordinary people of a later age can get no more instruction for practical missionary work than they receive from the history of the Cid, or from the exploits of King Arthur. It was really intended to throw light on the path of those who should come after.

But it is argued that as a matter of fact St. Paul was an exceptional man living in exceptional times, preaching under exceptional circumstances; that he enjoyed advantages in his birth, his education, his call, his mission, his relationship to his hearers, such as have been enjoyed by no other; and that he enjoyed advantages in the peculiar constitution of society at the moment of his call such as to render his work quite exceptional. To this I must answer (1) that St. Paul's missionary method was not peculiarly St. Paul's. He was not the only missionary who went about establishing Churches in those early days. The method in its broad outlines was followed by his disciples, and they were not all men of exceptional genius. It is indeed universal, and outside the Christian Church has been followed by reformers, religious, political, social, in every age and under most diverse conditions. It is only because he was a supreme example of the spirit, and power with which it can be used, that we can properly call the method St. Paul's. (2) That we possess to-day an advantage of inestimable importance in that we have the printing press and the whole of the New Testament where St. Paul had only the Old Testament in Greek. (3) That however highly we may estimate St. Paul's personal advantages or the assistance which the conditions of his age afforded, they cannot be so great as to rob his example of all value for us. In no other work do we set the great masters wholly on one side, and teach the students of to-day that whatever they may copy, they may not copy them, because they lived in a different age under exceptional circumstances and were endowed with exceptional genius. It is just because they were endowed with exceptional genius that we say their work is endowed with a universal character. Either we must drag down St. Paul from his pedestal as the great missionary, or else we must acknowledge that there is in his work that quality of universality.

The cause which has created this prejudice against the study of the Pauline method is not far to seek. It is due to the fact that every unworthy, idle and slipshod method of missionary work has been fathered upon the Apostle. Men have wandered over the world, "preaching the Word," laying no solid foundations, establishing nothing permanent, leaving no really instructed society behind them, and have claimed St. Paul's authority for their absurdities. They have gone through the world, spending their time in denouncing ancient religions, in the name of St. Paul. They have wandered from place to place without any plan or method of any kind, guided in their movements by straws and shadows, persuaded they were imitating St. Paul on his journey from Antioch to Troas. Almost every intolerable abuse that has ever been known in the mission field has claimed some sentence or act of St. Paul as its original.

It is in consequence of this, because in the past we have seen missionary work made ridiculous or dangerous by the vagaries of illiterate or unbalanced imitators of the Apostle, that we have allowed ourselves to be carried to the opposite extreme, and to shut our eyes to the profound teaching and practical wisdom of the Pauline method.

Secondly, people have adopted fragments of St. Paul's method and have tried to incorporate them into alien systems, and the failure which resulted has been used as an argument against the Apostle's method. For instance, people have baptized uninstructed converts and the converts have fallen away; but St. Paul did not baptize uninstructed converts apart from a system of mutual responsibility which ensured their instruction. Again, they have gathered congregations and have left them to fend for themselves, with the result that the congregations have fallen back into heathenism. But St. Paul did not gather congregations, he planted Churches, and he did not leave a Church until it was fully equipped with orders of Ministry, Sacraments and Tradition. Or again, they have trusted native helpers with the management of mission funds, and the natives have grievously misused them; but

St. Paul did not trust natives with the management of Church funds. He had no funds with which to entrust them. These people have committed funds in trust to individual natives and have been deceived; but St. Paul left the Church to manage its own finance. These people have made the natives responsible to *them* for honest management; but St. Paul never made any Church render an account of its finances to him. Or again, Europeans have ordained ill-educated natives and have repented of it. But they have first broken the bonds which should have united those whom they ordained to those to whom they were to minister, and then have expected them to be ministers of a foreign system of Church organization with which neither the ministers nor their congregations were familiar. St. Paul did not do this. He ordained ministers of the Church for the Church, and he instituted no elaborate constitution. When these false and partial attempts at imitating the Apostle's method have failed, men have declared that the Apostolic method was at fault and was quite unsuited to the condition and circumstances of present-day missions. The truth is that they have neither understood nor practised the Apostle's method at all.

There is yet another and a more weighty reason: St. Paul's method is not in harmony with the modern Western spirit. We modern teachers from the West are by nature and by training persons of restless activity and boundless self-confidence. We are accustomed to assume an attitude of superiority towards all Eastern peoples, and to point to our material progress as the justification of our attitude. We are accustomed to do things ourselves for ourselves, to find our own way, to rely upon our own exertions, and we naturally tend to be impatient with others who are less restless and less self-assertive than we are. We are accustomed by long usage to an elaborate system of Church organization, and a peculiar code of morality. We cannot imagine any Christianity worthy of the name existing without the elaborate machinery which we have invented. We naturally expect our converts to adopt from us not only essentials but accidentals. We desire to impart not only the Gospel, but the Law and the Customs. With that spirit, St. Paul's methods do not agree, because they were the natural outcome of quite another spirit, the spirit which preferred persuasion to authority. St. Paul distrusted elaborate systems of religious ceremonial, and grasped fundamental principles with an unhesitating faith in the power of the Holy Ghost to apply them to his hearers and to work out their appropriate external expressions in them. It was inevitable that methods which were the natural outcome of the mind of St. Paul should appear as dangerous to us as they appeared to the Jewish Christians of his own day. The mere fact that they can be made to bear a shallow resemblance to the methods of no method is sufficient to make the apostles of order suspicious. In spite of the manifest fact that the Catholic Church was founded by them, they appear uncatholic to those who live in daily terror of schism. It seems almost as if we thought it uncatholic to establish the Church too fast.

But that day is passing. In face of the vast proportions of the work to be done, we are day by day seeking for some new light on the great problem how we may establish the Catholic Church in the world. In this search, the example of the Apostle of the Gentiles must be of the first importance to us. He succeeded in doing what we so far have only tried to do. The facts are unquestionable. In a very few years, he built the Church on so firm a basis that it could live and grow in faith and in practice, and it could work out its own problems, and overcome all dangers and hindrances both from within and without.

Notes

1. Henry Venn, "On Steps Towards Helping a Native Church to Become Self-Supporting, Self-Governing and Self-Extending," *To Apply the Gospel: Selections from the Writings of Henry Venn,* Max Warren, ed. (Grand Rapids: William B. Eerdmans Publishing Company, 1971), pp. 74-78. Used by permission.

2. Ibid., pp. 13, 35, 36, 78; Warren, "Henry Venn," *Concise Dictionary,* p. 636.

3. Warren, *To Apply the Gospel,* pp. 15-49; William Knight, *Memoir of the Rev. Henry Venn* (London: Longmans, Green and Co., 1880).

4. Ibid.; Warren, "Henry Venn," p. 636; Eugene A. Stock, *The History of the Church Missionary Society,* Vol. I (London: Church Missionary Society, 1899), pp. 367-504, Vol. II.

5. Rufus Anderson, "Principles and Methods of Modern Missions," *Foreign Missions: Their Relations and Claims* (1869) in R. Pierce Beaver, ed., *To Advance the Gospel: Selections from the Writings of Rufus Anderson* (Grand Rapids: William B. Eerdmans Publishing Company, 1967), pp. 97-102. Used by permission.

6. Ibid., pp. 9-38; Beaver, "Rufus Anderson," *Concise Dictionary,* p. 21.

7. Beaver, *To Advance the Gospel,* pp. 39-44.

8. Ibid., pp. 9, 10; see Robert E. Speer, *Missionary Principles and Practice* (New York: Fleming H. Revell Company, 1902) and *Studies of Missionary Leadership* (Philadelphia: Westminster Press, 1914).

9. I Corinthians iv. 15.

10. John L. Nevius, "The Old System Criticised," *Planting and Development of Missionary Churches* (Nutley, New Jersey: The Presbyterian and Reformed Publishing Company, n.d.), pp. 7-18. Used by permission.

11. Ibid., preface to the fourth edition; Stephen Neill, "Nevius Plan," *Concise Dictionary,* pp. 437-438.

12. For the position of Anderson, see Beaver, *To Advance the Gospel,* pp. 105-106.

13. Neill, "Nevius Plan," pp. 437-438; H. S. C. Nevius, *The Life of John Livingstone Nevius* (Chicago: Fleming H. Revell Company, 1895).

14. Roland Allen, "Introductory," *Missionary Methods: St. Paul's or Ours?* Copyright 1959. Moody Press, Moody Bible Institute of Chicago. Used by permission.

15. Noel Q. King, "Roland Allen," *Concise Dictionary,* pp. 14-15.

VII

Missionary Tracts and Sermons

General Introduction

In addition to missionary biographies, journals, diaries, and letters, missionary tracts and sermons have made indelible impressions upon the church and have repeatedly inspired renewed concen for the world missionary cause. The following pages contain some of the tracts which have come down to us from the early church fathers. These tracts reveal the widespread advance of the faith in those early centuries and the strong consciousness of the early church leaders concerning the significance of this missionary advance.

We also include some of the great missionary sermons which came in the wake of the missionary explosion which began with the Moravian movement under Zinzendorf and continued in the extraordinary missionary statesmanship of John R. Mott. We noted earlier the impact made by Carey's challenging sermon, "Expect Great Things from God; Attempt Great Things for God." Another sermon which made a significant impact was given by William Conner Magee, Dean at the Royal Chapel of Dublin, on the anniversary of the Church Missionary Society. It was entitled, "The Missionary Trials of the Church." Other examples of missionary sermons which made their impact felt are "The Moral Dignity of Mission Enterprise" by Francis Wayland, "Apostolic Missions" by Joseph Angus, and "Heroism of Foreign Missions" by Phillips Brooks.

30

Against Heresies [1]
Irenaeus

Introduction

Irenaeus (137?-190) was from Asia Minor. Little is known of him before he became bishop of Lyons in 177. Before that he had been a presbyter. He knew Polycarp, and this was his link with the apostolic fathers. He is considered by some to be the greatest and most influential church leader after the apostolic period and before Eusebius. Though most of his works are lost, what he wrote had a great influence upon his day and the generations that followed. His principal literary work is *Against Heresies.* Its significance as a missionary tract is the fact that it speaks of the "worldwide" spread of the faith and makes reference to the advance of Christianity in this early period into Spain, Germany, Egypt, Libya, and the East (referring to the East of Palestine). Irenaeus, whose name means "Peace," fought heresies and strove for the unity of the church, though he did not favor uniformity and opposed the growing tendency to centralize the church under the power of the bishop of Rome. [2]

Unity of the Faith of the Church Throughout the Whole World

1. The Church, though dispersed throughout the whole world, even to the ends of the earth, has received from the apostles and their disciples this faith: [She believes] in one God, the Father Almighty, Maker of heaven, and earth, and the sea, and all things that are in them; and in one Christ Jesus, the Son of God, who became incarnate for our salvation; and in the Holy Spirit, who proclaimed through the prophets the dispensations of God, and the advents, and the birth from a virgin, and the passion, and the resurrection from the dead, and the ascension into heaven in the flesh of the beloved Christ Jesus,

our Lord, and His [future] manifestation from heaven in the glory of the Father "to gather all things in one," and to raise up anew all flesh of the whole human race, in order that to Christ Jesus, our Lord, and God, and Saviour, and King, according to the will of the invisible Father, "every knee should bow, of things in heaven, and things in earth, and things under the earth, and that every tongue should confess" to Him, and that He should execute just judgment towards all; that He may send "spiritual wickednesses," and the angels who transgressed and became apostates, together with the ungodly, and unrighteous, and wicked, and profane among men, into everlasting fire; but may, in the exercise of His grace, confer immortality on the righteous, and holy, and those who have kept His commandments, and have perse-vered in His love, some from the beginning [of their Christian course], and others from [the date of] their repentance, and may surround them with everlasting glory.

2. As I have already observed, the Church, having received this preaching and this faith, although scattered throughout the whole world, yet, as if occupying but one house, carefully preserves it. She also believes these points [of doctrine] just as if she had but one soul, and one and the same heart, and she proclaims them, and teaches them, and hands them down, with perfect harmony, as if she possessed only one mouth. For, although the languages of the world are dissimilar, yet the import of the tradition is one and the same. For the Churches which have been planted in Germany do not believe or hand down anything different, nor do those in Spain, nor those in Gaul, nor those in the East, nor those in Egypt, nor those in Libya, nor those which have been established in the central regions of the world. But as the sun, that creature of God, is one and the same throughout the whole world, so also the preaching of the truth shineth everywhere, and enlightens all men that are willing to come to a knowledge of the truth. Nor will any one of the rulers in the Churches, however highly gifted he may be in point of eloquence, teach doctrines different from these (for no one is greater than the Master); nor, on the other hand, will he who is deficient in power of expression inflict injury on the tradition. For the faith being ever one and the same, neither does one who is able at great length to discourse regarding it, make any addition to it, nor does one, who can say but little, diminish it.

3. It does not follow because men are endowed with greater and

less degrees of intelligence, that they should therefore change the sub-
ject-matter [of the faith] itself, and should conceive of some other
God besides Him who is the Framer, Maker, and Preserver of this
universe (as if He were not sufficient for them), or of another Christ,
or another Only-begotten. But the fact referred to simply implies this,
that one may [more accurately than another] bring out the meaning
of those things which have been spoken in parables, and accommodate
them to the general scheme of the faith; and explain [with special
clearness] the operation and dispensation of God connected with human
salvation; and show that God manifested longsuffering in regard to
the apostasy of the angels who transgressed, as also with respect to
the disobedience of men; and set forth why it is that one and the
same God has made some things temporal and some eternal, some
heavenly and others earthly; and understand for what reason God,
though invisible, manifested Himself to the prophets not under one
form, but differently to different individuals; and show why it was
that more covenants than one were given to mankind; and teach what
was the special character of each of these covenants; and search out
for what reason "God hath concluded every man in unbelief, that
He may have mercy upon all"; and gratefully describe on what account
the Word of God became flesh and suffered; and relate why the advent
of the Son of God took place in these last times, that is, in the end,
rather than in the beginning [of the world]; and unfold what is contained in the Scriptures concerning the end [itself], and things to come;
and not be silent as to how it is that God has made the Gentiles,
whose salvation was despaired of, fellow-heirs, and of the same body,
and partakers with the saints; and discourse how it is that "this mortal
body shall put on immortality, and this corruptible shall put on incor-
ruption"; and proclaim in what sense [God] says, "That is a people
who was not a people; and she is beloved who was not beloved";
and in what sense He says that "more are the children of her that
was desolate, than of her who possessed a husband." For in reference
to these points, and others of a like nature, the apostle exclaims: "Oh!
the depth of the riches both of the wisdom and knowledge of God;
how unsearchable are His judgments, and His ways past finding out!"
But [the superior skill spoken of] is not found in this, that any one
should, beyond the Creator and Framer [of the world], conceive of

the Enthymesis of an erring Æon, their mother and his, and should thus proceed to such a pitch of blasphemy; nor does it consist in this, that he should again falsely imagine, as being above this [fancied being], a Pleroma at one time supposed to contain thirty, and at another time an innumerable tribe of Æons, as these teachers who are destitute of truly divine wisdom maintain; while the Catholic Church possesses one and the same faith throughout the whole world, as we have already said.

31

The Stromata[3]
Clement of Alexandria

Introduction

The date of the birth of Clement of Alexandria is unknown, but the general date of his death is around 220. Because of his classical writing style, scholars believe he was a native of Athens. He was a pagan philospher before he became a Christian. He traveled widely and studied under some of the greatest teachers of the day. His most revered teacher was Pantaenus, whom he succeeded as the leader of the Alexandrian School of Christian philosophy when Pantaenus left to make his missionary tour of the East (see part II, 5). He taught with distinction in Alexandria until 202 when persecution forced him to flee Egypt. He went first to Jerusalem then to Antioch where he continued his influential career as a teacher and leader. Some of the leading churchmen of the next generation were his pupils: Origen who succeeded him at Alexandria, Bishop Alexander of Jerusalem, Hippolytus, and others. His greatest works are *The Exhortation of the Heathen*, *The Instructor*, *The Stromata* (or *Miscellanies*). The missionary importance of *The Stromata* is found in book VI, chapter XVIII, in the section which contrasts the relative influence of Christianity compared to philosophy. Philosophy had remained in Greece, but Christianity had spread "over the whole world." [4]

Universal diffusion of the Gospel a contrast to philosphy

The philosophers, however, chose to [teach philosophy] to the Greeks alone, and not even to all of them; but Socrates to Plato, and Plato to Xenocrates, Aristotle to Theophrastus, and Zeno to Cleanthes, who persuaded their own followers alone.

But the word of our Teacher remained not in Judea alone, as philosophy did in Greece; but was diffused over the whole world, over every nation, and village, and town, bringing already over to the truth whole houses, and each individual of those who heard it by him himself, and not a few of the philosophers themselves.

And if any one ruler whatever prohibit the Greek philosophy, it vanishes forthwith. But our doctrine on its very first proclamation was prohibited by kings and tyrants together, as well as particular rulers and governors, with all their mercenaries, and in addition by innumerable men, warring against us, and endeavouring as far as they could to exterminate it. But it flourishes the more. For it dies not, as human doctrine dies, nor fades as a fragile gift. For no gift of God is fragile. But it remains unchecked, though prophesied as destined to be persecuted to the end. Thus Plato writes of poetry: "A poet is a light and a sacred thing, and cannot write poetry till he be inspired and lose his senses." And Democritus similarly: "Whatever things a poet writes with divine afflatus, and with a sacred spirit, are very beautiful." And we know what sort of things poets say. And shall no one be amazed at the prophets of God Almighty becoming the organs of the divine voice?

Having then moulded, as it were, a statue of the Gnostic, we have now shown who he is; indicating in outline, as it were, both the greatness and beauty of his character. What he is as to the study of physical phenomena shall be shown afterwards, when we begin to treat of the creation of the world.

32

Apology[5]
Tertullian

Introduction

Tertullian (145-200) was a native of Carthage, the son of a proconsulor centurion. He was educated in Rome, apparently in law, which he practiced for a while, it appears, before he became a Christian in 185. He married soon after this. In 190 he became a presbyter. He was the first of the great Latin fathers and had a profound influence upon church leaders of his own and following generations. Cyrian did not let a day pass without reading a selection from his writings. Tertullian developed the ecclesiastical Latin later used by Jerome and the other Latin fathers. Ironically he left the Roman wing of the church and become a Montanist. He was a prolific writer, leaving a total of thirty-eight works, five books against Marcion alone. Tertullian's lines in chapter XXXVII of his *Apology* constitute a classic of missionary apologetic: "We are but of yesterday, and we have filled every place among you— cities, islands, fortresses, towns, market-places, the very camp, tribes, companies, palace, senate, forum,— we have left nothing to you but the temples of your gods." [6]

We Are But of Yesterday

If we are enjoined, then, to love our enemies, as I have remarked above, whom have we to hate? If injured, we are forbidden to retaliate, lest we become as bad ourselves: who can suffer injury at our hands? In regard to this, recall your own experiences. How often you inflict gross cruelties on Christians, partly because it is your own inclination, and partly in obedience to the laws! How often, too, the hostile mob, paying no regard to you, takes the law into its own hand, and assails us with stones and flames! With the very frenzy of the Bacchanals, they do not even spare the Christian dead, but tear them, now sadly changed, no longer entire, from the rest of the tomb, from the asylum we might say of death, cutting them in pieces, rending them asunder. Yet, banded together as we are, ever so ready to sacrifice our lives, what single case of revenge for injury are you able to point to, though, if it were held right among us to repay evil by evil, a single night with a torch or two could achieve an ample vengeance? But away with the idea of a sect divine avenging itself by human fires, or shrinking from the sufferings in which it is tried. If we desired, indeed, to act the part of open enemies, nor merely of secret avengers, would there be any lacking in strength, whether of numbers or resources? The Moors, the Marcomanni, the Parthians themselves, or any single people, however great, inhabiting a distinct territory, and confined within its own boundaries, surpasses, forsooth, in numbers, one spread over all the world! We are but of yesterday, and we have filled every place among you—cities, islands, fortresses, towns, market-places, the very camp, tribes, companies, palace, senate, forum,—we have left nothing to you but the temples of your gods. For what wars should we not be fit, not eager, even with unequal forces, we who so willingly yield ourselves to the sword, if in our religion it were not counted better to be slain than to slay? Without arms even, and raising no insurrectionary banner, but simply in enmity to you, we could carry on the contest with you by an ill-willed severance alone. For if such multitudes of men were to break away from you, and betake themselves to some remote corner of the world, why, the very loss of so many citizens, whatever sort they were, would cover the empire with shame; nay, in the very forsaking, vengeance would be inflicted. Why, you would be horror-struck at the solitude in which you would find yourselves, at such an all-prevailing silence, and that stupor as of a dead world. You would have to seek subjects to govern. You would have more enemies than citizens remaining. For now it is the immense number of Christians which makes your enemies so few,—almost all the inhabitants of your various cities being followers of Christ. Yet you choose to call us enemies of the human race, rather than of human error. Nay, who would deliver you from those secret foes, ever busy both destroying your souls and ruining your health? Who would save you, I mean, from the attacks of those spirits of evil, which without reward or hire we exorcise? This alone would be revenge enough for us, that you were henceforth left free to the possession of unclean spirits. But instead of taking into account what is due to us is for the important protection we afford you, and though we are not merely no trouble to you, but in fact necessary to your well-being, you prefer to hold us enemies, as indeed we are, yet not of man, but rather of his error.

33

Against Celsus [7]
Origen

Introduction

Origen was born in Alexandria around 185. His father was a teacher of rhetoric and grammar, and he saw to it himself that his precocious son received a good, well-rounded education. The same wave of persecution that caused Clement to leave Alexandria was responsible for the imprisonment of Origen's father when Origen was seventeen. The death of his father a year later forced Origen to assume the support of his mother and a number of smaller children (all of the family's property and wealth had been confiscated). At the incredible age of eighteen, Origen assumed the leadership of the school in Alexandria vacated by the great Clement. Among his pupils were such notables as Justin Martyr and Heraclas, later bishop of Alexandria.[8]

It was amazing that Origen—as popular as he was—escaped death in Alexandria. He did in time have to leave, however, and fled to Caesarea where he continued his teaching and writing. Though not ordained, he was asked by Bishops Alexander of Jerusalem and Theoctistus of Caesarea to give a series of lectures at a convocation sponsored by the two bishops. This irregular action infuriated Bishop Demetrius of Alexanderia who called a synod of church leaders and expelled him. Origen remained in Caesarea and continued his influential writings. However, even when his own pupil Heraclas succeeded Demetrius, the action of the synod was never reversed. Though he was a man of unusually high morals, he was never able to live down the charges of heresy. This stigma remained with him even after his death. Paradoxically his writings had significant impact and remain today as some of the classic documents of the early Christian centuries. His works were as broad as the range of his knowledge and career. He wrote exegetical, critical, apologetic, dogmatic, and practical works. His famous *Against Celsus* has significance for missions in that it speaks repeatedly of the widespread growth of the church from its humble beginning.[9]

Proof of Rapid and Widespread Growth of Christians

CHAP. X

But observe what he alleges as a proof of his statement: "Christians at first were few in number, and held the same opinions; but when they grew to be a great multitude, they were divided and separated, each wishing to have his own individual party: for this was their object from the beginning." That Christians at first were few in number, in comparison with the multitudes who subsequently became Christian, is undoubted; and yet, all things considered, they were not so very few. For what stirred up the envy of the Jews against Jesus, and aroused them to conspire against Him, was the great number of those who followed Him into the wilderness,—five thousand men on one occasion, and four thousand on another, having attended Him thither, without including the women and children. For such was the charm of Jesus' words, that not only were *men* willing to follow Him to the wilderness, but *women* also, forgetting the weakness of their sex and a regard for outward propriety in thus following their Teacher into desert places. Children, too, who are altogether unaffected by such emotions, either following their parents, or perhaps attracted also by His divinity, in order that it might be implanted within them, became His followers along with their parents. But let it be granted that Christians were few in number at the beginning, how does that help to prove that Christians would be unwilling to make all men believe the doctrine of the Gospel?

CHAP. XI

He says, in addition, that "all the Christians were of one mind," not observing, even in this particular, that from the beginning there were differences of opinion among believers regarding the meaning of the books held to be divine. At all events, while the apostles were still preaching, and while eye-witnesses of (the works of) Jesus were still teaching His doctrine, there was no small discussion among the converts from Judaism regarding Gentile believers, on the point whether they ought to observe Jewish customs, or should reject the burden of clean and unclean meats, as not being obligatory on those who had abandoned their ancestral Gentile customs, and had become believers in Jesus. Nay, even in the Epistles of Paul, who was contemporary with those who had seen Jesus, certain particulars are found mentioned as having been the subject of dispute,—viz., respecting the resurrection, and whether it were already past, and the day of the Lord, whether it were nigh at hand or not. Nay, the very exhortation to "avoid profane and vain babblings, and oppositions of science falsely so called: which some professing, have erred concerning the faith," is enough to show that from the very beginning, when, as Celsus imagines, believers were few in number, there were certain doctrines interpreted in different ways.

CHAP. XII

In the next place, since he reproaches us with the existence of heresies in Christianity as being a ground of accusation against it, saying that "when Christians had greatly increased in numbers, they were divided and split up into factions, each individual desiring to have his own party"; and further, that "being thus separated through their numbers, they confute one another, still having, so to speak, one *name* in common, if indeed they still retain it. And this is the only thing which they are yet ashamed to abandon, while other matters are determined in different ways by the various sects." In reply to which, we say that heresies of different kinds have never originated from any matter in which the principle involved was not important and beneficial to human life. For since the science of medicine is useful and necessary to the human race, and many are the points of dispute in it respecting the manner of curing bodies, there are found, for this reason, numerous heresies confessedly prevailing in the science of medicine among the Greeks, and also, I suppose, among those barbarous nations who profess to employ medicine. And, again, since philosophy makes a profession of the truth, and promises a knowledge of existing things with a view to the regulation of life, and endeavours to teach what is advantageous to our race, and since the investigation of these matters is attended with great differences of opinion innumerable heresies have consequently sprung up in philosophy, some of which are more celebrated than others. Even Judaism itself afforded a pretext for the origination of heresies, in the different acceptation accorded to the writings of Moses and those of the prophets. So, then, seeing Christianity appeared an object of veneration to men, not to the more servile class alone, as Celsus supposes, but to many among the Greeks who were devoted to literary pursuits, there necessarily originated heresies,—not at all, however, as the result of faction and strife, but through the earnest desire of many literary men to become acquainted with the doctrines of Christianity. The consequence of which was, that, taking in different acceptations those discourses which were believed by all to be divine, there arose heresies, which received their names from those individuals who admired, indeed, the origin of Christianity, but who were led, in some way or other, by certain plausible reasons, to discordant views. And yet no one would act rationally in avoiding medicine because of its heresies; nor would he who aimed at that which is seemly entertain a hatred of philosophy, and adduce its many heresies as a pretext for his antipathy. And so neither are the sacred books of Moses and the prophets to be condemned on account of the heresies in Judaism.

34

"Concerning the Proper Purpose of the Preaching of the Gospel" [10] Nicholaus Ludwig Count von Zinzendorf

Introduction

Nicholaus Ludwig von Zinzendorf (1700-1760) was one of the most charismatic forerunners of the modern mission movement. The precocious Zinzendorf spent six significant years (from 1710 to 1716) at Halle under the tutelage of August Hermann Francke, the great Pietist. Here he received the inspiration which led him at the age of twenty-two to establish on his estate in Herrnhut, Germany, a revolutionary missionary community. The group was formed of refugees from Moravia and came in time to be known as the Church of the Moravian Brethren. Zinzendorf was their second bishop. He led this small band of believers to sponsor the first significant company of missionaries in the history of Protestantism. The Moravians were the model which Carey held up to his Baptist brethren, and they directly influenced John Wesley. The Moravians, therefore, were the spark which ignited the flame of the evangelistic and missionary fires which have blazed across the earth for two hundred and fifty years.[11]

Moving in the strong pietistic tradition he had received from Francke, Zinzendorf developed a theory and a methodology around which he molded the Moravian community. He was a deeply sensitive spirit, a poet and a hymn writer as well as a leader and organizer. The community of faith which he organized and shaped reflected his spirit as well as his administrative skills. It was the model from which the early leaders of the modern mission movement drew their inspiration. Zinzendorf lives today as one of the sublime figures of mission history. The following sermon furnishes insight into some of the ideas of Zinzendorf. It also reflects something of the spirit of the man behind these ideas—ideas which changed the world of his day and which strongly influenced the centuries that followed.

Concerning the Proper Purpose of the Preaching of the Gospel

Preached on the same day, September 4, 1746

TEXT: MATTHEW 22:2, and LUKE 14:17. *"The kingdom of heaven may be compared to a king who gave a marriage feast for his son;" "and at supper-time he sent his servants to say to those who had been invited, 'Come; everything is ready.' "*(LT) [12]

The words which I have just read fall of their own accord into a division which is quite natural. A marriage requires a bridegroom, a bride, and guests. The servants who are sent out to call the guests give us less cause for concern, since they, in the spiritual marriage, must necessarily belong either to the bride or to the guests.

This passage does not say how the bride is called, how the souls are called who are looked upon as members of the bride. For everyone who has read the Bible knows that the bride is not just one soul. It is said often enough that it is not one person, but rather whole multitudes which constitute the wife of the Lamb, the bride of the Lamb.

Here there is no description of how the bride, how the members of the bride are now brought together; and if we look through the whole Bible, we will hardly come across one syllable in any one of the evangelists or in any one of the letters of the apostles concerning the nature and the circumstances of the call through which the members of the bride of Jesus are brought together. On the other hand, however, we find throughout the entire Holy Scripture of the Old and New Testaments many places indicating the bridal state and its nature and also how the Saviour busies Himself with such hearts once He has them. But how He obtains them in the first place is still a mystery between them both. The whole Bible, and especially the New Testament, is full of descriptions of the calling of the guests. It is the subject which Paul treats so extensively in the Epistle to the Romans. When he comes to the preaching of the Gospel, he calls himself a herald, and says, "The people must have a preacher. How can they hear without a preacher?" (Rom. 10:14, alt.).

It is, therefore, worthwhile to speak among men concerning the subject of the bride and bridegroom, of the invitation to the marriage, and of the guests who are invited. And because the last concerns us above all else, since we have to deal with the preaching of the Gospel, I shall deal with it first.

"He sent his servants out to say to those who had been invited, 'Come, for everything is ready' " (Luke 14:17). From another evangelist I have added the construction, "He sent out at supper-time" (Luke 14:17).

It is an important matter that the Gospel may not be preached whenever it enters a person's head to do so; rather, it too has its appropriate time. "When the time had fully come" (Gal. 4:4), is a biblical expression. The Saviour makes use of these words several times, "The time is fulfilled" (e.g., Mark 1:15); thus He says, as He weeps over Jerusalem, "at this your time" (Luke 19:42, LT). This agrees with the words of the text which stand in another evangelist: "at suppertime."

My friends! We must establish this principle, that the blessed, fruitful, and almost irresistible "calling in" of many thousands of souls presupposes a little flock in the house which cleaves to the Saviour with body and soul, souls which are already there, united with the Saviour, so that one may point to these very people with the finger when one wants to invite others. It is an advantage, a blessing, a sound preaching of the Gospel, when one can say, "Come, everything is ready. I can show you the people who are already there; just come and see." This is the suppertime, when bride and bridegroom are already prepared, have already spoken with each other, have already completed their blessed engagement, and now, in order to solemnize it still more, make their appearance at a place. One perceives a people of God with whom the bridegroom concerns himself, people who glory in him, as he does in them. Thus it has come so far that the city on the hill can no longer be hidden, and it is a light which one does not put under a bushel but sets upon a candlestick. Thus a preaching of the Gospel must come out of this little flock: "Come, everything is ready; the time to come is here. Whoever comes now, comes at the right time." This is very simply that which is called preaching the Gospel.

This is nothing other than the general and earnest call to all creatures: "Come, for everything is ready."

But in order that it be even less possible to imagine that this call is not serious, (which would anyway be inappropriate to think of God), the Saviour says expressly of the kind of people who did not partake of this supper, who did not attain to salvation in this time, "They would not come" (Matt. 22:3). This cannot reasonably be said of people who were not able to come and who were not meant by the call but were called only in jest. Rather, the call must have been in earnest, if it can be said, "They would not come." "Jerusalem, Jerusalem," said the Saviour, "how often would I have gathered your children together as a hen gathers her chicks under her wings; but you would not" (Luke 13:34).

Now it is true that sometimes this is the fault of the messengers. It is the servants' failure if they do not take great care in calling the people. They selected people who did appear to them to be worthy to come to the marriage; they selected without doubt, the most distinguished, the most clever, learned, and wealthy, thinking that these are honorable and good people; as things stand in the world these days, we must call these above all. If a poor man can be saved with a fifteen-minute exhortation, the person of distinction must certainly have several weeks, and they are gladly invested in him. It is indeed a great weakness to imagine that it is of greater importance that the soul of such a person of rank is saved than that of a common and poor person. As if there were a difference among souls. The Holy Scripture has always sought to take away such distinctions from the minds of men and has shown that it is a false idea as far as the preaching of the Gospel is concerned. Therefore, Paul, in the first letter to the Corinthians, treats this topic so extensively and says finally, "I entreat you, simply look into your congregation: Where are the wise? Where are the eminent? Where are the rich?" (I Cor. 1:20, 26, alt.). Thus he demonstrates to them how to proceed in preaching the Gospel, to avoid fruitless work and threshing empty straw. The rich and the eminent are not excluded; but they do not have the least prerogative. They have no privilege before others with respect to salvation but rather a hundred difficulties which others do not have, and therefore one must not stay too long with them; one must not go to them first. And what is true about people respected for natural reasons, is equally true of those who are respected for spiritual reasons, the devout and religious men. If one would think in this case, "That is a man who serves God," (ten or twelve years ago the phrase was "a pious man"), "one whom I must indeed seek to bring to the Saviour," it could result in a great loss of time. The Saviour showed by means of a parable how the matter stands. He says to His servants, "Go out to the highways and hedges, and compel people to come in, that my house may be filled (Luke 14:23). See where you can get them, the poor, the common men who have absolutely nowhere to go; those to whom it could never occur that a lot of care be devoted to them—call them; they will come; to them you will be welcome." This being done, they brought a great number of people together, and among them there was only one who was thrown out, and this single one was without any doubt the most highly regarded person among them. For the fact that he did not want to accept a wedding garment clearly shows that he was not one of the beggars, not one of the ragged loiterers, but rather that he was well dressed. It was an old custom to give people marriage garments; also the richest and most eminent people received a festival garment when they came to a marriage. It is not possible that one of the beggar-people would have rejected the garment and would not rather have rejoiced over it. If he came half naked and a garment was given to him, he would have thanked God that he received a garment.

But one, either a naturally respected or virtuous person, full of spiritual gifts, full of aptitudes and merits, did not find it necessary to accept a garment, because he thought perhaps that his own clothes were better than those which he was to have received, and he was expelled in disgrace. And this is certainly remarkable, that among the entire great multitude of invited people only a single one was expelled, and precisely because of his unsociableness, because he did not want to look like the rest, because he would not accept the festival garment that every one of the marriage guests had received. I do not really need to explain what kind of a garment that is:

> Christ's own blood and righteousness
> Is the well-known wedding dress,
> So that we can before God stand,
> When we shall enter that joyful land.

Now concerning the preaching of the Gospel, it is clearly and fully described to us in so many places in the Bible. It treats of none other than Jesus and consists in this, that the Bridegroom be distinctly set forth to the souls.

Now what is the Bridegroom's beauty? What is His principal quality? What should be said to those who are invited? Should His glory and power and majesty be expounded to them? This is not worthwhile; they know all this already from the fact that He is the king's son.

Therefore what really matters is that His beautiful form and inner qualities be described to them. And since at all solemnities in general people have a desire to see the principal person, we must know how to identify Him so clearly that as soon as they come they can see that "this is the Bridegroom."

This happens when He is described the way He really looks. For this purpose, fathers devised very nice parables for themselves, and if they are taken as parables, they are edifying. Among others, one relates that there was a bishop named Martin who, among many other singular occurrences that happened to him, also had this experience, that Satan appeared to him in the likeness of the Saviour, but in the form of a majestic king, surrounded with heavenly glory. He said to him, "Martin, you see how I love you and what an important servant I consider you, for I personally appear to you rather than other men." Martin is said to have answered, "If you are Christ, where are your wounds?" The reply was that he did not come to him as one wounded, as one from the cross, but rather he came from heaven; he wanted to show himself to him in his glory, as he sits at the right of his Father. To this Martin answered, "You are the devil; a Saviour who is without wounds, who does not have the mark of his sufferings, I do not acknowledge." This is a fine parable and a charming example, and if the story were true, it ought to have been handled just that way. For the Saviour is never in all eternity without His sign, without His wounds: the public showing which He makes has His holy wounds as its ground. After His resurrection, when He did go through doors without a key, when He did go through the walls, "then He showed them His hands and His side. Then the disciples were glad when they saw the Lord" (John 20:20).

If we, therefore, want to invite people to the marriage, if we want to describe the Bridegroom, it must be said like this: "I decided to know nothing among you except Jesus, as He hung upon the cross (I Cor. 2:2, alt.), as He was wounded. I point you to His nail prints, to the side, to the hole which the spear pierced open in His side. Do not be unbelieving; let it be as present to you as if He had been crucified before your eyes, as if He stood there before your eyes and showed you His hands and His side. As soon as this look strikes your heart, you run to the marriage feast and then no house nor property, no husband, no wife, no child, nor anything else can keep you back anymore. You will not rest until you get to see this man. 'Such a one,' you say to all your neighbors, 'such a one is my friend. My friend looks like this.' " And this happens whenever there is preaching.

But how does it go when there is no preaching, when men have no need to preach because the Holy Spirit Himself is working? That there can be such a method cannot be doubted by any man who has read the Bible and who listens to Paul, "It pleased God to reveal His Son in Me" (Gal. 1:15 and 16), and who calls John 3 to mind, where the Saviour says, "Do listen. When a man is begotten again, it is just as if a wind should come; you do perceive that the wind is there and you hear its sound; you go out to see where the wind is coming from, and then it is already gone" (John 3:7 f., alt.). The immediate begetting of God is such a secret, sudden, unknown reality, hidden from the eyes of all mankind, that it can never be described.

Therefore, my friends, Methodism,[13] which tells people how a man is begotten again, is in danger of becoming absurd. And for this reason a man's own endeavor to explain to people how he was begotten again is also totally futile, because the man himself does not know, nor can he know, how he has begotten again. One man is begotten again in his cradle; another in the mother's womb; the third in the midst of his dead, natural condition, in his ignorance; the fourth on the occasion of great good fortune; the fifth on the occasion of a misfortune: one young, the other old; one in his last hour, the other near the very first beginning of his life. In a word, the new begetting, when the Spirit from God comes into our heart, when Jesus Christ with His five wounds is formed in us, when we are allotted to Him in heaven above—this is a divine moment.

We see this in John, who in his mother's womb was filled with the Holy Spirit; the child Jesus, who was Himself hidden in His mother's womb, formed Himself in his soul and came into such a relationship with his soul, into such a harmony, that when Mary visited Elizabeth, one fellow brother leaped to meet the other. The expression which King David, the great theologian of his time, once used—"My body and soul sing for joy to the living God (Ps. 84:2, alt.); my body and soul throb for the living God"—showed itself here already in the unborn child; John's body and soul throbbed for Him. "Why is this granted me," said Elizabeth, "that the mother of my Lord should come to me? No sooner did I see you, no sooner did I greet you, than behold, my babe leaped to greet you. And oh, blessed are you who have believed all the promises; for all will come to pass as it is promised you" (Luke 1:43 ff., alt.).

This is one instance, and there are many of the same kind. The Saviour is tied to absolutely nothing. He will not be dictated to. Each instance takes its course. The Holy Spirit portrays Jesus to souls; He preaches His wounds. To one this happens distinctly, to another indistinctly. To Saul, the persecutor, who went around and massacred people who adhered to Jesus, who for this purpose had passports and mandates with him from the high priests, to him He appeared so distinctly, to him it was so clear in his soul that the crucified Jesus of Nazareth was the Saviour that he needed no further explanation, but laid hold of it immediately. Queen Candace's treasurer was reading about a slaughtered lamb that was so happy, hearty, and willing, etc. to go to the slaughter. "Tell me," he said (it was an obscure description, a picture which required sharp eyes), "tell me, about whom does the prophet say this? About himself or about someone else?" Philip answered immediately, "I will indeed tell you about it." And he made it clear to him and explained to him with human words the language of the Holy Spirit in the heart; he spoke to him the *arrheta rhemata*, the unspeakable words (II Cor. 12:4), the words in the heart. And he catches on immediately: "Baptize me into His death and into His wounds; here I am; what is to prevent it?" (Acts 8:36, alt.).

And just for this reason we are not to be very concerned about the bride which the Holy Spirit courts in this world for Jesus Christ; the proxy-marriage in the name of Jesus Christ takes its course, and no devil can obstruct it, let him do what he will. No worldly circumstance, no absolute prohibition of the Gospel in any country, no drought and famine of the divine Word can thwart it. He is sure of His souls; they are souls which live and move and have their being in Him.

They live no longer, but rather He lives in them. At that moment they die to corruption and sinning, and continue dying, as long as man is in the body, so that the spirit is rightly set free and is not connected by the slightest filament when it is called out of the body.

And the blessed work goes on forever and remains in the Spirit's hand, in His disposition. We have no need to be anxious about it. We need not be worried how the Saviour obtains His bride. He is sure of her; He keeps her eternally, and no one will snatch her from His hand; no one dare waken nor rouse her if it does not please her. "I have promised you this, that you should be mine" (Ezek. 16:8, alt.).

But what do those people experience? Though they cannot tell the moment of their begetting, though they cannot specify the hour, how do they feel? For so many movements of grace take place which resemble each other that one would have to become converted ten times, if at every great and exceptional grace one would think, this was my conversion. Each grace, each breath of grace that comes over us is blessed and highly blessed, and the more often it comes, the more we have to thank and praise Him and the more whole we become.

But all the less can the days and hours be given. For as the wind is there one moment and then gone again, so it is too with everyone who is begotten of the Spirit. But if one asks, "How are you now?"—if one asks a person begotten of God, a person begotten of the Father of Jesus Christ, a man begotten for the bride of Jesus Christ, "How are you now? What is before your eyes? What do you see?"—the answer is, "The slaughtered sheep, Jesus Christ." He sees just this; he lives in that very thing in which all the marriage people and all the guests must live who go to the marriage feast.

The bride and those invited have one object, one beauty, one virtuousness of the Bridegroom to admire. They admire that this man, the Son of God, the Creator of the world, should have wanted to die on the cross for His poor human beings, that He obtained His bride with His blood, that He brought back His fallen bride, His fallen wife, His adulteress and on the cross saved this His property, His possession, His creature as a spoil. This is also the impression which the bride-hearts have, which the souls have who throughout their whole life know nothing and want to know nothing other than their Bridegroom.

Therefore it would be a great mistake for anyone to suppose that the bride-hearts who day and night live, eat, drink, sleep, and get up with the Saviour would probably want to have something else; that they would not be taken up with His cross and suffering, torment and merit, and similar catechism concerns; rather that they would maintain such a familiarity with the angels and cherubim, with heaven and the heavenly Jerusalem, associate with them, and have visions of spirits or deep insights into the Revelation of John. But no, this is not at all the case. An invited guest may be more learned, wiser, and more experienced and have a deeper insight into all truths than many a heart that is bound to the Saviour in the closest manner. A soul most tenderly in love with the Saviour may be ignorant of a hundred truths and only concentrate most simply on Jesus' wounds and death. Oh, how ardently this soul mediates on this part of the body, which on the day of His coming will be the sign of the Son of Man, the hole in His side, His heart, out of which flowed blood and water. This is its wisdom, its knowledge, which reflects the soul like a mirror:

> O sacred head, now wounded,
> With grief and shame weighed down,
> Now scornfully surrounded
> With thorns thine only crown!
> O sacred head what glory,
> What bliss 'til now was thine.
> Yet though despised and gory,
> I joy to call thee mine.

This is the Bridegroom's form which so captivates the soul's heart that it has no time left to think of anything else; and the more the soul falls in love with this and becomes involved, the blinder it becomes to other things, to the glories of the world. It does not become hostile to them, nor does it censure them much; but rather it does not have very much to do with them. It does not think about this miserable life, because God delights its heart.

Therefore there is no known difference, according to Scripture, between the bride and those who are invited, neither in object nor feeling nor in the kind of conversation. The only difference is that the call to be the bride of Jesus Christ, to be the first-born, one engaged to the Lamb, one who knows nothing but Him and has not climbed higher than into the wounds and must first be led by the hand to everything else that he should or should not think (as Paul says, "When you should think this way or that, then God will certainly reveal it to you" [Phil. 3:15, alt.])—the only difference is that this call happens immediately and with less observance than does the ordinary conversion. The structuring, creation and preservation of such simple hearts of the Saviour is the immediate work of the Holy Spirit and indeed His alone.

But there are still millions of souls who come to participation in this salvation who are at the marriage and are also joyful, who draw a conclusion about the future from the present blessedness, and who join the supper as invited guests; and they are always called through the preaching of the Gospel.

Therefore there is no ground to debate whether God performs the work of conversion in a soul Himself or whether He makes use of men to this end. Certainly He is in need of no one, for He Himself can draw, can beget, can bring forth, through His Spirit all the souls whom He wants to give to His Son, whom He will marry to Him at the time when He will be the Consecrator, when the creature shall marry the Creator. And this He actually does. But these are not enough; they do not make a *numerus clausus,* a number which may not be exceeded. Rather, the number is innumerable; the multitudes who through the Gospel of the merits and death of Jesus receive the invitation to go to the marriage will exceed all thought. "Compel people to come in, that my house may be filled" (Luke 14:23), that innumerable more may share my salvation; "Come, O blessed of my Father, inherit the kingdom prepared for you," etc. (Matt. 25:34).

This is an admirable thing, to know that our Lord, as rich and great and generous as He is, nevertheless is not satisfied that He has His assured reward, the souls of whom He is sure; but, having already been crucified and dead, He wants to be looked at and to manifest Himself as the Saviour of all men. "Go into all the world and preach the gospel to the whole creation" (Mark 16:15); whoever will now believe you, whoever will hold to me, whomever I will please, whoever will come to love me, he shall be saved; he shall be delivered from his present evil world and from the wrath to come and shall enter into my rest.

This then is the ground and purpose of the preaching of the Gospel plain and clear.

Now when the souls who love the Lamb as the bride loves the

Bridegroom hear that there is preaching (although they do not need to be called, to have the Lamb painted before them, for they live and move in Him; they always have Him before their eyes, as David says, "I keep the Lord always before me" [Ps. 16:8]), then they rejoice with all their hearts when the Gospel is preached; they look forward to the guests, and they are as embarrassed as the Bridegroom if there might be only a few, for they want the house to be full.

And this is a blessed combination to see in one gathering such a crowd of souls in love with the Saviour, together with a number of guests, who will have supper together and together will greet the holy wounds. And may the Saviour also in this place present more living examples of this, as time passes, for his wounds' sake!

35

"The Star in the East" [14]
Claudius Buchanan

Introduction

Claudius Buchanan, a native of Scotland, was one of the chaplains of the East India Company. The controversial nature of his sermon, "The Star in the East," must be seen against the background of the East India Company's selfish opposition to missions in India. Buchanan preached his famous sermon while on a visit to England in 1809. It was published the same year and immediately became a revolutionary tract of the times. It shook the complacency of the British church and contributed significantly toward the reversal of the policy of the East India Company. It also had a wide circulation and influence in America. New American mission societies emerged partly because of its influence. It was a major factor in the decision of Judson to become a missionary.[15]

The Star in the East

"For we have seen his star in the east, and are come to worship him."—Matt. 2:2.

When, in the fulness of time, the Son of God came down from heaven to take our nature upon him, many circumstances concurred to celebrate the event, and to render it an illustratious epoch in the history of the world. It pleased the Divine Wisdom that the manifestation of the deity should be distinguished by a suitable glory; and this was done by the ministry of angels, by the ministry of men, and by the ministry of nature itself.

First. This was done by the ministry of angels; for an angel announced to the shepherds "the glad tidings of great joy which should be to all people"; and a multitude of the heavenly host sang "Glory to God in the highest, on earth, peace, good will toward men."

Secondly. It was done by the ministry of men; for illustrious persons, divinely directed, came from a far country, to offer gifts and to do honor to the new-born King.

Thirdly. It was done by the ministry of nature. Nature herself was commanded to bear witness to the presence of the God of nature. A star, or divine light, pointed out significantly from heaven the spot upon earth where the Savior was born.

Thus, I say, it pleased the Divine Wisdom by an assemblage of heavenly testimonies to glorify the incarnation of the Son of God.

All these testimonies were appropriate; but the journey of the eastern sages had in it a peculiar fitness. We can hardly imagine a more natural mode of honoring the event than this, that illustrious persons should proceed from a far country to visit the child which was born Savior of the world. They came, as it were, in the name of the Gentiles, to acknowledge the heavenly gift, and to bear their testimony against the nation which rejected it. They came as the representatives of the whole heathen world; not only of the heathens of the East, but also of the heathens of the West, from whom we are descended. In the name of the whole world, lying "in darkness, and in the shadow of death," they came inquiring for that light which they had heard was to visit them in the fulness of time. "And the star which they saw in the East went before them, till it came and stood over where the young Child was. And when they were come into the house, they fell down and worshiped him; and when they had opened their treasures, they presented unto him gifts, gold, and frankincense, and myrrh"; and they departed into their own country.

Do you ask how the star of Christ was understood in the East? or, why Providence ordained that peculiar mode of intimation?

Christ was foretold in old prophecy, under the name of the "star that should arise out of Jacob"; and the rise of the star of Jacob was notified to the world by the appearance of an actual star.

We learn from authentic Roman history, that there prevailed "in the East," a constant expectation of a prince, who should rise out of Judea and rule the world. That such an expectation did exist, has been confirmed by the ancient writings of India. Whence, then, arose this extraordinary expectation, for it was found also in the sibylline books of Rome?

The Jewish expectation of the Messiah had pervaded the East long before the period of his appearance. The Jews are called by their own prophet the "expecting people" (as it may be translated, and as some of the Jews of the East translate it), the "people are looking for and expecting One to come." Wherever, then, the ten tribes were carried throughout the East, they carried with them their expectation. And they carried also the prophecies on which their expectation was founded. Now, one of the clearest of these prophecies runs in these words: "There shall come a star out of Jacob." And as in the whole dispensation concerning the Messiah, there is a wonderful fitness between the words of prophecy and the person spoken of, so it pleased the Divine Wisdom that the rise of the star in Jacob should be announced to the world by the appearance of an actual star (for by what other means could the great event be more significantly communicated to the remote parts of the earth?), and this actual star, in itself a proper emblem of that "Light which was to lighten the Gentiles," conducted them to him who was called in a figure the star of Jacob, and the "glory of his people Israel"; and who hath said of himself (Rev. 22:16), "I, Jesus, am the bright and morning star."

But, again, why was the East thus honored? Why was the East, and not the West, the scene of these transactions? The East was the scene of the first revelation of God. The fountains of inspiration were first opened in the East. And, after the flood, the first family of the new world was planted in the East; I mean the east, in relation to Judea. Besides, millions of the human race inhabit that portion of the globe. The chief population of the world is in these regions. And in the middle of them the star of Christ first appeared. And, led by it, the wise men passed through many nations, tongues, and kindreds, before they arrived at Judea in the west; bearing tidings to the world that the Light was come, that the "Desire of all Nations" was come. Even to Jerusalem herself they brought the first intimation that her long-expected Messiah was come.

Now, my brethren, as the East was honored in the first age, in thus pointing out the Messiah to the world, so now again, after a long interval of darkness, it is bearing witness to the truth of his religion; not indeed by the shining of a star, but by affording luminous evidence of the divine origin of the Christian faith. It affords evidence, not only of the general truth of its history, but of its peculiar doctrines; and not of its doctrines merely, but of the divine power of these doctrines in convincing the understandings and converting the hearts of men. And in this sense it is that "we have seen his star in the East, and are come to worship him."

And when these evidences shall have been laid before you, you will see that the time is come for diffusing his religion throughout the world; you will "offer gifts" in his name for the promotion of the work; and you will offer up prayers in its behalf, "that God would be pleased to make his ways known, his saving health unto all nations."

. . . .

What conclusion, then, shall we draw from these facts? It is this: That the time for diffusing our religion in the East is come. We shall notice some other particulars which encourage us to think that the time is come.

1. The minds of men seem everywhere to be impressed with the duty of making the attempt. Nearly fifteen years have elapsed since it began, and their ardor is not abated. On the contrary, they gather strength as they proceed; new instruments are found, and liberal contributions are made by the people. Indeed, the consciences of men seem to bear witness that the work is of God.

The rapid success of this undertaking must appear almost incredible to those who are not acquainted with the fact. Translations of the Scriptures are carried on, not only in the languages of India, Persia and Arabia, but in those also of Burmah and China. Mount Caucasus, in the interior of Asia, is another center of translation for the East, particularly for the numerous nations of the Tartar race. The Scriptures are preparing for the Malayan isles, and for the isles of the Pacific sea. The great continent of Africa has become the scene of different missions and translations. North and South America are sending forth the Scriptures. They are sent to the uttermost parts of the earth. They have been sent to Greenland, Labrador and Australasia. We might almost say, "There is no speech nor language where their voice is not heard."

And this spirit, for the diffusion of the truth, is not confined to Britain. It is found among good men of every Christian nation. Perhaps on this day prayers are offered up in behalf of the work, in Europe, Asia, Africa, and America. We are encouraged, then, to believe that the time is come, in the first place, by the consent of good men. When I say good men, I mean religious and devout men, whose minds are not entirely occupied with the politics and affairs of this world, but who are "looking for the consolation of Israel"—as it is expressed in these words, "Thy kingdom come."

2. Another circumstance indicating that the time is at hand, is the general contemplation of the prophecies. The prophecies of Scripture are at this time pondered as seriously in Asia as in Europe. Even the Jews in the East begin to study the oracles of their prophet Isaiah. And what is more important, the prophecies begin to be published among heathen nations; and we may expect that every nation will soon be able to read the divine decree concerning itself.

3. The Holy Scriptures are translating into various languages. When the gospel was first to be preached to all nations it was necessary to give a diversity of tongues—a tongue for each nation; and this was done by the divine power. But in this second promulgation, as it were, of the gospel, the work will probably be carried on by a diversity of translations, a diversity of Scriptures; a translation for each nation. Instead of the gift of tongues, God, by his providence, is giving to mankind a gift of Scriptures.

4. Another circumstance, which seems to testify that this work is of God, is the commotion in the bands of infidelity against it. "Herod is troubled, and all Jerusalem with him." A spirit hath issued from the mouth of infidelity, which rageth against him whose star appeared in the East, and would destroy the work in its infancy. It rageth not against the Romish Church in the East, though that be Christian; nor against the Armenian church in the East, though that be Christian; nor against the Greek church in the East, though that be Christian;

but it rageth against the religion of the New Testament, that vital religion which aims at the conversion of the hearts of men.

Our Savior hath said, "The gospel shall be published among all nations." But these resist the divine Word and say it cannot be published in all nations. Our Lord hath said, "Go ye into all the world, and preach the gospel to every creature." But these allege that the gospel cannot be preached to every creature, for that "the bond of superstition is too strong, or that the influence of Christianity is too weak."

These are unguarded words, and ought not to be heard in a Christian country. These are presumptuous words, arraigning the dispensation of the Most High. Such words as these were once spoken by the philosophy of Greece and Rome, but the gospel prevailed, and first erected its dominion among them. In process of time the barbarous nations of Europe yielded to its sway, of which we are evidences at this day. And the nations of Asia will yield to the same power, and the truth will prevail, and the gospel shall be preached over the whole world.

5. The last circumstance which we shall mention, as indicating that the period is come for diffusing the light of revelation, is the revolution of nations, and "the signs of the times."

Men of serious minds, who are erudite in Holy Scripture, and in the history of the world, look forward to great events. They judge of the future from the past. They have seen great events—events which, twenty years ago, would have appeared as incredible as the conversion of the whole world to Christianity.

At no former period have the judgments of heaven been so evidently directed against the nations which are called Christian as at this day. It is manifest that God hath a controversy with his people, whatever be the cause. The heathen world enjoys a comparative tranquillity. But Christian nations are visited in quick succession by his awful judgments. What, then, is the cause of the judgments of God on his Christian people?

If we believe the declarations of God, in his holy Word, we shall ascribe the judgment of Christian nations, at this day, to their rejecting so generally the testimony of Christ.

. . . .

Let us then weigh well what it is which, in the present circumstances of the world, saves this nation. If it be the divine pleasure to save us, while other nations are destroyed, it cannot be on account of the greatness of our empire, or of our dominion by sea, or of our extended commerce. For why should the moral Governor of the world respect such circumstances as these? But if we are spared it will be, we believe, on account of our maintaining the pure religion of Christ as the religion of our land, and of our promoting the knowledge of that religion, and of the blessed principles which accompany it throughout the rest of the world. This may be a consideration worthy of divine regard. And this, though it be no pledge of our duration, is the chief assurance of our perpetuity. On this chiefly (viz., our being an instrument of good to the world) must depend our hope of surviving the shocks and convulsions which are now overwhelming the other nations of Europe.

. . . .

Behold, then, my brethren, the great undertaking for the promotion of which you are now assembled. If it were in the power of this assembly to diffuse the blessings of religion over the whole world, would it not be done? Would not all nations be blessed? You perceive that some take a lively interest in this subject, while others are less concerned. What is the reason of this difference? It is this: Every man who hath felt the influence of religion on his own heart will desire to extend the blessings to the rest of mankind; and no one who hath lived without a concern about religion will be solicitous to communicate to others a gift which he values not himself. At the same time, perhaps, he is not willing to be thought hostile to the work. But there is no neutrality here. "He that is not with Christ" in maintaining his kingdom on earth "is against him." And so it appeareth to "God, who searcheth the heart." Every one of us is now acting a part in regard to this matter, for which we must give an account hereafter. There is no one, however peculiar he may reckon his situation or circumstances, who is exempted from this responsibility. For this is the criterion of obedience in the sight of God, even our conduct is receiving or rejecting the "record which God hath given of his Son." And no man "receiveth this record" in sincerity and truth, who will not desire to make it known to others. You have heard of the conversion of Mahometans and Hindoos. Yes, our Lord hath said, "Many shall come from the east and from west, and shall sit down with Abraham, and Isaac, and

Jacob, in the kingdom of heaven, but the children of the kingdom shall be cast out."

Begin, then, at this time, the solemn inquiry, not merely into the general truth of Christ's religion, but into its divine and converting power. You observe that in this discourse I have distinguished between the name of Christianity and the thing. For it seems there are some who have departed from the ancient principles of our reformation, who admit the existence of the Spirit of God, but deny his influence, who agree not with the Apostle Paul that the "gospel cometh to some in word only," and to others in power, and in the Holy Ghost and in much assurance, and who seem to forget what our Savior hath said of the "broad road" and the "narrow way." Begin then, the important inquiry, for "the time is short," and this question will soon be brought to issue before an assembled world. In the meantime I shall offer to you my testimony on this subject.

The operation of the grace of God, in "renewing a right spirit within us" (Ps. 51) is a doctrine professed by the whole faithful church of Christ militant here on earth. The great Author of our religion hath himself delivered the doctrine in the most solemn manner to the world: "Verily, verily, I say unto you, except a man be born again, he cannot see the kingdom of God." Verily, verily, it is an undoubted truth, an unchangeable principle of the heavenly dispensation, that except a man be renewed in mind by the Spirit of God, he shall not have the power even to see or behold the kingdom of God. What though many in our day deny this doctrine? A whole nation denied a doctrine greater, if possible, than this. The very name and religion of Christ have been denied in our time. But if our Savior hath declared any one doctrine of the gospel more clearly than another, it is this of a spiritual conversion; and the demonstration of its truth is found in all lands where his gospel is known. Christians, differing in almost everything else, agree in this. Differing in language, customs, color and in country; differing in forms of worship and church government, in external rights and internal order, they yet agree in the doctrine of a change of heart, through faith in Christ, for this hath been the grand characteristic of Christ's religion among all nations, tongues, and kindreds, where the gospel hath been preached through all ages down to this day. This is, in fact, that which distinguishes the religion of God in Asia, from the religions of men. In every part of the earth where I myself have been this doctrine is proclaimed, as the hope of the sinner and the glory of the Savior. And again, in every place it is opposed, in a greater or less degree, by the same evil passions of the human heart. In rude nations, the same arguments are brought against it, in substance, which are used here in a learned country. Among ignorant nations a term of reproach is attached to serious piety, even as it is here among a refined people; thereby proving what our Lord hath taught—that the superior goodness inculcated by his gospel would not be agreeable to all men; and that some "would revile and speak evil of his disciples, for righteousness' sake"—thereby proving what the Apostle Paul hath taught, that "the cross of Christ is an offence" to the natural pride of the human heart; that "the carnal mind is enmity against God"; and that "the natural man receiveth not the things of the spirit of God, because they are spiritually discerned."

I have thought it right, my brethren, to deliver to you my testimony at this time; to assure you that the gospel which begins to enlighten the East, is not "another gospel," as the Apostle speaks, but the same as your own. There is one sun; there is one gospel. "There is one Lord, one faith, one baptism," and there is one judgment. May we be all prepared to give our answer on that day!

My brethren, you are now invited to contribute some aid toward the extension of the religion of Christ. You are now called on to give your testimony to its truth. You are now, as it were, to present "your gifts" before him who was born Savior of the world; and to send back those "glad tidings" to the East, which the East once sent to you, namely, that the light is come, that "the desire of all nations is come." Let every one who prays with his lips, "Thy kingdom come," prove to himself at this time his own sincerity, that he really desires in his heart that the kingdom of Christ should come. Blessed is the man who accounts it not only a duty, but a privilege, and so you will account it hereafter, when you shall behold all nations assembled before the judgment seat of Christ. You will then reflect with joy that you are enabled, at this time, "to confess his name before men," and to afford some aid for the "increase of his government" and glory upon earth. And let everyone who lends this aid accompany it with prayer, that the act may be blessed to himself in awakening his mind more fully to the unutterable importance of the everlasting gospel.

36

"Vindication of Missions in India" [16]
Alexander Duff

Introduction

Alexander Duff (1806-1878), a native of Scotland, was the pioneer missionary of the Church of Scotland. He went to India in 1829 and began a type of educational missions which became the model for the Christian mission in India and elsewhere. He was forced to leave India in 1834 because of poor health, and he gave the next few years to raising the missionary consciousness of the Church of Scotland. Upon his return to India in 1840, he resumed the leadership of the educational work he had begun earlier, edited the *Calcutta Review*, and developed new schools. On his second furlough, beginning in 1850, he was active in promoting missions in the English-speaking world. His tours over Britain and in America greatly stirred the Christian community for the cause of missions. In 1855 he returned to India where he labored with distinction until 1863.[17]

Upon Duff's return to Scotland he became the leading figure in the Foreign Mission Committee of the Free Church. He also distinguished himself by becoming the first full professor of missions, in Edinburgh in 1867. Although he is best known as an educational missionary and missionary statesman, he was an extremely articulate preacher. The following sermon, preached at Exeter Hall in 1837 on the anniversary of the Church of Scotland's Foreign Missions, is a classic example of his preaching skill. To read this sermon is to realize why he stirred his audiences so deeply and why he was able to promote the mission cause so effectively.[18]

Vindication of Missions in India

The motion in my hand referring to an increase of liberality and of laborers, I shall at once proceed to the subject, by asking, as in the sight of the Omniscient God, Can it be alleged or pretended that all Christians at present give what they really can? Or, that all have gone forth to the field of labor who are really qualified?

I pause for a reply. But, if things greatly change not from what they are, I may pause forever. Look at men's acts, and not at their words; for I am wearied and disgusted into very loathing at "great swelling words," which boil and bubble into foam and froth on the bosom of an impetuous torrent of oratory, and then burst into airy nothingness. Look at men's acts, and not at their great, swelling words; and tell me, What language do they speak?

Is it in very deed a thing so mighty for one of your merchant princes to rise up on this platform, and proclaim his intense anxiety that contributions should be liberal; and then stimulate those around him by the noble example of embodying his irrepressible anxiety in the magnificent donation of 10*s*, 20*s*, or 50*s!* when, at the very moment, without curtailing any of the real necessaries of life—without even abridging any one of its fictitious comforts or luxuries—he might readily consecrate his hundreds or thousands, to be restored more than a hundredfold on the great day of final recompense? And call you this an act of such prodigious munificence, that it must elicit the shouts and the pæans of an entranced multitude? Call you this an act of such thrilling disinterestedness, that it must pierce into hearts otherwise hermetically sealed against the imploring cries of suffering humanity? Call you this an act of self-sacrificing generosity, that it must be registered for a memorial in the Book of God's remembrance, with the same stamp of divine approbation as that bestowed on the poor widow in the gospel, who, though she gave but little, gave her ALL?

And is it in very deed a thing so mighty for a Christian pastor, whether bishop, priest, or deacon, or any minister of a church, to abandon for a season his routine of duty, and once in the year to come up, either to regale, or to be regaled, with the incense of human applause in this great metropolis—the emporium of the world's commerce—the seat of the world's mightiest empire—and the general rendezvous of men and things unparalleled in all the world besides?

Is it a thing so mighty for any one of these to stand up on this platform, and call on assembled thousands to rise to their true elevation, and acquit themselves like men in the cause of him who rides on the whirlwind and directs the storm? And, dismissing all ordinary forms and figures of speech as tame and inadequate, is it an act so heroic to stand on this platform, and break forth into apostrophes, which ring with the din of arms and shout of battle? And is it an act so heroic, at the safe distance of ten thousand miles, courageously to summon the gates of Pekin to lift up their heads, and its barricades and ramparts to rend asunder at the presence of the heralds of salvation? and, impersonify the Celestial Empire herself, boldly invoke her to send up without delay her hundreds of millions to the House of the Lord, exalted above the hills, and place her imperial crown on the head of him on whose head shall be all the crowns of the earth, and the diadem of the universe? Or is it an act of spiritual prowess so mighty, for one who never joined in the conflict, to stand up on this platform and rehearse the battles which have been fought in the missionary field, the victories which have been obtained, and the trophies which have been won? Is it an achievement of never-dying fame, to burst into rapture at the unrivaled honor of those brave veterans, who have already laid down their lives in storming the citadels of heathenism?

Hark! Here are a few blasts from a trumpet which has often pealed at our great anniversaries: "The Missionary's Life! Ah, an archangel would come down from the throne, if he might, and feel himself honored to give up the felicities of heaven for a season for the toils of a missionary's life! The Missionary's Work! Ah, the work of a minister at home, as compared with that of a missionary, is but as the lighting of a parish lamp, to the causing the sun to rise upon an empire that is yet in darkness! The Missionary's Grave! Ah, the missionary's grave is far more honorable than the minister's pulpit!"

After such outpourings of fervent zeal and burning admiration of valor, would you not expect that the limits of a kingdom were too circumscribed for the range of spirits so chivalrous? Would you not expect that intervening oceans and continents could oppose no barrier to their resistless career? Would you not expect that, as chieftains at the head of a noble army, numerous as the phalanxes which erewhile flew from tilt and tournament to glitter in the sunshine of the Holy Land, they should no more be heard of till they made known their presence by the terror of their power in shattering to atoms the towering walls of China, and hoisting in triumph the banners of the cross over the captured mosques of Araby and prostrate pagodas of India?

Alas! alas! what shall we say, when the thunder of heroism, which reverberates so sublimely over our heads from year to year in Exeter Hall, is found in changeless succession to die away in fainter and yet fainter echoes among the luxurious mansions, the snug dwellings, and goodly parsonages of Old England? Listen to the high-sounding words of the mightiest of our anniversary thunderers on this platform, and would ye not vow that they were heroes with whom the post of honor was the post of danger? Look at the astounding contrast in their practice, and will not your cheeks redden with the crimson flush of shame, to find that they are cowards, with whom the post of honor is, after all, the post of safety? And is this the way to wake the long-slumbering spirit of devotedness throughout the land? Is this the kind of call which will rouse the dormant energies of a sluggish church? Is this the kind of summons which will cause a rush of champions into the field of danger and of death? Is this the kind of example, which will stimulate a thousand Gutzlaffs to brave the horrors of a barbarous shore, and incite thousands of martyrs, and of Careys, and of Morrisons, to arm themselves on the consecrated spots where these foremost warriors fell?

I know not what the sentiments of this great audience may be on a subject so momentous; but, as for myself, I cannot, at whatever risk of offense to friends and of ribaldry from enemies—I cannot, without treason to my God and Savior—I cannot but give vent to the overpowering emotions of my own heart, when, in the face of England, Scotland, and Ireland, I exclaim: "Oh that my head were waters, and mine eyes were a fountain of tears, that I could weep over the fatal, the disastrous inconsistencies, of many of the most renowned of the leaders of the people!"

What, then, is to be done? When are the gigantic evils complained of to be efficiently remedied? Never! never! till the leading members of our churches be shamed out of their lavish extravagance, in conforming to the fashion of a world which is soon to pass away, and out of their close-fisted penuriousness as regards all claims which concern the eternal destinies of their fellows. Never! never! till the angels of our churches be shamed out of their sloth. For, rest assured, that people will get weary of the sound of the demand, "Give, give," which is eternally reiterated in their ears, when those who make it so seldom give, or, what is the same thing, give in such scanty driblets, that it seems a mockery of their own expostulations, and of the sound of command, "Go, go," when those who make it are themselves so seldom found willing to go!

How, then, is the remedy to be effected? Not, believe me, by periodical showers of words, however copious, which fall like snowflakes in the river—a moment white, then gone for ever! No! But by thousands of deeds, which shall cause the very scoffer to wonder, even if he should wonder and perish—deeds which shall kindle into a blaze the smouldering embers of Christian love; deeds which shall revive the days of primitive devotedness when men valiant for the truth despised earthly riches and conquered through sufferings, not counting their lives dear unto the death.

Show me your wealthy citizen, who makes a loud profession of the name of Christ, coming forth, not with niggardly hand doling out a miserable paltry pittance from his superabounding storehouse. Show me him ready to give proof of the sincerity of his profession, by casting down the half of his goods at the feet of Jesus for the poor and perishing; and, if there remain other claims uncanceled from former negligence, ready to requite the obligation fourfold. Show me him striving to emulate the Hebrew monarch, who burned with desire to build a temple to Jehovah, the God of Israel, and who, in the full ardor of his zeal and the rushing of the tide of gratitude, at once proceeded from desire to action; and he opened his ample treasury, and poured forth of its gold, and silver, and iron, and brass, and onyx-stones, and glittering stones, and all manner of precious stones, to be employed in erecting and adorning the goodly edifice: and, fired with the forth-putting of his own generosity, and borne away with the glare of his own holy enthusiasm, he communicated the sacred impulse to the hosts of his people, when, with the confident boldness of one who had himself made ample sacrifices, he cried out in their hearing, "And who then is willing to consecrate his service this day unto the Lord?" And may I not now appeal to you, as men and as Christians, whether self-sacrificing examples of this description would not do a hundred times more to melt down the frozen hearts of an age of superficial, fashionable evangelism, than a thousand sermons in our pulpits, and a thousand speeches from our platforms?

Again, show me the Christian men, who, unlike the archangels, who cannot leave their thrones, may, if they will, relinquish, in a single hour, all their stations of dignity, all their offices of State, and all their high temporal prerogatives. Show me the Christian men, the praises of whose condition resound through the annals of literature, ready to go forth, and on an errand of salvation ready to bend their lofty intellects to the capacities of the poor and illiterate. Show me the men, the fame of whose sacred eloquence never fails to attract overwhelming crowds of eager listeners, ready to go forth and preach the unsearchable riches of Christ, though it might be in broken accents and a stammering tongue. Show me the men, the skill of whose statesmanship calls forth the plaudits of admiring senates, ready to go forth on the godlike embassy of causing the Indian, and the Negro, and the rude barbarian, to know the divine and glorious conquest once achieved on Calvary. Show me the men whose brows are encircled with the mitre or the coronet, ready to cast both down at their Master's feet, and go forth into heathen lands, prepared to suffer and prepared to die, and in dying earn to themselves the nobler crown of martyrdom. Show me one and all of our loud-talking professors, from the peer of the realm down to the humblest pastor or member of a flock, not satisfied with reducing their services into the wretched inanity of an occasional sermon, or a speech easily pronounced and calling for no sacrifice. Show me one and all of these, joyfully prepared to respond to their Master's summons. And when the loud cry is raised, "Who will march to the battle-field? Who will go up to the help of the Lord against the mighty?" let us hear the prompt and eager reply from a thousand voices, "Lord, here am I! send me." And I appeal to you, as men and as Christians, whether examples like these of self-devotedness would not do a hundred times more to stir up the spirit of apostles and martyrs, which has been allowed to slumber for ages in their tombs, than thousands of sermons and thousands of speeches, though delivered in higher strains than ever angel sang.

But I shall be told that I am now trespassing beyond the bounds of reason and sobriety; yea, that I am soaring on waxen wings into the regions of wildest utopianism. "What!"—it will be said, and that too by numbers who make flaming professions of the name of Christ— "what! philosophers, and pulpit orators, and statesmen, and lords spiritual and temporal, who reckon it no small stretch of magnanimity and condescension to take missionaries, who theoretically constitute the highest but practically the lowest and most-despised caste of Christian pastors, under the ample shield of their patronage and protection!— what! expect them to descend from their eminences of honor, and go forth themselves, content with the humble fare, and arrayed in the humble attire of self-denying missionaries? Is not this the very climax of religious raving?"

And is it really so? Has it really come to this, among the thousands who bend the knee to the name of Jesus, that the very proposal that they should, one and all of them, be ready to imitate their Lord and Master, must be unceremoniously classed in the category of lunacy? And are we really bent on bringing heaven down to earth, instead of exalting earth to heaven? Are we in right earnest resolved to adjust the divine standard of what ought to be, by the human standard of what is? Do I now stand in an assembly of professing Christians? Well, *Who is this that cometh from Edom with dyed garments from Bozra?* It is *the Man, who is Jehovah's Fellow!* it *is Immanuel, God with us!* But who can portray the underived, the incomparable excellencies of him, in *whom dwelt all the fullness of the Godhead bodily?*

In this contemplation, we are at once lost in an unmeasurable ocean of overpowering glory. Imagination is bewildering—language fails. Go, take a survey of the earth on which we dwell; collect every object and every quality which has been pronounced fair, sweet, or lovely; combine these into one resplendent orb of beauty. Then leave the bounds of the earth; wing your flight through the fields of immensity; in your progress collect what is fair and lovely in every world, what is bright and dazzling in every sun; combine these into other orbs of surpassing brightness, and thus continue to swell the number of magnificent aggregates, till the whole immense extent of creation is exhausted. And after having united these myriads of bright orbs into one glorious constellation, combining in itself the concentrated beauty and loveliness of the whole created universe, go and compare an atom to a world—a drop to the ocean—the twinkling of a taper to the full blaze of the noon tide sun; and then may you compare even this all-comprehending constellation of beauty and loveliness with the boundless, the ineffable beauty and excellence of him, who *is the brightness of his Father's glory,* who is *God over all, blessed for ever.* And yet wonder, O heavens, and rejoice, O earth! this great and mighty and glorious Being did for our sakes condescend to veil his glory and appear on earth as *a man of sorrows, whose visage was so marred more than any man's, and his form more than the sons of men.* Oh, is not this LOVE!—self-sacrificing love! love, that is *higher than the heights above, deeper than the depths beneath?* Oh, is not this condescension—self-sacrificing condescension—condescension without a parallel and without a name? *God manifest in the flesh?* God manifest in the flesh, for the redemption of a rebel race! Oh, is not this the wonder of a world? And in view of love so ineffable, and condescension so unfathomable, tell me, oh, tell me, if it would seem aught so strange—I will not say in the eye of poor, dim, beclouded humanity—but in the eye of that celestial hierarchy which caused heaven's arches to ring with anthems of adoring wonder when they beheld the brightness of the Father's glory go forth eclipsed mysteriously to sojourn on earth and tread the wine-press alone, red in his apparel and his garments dyed in blood—tell me, oh, tell me, if in their cloudless vision it would seem aught so marvelous, so passing strange, did they behold the greatest and the mightiest of a guilty race, redeemed themselves at so great a price, cheerfully prepared to relinquish their highest honors and fairest possessions, their loveliest academic bowers and stateliest palaces; yea, did they behold royalty itself retire, and cast aside its robes of purple, its scepter and its diadem, and issue forth in the footsteps of the divine Redeemer into the waste, howling wilderness of sin, to seek and to save them that are lost.

Ye groveling sons of earth! call this fanaticism if you will. Brand it as wild enthusiasm. I care not for the verdict. From you I appeal to the glorious sons of light, and ask, "Was not this, in principle, the very enthusiasm of patriarchs, who rejoiced to see the day of Christ afar off, and were glad? Was not this the enthusiasm of prophets, whose harps, inspired by the mighty theme, were raised into strains of more than earthly grandeur? Was not this the enthusiasm of angels, who made the plains of Bethlehem ring with the jubilee of peace on earth and good will to the children of men? Was not this the enthusiasm of apostles and martyrs, who gloried in the flames of the funeral pile as their most illustrious apparel? Was not this the enthusiasm (with reverence be it spoken) of the eternal Son of God himself, when he came forth travailing in the greatness of his strength to endure the agony of bloody sweat?"

And if this be enthusiasm, which is kindled by no earthly fire, and which, when once kindled, burns without being consumed, how must the hopes of the church lie sleeping in the tomb, where it does not exist! Oh, until a larger measure of this divine enthusiasm be diffused through the churches of Christendom, never, never, need we expect to realize the reign of millennial glory, when all nature shall once more be seen glorying in the first bloom of Eden—where one bond shall unite, and one feeling animate, all nations—where all kindreds, and tribes, and tongues, and people shall combine in one song, one universal shout of grateful *Hallelujah unto him that sitteth upon the throne, and unto the Lamb for ever and ever.*

37

The Evangelization of the World in this Generation[19]
John R. Mott

Introduction

John Raleigh Mott (1865-1955), perhaps the greatest missionary statesman of modern times, had a remarkable life which spanned the last half of the nineteenth century and the first half of the twentieth century. A native of Iowa, he early became a national intercollegiate secretary for the YMCA, which organization he served in a number of capacities for sixty years. At the Mt. Hermon Student Conference in 1886, he was influenced by the great D. L. Moody and became one of the first hundred to sign the declaration for missionary service of the Student Volunteer Movement. Mott served as chairman of the continuing organization until 1920. In 1895 he founded the World Student Christian Federation, became its general secretary, and served as its chairman until 1929. He had the distinction of chairing the first three great world missionary conferences of the twentieth century: Edinburgh, 1910; Jerusalem, 1928; Madras, 1938. He was chairman of the Continuation Committee of the Edinburgh Conference and of the International Missionary Council.[20]

Mott was a man of enormous spiritual stature and unusual gifts. He was both a powerful evangelist and a keen organizer and administrator. He was a gifted speaker, and his leadership ability was rare. An indefatigable worker, his winsome spirit added grace to all he did. He wrote a number of books, mostly related to mission work. A missionary statesman extraordinary, one of the things for which he is best remembered was his burning passion to evangelize the world in his generation. The following chapter from his book on the subject reveals something of the ideas and the spirit that made the man.[21]

The Obligation to Evangelize the World

It is our duty to evangelize the world because all men need Christ.

The Christian Scriptures and the careful and extended observation of earnest men the world over agree that with respect to the need of salvation all nations and races are alike. The need of the non-Christian world is indescribably great. Hundreds of millions are to-day living in ignorance and darkness, steeped in idolatry, superstition, degradation and corruption. Reflect on the desolating and cruel evils which are making such fearful ravages among them. See under what a burden of sin and sorrow and suffering they live. Can any candid person doubt the reality of the awful need after reviewing the masterly, scientific survey by Dr. Dennis of the social evils of the non-Christian world? No one who has seen the actual conditions can question that they who are without God are also without hope.

The non-Christian religions may be judged by their fruits. While they furnish some moral principles and precepts of value, they do not afford adequate standards and motives by which rightly to guide the life, nor power to enable one to take the step between knowing duty and doing it. Though there are among the followers of these religions men of high and noble lives, in the sight of God all have sinned and stand in need of the Divine forgiveness and of Christ the Saviour. All other religions have failed to do what Christianity has done and is doing as a regenerating power in the individual and as a transforming force in society. It is a significant fact that the thousands of missionaries scattered throughout the world, face to face with heathenism and thus in the best position to make a scientific study of the problem, bear such a unanimous testimony as to the practical results of the non-Christian religions as should forever banish any doubt or reservation regarding their inadequacy to meet the world's need.

The Scriptures clearly teach that if men are to be saved they must be saved through Christ. He alone can deliver them from the power of sin and its penalty. His death made salvation possible. The Word of God sets forth the conditions of salvation. God has chosen to have these conditions made known through human agency. The universal capability of men to be benefited by the Gospel, and the ability of Christ to satisfy men of all races and conditions, emphasize the duty of Christians to preach Christ to every creature. The burning question for every Christian then is, Shall hundreds of millions of men now living, who need Christ and are capable of receiving help from Him, pass away without having even the opportunity to know Him?

It is not necessary that we go to the Scriptures, or to the ends of the earth, to discover our obligation to the unevangelized. A knowledge of our own hearts should be sufficient to make plain our duty. We know our need of Christ. How unreasonable, therefore, for us to assume that the nations living in sin and wretchedness and bondage can do without Him whom we so much need even in the most favored Christians lands.

It is our duty to evangelize the world because we owe all men the Gospel.

We have a knowledge of Jesus Christ, and to have this is to incur a responsibility toward every man who has it not. To have a Saviour who alone can save from the guilt and power of sin imposes an obligation of the most serious character. We received the knowledge of the Gospel from others, but not in order to appropriate it for our own exclusive use. It concerns all men. Christ tasted death for every man. He wishes the good news of His salvation made known to every creature. All nations and races are one in God's intention, and therefore equally entitled to the Gospel. The Christians of to-day are simply trustees of the Gospel and in no sense sole proprietors. Every Indian, every Chinese, every South Sea Islander has as good a right to the Gospel as anyone else; and, as a Chinese once said to Robert Stewart, we break the eighth commandment if we do not take it to him.[22] In the words of Mr. Eugene Stock, "Bring me the best Buddhist or Mohammedan in the world, the most virtuous, the most high-minded, and I think that man has a right to hear of the tremendous fact that a Divine Person came into the world to bring blessing to mankind. Whether he needs it or no, I will not stop to argue. I think he has a claim upon Christian people to tell him of that fact." [23] What a wrong against mankind to keep the knowledge of the mission of Christ to men from two-thirds of the race!

Our sense of obligation must be intensified when we ask ourselves the question, If we do not preach Christ where He has not been named, who will? "God has 'committed unto us the word of reconciliation,' and from whom shall the heathen now living ever hear that word, if the Christians of the present day fail to discharge the debt?" [24] We know their need; we know the only remedy; we have access to them; we are able to go.

The claims of humanity and universal brotherhood prompt us to make Christ known to those who live in darkness and in misery. The Golden Rule by which we profess to live impels us to it. The example of Christ, who was moved with compassion to meet even the bodily hunger of the multitudes, should inspire us to go forth with the Word of life to the millions who are wandering in helplessness in the shadow of death.

. . . .

The evangelization of the world in this generation is to Christians no self-imposed task; it rests securely upon Divine commandment. The Great Commission of Christ given by Him in the upper room in Jerusalem on the night after the resurrection, again a little later on a mountain in Galilee, and yet again, on the Mount of Olives, just before the ascension clearly expresses our obligation to make Christ known to all men. While this command was given to the disciples of Christ living in the first generation of the Christian era, it was intended as well for all time and for each Christian in his own time. That the command was not intended for the Apostles alone is seen from the promise with which it is linked, "Lo I am with you alway, even unto the end of the age." The practice of the Church in the Apostolic Age and Sub-Apostolic Age shows that the command was regarded as binding not only upon the Apostles but also upon all Christians. It was addressed to all in every place and throughout every generation who should call upon the name of the Lord Jesus Christ. It is true there is no express command to evangelize the world in this generation; but, as Mr. Stock has pointed out, "If we have a general command to make the Gospel known to those who know it not, there seems no escape from the conclusion that the duty to make it known to all—that is, all now alive—lies in the nature of the case." [25] Thus the expression, the evangelization of the world in this generation, simply translates Christ's last command into terms of obligation concerning our own lifetime.

In this command of our Lord we have "a motive power sufficient to impel disciples always with uniform force; which will survive romance; which will outlive excitement; which is independent of experiences and emotions; which can surmount every difficulty and disappointment; which burns steadily in the absence of outward encouragement, and glows in a blast of persecution; such a motive as in its intense and imperishable influence on the conscience and heart of a Christian shall be irrespective at once of his past history, of any peculiarities in his position, and of his interpretation of prophecy." [26] This command has been given to be obeyed. It is operative until it is repealed. The execution of it is not optional but obligatory. It awaits fulfilment by a generation that shall have courage and consecration enough to attempt the thing commanded. It should move to action all real Christians; for, in the words of Archbishop Whately, "If our religion is *not* true, we ought to *change* it; if it is true, we are bound to propagate what we believe to be the truth." [27] "Why call ye me, Lord, Lord, and do not the things which I say?" [28] "If ye love me ye will keep my commandments." [29]

It is our duty to evangelize the world because this is essential to the best life of the Christian Church.

If all men need the Gospel, if we owe the Gospel to all men, if Christ has commanded us to preach the Gospel to every creature, it is unquestionably our duty to give all people in our generation an opportunity to hear the Gospel. To know our duty and to do it not is sin. Continuance in the sin of neglect and disobedience necessarily weakens the life and arrests the growth of the Church. Who can measure the loss of vitality and power that she has already suffered within our own day from her failure to do all in her power for the world's evangelization? The Christians of to-day need some object great enough to engage all the powers of their minds and hearts. We find just such an object in the enterprise to make Christ known to the whole world. This would call out and utilize the best energies of the Church. It would help to save her from some of her gravest perils—ease, selfishness, luxury, materialism and low ideals. It would necessitate, and therefore greatly promote, real Christian unity, thus preventing an immense waste of force. It would react favorably on Christian countries. There is no one thing which would do so much to promote work on behalf of the cities and neglected country districts of the home lands as a vast enlargement of the foreign missionary operations. This is not a matter of theory; for history teaches impressively that the missionary epochs have been the times of greatest activity and spiritual vigor in the life of the home Church. So the best spiritual interests of American, Great Britain, Germany, Australasia and other Christian lands are inseparably bound up with the evangelization of the whole wide world. The dictates of patriotism, as well as of loyalty to our Lord, thus call upon us to give ourselves to the world's evangelization.

But the most serious and important consideration of all is that the largest manifestation of the presence of Christ with us as individual Christians, and with the Church at large, depends upon our obedience to His command. There is a most intimate and vital connection between "Go ye and make disciples of all the nations," and "Lo, I am with you alway." The gift of the Holy Spirit is associated in the New Testament with spreading the knowledge of Christ. More than that, the power of the Holy Spirit was bestowed for the express purpose of equipping Christians for the work of preaching the Gospel unto the uttermost parts of the earth, begining from Jerusalem. If the Church of to-day, therefore, would have the power of God come mightily upon her—and is not this the great need?—she will necessarily receive it while in the pathway of larger obedience to the missionary command.

The obligation to evangelize the world is an urgent one.

Every reason for doing this work of evangelizing at all demands that it be done not only thoroughly but also as speedily as possible. The present generation is passing away. If we do not evangelize it, who will? We dare not say the next generation will be soon enough. The Church has too long been in the habit of committing the heathen to the next generation. "It is not possible for the coming generation to discharge the duties of the present, whether it respects their repentance, faith, or works; and to commit to them our share of preaching Christ crucified to the heathen, is like committing to them the love due from us to God and our neighbor. The Lord will require of us that which is committed to us." [30]

The present generation is one of unexampled crisis in all parts of the unevangelized world. Missionaries from nearly every land urge that, if the Church fails to do her full duty in our lifetime, not only will multitudes of the present generation pass away without knowing of Christ, but the task of our successors to evangelize their generation will be much more difficult.

Our generation is also one of marvelous opportunity. The world is better known and more accessible, its needs more articulate and intelligible, and our ability to go into all the world with the Gospel is much greater than in any preceding generation. All this adds to our responsibility.

The forces of evil are not deferring their operations to the next generation. With world-wide enterprise and with ceaseless vigor they are seeking to accomplish their deadly work in this generation. This is true not only of the dire influences which have been at work in the unevangelized nations for centuries, but also of those which have come from so-called Christian lands. By the liquor traffic, by the opium trade and by the licentious lives and gambling habits of some of our countrymen we have greatly increased the misery and woe of the heathen. All non-Christian nations are being brought under the influences of the material civilization of the West, and these may easily work their injury unless controlled by the power of pure religion. The evangelization of the world in this generation is not, therefore, merely a matter of buying up the opportunity, but of helping to neutralize and supplant the effects of the sins of our own peoples.

Because of the infinite need of men without Christ; because of the possibilities of men of every race and condition who take Christ as the Lord of their lives; because of the command of our Lord which has acquired added force as a result of nineteen centuries of discovery, of opening of doors, of experience of the Christian Church; because of the shameful neglect of the past; because of the impending crisis and the urgency of the situation in all parts of the non-Christian world; because of the opportunity for a greatly accelerated movement in the present; because of the danger of neglecting to enter upon a great onward movement; because of the constraining memories of the Cross of Christ and the love wherewith He loved us, it is the solemn duty of the Christians of this generation to do their utmost to evangelize the world.

Notes

1. Irenaeus, "Unity of the Faith of the Church Throughout the World," *Against Heresies* in *The Apostolic Fathers with Justin Martyr and Irenaeus,* A. Cleveland Coxe, ed., *The Ante-Nicene Fathers,* Vol. I (Grand Rapids: William B. Eerdmans Publishing Company, 1950), pp. 330-332. Used by permission.

2. Ibid., pp. 309-313; T. Zahn, "Irenaeus," *The New Schaff-Herzog Encyclopedia of Religious Knowledge,* Vol. VI, pp. 28-31.

3. Clement of Alexandria, "Universal Diffusion of the Gospel a Contrast to Philosophy," *The Stromata* in *Fathers of the Second Century,* A. Cleveland Coxe, ed., *The Ante-Nicene Fathers,* Vol. II (Grand Rapids: William B. Eerdmans Publishing Company, 1951), pp. 519-520. Used by permission.

4. Coxe, Vol. II, pp. 165-169.

5. Tertullian, "We are but of yesterday, and we have filled every place among you" (ch. XXXVII), *Apology* in A. Cleveland Coxe, ed., *Latin Christianity: Its Founder, Tertullian,* Vol. III, *The Ante-Nicene Fathers* (Grand Rapids: William B. Eerdmans Publishing Company, 1951), p. 45. Used by permission.

6. Ibid., pp. 3-15.

7. Origen, "Proof of Rapid and Widespread Growth of Christians" (chs. X-XII) *Against Celsus* in A. Cleveland Coxe, ed., *Fathers of the Third Century,* Vol. IV, *The Ante-Nicene Fathers* (Grand Rapids: William B. Eerdmans Publishing Company, 1951), pp. 468-469. Used by permission.

8. Ibid., pp. 223-234.

9. Ibid.

10. Nicholaus Ludwig Count von Zinzendorf, "Concerning the Proper Purpose of the Preaching of the Gospel," *Nine Public Lectures on Important Subjects in Religion,* George W. Forell, trans, and ed. (Iowa City: University of Iowa Press, 1973), pp. 24-33. Used by permission.

11. A. J. Lewis, *Zinzendorf, the Ecumenical Pioneer* (Philadelphia: The Westminster Press, 1962); Heinz Motel, "Nicholaus Ludwig von Zinzendorf," *Concise Dictionary,* pp. 680-681.

12. Zinzendorf gives Matthew 22:1 ff. as the text. But the verse from Luke, which is cited later in the lecture, matches the German exactly. Matthew 22:1 has relevance only as an introduction, and Matthew 22:2 takes care of only the first half of the cited text.

13. Zinzendorf uses this term in the specific sense.

14. Claudius Buchanan, "The Star in the East," in *The Highway of Mission Thought,* T. B. Ray, ed. (Nashville: Sunday School Board of the Southern Baptist Convention, 1907), pp. 39-76.

15. Ibid., p. 38; Latourette, Vol. VI, pp. 100-101.

16. Alexander Duff, "Vindication of Missions in India," in *The Highway of Mission Thought,* T. B. Ray, ed. (Nashville: Sunday School Board of the Southern Baptist Convention, 1907), pp. 171-185.

17. Ibid., p. 172; A. J. Boyd, "Alexander Duff," *Concise Dictionary,* pp. 173-174.

18. Ibid; Beaver, "Mission Studies (Protestant)," *Concise Dictionary,* p. 410.

19. John R. Mott, "The Obligation to Evangelize the World," *The Evangelization of the World in this Generation* (New York: Student Volunteer Movement for Foreign Missions, 1905), pp. 17-29.

20. Robert Mackie, "John Raleigh Mott," *Concise Dictionary,* pp. 426-427; F. W. Price, "Northfield Conferences," *Concise Dictionary,* pp. 451-452.

21. Ibid.

22. *Church Missionary Intelligencer,* Vol. XXI., 254.

23. Letter in Archives of the Student Volunteer Movement.

24. "Memorial of the Student Volunteer Missionary Union to the Church of Christ in Britain." *The Student Volunteer* (of Great Britain), New Series, No. 15, p. 77.

25. *Church Missionary Intelligencer,* New Series, Vol. XXI., 254.

26. Dr. Herdman, in "Proceedings of the General Conference on Foreign Missions" (held at Mildmay, 1878), 99.

27. "Sermons on Various Subjects," 353.

28. St. Luke vi. 46.

29. St. John xiv. 15.

30. "The Duty of the Present Generation to Evangelize the World: An Appeal from the Missionaries at the Sandwich Islands to Their Friends in the United States," 34.

VIII

Historic Missionary Conferences

General Introduction

One of the most significant phenomena growing out of the modern missionary movement has been a series of significant world missionary conferences. The first three were predecessors of the famous Edinburgh conference of 1910. They were the Liverpool Conference of 1860, the London Conference of 1888, and the New York Conference of 1900. A direct result of the historic Edinburgh Conference was the creation of the International Missionary Council in 1921. This council sponsored five historic conferences: Jerusalem 1928, Madras 1938, Whitby (Toronto) 1947, Willingen (Germany) 1952, Ghana 1958.[1]

With its integration into the World Council of Churches in New Dehli in 1961, the International Missionary Council became the Commission on World Mission and Evangelism. The first world missionary conference sponsored by this new body was the conference at Mexico City in 1963, which set a new course in its emphasis upon "Witness in Six Continents." This was followed by the Bangkok Conference of 1972-1973. In the following pages we look more closely at the epoch-making conferences of Edinburgh, Jerusalem, and Madras.[2]

38

"Findings of the Commission"[3]
Edinburgh, 1910

Introduction

The World Missionary Conference of Edinburgh held in 1910 marked the transition from the nineteenth to the twentieth century. It was the forerunner of the organized Protestant ecumenical movement and set the stage for the series of significant world missionary conferences which followed in the succeeding decades. Although there were no Roman Catholics or Orthodox representatives, the more than twelve hundred delegates present represented a broad spectrum of the Christian world, from high-church Anglicans to the Salvation Army. Even though the conference was dominated by Westerners, there was a minority of Asians present.[4]

It was understandable that the conference would reflect its age, and that "foreign missions" would be viewed from a Western perspective. However, the conference projected a great forward look and paved the way for the innovations of the future conferences. The various national councils grew out of Edinburgh, and it resulted directly in the creation of the International Missionary Council, as we have observed. The full spectrum of mission concerns of the day were encountered. The foundation on which all of the conference developed was the theological basis of the missionary enterprise. We include on the following pages the Report of Commission I: "Carrying the Gospel to All the Non-Christian World." The fundamental issues raised in this document were to dominate the theological discussions of the next two mission conferences and beyond.[5]

Findings of the Commission

FOREWORD

1. The Commission, after studying the facts and after taking counsel with the leaders of the missionary forces of the Church at home and abroad, expresses its conviction that the present is the time of all times for the Church to undertake with quickened loyalty and sufficient forces to make Christ known to all the non-Christian world.

It is an opportune time. Never before has the whole world-field been so open and so accessible. Never before has the Christian Church faced such a combination of opportunities among both primitive and cultured peoples.

It is a critical time. The non-Christian nations are undergoing great changes. Far-reaching movements—national, racial, social, economic, religious—are shaking the non-Christian nations to their foundations. These nations are still plastic. Shall they set in Christian or pagan moulds? Their ancient faiths, ethical restraints, and social orders have been weakened or abandoned. Shall our sufficient faith fill the void? The spirit of national independence and racial patriotism is growing. Shall this become antagonistic or friendly to Christianity? There have been times when the Church confronted crises as great as those before it now on certain fields; but never before has there been such a synchronising of crises in all parts of the world.

It is a testing time for the Church. If it neglects to meet successfully the present world crisis by failing to discharge its responsibility to the whole world, it will weaken its power both on the home and foreign fields and seriously handicap its mission to the coming generation. Nothing less than the adequacy of Christianity as a world religion is on trial.

This is a decisive hour for Christian missions. The call of Providence to all our Lord's disciples, of whatever ecclesiastical connection, is direct and urgent to undertake without delay the task of carrying the Gospel to all the non-Christian world. It is high time to face this duty and with serious purpose to discharge it. The opportunity is inspiring; the responsibility is undeniable. The Gospel is all-inclusive in its scope, and we are convinced that there never was a time more favourable for united, courageous, and prayerful action to make the universality of the Gospel ideal a practical reality in the history of the Church.

2. The utter inadequacy of the present missionary force to discharge effectively the duty of world-wide evangelisation is evident. The present mission staff in the foreign field is not sufficient even to compass fully the work already in hand; much less is it prepared to accomplish any adequate expansion. On almost every field the efficiency and lives of the workers are endangered because of this effort to accomplish a task altogether too great for their numbers. The present status in some fields represents practically a deadlock; in many other fields there is no evidence of notable progress.

I. It is the high duty of the Church promptly to discharge its responsibility in regard to all the non-Christian world. To do this is easily within the power of the Church. Not to do it would indicate spiritual atrophy, if not treasonable indifference to the command of our Lord. Without attempting to estimate the necessary increase in income and foreign staff, it is the conviction of the Commission that the Church of Christ must view the world field in its entirety and do it full justice. There should be nothing less than a vast enlargement in the number of qualified workers, a thorough and courageous adaptation of means and methods to meet the situation, a wise unification in plans and forces, and a wholehearted fulfilling of the conditions of spiritual power.

II. The Commission, after a careful study of the missionary situation, and of the various considerations which should govern such a recommendation, would direct attention to the following fields as of special urgency in respect of the prosecution of missionary work:

1. Fields on which *the Church as a whole* should concentrate attention and effort.

(a) In China there is at this moment a unique opportunity which is fraught with far-reaching issues for the future not only of China and of the whole East, but also of Christendom.

(b) The threatening advance of Islam in Equatorial Africa presents to the Church of Christ the decisive question whether the Dark Continent shall become Mohammedan or Christian.

(c) The national and spiritual movements in India, awakening its ancient peoples to a vivid consciousness of their needs and possibilities, present a strong challenge to Christian missions to enlarge and deepen their work.

(d) The problems of the Mohammedan World, especially in the Near East, which, until recently, received little consideration from the Church at large, have been lifted unexpectedly into prominence and urgency, as well as into new relations, by the marvellous changes which have taken place in Turkey and Persia. One of the important tasks before the Church at this time is to deal adequately with these problems.

2. Fields which do not claim the attention of the Church as a whole,

but which demand additional effort on the part of the societies already in some measure occupying them.

In Korea an evangelistic movement extending rapidly over the land calls for a great strengthening of the missionary force. In Japan the mission work which has been centred in the great towns and among the higher middle classes requires to be expanded effectively over the country, and among all classes. In Malaya Christian missions must strain every nerve to prevent Islam from gaining the heathen tribes, and to win them for Christ. Siam and Laos also present an urgent appeal for an aggressive advance. In Melanesia a multitude of tribes in New Guinea and other islands are opening in quick succession to Christian influences. In various fields of pagan Africa, the Christian missions which have been planted are confronted by immense opportunities among those who are waiting for Gospel teaching, but who cannot be reached by the forces now on the field.

The rapid disintegration of the animistic and fetishistic beliefs of primitive peoples in most of the lands in the preceding lists presents an important problem. Most of these peoples will have lost their ancient faiths within a generation, and will accept that culture-religion with which they first come in contact. The responsibility of the Church is grave to bring the Gospel to them quickly, as the only sufficient substitute for their decaying faiths.

3. The Jewish people have a peculiar claim upon the missionary activities of the Christian Church. Christianity is theirs pre-eminently by right of inheritance. The Church is under special obligation to present Christ to the Jew. It is a debt to be repaid, a reparation to be fully and worthily made. The attempts to give the Gospel to this widely scattered yet still isolated people have been hitherto inadequate. The need is great for a change in the attitude of the Church towards this essential part of the Great Commission. The call is urgent in view of the enormous influence which the Jew is wielding in the world, especially throughout Christendom. The winning of this virile race with its genius for religion will be the strengthening of the Church of Christ and the enrichment of the world.

The enumeration of these fields might seem to suggest that the Church is not able to deal adequately and simultaneously with the entire non-Christian world. But the Commission declines to concede that this is so. After facing the facts we share the conviction of the large majority of our correspondents that the Church of Christ, if it puts forth its strength, is well able to carry the Gospel to all these fields immediately. While we recognise the greater urgency in the case of certain fields, we find it impossible, in the light of the needs of men, the command of Christ, and the resources of the Church, to delay giving to any people the opportunity to learn of Him. The point of chief emphasis is, that what the Church expects to do anywhere it must do soon. What is needed is a regular, sustained advance all along the line, in which all agencies shall be utilised and multiplied until they are co-extensive with the need of the entire world.

III. The unoccupied fields of the world have a claim of peculiar weight and urgency upon the attention and missionary effort of the Church. In this twentieth century of Christian history there should be no unoccupied fields. The Church is bound to remedy this lamentable condition with the least possible delay. Some of these unoccupied fields are open to the Gospel, such as Mongolia and many regions of Africa. In certain fields there are difficulties of access to be overcome. Both in Africa and Asia there are large regions belonging to the French Empire in which there are no Christian missions. There are other fields where political difficulties seem at present to prevent occupation, such as Tibet, Nepal, Bhutan, and Afghanistan. But the closed doors are few compared with the open doors unentered. It is the neglected opportunities that are the reproach of the Church. A large proportion of the unoccupied fields are to be found within the Mohammedan world, not only in Northern Africa and in Western Asia, but also in China. Indeed by far the greater part of the Mohammedan world is practically unoccupied. The claims of Christ upon the love and reverence of Moslem hearts should be faithfully and patiently pressed, with a zeal which will not yield to discouragement, and with passionate intercession which God will be pleased to hear and honour. The unreceptive and even defiant attitude of Islam towards Christianity, and its unwillingness to acknowledge the supreme Lordship of Christ, will yield to the Gospel if Christians do their duty. Its long dominance and intolerance are apparently being undermined by remarkable events. The present accessibility of Islam, the fruitfulness of the efforts already made, and the missionary energy of the Moslem propaganda favour direct, earnest, and unceasing efforts to convince the Mohammedans that Christ alone is worthy of their allegiance and worship. Emphasis should be laid on the need of special preparation on the part of all who are to devote themselves to this great undertaking.

IV. In view of the world-wide task confronting the Church of Christ, the proper disposition of the missionary forces in order to an effective advance becomes a question of vital importance. (1) With regard to the work of individual missionaries or missions, this question will be differently decided according to the countries and the peoples to be evangelised and the type of the evangelising mission, the principle being that the sphere should be sufficiently restricted to enable the missionary or the mission effectively to influence the people. (2) With regard to the work in large areas well occupied for decades, such as South Africa, some port cities, and other great centres in such countries as Japan, China, and India, a new and careful survey is necessary, if the undesirable crowding of missions and stations in limited areas (due in most cases to the unfavourable conditions at the beginning of the work) is to be remedied by a proper rearrangement of the stations and redistribution of the workers. (3) With regard to the totally unoccupied or partially occupied fields which on all sides invite missionary extension, the wise policy is to extend by expanding the work already in hand, and when establishing new work to begin at strong strategic centres.

V. As the missionary forces are divided into numerous independent organisations which are conducting foreign missions in different lands and with diverse methods, it is of the utmost importance that they should be in close touch with each other, that they should be familiar with each other's work and methods, and that they should profit by each other's failures and successes.

The Commission recommends that an International Committee should be formed for the consideration of international missionary questions. This Committee, in addition to serving as an agency for dealing with questions on which the various missionary societies desire to take co-operative action, would act as a council for investigation and advice about such matters as the unreached portions of the world, the actual occupation of different fields, and the success and failure of missionary methods. This Committee would naturally avail itself of the co-operation of existing councils and organisations both on the home and foreign fields.

VI. The Church on the mission field must be the chief evangelistic agency if the Gospel is to be preached to all men in our day. The evangelisation of the non-Christian world is not alone a European, an American, an Australasian enterprise; it is equally an Asiatic and an African enterprise. While the number of well-qualified foreign missionaries must be greatly increased in order to plant Christianity, to establish the native Church, to place at its disposal the acquired experience of the Christian Church, and to enlist and train effective leaders, nevertheless the great volume of work involved in making Christ known to the multitudinous inhabitants of the non-Christian world must be done by the sons and daughters of the soil. It is essential, therefore, on every mission field to seek to permeate the whole life of the Church from its beginning with the evangelistic spirit, and further, in proportion as the Church increases, to develop strongly a native evangelistic staff, working in co-operation with the foreign force. For this end training-schools and classes must be multiplied and developed. In this way leaders may be prepared who will conduct a more effective indigenous training of catechists, evangelists, and Bible-women, thus providing a sufficient force for a greatly enlarged evangelistic propaganda. Conferences on evangelistic work should be held within large areas admitting of concerted action. Moreover, if the Church is to abound with the spirit of self-propagation and prove an aggressive force, more attention must be given to building up its spiritual life and to establishing its members in the cardinal doctrines of the Christian faith.

VII. A crucial factor in the evangelisation of the non-Christian world is the state of the Church in Christian lands. On this point there is almost unanimous agreement among missionaries abroad and leaders at home. In the initial stages, at least, the Church at home determines the quality of the faith, ideals, and practices which are being propagated. It chooses and commissions workers who are to plant Christianity in the non-Christian fields and influences their character and spirit. It likewise does much to determine the nature of the impact of Christendom upon the non-Christian world through political, commercial, industrial, and social relations and activities. Until there is a more general consecration on the part of the members of the Home Church, there can be no hope of such an expansion of the missionary enterprise as to result in making the knowledge of Jesus Christ readily accessible to every human being. Further, it is only through this more complete obedience to Him that the missionary movement can become irresistible and triumphant in the fields where it is already at work. To ensure such an outflow of the vitalising missionary forces of the Church, its own life must be adequately energised. Whatever, therefore, can be done to make the Home Church conform in spirit and in practice to the New Testament teachings and ideals will contribute in the most powerful manner to the realisation of the great aim of the world's evangelisation. A new and resolute awakening of the Church to the richness of its heritage in the Gospel and to the duty of an ardent, universal, and untiring effort to make disciples of all nations, is the clear message of God to the Church of to-day.

VIII. Beyond doubt the most fundamental requirement of the missionary enterprise is a greater appropriation of the power of the Spirit of God. Important as are those aspects of the undertaking which deal with the statistics, the machinery and the strategy of missions, the leaders of the movement should concern themselves far more with the spiritual dynamics of missions. The most direct and effective way to promote the evangelisation of the world is to influence the workers, and indeed the whole membership of the Church at home and abroad, to yield themselves completely to the sway of Christ as Lord, and to establish and preserve at all costs those habits of spiritual culture which ensure lives of Christlike witnessing and of spiritual power. To this end there should be promoted retreats for groups of leaders, Bible institutes, conferences for the deepening of the spiritual life of Church members, and the ministry of private and united intercession.

All workers in foreign missions should seek a fresh and constant realisation of the truth that they are fellow-workers with God. In accordance with the word of our Lord, "My Father worketh hitherto and I work," they should seek a clearer understanding of the working of God in governing the world, creating great opportunities, removing grave obstacles, opening effectual doors, and developing favourable conditions and influences. And they should seek to realise with reverent wonder that through them Jesus Christ in His grace is at the present time working out the fulfilment of His own word, "I, if I be lifted up from the earth, will draw all men unto Me." Our Living Lord is the Supreme Worker in all mission work; His alone is the power; and all true work on our part is in reliance on His promise, "Lo, I am with you always."

39

"The Christian Message" [6]
Jerusalem, 1928

Introduction

The first world convocation of the International Missionary Council after its formations was held in Jerusalem, on the Mount of Olives, at Easter time, in 1928. Although its numbers were considerably smaller than Edinburgh, it was far more representative of the world community, with almost one fourth of the 231 delegates coming from Asia, Africa, and Latin America. The conference agenda reflected the emerging issues of the twentieth century.[7]

The findings were published in eight volumes. Besides volume I, they are: II. *Religious Education;* III. *The Relation between the Younger and the Older Churches;* IV. *The Christian Mission in Light of Race Conflict;* V. *The Christian Mission in Relation to Industrial Problems;* VI. *The Christian Mission in Relation to Rural Problems;* VII. *International Missionary Cooperation;* VIII. *Addresses on General Subjects* (regional reports from Africa, Asia, Latin America, etc.). Because of the growing theological relativism of the day, many feared that the agenda would lead to a surrender to the "social gospel." Consequently, strong theological statements were proposed, emphasizing the uniqueness of the Christian gospel. The following chapter from volume I reflects this strong theological position.[8]

The Christian Message

GO AND MAKE DISCIPLES OF ALL NATIONS

Throughout the world there is a sense of insecurity and instability. Ancient religions are undergoing modificaton, and in some regions dissolution, as scientific and commercial development alter the current of men's thought. Institutions regarded with age-long veneration are discarded or called in question; well-established standards of moral conduct are brought under criticism; and countries called Christian feel the stress as truly as the peoples of Asia and Africa. On all sides doubt is expressed whether there is any absolute truth or goodness. A new relativism struggles to enthrone itself in human thought.

Along with this is found the existence of world-wide suffering and pain, which expresses itself partly in a despair of all higher values, partly in a tragically earnest quest of a new basis for life and thought, in the birthpangs of rising nationalism, in the ever-keener consciousness of race- and class-oppression.

Amid widespread indifference and immersion in material concerns we also find everywhere, now in noble forms and now in license or extravagance, a great yearning, especially among the youth of the world, for the full and untrammeled expression of personality, for spiritual leadership and authority, for reality in religion, for social justice, for human brotherhood, for international peace.

In this world, bewildered and groping for its way, Jesus Christ has drawn to Himself the attention and admiration of mankind as never before. He stands before men as plainly greater than Western civilization, greater than the Christianity that the world has come to know. Many who have not hitherto been won to His Church yet find in Him their hero and their ideal. Within His Church there is a widespread desire for unity centered in His Person.

OUR MESSAGE

Against this background and in relation to it, we have to proclaim our message.

Our message is Jesus Christ. He is the revelation of what God is and of what man through Him may become. In Him we come face to face with the Ultimate Reality of the universe; He makes known to us God as our Father, perfect and infinite in love and in righteousness; for in Him we find God incarnate, the final, yet ever-unfolding, revelation of the God in whom we live and move and have our being.

We hold that through all that happens, in light and in darkness, God is working, ruling and over-ruling. Jesus Christ, in His life and through His death and resurrection, has disclosed to us the Father, the Supreme Reality, as almighty Love, reconciling the world to Himself by the Cross, suffering with men in their struggle against sin and evil, bearing with them and for them the burden of sin, forgiving them as they, with forgiveness in their own hearts, turn to Him in repentance and faith, and creating humanity anew for an ever-growing, ever-enlarging, everlasting life.

The vision of God in Christ brings and deepens the sense of sin and guilt. We are not worthy of His love; we have by our own fault opposed His holy will. Yet that same vision which brings the sense of guilt brings also the assurance of pardon, if only we yield ourselves in faith to the spirit of Christ so that His redeeming love may avail to reconcile us to God.

We re-affirm that God, as Jesus Christ has revealed Him, requires all His children, in all circumstances, at all times, and in all human relationships, to live in love and righteousness for His glory. By the resurrection of Christ and the gift of the Holy Spirit God offers His own power to men that they may be fellow workers with Him, and urges them on to a life of adventure and self-sacrifice in preparation for the coming of His Kingdom in its fulness.

We will not ourselves offer any further formulation of the Christian message, for we remember that as lately as in August, 1927, the World Conference on Faith and Order met at Lausanne, and that a statement on this subject was issued from that Conference after it had been received with full acceptance. We are glad to make this our own.

"The message of the Church to the world is and must always remain the Gospel of Jesus Christ.

"The Gospel is the joyful message of redemption, both here and hereafter, the gift of God to sinful man in Jesus Christ.

"The world was prepared for the coming of Christ through the activities of God's Holy Spirit in all humanity, but especially in His revelation as given in the Old Testament; and in the fulness of time the eternal Word of God became incarnate and was made man, Jesus Christ, the Son of God and the Son of Man, full of grace and truth.

"Through His life and teaching, His call to repentance, His proclamation of the coming of the Kingdom of God and of judgment, His suffering and death, His resurrection and exaltation to the right hand of the Father, and by the mission of the Holy Spirit, He has brought to us forgiveness of sins, and has revealed the fulness of the living God and His boundless love toward us. By the appeal of that love, shown in its completeness on the Cross, He summons us to the new life of faith, self-sacrifice, and devotion to His service and the service of men.

"Jesus Christ, as the crucified and the living One, as Saviour and Lord, is also the center of the world-wide Gospel of the Apostles and the Church. Because He Himself is the Gospel, the Gospel is the message of the Church to the world. It is more than a philosophical theory; more than a theological system; more than a program for material betterment. The Gospel is rather the gift of a new world from God to this old world of sin and death; still more, it is the victory over sin and death, the revelation of eternal life in Him who has knit together the whole family in heaven and on earth in the communion of saints, united in the fellowship of service, of prayer, and of praise.

"The Gospel is the prophetic call to sinful man to turn to God, the joyful tidings of justification and of sanctification to those who believe in Christ. It is the comfort of those who suffer; to those who are bound it is the assurance of the glorious liberty of the sons of God. The Gospel brings peace and joy to the heart, and produces in men self-denial, readiness for brotherly service, and compassionate love. It offers the supreme goal for the aspirations of youth, strength to the toiler, rest to the weary, and the crown of life to the martyr.

"The Gospel is the sure source of power for social regeneration. It proclaims the only way by which humanity can escape from those class- and race-hatreds which devastate society at present into the enjoyment of national well-being and international friendship and peace. It is also a gracious invitation to the non-Christian world, East and West, to enter into the joy of the living Lord.

"Sympathizing with the anguish of our generation, with its longing for intellectual sincerity, social justice, and spiritual inspiration, the Church in the eternal Gospel meets the needs and fulfils the God-given aspirations of the modern world. Consequently, as in the past so also in the present, the Gospel is the only way of salvation. Thus, through His Church, the living Christ still says to men, 'Come unto me! . . . He that followeth me shall not walk in darkness, but shall have the light of life.' "

THE MISSIONARY MOTIVE

If such is our message, the motive for its delivery should be plain. The Gospel is the answer to the world's greatest need. It is not our discovery or achievement; it rests on what we recognize as an act of God. It is first and foremost "Good News." It announces glorious Truth. Its very nature forbids us to say that it may be the right belief for some but not for others. Either it is true for all, or it is not true at all.

But questions concerning the missionary motive have been widely raised, and such a change in the habits of men's thoughts as the last generation has witnessed must call for a re-examination of these questions.

Accordingly we would lay bare the motives that impel us to the missionary enterprise. We recognize that the health of our movement and of our souls demands a self-criticism that is relentless and exacting.

In searching for the motives that impel us we find ourselves eliminating decisively and at once certain motives that may seem, in the minds of some, to have become mixed up with purer motives in the history of the movement. We repudiate any attempt on the part of trade or of governments, openly or covertly, to use the missionary cause for ulterior purposes. Our Gospel by its very nature and by its declaration of the sacredness of human personality stands against all exploitation of man by man, so that we cannot tolerate any desire, conscious or unconscious, to use this movement for purposes of fastening a bondage, economic, political, or social, on any people.

Going deeper, on our part we would repudiate any symptoms of a religious imperialism that would desire to impose beliefs and practices on others in order to manage their souls in their supposed interests. We obey a God who respects our wills and we desire to respect those of others.

Nor have we the desire to bind up our Gospel with fixed ecclesiastical forms which derive their meaning from the experience of the Western church. Rather the aim should be to place at the disposal of the younger churches of all lands our collective and historical experience. We believe that much of that heritage has come out of reality and will be worth sharing. But we ardently desire that the younger churches should express the Gospel through their own genius and through forms suitable to their racial heritage. There must be no desire to lord it over the personal or collective faith of others.

Our true and compelling motive lies in the very nature of the God to whom we have given our hearts. Since He is love, His very nature is to share. Christ is the expression in time of the eternal self-giving of the Father. Coming into fellowship with Christ we find in ourselves an overmastering impulse to share Him with others. We are constrained by the love of Christ and by obedience to His last command. He Himself said, "I came that they may have life, and may have it abundantly," and our experience corroborates it. He has become life to us. We would share that life.

We are assured that Christ comes with an offer of life to man and to societies and to nations. We believe that in Him the shackles of moral evil and guilt are broken from human personality and that men are made free, and that such personal freedom lies at the basis of the freeing of society from cramping custom and blighting social practices and political bondage, so that in Christ men and societies and nations may stand up free and complete.

We find in Christ, and especially in His Cross and Resurrection, an inexhaustible source of power that makes us hope when there is no hope. We believe that through it men and societies and nations that have lost their moral nerve to live will be quickened into life.

We have a pattern in our minds as to what form that life should take. We believe in a Christ-like world. We know nothing better; we can be content with nothing less. We do not go to the nations called non-Christian, because they are the worst of the world and they alone are in need; we go because they are a part of the world and share with us in the same human need—the need of redemption from ourselves and from sin, the need to have life complete and abundant and to be remade after this pattern of Christlikeness. We desire a world in which Christ will not be crucified but where His Spirit shall reign.

We believe that men are made for Christ and cannot really live apart from Him. Our fathers were impressed with the horror that men should die without Christ—we share that horror; we are impressed also with the horror that men should live without Christ.

Herein lies the Christian motive; it is simple. We cannot live without Christ and we cannot bear to think of men living without Him. We cannot be content to live in a world that is un-Christ-like. We cannot be idle while the yearning of His heart for His brethren is unsatisfied.

Since Christ is the motive, the end of Christian missions fits in with that motive. Its end is nothing less than the production of Christlike character in individuals and societies and nations through faith in and fellowship with Christ the living Saviour, and through corporate sharing of life in a divine society.

Christ is our motive and Christ is our end. We must give nothing less, and we can give nothing more.

THE SPIRIT OF OUR ENDEAVOR

Our approach to our task must be made in humility and penitence and love: in humility, because it is not our own message which we bring, but God's, and if in our delivery of it self-assertion finds any place we shall spoil that message and hinder its acceptance; in penitence, because our fathers and we ourselves have been so blind to many of the implications of our faith; in love, because our message is the Gospel of the Love of God, and only by love in our own hearts for those to whom we speak can we make known its power or its true nature.

Especially do we confess the sluggishness of the older churches to realize and discharge their responsibility to carry the Gospel to all the world; and all alike we confess our neglect to bring the ordering of men's lives into conformity with the spirit of Christ. The Church has not firmly and effectively set its face against race-hatred, race-envy, race-contempt, or against social envy and contempt and class-bitterness, or against racial, national, and social pride, or against the lust for wealth and exploitation of the poor or weak. We believe that the Gospel "proclaims the only way by which humanity can escape from class- and race-hatred." But we are forced to recognize that such a claim requires to be made good and that the record of Christendom hitherto is not sufficient to sustain it. Nor has it sufficiently sought out the good and noble elements in the non-Christian beliefs, that it might learn that deeper personal fellowship with adherents of those beliefs wherein they may be more powerfully drawn to the living Christ. We know that, even apart from conscious knowledge of Him, when men are true to the best light they have, they are able to effect some real deliverance from many of the evils that afflict the world; and this should prompt us the more to help them to find the fulness of light and power in Christ.

But while we record these failures we are also bound to record with thankfulness the achievements of the Christian Church in this field. The difference between the Europe known to St. Paul and the Europe known to Dante, to Luther, to Wesley is plain for all to see. From every quarter of the globe comes testimony to the liberation effected by Christ for women. Since the vast changes made by the development of industrialism have come to be appreciated, every country has had its Christian social movements and the Universal Conference on Life and Work, held at Stockholm in 1925, revealed how widespread and influential these have become. Truly our efforts have not been commensurate with the needs of the world or with the claim of Christ; but in what has been accomplished and attempted we have already great encouragement for the days to come. In particular there is a growing sensitiveness of conscience with regard to war and the conditions that may lead up to it. For all these indications of the growing power of the spirit of Christ among Christians we thank God. And we call on all Christian people to be ready for pioneering thought and action in the name of Christ. Too often the Church has adopted new truth, or new goals for enterprise, only when the danger attached to them is over. There is a risk of rashness; but there is also possible an excessive caution by which, because His Church hangs back, the glory of new truth or enterprise which rightly belongs to Christ is in men's thoughts denied to Him.

The Call to the World

Filled with conviction that Jesus Christ is indeed the Saviour of the world, and conscious of a desperate need in ourselves and in all the world for what He only can supply, we call upon our fellow Christians and all our fellow men to turn again to Him for pardon and for power.

1. To all the churches of Christ we call: that they stand firmly upon the rock of Christian conviction and wholeheartedly accept its missionary obligations; that they go forward in full loyalty to Christ to discover and to express, in the power and freedom of the Holy Spirit, the treasures in His unsearchable riches which it is the privilege and duty of each to win for the Universal Church; that they strive to deliver the name of Christ and of Christianity from complicity in any evil or injustice.

Those who proclaim Christ's message must give evidence for it in their own lives and in the social institutions which they uphold. It is by living Christ among men that we may most effectively lift Him up before them. The Spirit that returns love for hate, and overcomes evil with good, must be evidently present in those who would be witnesses for Christ. They are also bound to exert all their influence to secure that the social, international, and inter-racial relationships in the midst of which their work is done be subordinate to and expressive of His Spirit. Especially must it be a serious obstacle to missionary effort if a non-Christian country feels that the relation of the so-called Christian countries to itself is morally unsound or is alien from the principles of Christ, and the Church must be ready for labor and sacrifice to remove whatever is justly so condemned.

The task before us is beyond our powers. It can be accomplished only by the Holy Spirit, whose power we receive in its completeness only in the fellowship of Christ's disciples. We call all followers of Christ to take their full share as members of His Body, which is the Church; no discontent with its organization or tradition or failings should be allowed to keep us outside its fold; the isolated Christian is improverished in his spiritual life and impotent in his activities; our strength, both inward and outward, is in the living fellowship. But in these hurried and feverish days there is also more need than ever for the deepening of our spiritual life through periodical detachment from the world and its need in lonely communion with God. We desire also to call for a greater volume of intercessory prayer. The whole Church should be earnest and instant in prayer, each part for every other, and all together for the Church's unity and for the hallowing of God's Name throughout the world.

Further, we call on Christians in all lands who are trained in science, art, or philosophy to devote their talents to the working out of that Christian view of life and the world which we sorely need to secure us against instability, bewilderment, and extravagance.

Lastly, we urge that every possible step be taken to make real the fellowship of the Gospel. The churches of the West send missions and missions-of-help to the churches of Africa and Asia. We believe that the time is come when all would gain if the younger churches were invited to send missions-of-help to the churches of Europe and America, that they may minister of their treasure to the spiritual life of those to whom they come.

2. To non-Christians also we make our call. We rejoice to think that just because in Jesus Christ the light that lighteth every man

shone forth in its full splendor, we find rays of that same light where He is unknown or even is rejected. We welcome every noble quality in non-Christian persons or systems as further proof that the Father, who sent His Son into the world, has nowhere left Himself without witness.

Thus, merely to give illustration, and making no attempt to estimate the spiritual value of other religions to their adherents, we recognize as part of the one Truth that sense of the Majesty of God and the consequent reverence in worship, which are conspicuous in Islam; the deep sympathy for the world's sorrow and unselfish search for the way of escape, which are at the heart of Buddhism; the desire for contact with Ultimate Reality conceived as spiritual, which is prominent in Hinduism; the belief in a moral order of the universe and consequent insistence of moral conduct, which are inculcated by Confucianism; the disinterested pursuit of truth and of human welfare which are often found in those who stand for secular civilization but do not accept Christ as their Lord and Saviour.

Especially we make our call to the Jewish people, whose Scriptures have become our own, and "of whom is Christ as concerning the flesh," that with open heart they turn to that Lord in whom is fulfilled the hope of their nation, its prophetic message, and its zeal for holiness. And we call upon our fellow Christians in all lands to show to Jews that lovingkindness that has too seldom been shown towards them.

We call on the followers of non-Christian religions to join with us in the study of Jesus Christ as He stands before us in the Scriptures, His place in the life of the world, and His power to satisfy the human heart; to hold fast to faith in the unseen and eternal in face of the growing materialism of the world; to coöperate with us against all the evils of secularism; to respect freedom of conscience so that men may confess Christ without separation from home and friends; and to discern that all the good of which men have conceived is fulfilled and secured in Christ.

Christianity is not a Western religion, nor is it yet effectively accepted by the Western world as a whole. Christ belongs to the peoples of Africa and Asia as much as to the European or American. We call all men to equal fellowship in Him. But to come to Him is always self-surrender. We must not come in the pride of national heritage or religious tradition; he who would enter the Kingdom of God must become as a little child, though in that Kingdom are all the treasures of man's aspirations, consecrated and harmonized. Just because Christ is the self-disclosure of the One God, all human aspirations are towards Him, and yet of no human tradition is He merely the continuation. He is the desire of all nations; but He is always more, and other, than they had desired before they learned of Him.

But we would insist that when the Gospel of the Love of God comes home with power to the human heart, it speaks to each man, not as Muslim or as Buddhist, or as an adherent of any system, but just as man. And while we rightly study our religions in order to approach men wisely, yet at the last we speak as men to men, inviting them to share with us the pardon and the life that we have found in Christ.

3. To all who inherit the benefits of secular civilization and contribute to its advancement we make our call. We claim for Christ the labors of scientists and artists. We recognize their service to His cause in dispersing the darkness of ignorance, superstition, and vulgarity. We appreciate also the noble elements that are found in nationalist movements and in patriotism, the loyalty, the self-devotion, the idealism, which love of country can inspire. But even these may lead to strife and bitterness and narrowness of outlook if they are not dedicated to Christ; in His universal Kingdom of Love all nations by right are provinces, and fulfil their own true destiny only in His service. When patriotism and science are not consecrated they are often debased into self-assertion, exploitation, and the service of greed. Indeed, throughout all nations the great peril of our time arises from that immense development of man's power over the resources of nature which has been the great characteristic of our epoch. This power gives opportunity for wealth of interest, and, through facilities of communication, for freedom of intercourse such as has never been known. But it has outgrown our spiritual and moral control.

Amid the clashes of industrial strife the Gospel summons men to work together as brothers in providing for the human family the economic basis of the good life. In the presence of social antipathies and exclusiveness the Gospel insists that we are members of one family, and that our Father desires for each a full and equal opportunity to attain to His own complete development, and to make his special contribution to the richness of the family life. Confronted by international relations that constantly flout Christ's law of love, there is laid on all who bear His name the solemn obligation to labor unceasingly for a new world-order in which justice shall be secured for all peoples, and every occasion for war or threat of war be removed.

Such changes can be brought about only through an unreserved acceptance of Christ's way of love, and by the courageous and sacrificial living that it demands. Still ringing in our ears is the call, "Be not fashioned according to this world: but be ye transformed by the renewing of your mind."

Conclusion

In our conference together we have seen more clearly the fulness and sufficiency of the Gospel and our own need of the salvation of Christ. The enlarging thoughts of the generation find the Gospel and the Saviour ever richer and greater than men had known.

This deepened assurance of the adequacy and universality of the Gospel, however, is not enough. More effective ways must be found for its proclamation, not to systems of opinion only, but to human beings, to men and women for whom Christ died. The most thorough and convincing intellectual statement of Christianity is necessary, but such statements cannot suffice. The Gospel must be expressed also in simplicity and love, and offered to men's hearts and minds by word and deed and life, by righteousness and loving-kindness, by justice, sympathy, and compassion, by ministry to human needs and to the deep want of the world.

As together, Christians of all lands, we have surveyed the world and the needs of men, we are convinced of the urgent necessity for a great increase in the Christian forces in all countries, and for a still fuller measure of coöperation between the churches of all nations in more speedily laying the claim of Christ upon all the unoccupied areas of the world and of human life.

We are persuaded that we and all Christian people must seek a more heroic practice of the Gospel. It cannot be that our present complacency and moderation are a faithful expression of the mind of Christ, and of the meaning of His Cross and Resurrection in the midst of the wrong and want and sin of our modern world. As we contemplate the work with which Christ has charged His Church, we who are met here on the Mount of Olives, in sight of Calvary, would take up for ourselves and summon those from whom we come and to whom we return to take up with us the Cross of Christ, and all that for which it stands, and to go forth into the world to live in the fellowship of His sufferings and by the power of His resurrection, in hope and expectation of His glorious Kingdom.

40

"A Message to All Peoples" [9]
Madras, 1938

Introduction

A decade after Jerusalem, on the eve of World War II, the International Missionary Council convened at Christmastime, 1938, on the campus of Madras Christian College in the Madras suburb of Tambaram. Sixty-nine countries were represented, and over half of the approximately five hundred delegates were from Asia, Africa, and Latin America. Some of the most articulate voices of the conference were church leaders from these countries. It was perhaps the most truly international meeting ever held up to that time. The findings of the conference were published in seven volumes titled respectively: *The Authority of the Faith, The Growing Church, Evangelism, The Life of the Church, The Economic Basis of the Church, The Church and State, Addresses and Other Records* (reports on various types of work by nationals from different countries, etc.).[10]

Even though the conference dealt seriously with such matters as economics and church-state relations, the theological debate on the relationship of Christianity to non-Christian religions dominated the conference. It convened in the midst of the controversy provoked by the theological relativism of William Ernest Hocking's *Rethinking Missions* and the reply to it by the biblical realism of Hendrik Kraemer's *The Christian Message in a Non-Christian World*. Since the next part of this study will be given exclusively to this debate, we shall include in the following pages a brief statement adopted at the final session. It is a message which reflects the hope of the conference after the stormy issues it had faced and as it looked out over a complex and increasingly secularized world with the prayer that the church might surround this needy world with the love of God in Christ.[11]

A Message to All Peoples
(Adopted by the Council at its closing session)

The International Missionary Council, meeting at Tambaram in India, sends greetings to the peoples of all lands.

We are four hundred and seventy delegates gathered from seventy nations and from many races of the earth to consider how we may better make known to the world the love of the eternal God as He has revealed Himself in Jesus Christ.

The reports that have been brought to us from every quarter of the globe have made us realise that the ancient pestilences which destroy mankind are abroad with a virulence unparalleled. In every country the fact of war or the fear of it casts its paralysing shadow over human hope. Race hatred, the ugly parent of persecution, has been set up as a national idol in many a market place and increasingly becomes a household god. Everywhere the greed of money continues to separate those who have from those who have not, filling the latter with angry plans of revolution and the former with the nervousness of power.

Again and again a sense of penitence has come over us as we have realised that these consuming evils are all of them man-made. They bear upon them the marks of human manufacture as clearly as the motor car or the aeroplane. Neither flood nor earthquake nor dark mysterious force outside of our control produces wars or economic tensions. We know that we live involved within a chaos which we ourselves have made.

Again and again we have been forced to note that the evils that we face are not the work of bad men only, but of good as well. The gravest of our disasters have been brought upon us not by men desiring to make trouble for mankind but by those who thought they did their best in the circumstances surrounding them. We do not know the man wise enough to have saved the world from its present sufferings— and we do not know the man wise enough to deliver us now.

But it is just at this point that we are forced back upon our Faith and rescued from pessimism to a glorious hope. We know that there is One who, unlike ourselves, is not defeated and who cannot know defeat. In the wonder of Christ's revelation we see God not as a remote and careless deity sufficient to Himself, but as a Father with a love for mankind, His children, as indescribable as it is fathomless. We who have looked at Christ, His Messenger, His Son, torn with suffering on a cross on which only His love for man has placed Him, have a tragic but transfiguring insight into the richness and reality of God's passion for His own. It is this insight which has taken the Christians to glad martyrdoms through the centuries and sent them to the ends of the earth to spread the great Good News. And in humility we record our gratitude that even in this present time evidences multiply that men and women still go forth as faithful and untiring ambassadors of Christ.

It is clear that only God can save the peoples, and that the God and Father of our Lord Jesus Christ not only can but will. It must become clearer to us all, however, that the instruments He demands are not men and women of ideals as such, but those who constantly in prayer and worship verify those same ideals before His august will— verify and improve and never cease to re-verify them. It is not the merely moral person whom God requires in the present crisis, or in any other, but the person who keeps his morality alive and growing through the constant refreshing of His creative touch. We can, none of us, become faultless agents of His grace, but the only hope before the world lies in those who at least attempt to know Him and to follow in His way.

National gods of any kind, gods of race or class, these are not large enough to save us. The recognition of God in Christ by no means robs a man of his nation or his family or his culture. When Christ is taken seriously by a nation or an ancient culture, He destroys no whit of good within it but lifts it rather to its own highest destiny. He does destroy exclusiveness, but in its place He causes a new quality to grow—good will—a good will which is wider than national or cultural loyalities and corresponds to the largeness of God's love.

In our midst we have seen anew that devotion to the things of Christ will work a miracle among men and women. We have prayed, and as we prayed the barriers of nationality and class have melted. Knit by the Holy Spirit the one to the other and all to God, we have known the meaning of fellowship. We feel this to be a promise of what may be in all the earth.

We call upon our fellow Christians throughout the world to join us in a new dedication. Surely God is summoning us in these times to let go our self-sufficiency, to frequent His altars, to learn of Him, and to make His ways known in all the relationships of life. To make Him known in the State involves labour for the establishment of justice among all the people. In the world of commerce it involves the ending of unregulated competition for private gain and the beginning of emulation for the public good. Everywhere it involves self-sacrificial service. God grant to His Church to take the story of His love to all mankind, till that love surround the earth, binding the nations, the races and the classes into a community of sympathy for one another, undergirded by a deathless faith in Christ.

Notes

1. W. Richey Hogg, "World Missionary Conferences," *Concise Dictionary*, pp. 133-138.

2. Ibid.; "Edinburgh to Melbourne," *International Review of Missions* (Geneva, Switzerland, July, 1978).

3. "Findings of the Commission," *World Mission Conference, 1910, Report of Commission I, Carrying the Gospel to All the Non-Christian World* (New York: Fleming H. Revell Company), pp. 362-370. Used by permission.

4. Hogg, pp. 134-135.

5. *World Missionary Conference Edinburgh, 1910* (Official Handbook) (Edinburgh: World Missionary Conference Office); Harry Sawyer, "The First World Missionary Conference: Edinburgh, 1910," *International Review of Missions* (July, 1978), pp. 255-272; Hogg, 134-135.

6. "The Christian Message" (ch. XIII), *The Jerusalem meeting of the International Missionary Council, March 24-April 28*, Vol. I, *The Christian Life and Message in Relation to Non-Christian Systems of Thought and Life* (New York: International Missionary Council, 1928), pp. 400-414. Used by permission.

7. Ibid.; Hogg, pp. 135-136.

8. *The Jerusalem Meeting*, p. ii; Hogg, pp. 135-136.

9. "A Message to All Peoples," *International Missionary Council Meeting at Tambaram, Madras,*

December 12-29, 1938, Vol. VII, *Addresses and Other Records* published by Oxford University Press for the International Missionary Council (1939). Reprinted by permission of Oxford University Press.

10. *International Missionary Council Meeting at Tambaram, Madras,* Vol. I, *The Authority of the Faith,* p. iv; Hogg, pp. 136-137.

11. Hogg, pp. 136-137.

IX

Mission Encounter with Non-Christian Religions

General Introduction

Growing out of the theological discussions of the Jerusalem Conference, the Laymen's Foreign Missions Inquiry was formed in 1930. The second stage of the Inquiry was developed by a fifteen-member Commission of Appraisal, chaired by William Ernest Hocking of Harvard. The commission was assigned the responsibility of studying the function of missions in that day. The report was published in 1932 under the signature of Hocking who was the principal writer. The most controversial part of the report related to the attitude of Christians toward non-Christian religions. It expressed the sentiment that "the relation between religions must take unceasingly hereafter the form of a common search for truth"; that the Christian missionary "will look forward, not to the destruction of these (non-Christian) religions, but to their continued co-existence with Christianity, each stimulating the other in growth toward the ultimate goal, unity in the completest religious truth." [1]

In 1936 Hendrik Kraemer was commissioned by the International Missionary Council to address the same subject in preparation for the Madras meeting. The result was *The Christian Message in a Non-Christian World* published in 1938. It took sharp issue with *Re-thinking Missions*. Kraemer's position was that all non-Christian religions were the attempt of man to understand the meaning of existence, but that Christianity, defined as the revelation of God in Christ, was God's self-disclosure to man, which can only be received by faith. He, therefore, took the position of Christianity's radical discontinuity with all expressions of non-Christian religion, concluding that the only point of contact was the missionary himself or herself. In the Madras reports, the first article of the first volume *(The Authority of the Faith)* was written by Kraemer. In "Continuity or Discontinuity," he took the same position he had taken in his book which had been published earlier. [2]

As a continuation of the debate after Madras, Edmund Davison Soper in *The Philosophy of the Christian World Mission* sought to synthesize the two radical views in his own mediating position. He described Hocking's position as "continuity with doubtful uniqueness" and Kraemer's position as "uniqueness with no continuity." He then described his own position as "uniqueness together with continuity." The following pages provide selections from Hocking and Kraemer which set forth in some detail their sharply contrasting positions.[3]

41

Re-thinking Missions: A Laymen's Inquiry After One Hundred Years[4]   William Ernest Hocking

Introduction

William Ernest Hocking (1873-1966) was born in Cleveland, Ohio. He was educated at Harvard and after a few years of teaching at Yale returned there where he taught until retirement. An active Christian layman, his philosophical works reflected his religious interest: *The Meaning of God in Human Experience* (1912). As chairman of the Laymen's Inquiry, he traveled extensively in Asia, making a firsthand investigation of the mission field. His editorship of the findings of the commission placed him at the storm center of a long controversy. However, his later works—*Living Religions and a World Faith* (1940) and *The Coming World Civilization* (1956)—reflected a much more evangelical position than *Re-thinking Missions*, which seemed to undercut the very motive for Christian mission.[5]

Christianity, Other Religions and Non-Religion

At the beginning of our century of Protestant missions, Christianity found itself addressing men attached to other religions: its argument was with these religions. At present, it confronts a growing number of persons, especially among the thoughtful, critical of or hostile to all religion. Its further argument, we judge, is to be less with Islam or Hinduism or Buddhism than with materialism, secularism, naturalism. The growth of this third factor, non-religion, alters the relation of the other two: Christianity and the environing religions face at the same moment the same menace, the spread of the secular spirit; the former opponents have become to this extent allied by the common task. It is not surprising if our missions find this realignment difficult, perhaps embarrassing; it compels a thorough re-analysis of the purpose of missions in reference to other faiths.

. . . .

6. *The Attitude Toward Error*

a. The errors. In all the great religious systems of Asia one learns to make distinctions—and is prepared to find them very wide—between the religion of the people, the religion of the priestly class and of the professional holy men, the religion of the scholars and reformers, and the religion of the intelligent laity. Of these, the religion of the priesthood is in general the least edifying: there are always exceptional men, but the priestly average is not much better instructed nor more spiritual than it is required to be by the intelligence and conscience of the public with which it deals. And except in Japan, the requirements of the mass of the people are those of an uninstructed peasantry. The priesthood has a vested interest in the maintenance of all the beliefs which sustain the observances of the temples: it is recruited and trained with these observances chiefly in view. If the religion is a state religion, its priests will be also trained with a semi-political role in view, almost invariably resulting in the degradation of religion. There is many a Hindu scholar who has no personal contact with the worship of the temples. There are Buddhist monasteries in China and Japan where the business of the temple is in another world, mentally, from the adjacent business of the library, the school and the hall of meditation. As long as Asia may be obliged to accept for its peasant masses the twin curses of poverty and ignorance, so long must we expect to find the third curse, the unspiritual priest.

It is always possible that the right attitude toward an ecclesiastical system, as distinguished from the religion it frames, may be one of clear hostility. There are times when the policy of implacable antagonism is the way of true friendship to the religious interest itself. The decision will depend in each case on the degree of health within the system. In Hinduism, the power of the priestly class and its general influence are probably more deplorable than those of the corresponding class in the old regimes of Russia and Turkey. The motives for purging the temples are proportionately great. But there is a question for the Christian at this point: Is he the qualified and appointed judge?

He has to remember first of all that there are forces within Indian life occupied with just this problem, laboring with competence and understanding for reform from within. He must consider that no great system lives through the centuries on the strength of its diseases, but on the strength of some fitness to the total civilization: until he has thought through this function he should hesitate to adopt an iconoclastic view. It would be a sad error of judgment if, at the moment of a strong and promising movement of internal renovation, the Christian Church should aim at destroying or displacing the old structure.

It is clearly not the duty of the Christian missionary to attack the non-Christian systems of religion. Nor is it his primary duty to denounce the errors and abuses he may see in them: it is his primary duty to present in positive form his conception of the true way of life and let it speak for itself. Nevertheless, it is more respectful to non-Christians, as men, to criticize plainly whatever deserves criticism, especially when it touches the kernel of the religious life, than it is to be silent. Gandhi has recently said "My fierce hatred of child marriage I gladly say is due to Christian influence . . . Before I knew anything of Christianity, I was an enemy of untouchability . . . My feelings gathered momentum owing to the fierce attack from Christian sources on this evil." What is necessary is that the missionary should realize that in his criticism he is joining Hindus in rectifying abuses which have invaded the structure of their religion. And further, that the Hindu can do far more toward any such reform than can he, the Christian, as an outsider. The Christian view may aid in resolving a Gandhi to an act of mercy in the slaughter of a suffering cow: but Gandhi's deed will do more to revise Hindu custom than all the criticisms of all the Christians.

The Christian will therefore regard himself a co-worker with the forces which are making for righteousness within every religious system. If he can in any way aid or encourage these forces, he will regard it a part of his Christian service to spend thought and energy in this way.

Desiring to be considered a co-worker rather than an enemy, he will especially refrain from misrepresentation abroad of the evils he desires to cure, and more particularly from dwelling on these evils without mentioning also the efforts being made by nationals to correct them.

. . . .

8. *The Attitude Toward Reform*

b. Growth in non-Christian religions: borrowings. Whenever two vigorous religions are in contact, each will tend to borrow from the other—terms, usages, ideas, even gods and articles of faith. After centuries of such borrowing they show strong resemblances, like Taoism and Buddhism in China, while holding to some precious points of difference. Commonly the borrowing is without acknowledgement: each religion takes what it can use from the other, or from the common fund of popular usage, and gives it a turn and a derivation suited to its own history. So Christianity in its early days adopted Christmas tree, or Yule festival, or imagery from the mysteries, or philosophical tools from the stock of Greece and Rome. Sometimes the new acquisitions are merely set up outside or loaded into the general warehouse without logical regard to what is already there: Hinduism has frequently added to its inner variety in this way. Sometimes they take root and grow on the existing stock, because they belong there by natural stages of advance.

In the presence of Christianity, it is not surprising that the living religions of the East should grow in this way, especially Hinduism and Buddhism. They are not as a rule averse to acknowledging the debt, even while claiming that what they borrow is their own by right. In this way, little by little, much of Christianity is assimilated by these religions without calling it Christianity. Not merely modes of worship, preaching, Sunday schools, hymns, popular fables, but aspects of the conception of God, ethical notions, the honoring of Christ, may be taken over.

What should be the attitude of the Christian mission to this process?

At best, it would appear to be a striking success of its own work: a transfer of the substance apart from the name. With what are we concerned except for the spread through the world of what Christianity *means?*

Nevertheless, there are misgivings. In part from a fear that the adoption will be imitative, unreal, or half-understood, leaving men satisfied with what resembles Christianity without its reality. In part from a very different fear, namely, that the adoption will be real as far as it goes, the non-Christian religion thereby receive new vigor, the contrast between it and Christianity be lessened, the motives which have led its members to come over into the Christian fellowship correspondingly minimized. Those who feel this latter fear are evidently thinking in terms of competition. We have in mind a missionary who defines the God of Islam as a God of power, whereas the Christian God is a God of love. He is accordingly disturbed when he finds a Moslem teaching that the compassion of Allah is the same as the love of God: he inclines to cry plagiarism! and to warn all Moslems that the idea of God as loving Father is Christian and private property!

The situation is particularly pointed in Japan, where Buddhism with a keen, aggressive, well-equipped leadership shows the greatest readiness to appropriate Christian ideas and practices. If this means an advance in true religion among the Japanese people, how can the Christian have anything but welcome for the result? Yet the numerical advance of the Christian organization is retarded by this very success: hence there enters an element of rivalry. To those primarily interested in the extension of church membership, this growth within Buddhism is likely to be read as a challenge calling for something like a counter-aggression. Concern for the institution here threatens to part company with concern for the souls of men.

It is time for the Christian movement to have overcome these unworthy fears springing from a sense of proprietorship. The unique thing in Christianity is not borrowable nor transferable without the transfer of Christianity itself. Whatever can be borrowed and successfully grown on another stock does in fact belong to the borrower. For a part of the life of any living religion is its groping for a better grasp of truth. The truth which rectifies the faults of any religious system is already foreshadowed in its own search. Hence all fences and private properties in truth are futile: the final truth, whatever it may be, is the New Testament of every existing faith.

We desire the triumph of that final truth: we need not prescribe the route. It appears probable that the advance toward that goal may be by way of the immediate strengthening of several of the present religions of Asia, Christian and non-Christian together. The Christian who would be anxious in view of such a result displays too little confidence in the merits of his own faith. Whatever is unique in it, and necessary to the highest religious life of men can be trusted to show its value in due time and in its own way. Meantime, if through growing appreciation and borrowing, the vitality of genuine religion is anywhere increased he may well rejoice in that fact. He will look forward, not to the destruction of these religions, but to their continued co-existence with Christianity, each stimulating the other in growth toward the ultimate goal, unity in the completest religious truth.

. . . .

10. *Instituting the Sharing Process*

But perhaps the chief hope for an important deepening of self-knowledge on the part of Christendom is by way of a more thoroughgoing sharing of its life with the life of the Orient. Sharing may mean spreading abroad what one has: but sharing becomes real only as it becomes mutual, running in both directions, each teaching, each learning, each with the other meeting the unsolved problems of both.

That the non-Christian religions do contain elements of instruction for us, imperfect exponents as we are of the truth we have, cannot be doubted. We have just illustrated this in what we have said of meditation. There are many other respects in which we may well be the learners. Buddhism's unworldliness, in many ways a disadvantage, still represents an ingredient of all true religion, prominent in early and mediaeval Christianity, from which the "social gospel" may become too far estranged. And with it goes an undeviating concern for metaphysical truth which we of the West have been tempted at times to abandon in the interest of "practicality." In this, it may be Buddhism that is truly practical: for it is the depths of the universe which most directly stir the depths of selfhood, and the stability of the inner life is the source of all strength for outer action. It is Zen Buddhism, we remember, a cult of quietude and discipline, which has given to Japan so many strong men in public life.

One great reason for the presence of Christianity in the Orient is an interest in its own developing interpretation, as it could hardly grow in America alone, through free intercourse with various other types of religious experience. The relation between religions must take increasingly hereafter the form of a common search for truth.

It is our view that this function should be in part performed through a type of institution distinct from and supplementary to the present type of teaching mission.

We have in mind the establishment of centers here and there as persons and occasions offer, for the avowed purpose of facilitating such cooperative religious inquiry through give and take between persons of various faiths. We are not thinking of institutions which bind and hold men together in unions of fixed membership; such institutions exist, and they have a way of going dull. We think rather of places fitted for hospitality toward persons desiring to come and go freely, where men concerned with these themes may meet one another, perhaps live together for a time, eat together, study together, work together, and also have plenty of opportunity for solitary thought and reading. As the function is a natural one, there have always been ways, more or less adequate, of providing for it. It is now time to do it well.

Doing it well would imply a place where quiet and retreat are possible. At the same time, it might with advantage have a special activity of its own, bringing together a nucleus of permanent personnel. It might be a place of study and research such as we have suggested. But the business of the place would be conversation, ample, repeated, unhurried, with intervals of reflection and work.

Out of these conversations and thoughts there should come, in the first place, a steady growth of mutual understanding and respect among these seekers of various faiths; then that deepening of self-knowledge which is inseparable from a better knowledge of others; and from time to time, as the supreme success, the birth of an idea which shall stir and strengthen religion in the race.

. . . .

42

The Christian Message in a Non-Christian World [6]
Hendrik Kraemer

Introduction

Hendrik Kraemer (1888-1965), renowned Dutch theologian and missiologist, exercised one of the greatest influences on Protestant mission thought of any person in the twentieth century. A layman, he went to Indonesia in 1922 under sponsorship of the Netherlands Bible Society. There he acquired great expertise in Indonesian Islam. A brilliant Oriental linguist, he developed a profound understanding of the religions of the East. Although he is best known for his influential work *The Christian Message in a Non-Christian World* and its sequel *Religion and the Christian Faith* (1956), he wrote other works on such themes as the laity and communication.[7]

In 1937 he became professor of phenomenology of religion at Leyden, and during the war the Germans placed him in a concentration camp. In 1947 he became the first director of the Ecumenical Institute at the Chateau de Bossey. Though a profound scholar, he was deeply concerned about practical problems on the mission field, such as hindrances to the development of indigenous churches. After his retirement he continued his writing and was an invaluable "advisor at large" for the Christian world mission cause.[8]

The Attitude Towards the Non-Christian Religions

The Christian religion in its real sense, that is, as the revelation in Christ with all that that involves as to faith and ethics, revolves around two poles.

The first pole is knowledge of God of a very special kind that upsets all other conceptions of God or of the Divine. The God revealed and active in Christ is the holy, reconciling God. He is the God who, in His act of reconciling the world and man unto Himself, manifested His holiness as well as His love. He set a new course so as to re-establish His rightful dominion of men on the foundation of a new relation of "love which has no dread in it."

The second pole is a knowledge of man, also of a very special kind and revolutionary in comparison with any other conception of man. Man, in the light of the revelation in Christ, is God's creature, destined to be His child and co-worker, hence of great worth and great qualities. His nature and condition, however, have become perverted by a radical self-centredness, explained in the Bible as the will to be "like God, knowing good and evil," the root of sin and death in the world. Man's God-rooted origin and end, and his splendid God-given qualities, assert themselves still in the ways in which he tries to master and regulate life, as manifested in his great achievements in the field of culture, art, science, political, social and economic life. The perversion of sin, which permeates all his achievements with the will that makes for god-likeness, causes that in all things, not excepting the greatest and sublimest in any sphere of life, man is trying to evade his fundamental problem, namely, this perversion of sin. Yet at the same time, in these evasions he is trying to overcome and conquer—though unsuccess-fully—by his own devices this his fundamental problem. Therefore human life in all its manifestations, abject as well as sublime, lies under the judgment of God and can only be redeemed and fundamen-tally renewed by recognizing wholeheartedly this judgment and the love and faith of God which are embodied therein. The whole-hearted recognition and acceptance of God's judgment and love by man is called faith, and the life built on that kind of faith is called the new life of the Spirit.

. . . .

Now it is our task to determine against this background our attitude towards the non-Christian religions.

The problem of this attitude is, for various reasons, one of the great-est and gravest which the Christian Church all over the world and the missionary cause have to face at the present time. Properly speak-ing, it is part of the root-problem which occupies us through our whole discussion—that is, the Christian Church and the Christian religion in their relation to the world and its spheres of life. The question behind this root-problem is always in some form or another: What do you think about man, his nature, his possibilities, his achievements? It is very pertinent to remind ourselves of this, for two reasons.

First, the non-Christian religions are not merely sets of speculative ideas about the eternal destiny of man. The departmentalization of religion in the modern world as a result of the secularist differentiation of life-spheres strongly forces this erroneous conception of religion on the general mind. These non-Christian religions, however, are all-inclusive systems and theories of life, rooted in a religious basis, and therefore at the same time embrace a system of culture and civilization and a definite structure of society and state. To pronounce from the standpoint of the Christian faith upon our attitude towards the non-Christian religions necessarily means to pronounce upon the relation of the Christian faith to culture, state, society—in short, to the world and its spheres of life.

Secondly, the course usually followed—and which we shall follow too—when discussing the attitude of Christianity towards the non-Christian religions is that of expressing the whole problem in terms of the problems of general revelation and natural theology. This theological limitation of the discussion is all to the good, because it concentrates thought on the fundamental religious problems, effecting thereby a greater clarity of insight. It ought, however, constantly to be kept in mind that it is embedded in the all-embracing problem of the Christian religion or the Christian church in its relation to the world. The great advantage that is to be derived from sticking to this commanding view is that the burning missionary problem of the attitude towards the non-Christian religions is a specimen of the great problem with which the Christian Church all over the world in different ways is inescapably confronted. In the condition of universal transition and revolutionary revision of culture, structure of state, society and economic order in which the world of to-day finds itself, the Church has to state anew its position in and obligation towards these spheres of life and their *present* pre-suppositions, pretensions, tendencies and values.

The confusion left behind in many minds from the discussion in the Jerusalem Meeting of the I.M.C. in 1928 of the papers on the values of the different religions was due to the fact that the value of those religions was discussed in a too-isolated way and the religions were not therefore given their appropriate setting. The questions that, from the Christian point of view, i.e. the view-point of revelation, lie at the back of such terms as general revelation and natural theology may be expressed as follows. Are nature, reason and history sources of revelation in the Christian sense of the word? If so, what is the relation of the Christian revelation and its implications to the body of human self-unfolding which takes place in philosophy, religion, culture, art, and the other domains of life? Whether the answer of the Christian Church is in the terms of a resolute renunciation of the world, as in the first centuries, or in those of a form of co-operation as in the Middle Ages, or is still different, depends wholly on the concrete circumstances of a given period and which aspect of its obligation as a Church, which lives by only one supreme loyalty, has to be operative in this given period.

There are, however, two conditions never to be lost sight of. In the first place, Christianity, under all circumstances, must always be aware that it is built on the prophetic and apostolic witness to a divine, transcendental order of life that transcends and judges by virtue of its inherent authority the whole range of historical human life in every period.

In the second place, whether the attitude is one of renunciation, of reserve or of intimate relation, it has to be essentially a *positive* attitude, because the world remains the domain of God who created it. After its rebellion against Him, He did not let it go but held it fast in His new initiative of reconciliation. It must be a positive attitude also because the Christian Church, as the witness to and representative of the new order of salvation and reconciliation, has been set by God *in* this world in order to be and work for the sake of this world. Jesus taught us to pray, "God's will be done on earth as it is in heaven," and this petition will always be the Magna Charta of the Church's obligation to occupy itself strenuously and positively with the world and its spheres of life, including the non-Christian religions.

The two conditions just mentioned indicate clearly the dialectical relation in which Christianity, if true to its nature and mission, ought to stand to the world—the combination of a fierce "yes" and at the same time a fierce "no" to the world: the *human* and *broken* reflection of the divine "no" and "yes" of the holy God of reconciliation, who held the world under His absolute judgment and at the same time claimed it for His love.

. . . .

The argument of value does not coincide in any way whatever with that of truth. The non-Christian religions can just as well as Christianity show up an impressive record of psychological, cultural and other values, and it is wholly dependent on one's fundamental axioms of life whether one considers these non-Christian achievements of higher value for mankind than the Christian. The weakness of the value-argument in relation to the problem of ultimate and authoritative truth is still more patent if one remembers that from the standpoint of relative cultural value fictions and even lies have been extraordinarily valuable and successful. To-day we are taught unforgettable lessons on this score. Learned, ingenious, enthusiastic apologies for Christianity or religion, which shun the problem of truth because of its difficulty and satisfy themselves with important secondary motivations, are bred in ambiguity. A pragmatist position means ultimate scepticism or agnosticism and involves the surrender of the problem of truth. At the end the problem of truth stares us always sternly in the face, because man's deepest and noblest instincts refuse to extinguish the mark of his divine origin, namely, his thirst for and want of imperishable truth. The subjectively-motivated superiority of religious truths, experiences and values can never substantiate the claim for truth or justify and keep alive a missionary movement. The only possible basis is the faith that God has revealed *the* Way and *the* Life and *the* Truth in Jesus Christ and wills this to be known through all the world. A missionary movement and obligation so founded is alone able to remain unshaken and undiscouraged, even when it is without visible result as, for example, is so largely true in the case of Islam.

And how are we to justify this faith? The only valid answer, which is at the same time according to the character and nature of faith, is that it will become justified in the end when God will fulfil His purpose. For "Faith is a well-grounded assurance of that for which we *hope*, and a conviction of the reality of things which we do *not* see" (Heb. xi. 1). To demand a rational argument for faith is to make reason, that is, man, the standard of reference for faith, and ends in a vicious circle. Ultimate convictions never rest on a universally lucid and rational argument, in any philosophy and in any religion, and they never will.

To adhere to a certain view of life and of the world has always meant a choice and a decision; not a rational step in the sense of being universally demonstrable as a mathematical truth. Religion and philosophy deal with different things from mathematics and physical science. They deal with man and his desires, his passions and aspirations; or—to put it more adequately—loving, hating, coveting, aspiring man tries to deal with himself in religion and philosophy, and this involves every moment ethical and religious choices and decisions. The Christian's ultimate ground of faith is: "The Spirit bears witness along with our own spirits that we are children of God" (Rom. viii. 16); and he can die for that.

It has to be emphatically stated that the science of comparative religion, which brought and brings this confusion and anxiety, has exercised in many respects a highly salutary influence on religious life and our notions of it. Many fruits of the great humanistic movements of the last few centuries have made for a noble quest for truth, and for the liberation and widening of the human mind. So the science of comparative religion has effected in many directions a beneficent purification of religious insight. This remains true notwithstanding the many misguided notions and aberrations that it naturally entertained as being an occupation of human beings. In God's Hand it has become a means to unveil the stupendous richness of the religious life of mankind, in the good sense of the word as well as in the bad; to foster a spirit of openness and honesty towards this alien religious life; to undermine the unchristian intellectualistic and narrow-minded arrogance towards these other religions; to open the eyes to the often all-too-human element in Christianity in its historical development and reality, often as degrading as the baser elements in the other religions; to make aware of the petrification of faith and church-life into which the Christian Church slips as easily as other religions fall short of their original stimuli. Whosoever has learnt, with the aid of the science of comparative religion, to look honestly in the face the empirical reality of Christianity—I am not now speaking about the Christian revelation and its reality—and of the other religions, and has understood that Christianity as an historical religious body is thoroughly human, that is, a combination of sublime and abject and tolerable elements, will feel deeply that to speak glibly of the superiority of Christianity is offensive. Of course, there are many traits in which Christianity in its historical manifestation is superior to other religions; but of other traits the same can be said in regard to the non-Christian religions. The truly remarkable thing about Christianity as an historic and empirical reality, which differentiates it from all other religions, is rather that radical self-criticism is one of its chief characteristics, because the revelation in Christ to which it testifies erects the absolute superiority of God's holy Will and judgment over *all* life, historical Christianty included.

The feeling of superiority is essentially a cultural, and not at all a religious, product; and decidedly not a Christian one. A feeling of superiority can only thrive on a definite consciousness of achievement. The famous student of religion, Troeltsch, who declined the Christian claim of representing the ultimate, exclusive truth as revealed in Jesus Christ, yet who nevertheless maintained a so-called relative absoluteness for Christianity, was virtually giving expression to his innate feeling of Western cultural achievement. There is no reason why a Hindu or a Chinese, being nurtured in his particular atmosphere, should not claim, after a comparative survey of the cultures and religions of the world, the same relative absoluteness with regard to his religion.

In the light of the Christian revelation, however, it is impossible and unnatural to think in terms of achievement, whether ethical or religious; for the heart of the Gospel is that we live by divine grace and forgiveness, and that God has *made* Jesus Christ for us "wisdom from God," "righteousness," "sanctification" and "redemption" in order that "he who boasts, let his boast be in the Lord" (1 Cor. i. 30, 31) and not in any achievement of his own. Speaking strictly as a Christian, the feeling of superiority is the denial of what God meant and did through the Gospel. That in Christianity and in the mission field the superiority-feeling has so many vicitms indicates the intellectualist distortion of the Gospel into which pious Christians can lapse, by forgetting that to be a Christian means always and in all circumstances to be a forgiven sinner and never the *beatus possidens* of ready-made truth. In one of the preparatory papers for the Oxford Conference, Niebuhr makes the acute observation, which is pertinent to this attitude: "The final symbol of the perennial character of human sin is in the fact that the theologies, which preach humility and contrition, can nevertheless be vehicles of human pride."

. . . .

The Christian revelation places itself over against the many efforts to apprehend the totality of existence. It asserts itself as the record of God's self-disclosing and recreating revelation in Jesus Christ, as an apprehension of existence that revolves around the poles of divine judgment and divine salvation, giving the divine answer to this demonic and guilty disharmony of man and the world.

THE PROBLEM OF NATURAL THEOLOGY

This fact of the universal religious consciousness of humanity and of its products and achievements has been a serious problem for Christianity since the beginning. For a very simple and obvious reason. Christianity as *the* religion of revelation is necessarily at close grips with the problem of truth. The Apologists and Fathers of the first Christian centuries propounded two opposite solutions to the problem; either they assumed the operation of diffused reason *(logos spermatikos)* in the non-Christian world or they denounced the non-Christian religious world as the product of demonic influences.

The most massive attempt to embrace the religious life of mankind and the Christian revelation in one harmonious system of thought has been Aquinas's hierarchical system of the sphere of natural and rational religious truth and that of the supernatural and superrational realm of revelation, on the assumption that the first grade of natural theology has the function of a *præambula fidei* and a *præparatio evangelica*. The main objection to this imposing system is not that it is rationalistic. Its value lies rather in its legitimate endeavour to recognize the rights of reason and of the undeniable human urge for ordered and progressive life, and so to vindicate that rationalism within due proportions has a valid and important place in human life and thinking. Thomas Aquinas did not aim at rationalizing the data of revelation. He was too good a Christian not to maintain the mystery of revelation, for in his opinion a "vetula" (an old uneducated woman) who lived by the mysteries of the Christian revelation had deeper knowledge and certitude about the fundamental problems of existence than his beloved philosopher of antiquity.

The fundamental weakness of Thomas's system is, from the standpoint of Biblical realism, a religious one. Under the influence of Aristotelian philosophy he entertained an intellectualist conception of revelation, considering it to offer a set of supernatural truths, inaccessible to reason (for example, the Trinity). This conception is a denial of the existential and dynamic character of Biblical revelation. Further than that, in order to construe his harmony he made the order of grace and revelation a perfected stage of nature and of reason. *Gratia non tollit sed perficit naturam* (grace does not abrogate but perfects nature), was his maxim. In doing this he destroyed the insuperable barrier between natural and supernatural truth that he previously erected, and ignored—a fundamental religious mistake—the fact that, according to Biblical realism, the opposite of grace is not nature or reason, but sin. The real cause of this unpardonable mistake is that his starting-point is the ontological conception of Greek philosophy about God, that God is Pure Essence and the Unity of all Being—and not the prophetic voluntaristic conception of the Bible. The urge for rational unity of thought was the impelling force in his ontological hierarchy and drove him into the arms of philosophical monism, setting the religious life of mankind and the revelation in Christ in the relation of horizontal grading to each other. The revelation in Christ, however, is vertically related to all human religious life and wisdom, because it is the "wisdom of God" which is "sheer folly" to the Greeks, and not the perfection or crown of human reason or religion. In Thomas's system revelation and its content becomes, logically speaking, a much-needed supplement to the insufficiency of reason in the realm of super-natural truth, and not the crisis of all religion and all human reasoning, which it is in the sphere of Biblical realism.

. . . .

The opposite standpoint is the subject of vigorous theological debate in the last ten years. Karl Barth's theology is an energetic endeavour to assert and lay bare the exclusive nature of Biblical religious truth as wholly *sui generis*. Its outstanding merit in the present deluge of relativist thinking is that it states the problem of revelation as a matter of life or death for Christianity and theology. It is deeply sensitive to the radically religious character of Biblical realism and proclaims it with prophetic aggressiveness and fervour. Its voice deserves the most serious attention to-day, because this theology offers a much-needed purification of Christian thinking.

. . . .

The way in which this special revelation in Christ contradicts and upsets all human religious aspiration and imagination is an indirect indication of its special and *sui generis* quality and significance. The protest which all philosophies and religions have raised, raise and will raise against the cardinal elements of the Christian faith demonstrates that the God of the philosophers and the scholars, however lofty their conception may be, is *not* the God and Father of Jesus Christ.

. . . .

To sum up, from the standpoint of Biblical realism the attitude towards the non-Christian religions, and likewise the relation of the Christian Church to the world in all its domains, is the combination of a prophetic, apostolic heraldship of truth for Christ's sake with a priestly apostolic ambassadorship of love for His sake. The right attitude of the Church, properly understood, is essentially a missionary one, the Church being set by God in the world as ambassador of His reconciliation, which is the truth that outshines all truth and the grace that works faithful love.

POINTS OF CONTACT

Whenever the problem of the missionary attitude towards the non-Christian religions is discussed, the "point of contact" inevitably appears on the scene. The task of a good missionary is naturally considered to be that of eagerly looking for points of contact. Every missionary who has his heart in his work is all his life deeply concerned about points of contact. His apostolic and missionary obligation and desire to reach men with the Message, to stir a response, to set the chords of men's inner conscience vibrating, to find an entrance for the Gospel into their minds, to "make the way ready for the Lord," foster this concern. This concern is legitimate and should not be weakened by the knowledge that no mortal man can work faith in God and in Christ in another man, and that it is the Holy Spirit alone that can work faith and "convince of sin, righteousness and judgment."

. . . .

One might state this important aspect of the problem of concrete points of contact in this somewhat unusual way: that there is only one point of contact, and if that one point really exists, then there are many points of contact. This one point of contact is the disposition and the attitude of the missionary. It seems rather upsetting to make the missionary the point of contact. Nevertheless it is true, as practice teaches. *The strategic and absolutely dominant point in this whole important problem, when it has to be discussed in general terms, is the missionary worker himself.* Such is the golden rule, or, if one prefers, the iron law, in this whole matter. The way to live up to this rule is to have an untiring and genuine interest in the religion, the ideas, the sentiments, the institutions—in short, in the whole range of life of the people among whom one works, *for Christ's sake and for the sake of those people.* Whosoever disobeys this rule does not find any real point of contact. Whosoever obeys it becomes one with his environment, and has and finds contacts. Obedience to it is implied in the prime missionary obligation and passion, to wit, preparing the way for Christ and being by God's grace a pointer to Him. Only a genuine and continuous interest in the people as they are creates real points of contact, because man everywhere intuitively knows that, only when his actual being is the object of humane interest and love, is he looked upon in actual fact, and not theoretically, as a fellow-man. As long as a man feels that he is the object of interest only for reasons of intellectual curiosity or for purposes of conversion, and not because of himself as he is in his total empirical reality, there cannot arise that humane natural contact which is the indispensable condition of all real religious meeting of man with man. In these conditions the door to such a man and to the world he lives in remains locked, and the love of Christ remains for him remote and abstract. It needs translation by the manifestation of the missionary's genuine interest in the whole life of the people to whom he goes.

The problem of the concrete points of contact is thus in its practical aspect to a very great extent a problem of missionary ethics, and not only a problem of insight and knowledge.

. . . .

Notes

1. Gerald H. Anderson, "Layman's Foreign Mission Inquiry," *Concise Dictionary,* pp. 339-340.

2. Gerald H. Anderson, *The Theology of the Christian Mission,* pp. 10-12; *The Authority of the Faith,* pp. 1-23.

3. Anderson, *The Theology of the Christian Mission,* p. 12.

4. Abridged from Chapter 2 (pp. 29-48) in *Re-Thinking Missions: A Laymen's Inquiry after One Hundred Years* by The Commission of Appraisal, William Ernest Hocking, Chairman. Copyright, 1932 by Laymen's Foreign Missions Inquiry. By permission of Harper & Row, Publishers, Inc.

5. Latourette, "William Ernest Hocking," *Concise Dictionary,* p. 254.

6. Hendrik Kraemer, "The Attitude Towards the Non-Christian Religions" (ch. IV), *The Christian Message in a Non-Christian World* (New York: International Missionary Council, 1947), pp. 101-141. Used by permission.

7. Stephen Neill, "Hendrik Kraemer," *Concise Dictionary,* pp. 328-329.

8. Ibid., p. 329.

X

Historic Missionary Encyclicals

General Introduction

Even though this collection comes together out of a Protestant perspective, we would be remiss not to give some place to the significance of Roman Catholic missions since the Protestant Reformation. Indeed, we have included earlier notables: Las Casas, Xavier, and Ricci. Limited space prohibited our including such significant figures as Alexander de Rhodes and Robert de Nobili of the same general period. In more recent times there have been other towering figures relating to the missionary enterprise: Charles de Foucauld, Charles Lavigerie, James Anthony Walsh, cofounder of the Catholic Foreign Mission Society of America (Maryknoll), and many others.

In the first three centuries after the Reformation, Roman Catholics dominated the missionary enterprise, mostly under the patronage of the two great maritime colonial powers of the period: Spain and Portugal. The Jesuits were the most prominent missionaries of this early period. With the formation of the Congregation for the Propagation of the Faith in 1622, France became more prominent. At the beginning of the eighteenth century, Roman Catholic missions was at the height of its glory—but that very century brought an incredible reversal. The Enlightment, the French Revolution, the Napoleonic seizure of the papal states, conflict with Protestant powers, and suppression of the Jesuits in the major Catholic countries and later by Rome itself, almost decimated the missionary ranks. By 1773 some 3,500 Jesuits were recalled from the fields, and by 1800 the Propaganda had only three hundred missionaries.[1]

The recovery of Roman Catholic missions in the late nineteenth and in the twentieth centuries has been as dramatic as the earlier losses. In 1969 there were 100,000 missionaries serving around the world. Today there are over 6,600 overseas missionaries from the United States alone.[2] Since Vatican II, barriers have begun to collapse between

Catholics and Protestants. The charismatic movement has been a common denominator drawing individuals from both communities together. A renewed interest in the Bible on the part of Catholics, a series of serious Roman Catholic-Southern Baptist scholars dialogues, the active participation of Catholics in a growing number of ecumenical affairs—these and many other developments are bringing Catholics and Protestants together as never before.

One of the most significant developments in this new cooperation is in the area of missions. For example, Australian Baptist and Catholic nurses joined the nurses of the Southern Baptist mission of Dacca to minister to the Pakistani refugees. Catholics are prominent in the International Association for Mission Study, the American Society of Missiology, and the Association of Professors of Missions—organizations that include (in leadership positions) such groups as Southern and Conservative Baptists and Nazarenes, as well as traditional ecumenists. The Maryknoll Community and its publication arm, Orbis Books, the Paulist Fathers and the Paulist Press, and other Catholic forces are making one of the most significant contributions to the world mission cause in the international Christian community today. Paulist Press and William B. Eerdmans Publishing Company collaborate in the annual publication of the significant series, *Mission Trends,* jointly edited by Methodist Gerald H. Anderson and Paulist Thomas Stransky.

One of the most significant phenomena in the promotion of Roman Catholic missions over the centuries has been the missionary encyclicals of the popes. The first of these encyclicals was the Bull of Honorius III, dated February 25, 1221, in which the pope sent a letter to the thirteen metropolitans of the Church at that time urging them to send out missionaries. In more recent times there have been encyclicals by Leo XIII (1880), Benedict XV (1919), Pius XI (1926), Pius XII (1951 and 1957), John XXIII (1959), and Paul VI *("Evangelii Nuntindi").* In the following pages we include the encyclicals of Benedict XV and John XXIII.[3]

43

"Maximum Illud," [4] 1919 Benedict XV

Introduction

Giacomo Giambattista della Chiesa (1854-1922) was born in Genoa, Italy. A brilliant student, he received the Doctor of Laws degree at the University of Genoa before he was twenty-one. He later earned two other doctorates, in theology and canon law. He distinguished himself in many ways as a priest, bishop, and cardinal. In 1914, he became pope and took the name Benedict XV. He served during the stormy days of World War I. His first encyclical was on the theme "Love One Another," written at the beginning of the hostilities in Europe. The value of his missionary encyclical of 1919 as a historical document is in the emphasis it places upon the founding and development of indigenous churches and in the fact that it broke a forty-year silence from the papacy in regard to a missionary encyclical.[5]

Maximum Illud

1) Before he returned to His Father, Our Lord Jesus Christ addressed to His disciples the words: "Go into the whole world and preach the gospel to all creation" (Mark 16:15). With these words He committed to them a duty, a momentous and a holy charge, that was not to lapse with the death of the Apostles but would bind their successors, one after another, until the end of the world—as long, that is, as there remained on this earth men whom the truth might set free. Entrusted with this mandate, "they went forth and preached everywhere" (Mark 16:20) the word of God, so that "through all the earth their voice resounds, and to the ends of the world, their message" (Psalm 18:5). From that time on, as the centuries have passed, the Church has never forgotten that command God gave her, and never yet has she ceased to dispatch to every corner of the world her couriers of the doctrine

He entrusted to her, and her ministers of the eternal salvation that was delivered through Christ to the race of men.

Great Apostles of the Gospel

2) Even in the first three centuries, when persecution after persecution, inspired by Hell, fell upon the infant Church in a raging attempt to crush her, even then when the whole of civilization was deluged with Christian blood, out on the far frontiers of the Empire the heralds of the gospel journeyed, announcing their tidings. Then, after peace and religious freedom had been officially granted to the Church, her apostolate to the world made far greater progress. In this achievement a number of men of striking sanctity played outstanding roles. One of them was Gregory the Illuminator, who brought the Faith to Armenia. Another was Victorinus, the apostle of Styria. Frumentius, who evangelized Ethiopia, was a third. Later on Patrick brought forth the Irish in Christ; Augustine introduced the Faith among the English; and Columba and Palladius preached the gospel to the Scots. Later still Clement Willibrord, the first Bishop of Utrecht, brought the radiance of the gospel to Holland; Boniface and Anagar carried the Faith to the Germans; and Cyril and Methodius won Slavonia for the Church.

Purpose of This Letter

7) The pitiable lot of this stupendous number of souls is for Us a source of great sorrow. From the days when We first took up the responsibilities of this apostolic office We have yearned to share with these unfortunates the divine blessings of the Redemption. So We are delighted to see that, under the inspiration of the Spirit of God, efforts to promote and develop the foreign missions have in many quarters of the world increased and intensified. It is Our duty to foster these enterprises and do all We can to encourage them; and this duty coincides perfectly with Our own most profound desires. Before writing this letter, venerable Brethren, We begged the Lord for His light and His aid. While writing it, We had two purposes in mind: to encourage you, your clergy, and your people in these efforts, and secondly, to point out methods you can adopt to further the fulfillment of this momentous undertaking.

8) First We want to address those who are in charge of the missions, whether as Bishops or as Vicars or Prefects Apostolic. All the responsibility for the propagation of the Faith rests immediately upon them, and it is to them especially that the Church has entrusted her prospects of expansion. We know very well the burning intensity of their zeal for the apostolate, and We are also well aware of the immense difficulties they have had to overcome and the crises they have had to face, especially in the last few years. This was the price they had to pay to remain at their stations and outposts and to go on extending the Kingdom of God. And so they paid it willingly.

. . . .

A Primary Concern

11) Furthermore, the superior of a mission should make it one of his primary concerns to expand and fully develop his mission. The entire region within the boundaries of his mission has been committed to his care. Consequently, he must work for the eternal salvation of every person living there. If, out of an immense populace, he has converted a few thousand people, he has no reason to lapse into complacency. He must become a guide and a protector for these children he has brought forth in Jesus Christ; he must see to their spiritual nourishment and he must not let a single one of them slip away and perish. But he must do more than this. He must not consider that he is properly discharging the duties of his office unless he is working constantly and with all the vigor he can muster to bring the other, far more numerous, inhabitants of the area to partake of the Christian truth and the Christian life.

An Effective Means

In this connection, the preaching of the gospel can be brought more immediately and more effectively to everyone in an area if more mission stations and posts are established as soon as it is practible to do so. Then, when the time comes to divide the mission, these will be ready to serve as centers for new Vicariates and Prefectures. While We are on this subject, We wish to single out for commendation some Vicars Apostolic who have richly earned it: those who have kept this future development steadily in mind and are constantly engaged in the work of readying new provinces for the kingdom of God. If they find that their own order or congregation is not supplying enough manpower for the task, they are perfectly willing to call in helpers from other religious groups.

12) On the other hand, We can hardly commend a man who takes the section of the Lord's vineyard that has been allotted to him for cultivation, and proceeds to treat it as a piece of private property, a domain not to be touched by the hands of an outsider. Dwell for a moment upon the severity of God's judgment on a man like this, particularly if the case is like some that have been brought to Our attention at different times—a rather small community of the faithful surrounded by an immense population of infidels, infidels whom the superior cannot catechize because he does not have enough men for the work and refuses to accept the help of others. The man entrusted with a Catholic mission, if he is working single-mindedly for the glory of God and the salvation of souls, goes out whenever it is necessary and searches, searches everywhere, for helpers in his holy ministry. He does not care who they are; he does not care whether they belong to his order or to another, or whether or not they are of his nationality, "provided only that, in every way . . . Christ is being proclaimed" (Philippians 1:18). And he does not limit his welcome to men, either. He will bring in sisters to open schools, orphanages, and hospitals, to found their hostels and establish other charitable institutions. He is happy and eager to do this, because he realizes how remarkably works of this kind, with God's help, contribute to the spread of the Faith.

13) In the pursuit of his objectives the conscientious mission head refuses, too, to limit his interests to the boundaries of his own mission and to act as though he considered everything going on elsewhere as no concern of his. Fired with the charity of Christ, he feels that anything that affects Christ's glory affects him, and he does all he can to develop close and friendly relations with his colleagues in neighboring districts. For situations frequently arise that affect all the missions in some particular area, and that demand joint action if they are to be handled successfully. But even apart from this, the Church would benefit a great deal

if the men in charge of missions met at fixed intervals as frequently as they could to confer and to encourage one another.

Local Clergy

14) There is one final, and very important, point for anyone who has charge of a mission. He must make it his special concern to secure and train local candidates for the sacred ministry. In this policy lies the greatest hope of the new churches. For the local priest, one with his people by birth, by nature, by his sympathies and his aspirations, is remarkably effective in appealing to their mentality and thus attracting them to the Faith. Far better than anyone else he knows the kind of argument they will listen to, and as a result, he often has easy access to places where a foreign priest would not be tolerated.

15) If, however, the indigenous clergy is to achieve the results We hope for, it is absolutely necessary that they be well trained and well prepared. We do not mean a rudimentary and slipshod preparation, the bare minimum for ordination. No, their education should be complete and finished, excellent in all its phases, the same kind of education for the priesthood that a European would receive. For the local clergy is not to be trained merely to perform the humbler duties of the ministry, acting as the assistants of foreign priests. On the contrary, they must take up God's work as equals, so that some day they will be able to enter upon the spiritual leadership of their people.

. . . .

Concern for Training of Local Clergy

17) The Apostolic See has always urged the directors of missions to realize that this is a very serious obligation of their office and vigorously to put it into action. Here in Rome the colleges—both the old colleges and the newer ones—that train clerics for the foreign missions, have already shown their earnestness in the matter. This is particularly true of those training men for the Oriental rites. And yet it is a deplorable fact that, even after the Popes have insisted upon it, there still remain sections of the world that have heard the Faith preached for several centuries, and still have a local clergy that is of inferior quality. It is also true that there are countries that have been deeply penetrated

by the light of the Faith, and have, besides, reached such a level of civilization that they produce eminent men in all the fields of secular life—and yet, though they have lived under the strengthening influence of the Church and the gospel for hundreds of years, they still cannot produce Bishops for their spiritual government or priests for their spiritual guidance. From these facts it is obvious that in some places the system ordinarily used in training future missionaries has up to now been feeble and faulty. To correct this difficulty, We are ordering the Sacred Congregation for the Propagation of the Faith to apply remedies adapted to the various regions of the world, and to see to the founding of seminaries for both individual regions and group of dioceses. Where seminaries already exist, this Congregation will see to it that they are adequately administered. However, the task to which the Congregation is to devote itself with particular care is the supervision of the growth and development of the local clergy in our Vicariates and other missions.

To the Missionaries

18) Now We turn to you, beloved sons, the working-men of the Lord's vineyard. In your hands lies the immediate responsibility for disseminating the wisdom of Christ, and with this responsibility the salvation of innumerable souls. Our first admonition is this: never for a moment forget the lofty and splendid character of the task to which you have devoted yourselves. Your task is a divine one, a task far beyond the feeble reach of human reasoning. You have been called to carry light to men who lie in the shadow of death and to open the way to heaven for souls that are hurtling to destruction. Assure yourselves that God was speaking to you, to each one of you, when He said: "Forget your people and your father's house" (Psalm 44:11). Remember that your duty is not the extension of a human realm, but of Christ's; and remember too that your goal is the acquisition of citizens for a heavenly fatherland, and not for an earthly one.

A Spiritual Goal

19) It would be tragic indeed if any of our missionaries forgot the dignity of their office so completely as to busy themselves with the interest of their terrestrial homeland instead of with those of their

homeland in heaven. It would be a tragedy indeed if an apostolic man were to spend himself in attempts to increase and exalt the prestige of the native land he once left behind him. Such behavior would infect his apostolate like a plague. It would destroy in him, the representative of the Gospel, the sinews of his love for souls and it would destroy his reputation with the populace. For no matter how wild and barbarous a people may be, they are well aware of what the missionary is doing in their country and of what he wants for them. They will subject him in their own way to a very searching investigation, and if he has any object in view other than their spiritual good, they will find out about it. Suppose it becomes clear that he is involved in worldly schemes of some kind, and that, instead of devoting himself exclusively to the work of the apostolate, he is serving the interests of his homeland as well. The people immediately suspect everything he does. And in addition, such a situation could easily give rise to the conviction that the Christian religion is the national religion of some foreign people and that anyone converted to it is abandoning his loyalty to his own people and submitting to the pretensions and domination of a foreign power.

. . . .

The Missionary's Model

28) Like his model, the Lord Jesus, the good missionary burns with charity, and he numbers even the most abandoned unbelievers among God's children, redeemed like everyone else with the ransom of the divine blood. Their lowly difference does not exasperate him; their immorality does not dishearten him. His bearing toward them is neither scornful nor fastidious; his treatment of them is neither harsh nor rough. Instead, he makes use of all the arts of Christian kindness to attract them to himself, so that he may eventually lead them into the arms of Christ, into the embrace of the Good Shepherd. He makes it a custom to ponder the thought expressed in Holy Scripture: "Thy kindly influence, Lord, Thy gracious influence is all about us. At the first false step, none is so ready to rebuke us, to remind and warn us of our error, bidding us come back and renew our loyalty to Thee . . . With such power at Thy disposal, a lenient judge Thou provest thyself, riding us with a light rein, and keeping Thy terrors in reserve"

(Wisdom 12:1-2, 18). What obstacle can arise, what annoyance or danger exists that could deter this emissary of Jesus Christ from fulfilling the task he has begun? There is none. This man, who has attained great favor with God by his free choice of the lofty work he has taken upon himself, will cheerfully endure whatever adversity or hardship befalls him. Toil, scorn, want, hunger, even a dreadful death—he will gladly accept them all, as long as there remains a slight chance that he can free even one soul from the jaws of hell.

29) The missionary who is motivated and inspired by the example of Christ Our Lord and of the Apostles can go out confidently to his ministry. But he must recognize that the basis of his confidence rests entirely on God. As We have said before, this whole work is a divine work. Only God can enter men's hearts and illumine their minds with the radiance of truth; only God can enkindle their wills with the spark of virtue; only God can give them the strength to pursue the truth and do the good they have seen. The emissary will spend himself in vain unless his Lord helps him as he works. Yet he has every reason to go bravely on with the task allotted to him, for he can rely on divine grace—that grace which is never withheld from the man who asks for it.

. . . .

Society for the Propagation of the Faith

37) We warmly urge Catholics to give generous assistance to the organizations that have been established for the support of the missions. The first of these is the Society for the Propagation of the Faith, an organization that has repeatedly earned the commendation of Our predecessors. In the hope that its work will be even more fruitful in the future We recommend it to the particular attention of the Sacred Congregation for the Propagation of the Faith. For this organization has to supply a goodly proportion of the funds needed for the missions, both the missions already established and those that will be organized in the future. We are confident that in times like these when spokesmen for erroneous doctrines are numerous and affluent the Catholic world will not permit its own missionaries, the sowers of the seeds of truth, to go without resources.

. . . .

Missionary Union of the Clergy

40) But if these hopes of Ours, venerable Brethren, are to be assured of very great success, you must adopt some special measure to direct the thoughts of your clergy toward the missions. The faithful are generally ready and willing to come to the assistance of this willingness so that the missions will gain as much as possible by it. To accomplish this end, We desire the establishment, in all the dioceses of the Catholic world, of the organization is called the Missionary Union of the Clergy. This organization is under the direction of the Sacred Congregation for the Propagation of the Faith, and We have given the Congregation all the authorization necessary for its work. The Union was organized a short time ago in Italy, and has rapidly taken root in other places. Its work has Our complete approval, and We have already demonstrated Our pontifical approbation by granting it a number of privileges. With good reason, for the Union's methods are admirably suited to the task of fostering among the clergy the readiness and ability to instill in Christian hearts a concern for the salvation of the non-Catholic multitudes and to promote the various enterprises that the Holy See has approved as effective channels for assistance to the missions.

Conclusion

41) We have now said, venerable Brethren, what We wanted to say to you about the work of propagating the Catholic Faith through the world. If all Catholics, both the missionaries in the field and the faithful at home, meet the obligations of this task as they should, then We have good reason to hope that our missions will quickly recover from the severe wounds and losses inflicted by the war, and that they will in a short time again show their old strength and vigor. As We look into the future, We seem to hear the Lord's voice, urging Us to "Launch out into the deep water" (Luke 5:4), as He urged Peter long ago. Our paternal charity spurs Us to the work of leading into His welcoming arms the multitudes now living with Us in this world. For the Church is sustained by the Spirit of God, and under the influence of this Spirit she remains always strong and vigorous. Then too, the work of the thousands of apostolic men who have labored in the past and are laboring now to promote her growth cannot fail to have its effect. And their example will attract numerous others to imitate them, and

to go out, supported by the generosity and devotion of the good Christian people, to reap for Christ a rich harvest of souls.

44

"Princeps Pastorum" 1959 John XXIII [6]

Introduction

Angelo Giuseppe Roncalli (1881-1963) was born in the small village of Sotto il Monte near Bergamo. He studied at Lombard College and the Roman Seminary in Rome. Early in his career, he taught and also served in the military. In 1921, while spiritual director of the seminary of Bergamo, he was invited by Benedict XV to reorganize the Society for the Propagation of the Faith. He traveled extensively in pursuit of his duties in this capacity. After this he held a number of significant diplomatic posts for the Vatican. In 1953 he became Cardinal and Patriarch of Venice.[7]

Roncalli became pope in 1958 and took the name John XXIII. Already seventy-seven, he was expected to be a "care-taker" pope. However, though he served fewer than five years—he made one of the greatest impacts on the world of any person in modern times. He probably was more widely accepted by the non-Catholic world than any pope in history. He was personally charming, and his charisma was indisputable. His travels and various exposures to the world and its needs uniquely fitted him for the significant role he played in leading a revolution in the Catholic Church and making a unique mark in history. He will of course always be most intimately linked with Vatican II, and rightly so. Closely linked with that epochal event, with its strong missionary emphasis, is John's encyclical of 1959, "Princeps Pastorum." It preceded

Vatican II and helped to pave the way for the significant pronouncements it would make on the mission
of the church.[8]

"Princeps Pastorum"

On the day when "the Prince of the Shepherds"[9] entrusted to Us
His lambs and sheep,[10] God's flock, which dwells all over the earth,
We responded to the sweet invitation of His love with a sense of
Our unworthiness but with trust in His all-powerful assistance. And
the magnitude, the beauty, and the importance of the Catholic missions
have been constantly on Our mind.[11] For this reason, We have never
ceased to devote to them Our greatest solicitude and attention. And
at the close of the first year marking the anniversary of Our reception
of the triple tiara, in the sermon which We delivered on that solemn
occasion We mentioned as among the happiest events of Our pontificate
the day, October 10th, on which over four hundred missionaries gathered in the most holy Vatican Basilica to receive from Our hands the
crucifix, image of Jesus Christ Crucified, before leaving for distant parts
of the world to illumine them with the light of Christianity.

Early interest

The most provident Lord, in His secret and loving designs, willed
that, in its very first years, Our priestly mission should be oriented
toward the furthering of this cause; in fact, immediately after the conclusion of the first World War, Our predecessor Benedict XV called
Us to Rome from Our diocese, so that We could devote Our zeal to
the Pontifical Congregation for the Propagation of the Faith, a function
which We most willingly performed during four years of Our priestly
life. We happily recall Whitsunday in 1922, the third centenary of
the foundation of the Congregation for the Propagation of the Faith,
which is especially entrusted with the task of carrying the beneficial
light of the Gospel, and heavenly grace, to the farthest reaches of
the earth. It was with great joy that We participated in the Congregation's centennial festivities on that day.

. . . .

Subject of this letter

With these and many other sweet memories in Our mind, and aware of the grave duties imposed upon the Supreme Shepherd of the flock of God, We would like, venerable brethren—seizing an occasion offered by that memorable apostolic letter, *Maximum illud,*[12] with which, forty years ago, Our predecessor Benedict XV furthered the cause of the Catholic missions by establishing new rules and enkindling the faithful with new zeal—We would like, We repeat, to speak to you with a fatherly heart, by means of this letter, on the necessity and hopes of extending God's kingdom to the many parts of the world where missionaries labor zealously, sparing no effort in order that new branches of the Church may grow and produce wholesome fruits.

Our predecessors Pius XI and Pius XII also issued decrees and exhortations to the furtherance of this cause,[13] which We confirmed with like authority and like charity when We issued Our first encyclical letter, *"Ad Petri Cathedram."*[14] We think, however, and We feel sure that We will never do enough to carry out the wishes of the divine Redeemer in this matter until all sheep are happily gathered in one fold under the leadership of one shepherd.[15]

A cry for help

When We turn Our mind and Our heart to the supernatural blessings of the Church that are to be shared with those people whose souls have not yet been suffused with the light of the Gospel, there appear before Our eyes either regions of the world where bountiful crops grow, thrive, and ripen, or regions where the labors of the toilers in God's vineyard are very arduous, or regions where the enemies of God and Jesus Christ are harassing and threatening to destroy Christian communities by violence and persecutions, and are striving to smother and crush the seed of God's word.[16] We are everywhere confronted by appeals to Us to ensure the eternal salvation of souls in the best way We can, and a cry seems to reach Our ears: "Help us!" [17] Innumerable regions have already been made fruitful by the sweat and blood of messengers of the Gospel "from every nation under heaven," [18] and native apostles, with the help of divine grace, are blossoming like new buds and are bringing forth saving fruits. We desire to reach those regions with Our words of praise and encouragement, and with

Our affection. We also wish to give them Our instructions and admonitions, which are prompted by firm hope based on the infallible promise of Our divine Master, that is contained in these words: "Behold, I am with you all days, even unto the consummation of the world." [19] "Take courage, I have overcome the world." [20]

. . . .

Growth of native clergy

This exhortation of Benedict XV, which was repeated by Our predecessors Pius XI and Pius XII, with the help of God's divine Providence has had visible and copious results. We want you to join Us in rendering thanks to God for the fact that a numerous and elect legion of bishops and priests has arisen in the mission territories, Our brethren and beloved sons, who fill Our heart with great expectations. If We cast even a cursory glance on the ecclesiastical situation in the areas which are entrusted to the Sacred Congregation for the Propagation of the Faith, with the exception of those at present under persecution, We note that the first bishop of east Asian origins was consecrated in 1923, and the first vicars apostolic of African Negro descent were named in 1939. By 1959, We count 68 Asian and 25 African bishops. The remaining native clergy grew in number from 919 in 1918 to 5553 in 1957 in Asia, and during the same period in Africa from 90 in 1918 to 1811 in 1957. With such an admirable increase in the numbers of the clergy did the Lord of the harvest [21] desire to reward adequately the labors and merits of those who zealously did mission work, either individually or in co-operation with many others, responding with a generous heart to the repeated exhortations of this Apostolic See.

. . . .

Place of foreign missionaries

However, Christian communities to which missionaries still devote their zeal, although already governed by their own hierarchy, are still in need of the work of missionaries from other countries, either because of the vastness of the territory, or the increasing number of converts, or the multitude of those who have not yet benefited from the doctrine of the Gospel. To such missionaries, no doubt, apply these words of Our immediate predecessor: "These cannot be considered foreigners, for all Catholic priests who truly answer their vocation feel themselves native sons wherever they work, in order that the Kingdom of God may flourish and develop." [22] Let them therefore work united by the bond of that loving, brotherly, and sincere charity which mirrors the love they must feel toward the divine Redeemer and His Church; and, in prompt and filial obedience to their bishops, whom "the Holy Spirit placed . . . to rule the Church of God," [23] they must be "of one heart and one soul," [24] grateful to each other for the mutual cooperation and help; indeed, if they act in this manner, it should be apparent to everyone's eyes that they are the disciples of Him who, in His own and most distinctive "new" commandment, exhorted all to a mutual and always increasing love.[25]

II

Our predecessor Benedict XV, in his apostolic letter *"Maximum illud,"* especially exhorted Catholic mission authorities to mold and shape the minds and souls of the clergy selected from the local population, and to do so in such a way that their formation and education would turn out "perfect and complete in every respect." [26] "In fact," he wrote, "a native priest, having a place of birth, character, mentality, and emotional make-up in common with his countrymen, is in a privileged position for sowing the seeds of the Faith in their hearts: indeed, he knows much better than a stranger the ways of persuasion with them." [27]

Personal sanctification

Regarding the requirements of a perfect priestly formation and education, it is necessary that seminarians be induced, tactfully but firmly, to espouse those virtues which are the prime qualification of the priestly calling, "that is, the duty to achieve personal sanctification." [28] The newly-ordained native clergy of those countries must enter into pious competition with the clergy of those older dioceses which have long been producing priests in their midst who were such mirrors of virtue that they are proposed as examples to the clergy of the whole Church. In fact, it is through sanctity that priests can and must be the light of the world and the salt of the earth.[29] In other words, they can, especially by their sanctity, show their own countrymen and the whole world the beauty and the supernatural power of the Gospel; they can teach all men that a perfect Christian life is a goal toward which all of God's children must strive, struggling and persevering with all their strength, regardless of their place of birth, their walk of life, or the degree of civilization they enjoy.

Native teachers in seminaries

Furthermore, Our fatherly soul harbors the happy hope that everywhere the local clergy will be able to select from among its ranks just and holy men capable of governing, forming, and educating their own seminarians. That is the reason why We are already instructing the bishops and the mission authorities to choose without hesitation from among the local clergy those priests who, for their exceptional virtue and wise actions, qualify as teachers in the local seminaries and are able to lead their students to sanctity.

Adaptation to locality

Furthermore, venerable brethren, as you well know, the Church has prescribed at all times that priests must prepare for their calling by means of a solid intellectual and spiritual education. Indeed, no one will doubt, especially in our time, that young people of all races and from all parts of the world are capable of absorbing such an education; this fact has already been clearly demonstrated. Without doubt, the formation to be given to this clergy must take into account the circumstances which obtain in different areas and nations. This extremely wise norm applies to all students for the priesthood; it is advisable that young seminarians never be "educated in places too far removed from human society," [30] because "once they step out into the world, they will have problems in dealing both with simple people and with intellectuals; this will often cause them to assume the wrong attitude toward the Christian population, or to regard the formation they received as a bad one." [31] Indeed, it is necessary that youths not only conform to the ideal of priestly spiritual perfection in everything, but also that they "gradually and prudently penetrate the mentality and feelings of the people" [32]—of the people, We repeat, whom they must enlighten with the truth of the Gospel and lead to perfection of life, with the help of God's grace. Therefore, it is necessary that seminary superiors conform to this plan of training and education while yet welcoming those material and technical facilities which the genius of mankind has made the patrimony, as it were, of every civilization in order to insure an easier and better life and to preserve the bodily health and safety of mankind.

Training for responsibility

The formation of the local clergy, as Our same predecessor, Benedict XV, wrote, must enable them, in compliance with the first requirement of their divine calling, "to assume rightly the rule of their people" [33]— to lead their people, by the influence of their teaching and their ministry, along the path to eternal salvation. To this end, We highly recommend that everyone, whether local or foreign, who contributes to the formation in question, do his conscientious best to develop in these students a sense of the importance and difficulty of their mission, and a capability for wisely and discreetly using the freedom allowed to them. This should be done so that they may be in a position to assume, quickly and progressively, all the functions, even the most important ones, pertaining to their calling, not only in harmonious cooperation with the foreign clergy, but also on an equal footing with them.[34] Indeed, this is the touchstone of the effectiveness of their formation, and will be the best reward for the efforts of all those who contributed to it.

Missiology

Indeed, in considering all the elements pertaining not only to the right intellectual and spiritual formation of the students for the priesthood but also to the needs and to the special mentality and emotional make-up of their own people, this Apostolic See has always recommended, both to the foreign and to the local clergy, that they should study the discipline of missiology. Our predecessor Benedict XV established chairs of this discipline in the Pontifical Urban Athanaeum of the Propagation of the Faith;[35] and Our immediate predecessor, Pius XII, remarked with satisfaction on the founding of the Institute of Missiology in the same university; "not a few faculties and chairs of missiology," he said, "have been established in Rome and in other places." [36] Therefore, in the curricula of the seminaries of mission countries, there will be no lack of studies pertaining to the various missiological disciplines, nor of technical training in all the practical skills which are considered useful for the future work of the clergy in those countries. Therefore it is absolutely necessary that their training not only conform to the best ecclesiastical traditions of a solid and undiluted education, but also that it open up and sharpen the minds of the seminarians in such a way as to enable each individual to evaluate correctly his own and his country's particular kind of culture, especially as it pertains to philosophical and theological teachings and their relation to the Christian religion.

The Church and cultures

"The Catholic Church," stated Our same predecessor, "has never fostered an attitude of contempt or outright rejection of pagan teachings but, rather, has completed and perfected them with Christian doctrine, after purifying them from all dross of errors. So, too, the Church, to a certain extent, consecrated native art and culture . . . , as well as the special customs and traditional institutions of the people . . . ; she has even transformed their feast days, the missions with an excessive quantity of secular projects. Economic assistance must be limited to necessary undertakings which can be easily maintained and utilized, and to projects whose organization and administration can be easily transferred to the lay men and women of the particular nation, thus allowing the missionaries to devote themselves to their task of propagating the faith, and to other pursuits aimed directly at personal sanctification and eternal salvation.

Notes

1. Peter Dirven, "Roman Catholic Missions," *Concise Dictionary,* pp. 414-415.

2. *Mission Handbook, 1978* (Washington: United States Catholic Mission Council, 1978), p. 18; Dirven, p. 416.

3. Thomas J. M. Burke, S. J., ed., *Catholic Missions: Four Great Missionary Encyclicals* (New York: Fordham University Press, 1957), pp. 9, 11-15, 18-19, 21-23; Josef Glazik, "Mission Encyclicals of the Popes," *Concise Dictionary,* pp. 406-407.

4. Reprinted by permission of the publisher from *Catholic Missions: Four Great Missionary Encyclicals,* edited by Rev. Thomas J. M. Burke, S. J. (New York: Fordham University Press, 1957), Copyright © 1957 by Fordham University Press (revised printing, 1959), pp. 9-23; translated by William Connolly, S. J. Used by permission.

5. Walter H. Peters, *The Life of Benedict XV* (Milwaukee: The Bruce Publishing Company, 1959); Glazik, p. 406.

6. John XXIII, "Priceps Pastorum," *The Staff of the Pope Speaks, Magazine*, ed., *The Encyclicals and Other Messages of John XXIII*, ©, 1964 Our Sunday Visitor, Inc. Reprinted with permission of the publisher, Our Sunday Visitor, Inc.

7. Ibid., pp. 1-6.

8. Ibid. See also Calvert Alexander, S. J., *The Missionary Dimension: Vatican II and the World Apostolate* (Milwaukee: The Bruce Publishing Company, 1967).

9. 1 *Peter* 5, 4.

10. Cf. *John* 21, 15-17.

11. Cf. *"Homilia in die Coronationis habita,"* AAS 50 (1958) 886.

12. Cf. *AAS* 11 (1919) 440 ff.

13. Cf. Pius XI's encyclical *"Rerum Ecclesiae,"* AAS 18 (1926) 65 ff.; Pius XII's encyclicals *"Evangelii praecones,"* AAS 43 (1951) 497 ff., and *"Fidei donum,"* AAS 49 (1957) 225 ff. An English translation of the latter is in TPS IV, 295-312.

14. Encyclical *"Ad Petri Cathedram,"* AAS 51 (1959) 497 ff.; p. 24 ff. above.

15. Cf. *John* 10, 16.

16. Cf. *Matt.* 13, 19.

17. *Acts* 16, 9.

18. *Acts* 2, 5.

19. *Matt.* 28, 20.

20. *John* 16, 33.

21. Cf. *Matt.* 9, 38.

22. Letter of Pius XII to Cardinal Adeodatus Piazza, *AAS* 47 (1955) 542; *TPS* V, 253-4.

23. *Acts* 20, 28.

24. *Acts* 4, 32.

25. Cf. *John* 13, 34 and 15, 12.

26. *AAS* 11 (1919) 445.

27. *Ibid.*

28. Pius XII's apostolic letter *"Menti Nostrae,"* AAS 42 (1950) 477.

29. Cf. *Matt.* 5, 13-14.

30. Pius XII's apostolic letter *"Menti Nostrae,"* AAS 42 (1950) 686.

31. *Ibid.*

32. *Ibid.*, p. 687.

33. Apostolic letter *"Maximum illud,"* AAS 11 (1919) 445.

34. Cf. Pius XII's apostolic letter *"Menti Nostrae,"* AAS 42 (1950) 686.

35. *Ibid.*, p. 448.

36. Encyclical *"Evangelii praecones,"* AAS 43 (1951) 500.

XI

Voices from the Younger Churches

General Introduction

From the beginning of the modern mission movement, outstanding leaders emerged from the churches planted by the missionaries. They in turn became planters and developers of Christian churches. Within these so-called "younger churches," articulate voices began to be heard. At first they were not given a prominent place on the platforms and within the forums of the great missionary assemblies. Only seventeen Asians were among the 1,200 delegates at Edinburgh in 1910. The Jerusalem Conference of 1928, however, witnessed almost one fourth of the delegates from Asia, Africa, and Latin America. By the time of the Madras Conference in 1938, over half the delegates were from the younger churches. Such men at T. C. Chao and Tao Fong Shan of China, D. G. Moses and V. S. Azariah of India, Toyohiko Kagawa of Japan, G. Baez Camargo of Mexico, K. L. Kisosonkole of Uganda, and D. T. Niles of Ceylon were prominent in the deliberations of the Conference.

Since then the number of voices has proliferated so that today literally hundreds of leading churchmen from the younger churches are taking their places among the significant Christian voices of "the six continents." The prominence of non-Westerners at the world missionary conferences since Madras and their prominence at such significant international assemblies as the International Congress on World Evangelization in Lausanne in 1974 reflect the increasing importance of the Third World voice in contemporary Christianity. The convening in Accra, Ghana, December 17-23, 1977, of the Pan African Conference of Third World Theologians was a clear signal of the emerging strength of that Third World voice of the faith.

Among those who are no longer with us, space will permit the listing of only a few. Representative of the great company of African leaders are Samuel Adjai Crowther of Nigeria, William Wade Harris of Liberia,

401

D. Don Tengo Jabavu of South Africa, Simon Kimbangu of the Congo (Zaire), Apolo Kivebulaya of Uganda, and John Tsizehena of Madagascar. Among the Asians the list is almost endless. The following are representative: Jashwant Chitambar, P. D. Devanandan, H. A. Krishna Pillai, Abraham Mar Thoma, and K. T. Paul of India; Cheng Ching-Yi and Gregory Lo of China; Kanzo Uchimuro, Masahisa Uemura, and Gumpei Yamamuro of Japan; Ko Tha Byu of Burma; and Tchi-Ho Yun of Korea. From Latin America Erasmo Braga and F. F. Soren of Brazil, Alejandro Trevino of Mexico, and Santiago Canclini of Argentina are representative of the strong voices of the immediate past. Among the leading women, Pandita Ramabai of India was one of the most prominent.

In the following pages we include the works of three men—a Latin American, an African, and an Asian—who continue to speak through the power of the pen. They represent the rich variety which has been expressed by the voices of the younger churches in the era which has just passed. Juan C. Varetto of Argentina was a Baptist patriarch whose preaching, teaching, and polemical writings were felt all over Latin America. Albert Luthuli, a South African chief whose family was the product of Christian missions, was a lay preacher who served on the Christian Council. Author of one of the most important documents on human rights of modern times, he saw the civil rights struggle essentially as a spiritual struggle. His spirit is being captured today in the liberation theology of the Third World which is being expressed increasingly in the context of the Christian mission.[1] D. T. Niles possessed that rare quality of being able to speak both for the younger churches and the Christian mission at large. He was able to criticize the "pot plant" Christianity which some missionaries "could not trust to the indigenous soil." [2] Yet he worked with and supported missionaries as strongly as any national—ever calling both nationals and missionaries to the higher role and goal of the Christian world mission.

45

Heroes and Martyrs of the Missionary Enterprise [3]
Juan C. Varetto

Introduction

Juan Crisóstomo Varetto (1879-1953) was born in Concordia, Entre Rios, Argentina of Genovese immigrant parents. Orphaned at fifteen, he moved to Buenos Aires where he became an Evangelical under the influence of the Methodists. In 1898 he became a Baptist. For forty years he was pastor of the First Baptist Church of La Plata. His ministry was characterized by strong evangelism, and his eloquence won for him invitations to preach all over South and Central America, the Caribbean, and even in Europe. He was a prolific writer. He wrote his first book, *Heroes and Martyrs,* in 1914, and it went through numerous editions. He was one of the first nationals in Latin America to write on the subject. His writings covered a broad range of subjects: Church history, biography, religious liberty, biblical studies, sermons, children's books, evangelistic tracts, mission themes, and polemical works. He edited the influential *El Expositor Bautista,* the official journal of Argentinian Baptists. Varetto was one of the most effective and influential leaders in the history of Latin American Protestantism. He is especially important because of his appreciation for the missionary enterprise and his contribution to Latin American literature on the subject. That tradition was continued through his daughter, his biographer, the wife of Santiago Canclini who until his recent death was known as "Mr. Baptist" of Argentina. Agustina Varetto de Canclini taught missions for twenty-five years at the International Seminary in Buenos Aires.[4]

The New World: Its Discovery and Occupation

In Tierra del Fuego

During Christmas week of 1831 the *Beagle* left Devonport headed for the southern tip of South America. On board was the famous naturalist, Charles Darwin, who was going to that area to carry out certain scientific investigations. However, the attention of all of the passengers was concentrated on three Indians from Tierra del Fuego who were under the protection of the captain. How do we explain the presence of these Indians in a ship which leaves England? In an earlier expedition, Captain Fitzroy had captured and carried to England four Indians, one of whom died in England. Being a Christian, and a man interested in missionary work, he treated these Indians well and resolved to carry them to England to educate them and then return them to Tierra del Fuego. One of them was very young and was given the name Jimmy Button. Another, a young girl, was called Fuegia Basket, and the third, York Minster. Returning with them on board was a missionary named Matthews who planned to remain with these three Fuegian Indians in order to evangelize the rest.

Having arrived once again at Tierra del Fuego, they disembarked and Darwin gave himself to his investigations being very surprised at the savage state of the inhabitants. Many times he expressed to Admiral James Sullivan "his conviction that it was completely useless to send missionaries to savages such as the Fueginos, probably the lowest examples of the human race."

The *Beagle* left the three Fueginos and Matthews, but returned to the Cape after ten days. Discovering the shocking fact that the Indians had threatened the life of the missionary, it made his stay impossible. The Indians had taken everything away from him and among other things had tried "to pull out everyone of the hairs which he had in his beard." Matthews later settled in New Zealand.

Others having failed in this attempt, the heroic Allen Gardiner appeared on the scene. From his childhood he had shown a great inclination toward the sea. When he was only six years old his mother found him one night sleeping on the floor. When she asked him why he was lying there, he answered that he wanted to accustom himself as a child to a hard life in order not to suffer someday when he had the opportunity to travel over the world. He joined the navy and rapidly ascended to the office of captain. But after that he resigned his commission and did not enter into active service. He became a Christian when he was twenty years old and made a decision to consecrate his life to the evangelization of the pagans, a calling which he was not able to accomplish until he was forty years old. He traveled to Africa, New Guinea, and many other territories, but his definite goal was to go to South America. He visited the western Andean section of Chile, but his projects there were received with much resistance. The opposition of the Catholic clergy obliged him to think about some other region where he could work without being resisted. The most southern part of the Continent seemed to be the most propitious place.

In 1842 he disembarked on the coast of the Straights of Magellan and, after looking for the Indians, established a relationship with a chief named Güisale who promised to protect him against any kind of attack. This beginning promised much for his work, and he resolved to return to England to communicate the result and to ask for cooperation from some missionary society. However, he failed in his attempts to search for help, and he resolved to start a society with different and isolated people who would respond to his plea. In 1844 in the city of Brighton, the South American Missionary Society was organized with the intent of establishing missionary work in the Patagonia. Soon Gardiner had returned to his mission field which he had elected, carrying with him provisions for some six months. On arriving he found that Chief Güisale had changed his mind and gave him a very cool reception and indifferent support. All of the means which Gardiner employed to regain his friendship failed, and the brave missionary had to give up and return once more to his country, although he intended to make another attempt later.

His friends, who had decided to help him, began to lose interest, saying that it was useless to spend money in another attempt. The Central Committee of the Mission proposed the abandonment of the enterprise. "Whatever may be your decision," responded Gardiner with the courage of a hero, "I have resolved to return to South America and to push aside the obstacles and exhaust every means to establish a mission among those Aborigines." Inspired by his courage, the committee resolved to continue and Gardiner once again crossed the Atlantic accompanied by the Spanish Protestant named Frederick González. This time he went inland to the territory of Bolivia where the liberal president gave him a very friendly welcome, promising to help him. However, new difficulties arose. A revolution broke out, and he had to return to his country in order to seek help. But, this time everyone turned their backs on him, because failure seemed to accompany all of his seemingly impossible projects.

But Gardiner was one of those men who would not give up! In 1848 he reappeared in Tierra del Fuego with a few followers and established a base at Banner Cove (today called Ensenada de la Bandera), where he built several small and provisional huts. The opposition of the Indians caused the failure of this new project, and Gardiner realized that the only way to evangelize the islands was to have a "floating mission"; that is, a boat in which to live and keep the provisions and from which the missionaries could disembark from time to time to work with the Indians. This meant that he would have to return once again to England and face the discouragment which characterized his friends who had formed the unfortunate Mission. However, this was the only way and Gardiner returned proposing his new enterprise. As expected, he received a cool and discouraging response, but Gardiner continued to knock on doors that seemed to be shut until he acquired what he needed to continue.

In September of 1850 a company of seven—three sailors named Pearse, Badcock, and Bryant; a medical doctor named Richard Williams, who left his profession to consecrate his life to work among the savages; John Maidment, a young person with apostolic ardor; Joe Erwin, a carpenter and shipbuilder, and Allen Gardiner—set sail for South America carrying with them two small boats about eight meters long with their corresponding small boats for landing purposes.

The lack of funds had obliged them to adjust their plans to these two small embarkations instead of a ship which they really needed. One of the small boats called *Pioneer* and the other *Speedwell*.

Having arrived at Tierra del Fuego, they disembarked at Ensenada de la Bandera, but the opposition of the Indians obliged them to return to their boats, losing many of their provisions. The constant and violent storms which are prevalent in this desolate region damaged the *Pioneer* to such a point that they had to abandon it on the beach. With a few tents, it served as their principal shelter. Their attempts at fishing, on which they had counted heavily for their food, did not give the desired results, and the rifles which they carried along in order to hunt could not be used because, lamentably, they had left behind the necessary gunpowder in the ship which had brought them. Soon, their provisions began to run out, and the ship which they counted on for replenishment never arrived. Each hour the situation became more critical. Each day seemed like a year for these seven heroes who soon began to realize that their fate was to die of hunger on the icy beaches of this southern extremity.

The *Speedwell* made a useless trip to Ensenada de la Bandera in order to look for provisions that they had left hidden. It was a very solemn moment, and painfully they began to realize that their enterprise was just about over. In some bottles which they found they placed a note asking for help, hoping someone would find it. And then they covered it over with a large rock on which they wrote the following words: "Dig below Go to Spaniard Harbour 1851."

This inscription served later to help the sailors who came to seek them find the bodies of these brave Christians.

Gardiner and Williams had the custom of keeping a diary which logged carefully the happenings of each day. This diary enables us to know something of what happened during the last days of these heroes.

In April they still had enough provisions to last for two months. Their faith in God never failed. In the diary of Williams, we find these words; "Sleeping or awake, I feel happier than I could ever express through the mere words of my tongue." On his birthday in the month of June, Gardiner wrote: "If I faint or die here I beg of you, O Lord, that you would lift up others and send more workers to this great harvest field."

Badcock was the first to die, asking Williams to sing him a hymn which says: "Lift up my soul." Six weeks later Erwin died. Soon Bryant passed away. The weak hands of his companions were still able to dig his grave. The twenty-eighth and twenty-ninth of August of 1851 they were still alive and Gardiner wrote the following words bidding farewell to his daughter: "The One who has kept me in perfect peace . . . I trust that the poor Fuegia will not be abandoned. If I have one desire to express it is that my comrades will not abandon the Mission to Tierra del Fuego but shall continue it with vigor."

In another part of the diary we find these words:

Yesterday I did not eat anything. Blessed by my Heavenly Father for the mercy which He has allowed me to enjoy: a comfortable bed, no pain, no fever, although it is almost impossible to turn over in my bed.

The last words of the diary are these: "Great and marvelous is the love of my good Heavenly Father for me. He has protected me to this point without food for my body but without my having to suffer hunger or thirst."

The sixth day of September he was still alive because a letter was found with this date.

Twenty days later a ship called the *John Davison*, commanded by Captain Smyley, arrived at Ensenada de la Bandera and guided by the message which they found in the bottles, they immediately went to the Cook River and there found a body in the boat and another on the shore. "The scene was extremely horrible," write the Captain. "The two captains that were with me in the boats cried like babies. Books, medicine, tools, everything it seemed was found scattered along the beach."

In such a manner this incomparable model of Christian constancy, this noble and magnanimous heart, this example of courage and love whose desire was to serve the Lord in this inhospitable territory came to a conclusion.

When the news of the disaster arrived in England a holy consternation took hold of all of the friends of the Mission. If his Christian friends had been more generous and had given to Gardiner the ship which he needed, this chapter in missionary history would not have had to be included. But, the bodies resting on the icy, rocky beaches of Tierra del Fuego spoke more eloquently than the burning words of Gardiner. The Mission voted to fulfill the desire of their hero by continuing the work. Soon large donations began to arrive and a ship was purchased which was adequate and was christened the "Allen Gardiner." A new group of missionaries dedicated themselves to the task and the Mission was very successful among these people who were soon to become extinct. Among the missionaries the one who stood out most was Mr. Thomas Bridges who, as the well-known Argentine writer Robert J. Payro' has said in "La Australia Argentia," "he has done a deep study of the language and customs of the Yagan Indians." "Probably" he adds, "to him we owe much of the information about these Indians published by other persons."

The Missionary Society did not limit itself to Tierra del Fuego; it has extended its work to many parts of the Continent: however, it maintains a preference for work among indigenous tribes.

46

Let My People Go [5]
Albert Luthuli

Introduction

Albert John Luthuli (1898-1967) of South Africa grew up in a Christian family and received a good education. He was a teacher the first seventeen years of his adult life. Though of a royal African line, he was elected by the people in 1935 to the chieftianship of the Abase Makolweni Tribe of the Groutville Mission Reserve. A lay preacher, he was also called to head the African National Congress, the largest anti-apartheid organization in the country with a widespread membership drawn from many sections of the nation. Through his leadership in this capacity, Chief Luthuli became the greatest civil rights leader in modern South African history.[6]

In 1952 Luthuli was dismissed from his chieftianship by the government because of his leadership in the congress. In his public statement upon his dismissal, he revealed his strong Christian conviction: "My only painful concern at times is that of the welfare of my family but I try even in this regard, in a spirit of trust and surrender to God's will as I see it, to say: 'God will provide.' It is inevitable that in the working for Freedom some individuals and some families must take the lead and suffer: The Road to Freedom Is Via the Cross." [7]

In 1953, a year later, he was banned from public speaking and removed to a remote area far from home and placed under semi-house arrest. The day of his release, he flew to Johannesburg for a speaking engagement and was arrested at the airport. He was banned this time for two years. A few months after his release, he was banned again. Charges against him were eventually dropped, and in 1958 he had a relatively free year. During this time large crowds of all races flocked to hear him. He was too popular, however, and in 1959 he was banned again, this time for five years. During this period, he was imprisoned for a time. In 1960 he won the Nobel Peace Prize, the only person from his country ever so honored. At the end of his ban, in 1964, he was banned for another five years. On July 21, 1967 frail and weak from his ordeals, he was struck by a freight train and killed.[8]

A close friend, and in a sense his white counterpart, Alan Paton, author of *Cry the Beloved Country*, delivered the funeral oration to seven thousand blacks and a few whites. Paton said of the fallen giant: "They took away his chieftainship, but he never ceased to be chief. They took away his temporal power, but he never ceased to have his spiritual power . . . . He had a voice like a lion, and it was because he had a lion's voice that he had to be silenced. So was silenced a great and noble man . . . . Although he was silenced, history will make his voice speak again, that powerful brave voice that spoke for those who could not speak."[9] The following selections from Luthuli's celebrated work, reveal both something of the ordeal of his life, especially in the later years, and also something of his inspiring spirit and remarkable faith.

Postscript: The Tempo Quickens

(This and the following chapter have been written since the Sharpeville shootings and the State of Emergency.)

At the beginning of June 1959, then, I was back home in Groutville, with the prospect before me of five years of isolation and frustration. It was a bleak outlook.

But the struggle must go on—ban or no bans. The Congress leaders lost little time in adapting themselves to the new situation, and I found myself busier at home in Groutville than I had been away from home.

One of our primary concerns at this time was the Potato Boycott. Since we reject violence as a method, we are always in search of telling and relevant ways of struggling against our degradation—ways that are peaceful, but at the same time impossible for the whites to ignore.

Before this time we had boycotted "Nationalist" products on the market with a measure of success. But it is not an easy matter to identify this or that product as "Nationalist." Some are obviously made in factories owned by the more extreme of our oppressors, but with others it is not easy to avoid injury to the wrong man's pocket, and we have never been callously indiscriminate in our attitudes.

When it came to the common potato, we were on ground where not many of the wrong people would suffer. Particularly in the Eastern Transvaal, but elsewhere also, the conditions under which African labourers work is nothing short of horrifying. The Eastern Transvaal does not include any large African reserves. In consequence, there is a shortage of labour. Never at a loss to come to the help of the white farmer in labour difficulties, the Government has found a solution. This is the system of Farm Gaols. It depends upon an unholy alliance between the police and the white farmers, and it is at its worst in the Eastern Transvaal. It also depends on the Pass Laws. Pass offenders—half a million men a year—are drafted out of gaols into the safekeeping of farmers. Both gaolers and farmers are delighted with the arrangement. The system helps to keep down the gaol population, and it provides the farms with an unending flow of completely rightless beasts of burden.

On the affected farms, African men—some are no more than boys—dig potatoes with their bare fingers. "Boss-boys" and overseers stand over them with whips, which they do not hesitate to use. The "convicts"—their crime is purely statutory—live in hovels, filthy little huts or filthy great barracks, under guard. Their diet is unmentionable, a good deal worse than prison fare for Africans—why keep them alive

when there are more where they came from? "Inspection" amounts
to a call on the white farmer, and a little chat over coffee on the
stoep. Murders, the result of prolonged beatings and semi-starvation,
or of sudden fits of anger, are committed. Some come to light.

I do not say these conditions prevail on every farm where there
are farm prisons and convict labour. I say that the system exists, and
I say that it is not only isolated farmers of bestial morality who take
advantage of it. And I say that the system exists because the Government approves of it.[10] It is their system.

It was against this system—against the Pass Laws which draft men
on to farms, often with no notice to their families, against Farm Gaols,
and against those farmers whose avarice flourishes on this iniquity—
that the Potato Boycott was directed. We made our call Union-wide,
and our original intention was to boycott all potatoes for one month.

Its success was instantaneous—and consider here that potatoes are
the staple diet of many Africans. It was certainly the hardest hitting
of all our boycotts. I think it caught the imagination of the people
because it dragged into the light of day specific and appalling human
suffering and misery.

. . . .

The Coalbrook mine disaster, with its appalling death toll, did not
lighten the darkness of our 1960 skies; and then came Sharpeville,
Langa, Nyanga.

It chanced that I was in Pretoria at this time. My evidence was
required in the Treason Trial as it entered its fourth year, and my
ban had been temporarily waived to allow me to give it. The burden
of my evidence was the burden of this book. It was a description of
what the Congress movement has stood for, of the reasons for our
actions, the method we have embraced, the goals which we mean to
achieve, and the South Africa we envisage.

Meanwhile, the A.N.C. [African National Congress] was preparing
itself for yet another nonviolent assault upon the Pass Laws. Our preparations were neither in their infancy nor yet fully mature, and it was
our intention, for reasons which I have explained earlier, not to launch
the new campaign until our people were thoroughly briefed and completely ready to participate and endure.

But the Pan-African Congress had also in mind a programme of
agitation against the passes. Their method was to go to police stations,

leaving their passes at home, and court arrest. Taking the country as a whole, they were organised only in a few centres. When it came to the point the police—in places[11] where they did not lose their heads—met the challenge by arresting a handful of leaders and ignoring their followers. The followers were thus placed in a position where they were still in possession of their passes, and their protest against them was being overlooked.

Fully conversant with the A.N.C. view that the people were not yet ready for the launching of this anti-pass campaign, Pan-Africanist leader Robert Sobukwe called on all Africans to follow him in leaving his pass at home and declaring this fact to the police. His call cut across A.N.C. plans for an orderly, carefully-mounted campaign with a deliberately-timed climax. Except in a small number of centres in the Transvaal and the Cape, the response to Sobukwe's appeal was mild. There was no sign that the campaign would snowball—and unless this had happened it could not have succeeded, since there was no country-wide organisation behind it.

But at Sharpeville the police perpetrated their murderous shooting. At Langa, Philip Kgosana turned back 30,000 demonstrators and thus avoided bloodshed, and at Nyanga the whole demonstration degenerated into prolonged riot and arson. Suddenly everything was in a different perspective. The guns of Sharpeville echoed across the world, and nowhere except among totalitarians was there any doubt about the true nature of what had occurred. The Government had placed beyond question the implacable, wanton brutality of their régime.

In the new situation created by the gunmen of Sharpeville, the A.N.C. at once went into action. From Pretoria, to which my banned state confined me, I called for a national day of mourning on 28th March, for the victims and their families. On this day I asked people to stay at home, and treat it as a day of prayer. The response was good, and in some centres it was magnificent.[12] Moreover, it was multi-racial, and went far beyond our usual allies. Many churches were open for prayer throughout the land, and students of all races participated in the mourning.

But passive mourning and active prayer seemed to the A.N.C. leadership to be not enough. The Pass system had claimed more victims, death and gaol being its allies. Congress called for the burning of passes. We did not desire to leave our shackles at home. We desired to be rid of them. I burned my Reference Book, others burned theirs, and the bonfires began to grow in number.

The Government replied promptly to the threat by declaring unlawful the two pass-carrying Congresses, and by proclaiming a State of Emergency. Units of the army were called out to reinforce the police. Arrests began on a large scale, and went on until 20,000 South Africans of all colours had been drafted into detention. A few evaded the police net and sat out the Emergency in more hospitable places, and a handful appears to have left for the duration.

My own arrest took place, like many others, in the small hours of the morning. I was staying in the home of white Pretoria friends, the Brinks—a home distinguished by a complete absence of any hint of colour-bar. My host entered my bedroom with the police in order to arouse me. He himself was already under arrest. I had to drag myself from sleep—no easy matter, since in these days I sat up late studying documents and preparing myself nightly for the next day's ordeal in the witness-box. The police lost no time in placing me under arrest. They could not, however, produce any warrant, and in fact the arrests were illegal since at that time the Emergency had not been gazetted.

After the house had been searched, we were taken out to the police car. Dr. Lang was picked up, but at the home of Fr. Mark Nye, an Anglican priest in charge of a mission which gave hospitality to the Treason Trial accused, the police drew a blank. He had heard he was "wanted" and had already surrendered himself.

We met up with Fr. Nye at the Pretoria Central Police Station, where we were shocked and horrified to find Miss Hannah Stanton also under arrest.

The morning was bitterly cold, especially for a man like me accustomed to the warm coastal belt. We longed in vain for a hot drink. Our reception was none too cordial. I was wearing conventional emblems of mourning for the Sharpeville victims—a black tie, and black crêpe. The white head warder ordered me in harsh tones to divest myself of them, adding that the wearing of decorations and the exchange of signs would not be tolerated. He made his point with somewhat unnecessary emphasis—nobody showed any reluctance to obey him. Later, when his crisis was over, this officer relaxed towards us and proved quite friendly.

More harshness awaited me. As we were being marched to our cells in the dim light of early morning, I was obliged to slow down to negotiate a flight of steps. I was instantly slapped hard across the face from behind. I stooped to gather my hat, and I was hit again. I was not afterwards able to identify my assailant with certainty—the light was poor—but I know him to have been a white policeman. At a subsequent inquiry other detainees testified to having seen this assault, and it emerged that others, too, had been struck. I was angered; but not surprised. Among Africans the South African Police have long been notorious for this sort of thing.

At first it looked as though my days as a detainee might be fairly "normal," even though the nights were spent in gaol. I was still giving evidence in the Treason Trial and expected for some time to appear regularly in court and meet the other accused and our defence lawyers. Two things altered this. In view of the banning of the Congresses, and the Emergency, our Defence Team withdrew, and from that time until near the end of the State of Emergency the defence was conducted by two of the accused—Duma Nokwe and Nelson Mandela. These two men, though not old in years, were among the foremost leaders of the A.N.C.

Secondly, my health declined. I was subject to an acute recurrence of high blood-pressure, apparently the result of the protracted daily strain of giving evidence. I was removed to the prison hospital where I remained throughout my detention. Nevertheless, I was able to continue to give evidence, though under difficulties, and the Bench gave me every consideration and indulgence. As long as it was necessary they allowed the court hours to be determined by what my doctors felt I could stand up to. I deeply regretted being the cause of thus lengthening the ordeal of the accused. I was greatly comforted in these days of stress by the solicitude of the defence attorney, Michael Parkington, and the diligent care and humane manner of Dr. M. de Villiers who attended me. The latter, especially, greatly eased the tension of those days, as far as Prison Regulations allowed.

Vigilant steps were taken to seal me off from other prisoners. (I believe this was true of some other detainees, too). Even African warders were under instructions not to speak to me. Especially as long as my illness kept me confined to bed for most of the day, I led a solitary life. Nevertheless, I do not remember my cell as a place of boredom. It became, in fact, a place of sanctuary, a place where I could make up for the neglect of religious meditation occasioned by the hurly-burly of public life. There was time, there was quietness, there was comparative solitude. I used it. Frail man that I am, I pray humbly that I may never forget the opportunity God gave me to rededicate myself, to consider the problems of our resistance to bondage, and above all to be quiet in His Presence. My whitewashed cell became my chapel, my place of retreat.

I was further nurtured in this regard by regular visits from the Rev. Mr. Junod, chaplain to condemned men in the Pretoria Central Prison,[13] and an ardent champion of Penal Reform in South Africa; and by two visits from a retired minister of the Dutch Reformed Church, Ds. Reynecke, whom I had known in our days on the Christian Council.

For the first three months of detention I saw nothing of the other detainees. Then, at the end of June, I was told that nothing in the regulations debarred me from being with them when they were in the prison yard for exercise. I used the opportunity at once, but only in a limited way, since my health prevented frequent visits. I made a point of being with them on Sundays at times of worship, and on occasions, after Mr. Junod had gone overseas, I conducted the services myself. Other prisoners did the same, and our communal worship was marked by a high level of seriousness—and by magnificent singing.

My liberty to associate with the other detainees lasted for no more than five weeks. Then, one afternoon, they demonstrated against the unexplained curtailment of their exercise time by refusing to march back into the lock-up. At this point the hospital detainees (there were two of us) asked to be taken back to our own cells. I had not long returned when I was taken to the officer in command, who accused me of having stirred up trouble among the detainees. He added that according to his officer in charge the detainees had been unruly ever since I was allowed among them. I hotly refuted this. The colonel said he would accept my word—but all the same, I was not again allowed these visits.

The most precious visits were those of my wife, who twice made the 1,000-mile journey to see me. The least welcome visitors were the three security police who called on me to charge me formally on 104 counts—one, burning my reference book; two, disobeying a law by way of protest; and three, 102 counts of inciting others to do the same. This case eventually came before the court in June. With repeated adjournments it dragged on until the end of the Emergency at the end of August, when I was found guilty on the first two counts and not guilty on the remaining 102. For burning my pass I was sentenced to six months without the option of a fine, suspended for three years because of my health. For disobeying a law by way of protest I was sentenced to a year or £100. I intended to make a statement before the imposing of sentence, but in the event I did not do this.

Thanks to the magnificent defence my lawyers provided in this trial, and thanks to the generosity of friends who paid my fine, I was soon a free man again—free to go home to Groutville and live under the terms of my ban. My relief was marred by knowledge of the damage done to the lives of so great a number of detainees, and by the continued imprisonment of many of my fellow-fighters for freedom, who languish in gaols throughout the land.

I carry away from my trial one moving memory—not of the court or the prosecution or even of the brilliant defence, but of the spectators. The area of the court accommodating them was always thronged, and I heard later that many people had to be turned away. Apartheid prevailed in the seating arrangements, of course; but the spectators were a multi-racial company all the same. There, in embryo, was a protrayal of my new South Africa, a company of men and women of goodwill, yearning to begin work on the building of a structure both permanent and real. Indeed, they have already begun.

Before I embarked on the first stage of my journey home I went back to the gaol which had been my home for five months, to bid farewell to the hospital staff and my warders, and to collect my belongings.

From there I was taken by white ladies of the Black Sash to the Anglican St. Benedict's Retreat House in Johannesburg. My inquisitiveness got the better of me. In response to my importuning, my Black Sash friends revealed how my fine had been paid. They had paid it. The Defence and Aid Fund, which came magnificently to the rescue of the detainees,[14] reimbursed them. Later I learned that Canon Collins of Christian Action had wired £100 from England to the Defence and Aid Fund. What an encouraging chain reaction of kindness!

I travelled to Natal by train in the company of a veteran of the Resistance, Dr. Conco, a Treason Trial defendant who had arranged his trip to be at my disposal as friend, medical adviser and equerry.

(Lest the term "equerry" should seem to stem from self-importance, I must explain that the idea that I am no longer a chief does not seem to have cut much ice among Africans. My people *still* refuse to let me travel alone!) My heart bleeds for Dr. Conco and men like him—a ruined medical practice, five years of anxiety and misery, constant absence from home, devastating impoverishment—and yet what courage!

We were besieged on the train. News that I was aboard got round. A white ticket collector helped to spread the tidings. As I moved along the crowded corridor he called out: "Make way, move out of the way. Don't you know this is Chief Luthuli? Don't you know your own leader? Stand out of the way!" Many called on Dr. Conco and me in our compartment, both Africans and Indians, some out of curiosity, some to express pleasure or allegiance, and at least one to report back to the Special Branch. We had left Johannesburg just after nine o'clock in the morning. It was midnight before we were free to retire.

In Durban I was joined by my wife who had, in spite of a severe fever, risen in the dark in Groutville and come in to Durban to meet me. It cost her a week in bed. For most of that day we were guests of Dr. Taylor at McCord's Hospital. At the close of the day we went back to Groutville and another warm welcome.

Epilogue

If friendships make a man rich, then I am rich indeed. I grieve over the ban which, until May, 1964, cuts me off from my many friends in all parts of South Africa. But I grieve more deeply for the men and women—their number is not known—whose desire for sanity in South Africa, whose insistence on no more than our human dignity, has led to banishment, deportation and gaol, while their families suffer poverty and acute distress. I have no illusions. Their number will grow.

But the struggle goes on, bans, banishments, deportations, gaol or not. We do not struggle with guns and violence, and the Supremacist's array of weapons is powerless against the spirit. The struggle goes on as much in gaol as out of it, and every time cruel men injure or kill defenceless ones, they lose ground. The Supremacist illusion is that this is a battle of numbers, a battle of race, a battle of modern armaments against primitives. It is not. It is right against wrong, good against evil, the espousal of what is twisted, distorted and maimed against the yearning for health. They rejoice in what hurts the weak man's mind and body. They embrace what hurts their own soul.

The task is not finished. South Africa is not yet a home for all her sons and daughters. Such a home we wish to ensure. From the beginning our history has been one of ascending unities, the breaking of tribal, racial and credal barriers. The past cannot hope to have a life sustained by itself, wrenched from the whole. There remains before us the building of a new land, a home for men who are black, white, brown, from the ruins of the old narrow groups, a synthesis of the rich cultural strains which we have inherited. There remains to be achieved our integration with the rest of our continent. Somewhere ahead there beckons a civilisation, a culture, which will take its place in the parade of God's history beside other great human syntheses, Chinese, Egyptian, Jewish, European. It will not necessarily be all black; but it will be African.

. . . .

The struggle must go on—the struggle to make the opportunity for the building to begin. The struggle will go on. I speak humbly and without levity when I say that, God giving me strength and courage enough, I shall die, if need be, for this cause. But I do not want to die until I have seen the building begun.

Mayibuye iAfrika! Come, Africa, come!

47

Upon the Earth [15]
D. T. Niles

Introduction

Daniel Thambyrajah Niles (1908-1970) was born in Jaffna, Ceylon of Tamil parents. He was the grandson of a distinguished Methodist minister. Daniel was educated in India and London and received honorary doctorates from institutions in Europe and America. He began his career as a Methodist evangelist and also served from time to time as a pastor. He held a number of significant positions: Evangelism secretary of the World Alliance of YMCA's 1929-1940, cochairman of the Youth Department of the World Council of Churches (1948-1952), executive secretary of the Department of Evangelism of the W.C.C. (1953-1959), chairman of the World Student Christian Federation (1953-1960), general secretary of the East Asian Conference of Churches (1957-1958). When he died he was chairman of the E.A.C.C.[16]

Niles distinguished himself internationally as a speaker and writer as well as a missionary statesman. He was an unusually articulate spokesman both for the younger churches and the Christian world mission. He authored one of the most quotable and quoted definitions of evangelism in modern times: "It is one beggar telling another beggar where to get food." [17] His books ranged from devotional biblical studies to treatises on non-Christian religions. However, most of his works were on mission themes. *Upon the Earth,* considered by some to be the finest work to that date on the strategy of the Christian mission, grew out of the issues of the world missionary conferences of Willigen (1952) and Ghana (1958). It is one of the series of *Foundations of the Christian Mission.* Niles could have had a life of ease, but he chose to live in a house which had no electricity. Though a world citizen and world Christian, he chose to live in the small fishing village near Jaffna where he was born. Here he spent his last days. Though he was too ill to be active, he continued to write up until the end, still sharing with the world the ideas of his keen mind and the devotion of his dedicated heart.[18]

The Kingdom of the Father Is Fulfilled

Our Father, Thy name be hallowed, Thy kingdom come, Thy will be done (Matt. 6:9-10).

Will this prayer, which is the constant prayer of the Church, find fulfilment? Will the time come when His name, by which every family in heaven and on earth is named (Eph. 3:15), is honoured among them; when His children will rejoice to hear His name and keep it sacred? Will the Father's Kingdom come, the Kingdom of glory, when all strife with sin shall be over and the rule of Christ shall have accomplished its purpose? (1 Cor. 15:24, 25.) Will the Father's will be done on earth as it is done in heaven; will His design for His whole creation (Col. 1:20) be achieved?

The New Testament answer to these questions is an unequivocal "Yes": a confidence derived from its determining faith that to the end God will be God, and that at the end God's purpose will triumph because it is God's. "The Son of God, Jesus Christ, is not Yes and No; but in Him it is always Yes. All the promises of God find their Yes in him" (2 Cor. 1:19, 20). "You shall know that I am the Lord," says God to Israel in exile (Ezek. 11:10). That is always God's final message to men—His word of warning to them in their self-confidence, His word of hope to them in their despair.

The hope to which the Gospel witnesses is not the result of any realistic calculation of present trends, nor of any prognosis based on an assessment of the problems that lie ahead; rather it is a hope offered as a hope to live by, a certainty in the future on which one can count and by which one can guide one's life. Peter, writing to his fellow Christians under pressure to deny their faith, proclaims to them "a salvation ready to be revealed in the last time" (1 Pet. 1:3-5). It is a salvation to depend on, a hope to be sustained by. "We have been born anew," he announces, "to a living hope through the resurrection of Jesus Christ from the dead, and to an inheritance kept in heaven for you." This kept inheritance is what the hope is about.

The Promised Inheritance

The Old Testament story is controlled by this fact of an inheritance.

God had promised an inheritance to Abraham. Once the promise was made, the inheritance was sure. It was there. For many years Abraham had no children, but an heir was certain because there was the inheritance.

The people of Israel were in bondage, but they would be free because their inheritance was waiting for them. For many years they wandered in the wilderness, but they would come at last and possess the promised land because it was promised.

Israel's faithlessness to God had brought them into exile. They lived in exile for many years. But they would return to their inheritance again because that inheritance was theirs.

In the New Testament, too, it is the inheritance that is always determinative. "Faith," says the writer to the Hebrews (11:1 f.), "is the title deed of our inheritance." It is that which has controlled through the generations the pilgrimage of faith. What is this inheritance? It is a new creation, a complete renewal of all that God has made;

We wait for new heavens and a new earth in which righteousness dwells (2 Pet. 3:13). And he who sat upon the throne said, Behold, I make all things new (Rev. 21:5).

It is the restoration in man of God's image, the offer to man even now of his new nature to be;

It does not yet appear what we shall be, but we know that when he appears we shall be like him (1 John 3:2).

You have put on the new nature which is being renewed in knowledge after the image of its Creator (Col. 3:10).

It is the reconstitution in Christ of the broken peace of the world. God's plan is a plan for the fullness of time to unite all things in Christ, things in heaven and things on earth (Eph. 1:10).

For in him all things were created and in him all things hold together (Col. 1:16, 17).

This inheritance is also the eternal city, man's final dwelling place, in which death shall have been conquered and man's fellowship with God reclaimed.

And I saw the holy city, new Jerusalem, coming down out of heaven from God; and I heard a great voice from the throne saying, Behold, the dwelling place of God is with men. And death shall be no longer (Rev. 21:2-4).

It is the return of the risen Christ, triumphant, to His union with His bride, the Church; and to the completion of the salvation of the world which He has wrought.

Little children, abide in him, so that when he appears we may have confidence and not shrink from him in shame at his coming (1 John 2:28).

The Spirit and the Bride say, Come. And let him who hears say, Come. Surely I am coming soon. Amen. Come, Lord Jesus! (Rev. 22:17, 20).

For there is one God, and there is one mediator between God and men, the man Christ Jesus, who gave himself as a ransom for all, the testimony to which was borne at the proper time (1 Tim. 2:5, 6).

This promise of the end which will certainly happen, however, is not left hanging in the air as a kind of deus-ex-machina event to give a happy ending to a tangled drama. The end promised is already begun. "You are those," says Paul, "on whom the end of the ages has come" (1 Cor. 10:11) so that we wait for its fulfilment with confidence. When our Lord began His ministry in Galilee, He announced a Kingdom that had arrived. "It has come near," He said, "it has come within reach. Stretch out your hand and touch it" (Mk. 1:15). The coming of the Kingdom was the coming of the King.

It is always difficult to present convincingly the message of the Christian hope but the task is made needlessly difficult by clinging to the language of apocalypticism when the New Testament itself points the way to Christocentric eschatology. Christ has come and, therefore, while we do not know when the end will be, we do know that the end is now. Now is the day of salvation. Everywhere, the preaching and the hearing of the Gospel is the sign of the eschatological presence. The presence of the work of anti-christ and of false christs also bears the same witness (Mk. 13:9-23).

This King who has come, the Gospel announces, was born by the Spirit. It is essential to see how closely the Gospel intertwines the action of the Son with the activity of the Spirit if one is not to miss the richness of the biblical teaching on the Kingdom. The Spirit came on Jesus when He was baptized. The Spirit led Him into the wilderness to think through the meaning of His mission. The Spirit of the Lord was upon Him as He began His ministry. He came to men in the power of the Spirit. And, when He had completed His mission by His death on the cross, the Spirit raised Him from the dead. Now, from His Kingdom on high, He has sent the Spirit into the world, that in the Spirit He may continue His work in the world until it is over, the Spirit Himself fulfilling in the world the ministry He began through the Christ. In the daring phrase of Paul, "the Lord is the Spirit" (2 Cor. 3:17), so that past event, present experience and future hope hold together as that one act of salvation by which human life is upheld.

The Gospel announces a new creation—already in Christ the new creation has begun (2 Cor. 5:17)—He is the new Man in whom all things will be renewed (Col. 3:10), in whom those who believe have the first-fruits of the Spirit (Rom. 8:23). The Gospel promises the restoration in man of God's image—already in the face of Christ the glory of God had been revealed (2 Cor. 3:18), so that we beholding that glory may be changed into His likeness. The Gospel declares the hope of a healed humanity—already Christ has broken down the middle wall of partition between those who were far and those who were nigh (Eph. 2:14). The Gospel proclaims the certainty of eternal life (1 Cor. 15:55, 56)—already death has been conquered by Christ, and the saints are already with Him in glory (1 Thess. 3:13).

"Now is the judgment of this world, now shall the ruler of this world be cast out": those are the words of Jesus (John 12:31). And, because He has said, "Now," we are able to say "Already." The end is certain because the end has begun; it is certain also because from this beginning the end is increasingly thrusting itself into every crevice of life. "Sealed with the promised Holy Spirit, which is the guarantee of our inheritance" the Holy Spirit works "until we acquire possession of it, to the praise of his glory" (Eph. 1:13, 14).

It is obvious, is it not, that if this be the teaching of the New Testament on the end-event as it has happened and as it will be completed, then the consequence of this truth for the mission of the Church and the obedience of the Christian is tremendous? Let us see what these consequences are.

A Mission with Compulsive Urgency

Throughout its history the mission of the Church has never commended itself as simply a good thing to undertake. Whenever and wherever it has been felt, it has been felt as an urgent necessity. Why?

Firstly, because the mission of the Church arises from the work of the Holy Spirit, so that he who is swept into this work finds himself in the power of another. We do not need to sustain ourselves by our conviction about the mission of the Church. To engage in that mission is to be sustained by the mission itself. Urgency belongs to the mission, so that the Church's sense of urgency is only derivative. When on D-day the allied forces landed on the French shore, every Frenchman became involved in an urgent undertaking. The urgency of the mission is simply due to the invasion of the Christ.

Secondly, the mission arises from the fact that because Jesus has died for all men, all men have died (2 Cor. 5:14), and they will remain dead until they are raised by the Holy Spirit to participation in the risen life of Christ. The mission of the Church is to proclaim this resurrection—its necessity and possibility—and to be the locus where the risen life of Christ can be found and experienced. The Gospel is not lest men die but because they are dead. It is a proclamation which answers the question: "Son of man, Can these bones live?" (Ezek. 37:3.) Such a proclamation is necessarily urgent. "If you believe in the resurrection of Jesus Christ," said an unbeliever to a Christian, "shout it out from the house tops."

Thirdly, the mission is to men whose response is being prepared by the Holy Spirit. That preparation demands that it be availed of. "In season and out of season," said Paul (2 Tim. 4:2); which means all the time and as widely as possible. Let it not happen that I was the neighbour to someone who was ready for the Gospel and that I passed him by. Since the essential ministry is the ministry of the Holy Spirit and the risen Christ, the Christian mission has necessarily to be performed with watchful urgency. Oftentimes the disciple does not know where the Lord is waiting for him, so that Christ's disciples have to spread themselves and be everywhere.

Fourthly, the mission is to make the pressure of Jesus Christ on the lives of men and of the world inescapable and insistent. This calls for strategy in the performance of that mission. Strategy means an over-all design, plans that must be carried out, decisions that must be obeyed. The mission is the mission of the Church, so that each individual Christian and every separate group find themselves under urgent command not to let down their fellows.

And lastly, the mission is also God's method of saving those who have believed. The disciple is saved as he participates in the operation of the Gospel. "The word of the cross" (our witness to it and our proclamation of it) says Paul, "is the power of God to us who are being saved" (1 Cor. 1:18). "Being saved"—that is the correct tense in which to express the Christian's experience of salvation. The movement of the Gospel is a continuous one, and what happens to the believer happens within this movement. No wonder Paul said, "I will explode if I do not preach the Gospel" (1 Cor 9:16).

Notes

1. See for example, Orlando Costas, *The Church and Its Mission: A Shattering Critique from the Third World* (Wheaton, Illinois: Tyndale House Publishers, Inc., 1974).

2. W. A. Visser 't Hooft, "D. T. Niles," *International Review of Missions* (Geneva, January, 1971), p. 116.

3. Juan C. Varetto, "The New World: Its Discovery and Occupation" (ch. 10), *Heroes and Martyrs of the Missionary Enterprise,* Justice Anderson, trans. (Buenos Aires: Board of Publication of the Baptist Evangelical Convention, 1958), pp. 202-213. Used by permission.

4. Agustina Varetto de Canclini, *Juan C. Varetto, Embajador de Cristo* (Buenos Aires: Editorial Evangelica Bautista, 1955).

5. Albert Luthuli, "Postscript: The tempo quickens" and "Epilogue," *Let My People Go* (New York: McGraw-Hill Book Company, Inc., 1962), pp. 217-218, 221-229, 232. Used by permission of Collins Publishers, London.

6. Ibid., pp. 7-12; Alan Paton, *The Long View* (New York: Frederick A. Praeger Publishers, 1968), p. 235.

7. Luthuli, Appendix A, "The Road to Freedom Is Via the Cross," p. 238.

8. Paton, pp. 201-202.

9. Ibid., pp. 265-267.

10. The Hon. C. R. Swart, Governor-General of the Union, made it his custom, while he was Minister of Justice, to open Farm Gaols officially. He was loud in their praise. They relieved the country of the expense of accommodating offenders, they helped farmers—and the rehabilitated criminals!

11. Such as Evaton.

12. Many Pan-Africanists were among those who respected this day.

13. He has since been dismissed by the Government.

14. This Fund was inspired by Bishop Reeves, financed from several countries, and administered by a committee under South African ex-Labour Parliamentarian, Alex Hepple.

15. D. T. Niles, "The Kingdom of the Father Is Fulfilled" (ch. 3), *Upon the Earth: The Mission of God and the Missionary Enterprise of the Churches* (New York: McGraw-Hill Book Company, Inc., 1962), pp. 80-86. Used by permission of Lutterworth Press.

16. Niles, *The Context in Which We Preach* (Geneva: John Knox House Association, 1956), p. 5; Kyaw Than, "D. T. Niles: Some Personal Reflections," *International Review of Missions,* p. 122.

17. Niles, *That They May Have Life* (New York: Harper and Brothers Publishers, 1951), p. 96.

18. Than, pp. 122-123.

Conclusion

We come to the end of our pilgrimage through the classics of Christian missions. As we conclude we are aware of a great host of missionary personalities who have not been mentioned. Of course, some of them left no formal writings and others preserved few letters. However, there is still a large body of missionary literature, some of it deserving to be considered classic, which could not be included because of the limitation of space. We cannot conclude, however, without reference to some of the leading personalities who have not been mentioned.

A number of earlier missionaries who have not been mentioned played vital roles in planting the Christian faith in Europe. Ulfilas (311-381) was missionary to the Goths (Germans). Columba (521-597) founded the Iona mission training center (Scotland). Benedict of Nursia founded his missionary order in 529. Columban (543-615) was missionary to the Franks. In 635 Aidan founded a mission training center near Scotland. Wilfrid began his evangelization of Sussex and the Isle of Wight in 686. Willibrord was sent to Frisia (Netherlands) in 690. Anskar (801-865) pioneered mission work in Scandinavia.

Bridging the centuries between the earlier and more recent periods in the Western Church were such significant personalities as the great Francis of Assisi (1182-1226). Among the women, one of the most renowned was Marie Guyard (1599-1672) who became famous for her leadership in Roman Catholic missions in Canada.

Even though we have not included any classics from the Eastern Orthodox Church, no list of significant missionary personalities would be complete without mentioning some of the leading figures in the missionary endeavors of the Eastern Church. The pioneer missionaries to Eastern Europe were Cyril and Methodius who began their evangelization of the Slavs in 860. In the Greek Church one of the towering figures was Stephen of Perm, missionary to the Zyryans (Finns) in

427

the fourteenth century. Among the leading personalities of more recent times in the Russian Church were Cyril Suchanov, colorful and creative missionary to Siberia (1741-1810). Following in his tradition was the capable Innokenti Veniaminov (1797-1879) who served in Siberia, the Aleutian Islands, and Alaska. One of the most renowned of all Orthodox missionaries was Nicolai Ivan Kasalkin, Archbishop of Tokyo, who served in Japan from 1861 to his death in 1912.

Worthy of special emphasis are the significant missionaries who served in the smaller branches of Eastern Christianity. Some of the more notable ones were Longinus who went to Nubia in 566, Alopen who carried Nestorian Christianity to China in 635, and Jordan Catalina who went to India in the fourteenth century.

We noted earlier the significant role played by women in the missionary enterprise. Among those not already mentioned, worthy of special note are Dr. Fanny Jane Butler of India, Mildred Cable of Central Asia, Christina Forsyth of South Africa, Isabelle Trotter of Algeria, Dr. Ida Scutter of the famous missionary Scutter family in India, and Dr. Clara Swain, the first woman missionary physician in the world.

The list of significant men who served as missionaries under the Protestant banner from the eighteenth century to the present would fill a large volume. They represent some of the most colorful personalities of history. We can only mention a few. Two men who preceded Carey to India were Bartholomew Ziegenbalg and Christian F. Schwartz. Two outstanding missionaries to South Africa were Francois Coillard and Andrew Murray, who has been one of the most widely read devotional writers of modern times. Two famous athletes who became two of the most colorful missionaries of modern history were: Charles Thomas Studd, a champion Cambridge cricketer who served in China and Africa; and Ion Grant Neville Keith-Falconer, champion bicyclist of Great Britain who served in the Middle East. Keith-Falconer, the son of the Earl of Kintore, was a noted Arabic scholar and a leading authority on shorthand. David Jones of Madagascar has become a legendary figure. Albert Schweitzer of French Equatorial Africa—physician, theologian, musician—was one of the most celebrated men of modern times. One of the most remarkable linguists in mission history was the colorful Hebrew Christian named Samuel Isaac Joseph Schereschewsky ("Brother Sherry"), missionary to China. One of the most inspiring men of modern times was Frank Laubach, early missionary to the Philippines and later passionate international crusader for literacy.

Then there is that unique company of men we call missionary statesmen. One of the prototypes was Zinzendorf. His successor was Augustus G. Spangenberg. Bridging the nineteenth and twentieth centuries along with Mott were William Paton and J. H. Oldham. More recent leaders have been Walter Freytag and Max Warren. A singularly impressive leader was the inspiring personality E. Stanley Jones, missionary to India, influential writer, and international evangelist.

Still there are more. We identify with the sentiment of the author of Hebrews 11 in his conclusion to the great role call of the faithful. "And what shall I more say? for the time would fail me to tell of" (v. 32) . . . John Paton of the New Hebrides, and of David Trumball of South America, and of T. J. Bowen of Nigeria, and of Hiram Bingham of the Gilbert Islands, and of Ludwig Nommensen of Sumatra, and of Hans Egede of Greenland, and of Wilfred Grenfell of Newfoundland and Labrador, and of . . . "who through faith subdued kingdoms, wrought righteousness, obtained promises, stopped the mouths of lions, quenched the violence of fire, escaped the edge of the sword, out of weakness were made strong, waxed valiant in fight, turn to flight the armies of the aliens" (vv. 33-34).

"And others . . . were slain with the sword" (vv. 36-37). Such were Jim Elliott and his young missionary colleagues who were killed by the Auca Indians of Ecuador while on a mission of love to them in 1956. Elliott, though cut short like Brainerd and Martyn before him, belongs to that long line of missionaries whose lives epitomize devotion. To read his diary is to be impressed with the striking similarity of its language to the vocabulary of devotion which we find in the Lulls, the Brainerds, the Zinzendorfs, the Martyns, the Livingstones, the Hudson Taylors. The language is the symbol of the life—this was their secret. The following words were found in the diary of Jim Elliott:

Oh, the fullness, pleasure, sheer excitement of knowing God on earth! I care not if I never raise my voice again for Him, if only I may love Him, please Him. Mayhap in mercy He shall give me a host of children that I may lead them through the vast star fields to explore His delicacies whose finger ends set them to burning. But if not, if only I may see Him, touch His garments, and smile into His eyes—ah then, not stars nor children shall matter, only Himself.

O Jesus, Master and Center and End of all, how long before that Glory is thine which has so long waited Thee? Now there is no thought of Thee among men; then there shall be thought for nothing else. Now other men are praised; then none shall care for any other's merits. Hasten, hasten, Glory of Heaven, take Thy crown, subdue Thy Kingdom, enthrall Thy creatures.[1]

Note

1. Elisabeth Elliott, *Through Gates of Splendor* (New York: Harper and Brothers Publishers, 1957) pp. 255–56. Used by permission.

Bibliography of English Sources

General Sources

Anderson, Gerald H., comp. *Bibliography of the Theology of Missions.* N. Y.: Missionary Research Library, 1960.

Beach, Harlan P. and Fahs, Charles H., eds. *World Missionary Atlas.* N. Y.: Institute of Social and Religious Research, 1925.

————., and St. John, Burton, eds. *World Statistics of Christian Missions.* N. Y.: The Committee and Council of the Foreign Mission Conference of North America, 1916.

Cox, Norman Wade, ed. *Encyclopedia of Southern Baptists.* Nashville: Broadman, 2 vols., 1958.

Coxwell, H. Wakelin, and Grubb, Kenneth, eds. *World Christian Handbook.* Nashville: Abingdon, 1968.

Dayton, Edward R., ed. *Mission Handbook: North American Protestant Ministries Overseas,* 11th ed. Monrovia, CA: M.A.R.C., 1976.

Dwight, H. O., Tupper, H. A., and Bliss, Edwin M., eds. *The Encyclopedia of Missions,* 2nd ed. N. Y.: Funk and Wagnalls, 1904.

Goddard, Burton L., ed. *The Encyclopedia of Modern Missions: The Agencies.* Camden, N. J.: Nelson, 1967.

Jackson, Samuel Macauley, ed. *The New Schaff-Herzog Encyclopedia of Religious Knowledge.* N. Y.: Funk and Wagnalls, 12 vols., 1908.

Loetscher, Lefferts A., ed. *Twentieth Century Encyclopedia of Religious Knowledge.* Grand Rapids: Baker, 2 vols., 1955.

Mission Handbook 1978. Washington: U. S. Catholic Mission Council.

Neill, Stephen; Anderson, Gerald H., and Goodwin, John, eds. *Concise Dictionary of the Christian World Mission.* London: Lutterworth, 1970.

New Catholic Encyclopedia. N. Y.: McGraw-Hill, 16 vols., 1967. Roberts, Alexander and Donaldson, James, eds. *The Ante-Nicene Fathers.* Grand Rapids: Eerdmans, 10 vols., 1950.

Schaff, Philip, ed., *A Select Library of the Nicene and Past Nicene Fathers of the Christian Church.* Grand Rapids: Eerdmans, 14 vols., 1956.
————., and Mace, Henry, eds. *A Select Library of Nicene and Post Nicene Fathers,* 2nd. series, 14 vols., 1952.
Shenk, Wilbert R. *Bibliography of Henry Venn's Printed Writings with Index.* Elkhart., Ind.: Institute of Mennonite Studies, 1975.

Biblical-Theological Basis of Missions

Allen, Roland. *The Ministry of the Spirit.* Grand Rapids: Eerdmans, 1962.
Anderson, Gerald H., ed. *Christian Mission in Theological Perspective.* N. Y.: Abingdon, 1967.
————., ed. *The Theology of the Christian Mission.* N. Y.: McGraw-Hill, 1962.
Anderson, Wilhelm. *Toward a Theology of Missions.* London: S.C.M., 1955.
Blauw, Johannes. *The Missionary Nature of the Church.* N. Y.: McGraw-Hill, 1962.
Boer, Harry R. *Pentecost and Missions.* Grand Rapids: Eerdmans, 1961.
Carver, William O. *The Bible, a Missionary Message.* N. Y.: Revell, 1921.
————. *Missions in the Plan of the Ages.* Nashville: Broadman, 1951.
De Dietrich, Suzanne. *The Witnessing Community.* Phil.: Westminster, 1958.
Forman, Charles W. *A Faith for all Nations.* Phil.: Westminster, 1957.
Glover, Robert H. *The Bible Basis of Missions.* Chicago: Moody, 1964.
Goerner, Henry Cornell. *Thus It Is Written.* Nashville: Broadman, 1953 (1944).
Gordon, A. J. *The Holy Spirit and Missions.* Harrisburg, Pa.: Christian Publications, 1968.
Hahn, Ferdinand. *Mission in the New Testament.* Naperville, Ill.: Allenson, 1963.
Kane, J. Herbert. *Christian Missions in Biblical Perspective.* Grand Rapids: Baker, 1976.
Lawrence, J. B. *The Holy Spirit in Missions.* Atlanta: Home Mission Board, S.B.C., 1947.
Love, Julian Price. *The Missionary Message of the Bible.* N. Y.: Macmillan, 1941.
Morgan, G. Campbell, *The Missionary Manifesto.* Grand Rapids: Baker, 1970.

Newbigin, Lesslie. *Trinitarian Faith for Today's Mission*. Richmond: John Knox, 1963.

Niles, Daniel T. *That They May Have Life*. N. Y.: Harper and Brothers, 1951.

———. *The Message and Its Messenger*. Nashville: Abingdon, 1966.

Peters, George W. *A Biblical Theology of Missions*. Chicago: Moody, 1972.

Rowley, H. H., *The Missionary Message of the Old Testament*. London: Carey, 1944.

Soper, Edmund D. *The Biblical Background of the Christian World Mission*. N. Y.: Abingdon-Cokesbury, 1951.

Speer, Robert E. *The Church and Missions*. N. Y.: Doran, 1926.

Tippett, Alan R. *Church Growth and the Word of God*. Grand Rapids: Eerdmans, 1970.

Vicedom, George F. *The Mission of God*. St. Louis: Concordia, 1965.

Warren, Max A. C. *The Gospel of Victory*. London: S.C.M., 1955.

Webster, Douglas. *Unchanging Mission: Biblical and Contemporary*. Phil.: Fortress, 1965.

Mission Histories: General

Aberly, John. *An Outline of Missions*. Phil.: Muhlenberg, 1945.

Barnes, L. C. *Two Thousand Years of Missions Before Carey*. Chicago: Christian Culture, 1900.

Carver, William O. *The Course of Christian Missions*. N. Y.: Revell, 1932.

Hardy, E. R. Jr. *Militant in Earth: Twenty Centuries of the Spread of Christianity*. N. Y.: Oxford, 1940.

Harnack, Adolf. *The Expansion of Christianity in the First Three Centuries*. N. Y.: Putnam's Sons, 2 vols., 1904.

Glover, Robert H., and Kane, J. Herbert. *The Progress of Worldwide Missions*. N. Y.: Harper and Row, 1960.

Hutcherson, Paul. *The Spread of Christianity*. N. Y.: Abingdon, 1922.

Kane, J. Herbert. *A Global View of Christian Missions: From Pentecost to the Present.*, rev. ed. Grand Rapids: Baker, 1971.

Latourette, Kenneth Scott. *Christianity Through the Ages*. N. Y.: Harper and Row, 1965.

———. *A History of the Expansion of Christianity*. N. Y.: Harper and Brothers, 7 vols., 1937-1945.

Mason, Alfred D. *Outlines of Mission History.* London: Hodder and Stoughton, 1912.

Matthews, Basil J. *Forward Through the Ages.* N. Y.: Friendship, 1951.

Neill, Stephen. *A History of Christian Missions.* N. Y.: McGraw-Hill, 1964.

Robinson, Charles H. *History of Christian Missions.* N. Y.: Scribner, 1915.

Warneck, Gustaf. *Outline of a History of Protestant Missions from the Reformation to the Present Time.* N. Y.: Revell, 1902.

Mission History: Special

Allen, W. O. B. and McClure, Edmund. *Two Hundred Years: The History of the Society for Promoting Christian Knowledge 1698-1898.* London: S.P.C.K., 1898.

Anderson, Gerald H., ed., *Studies in Philippine Church History.* Ithaca, N. Y.: Cornell University, 1969.

Anderson, Rufus. *History of the Missions of the American Board of Commissioners for Foreign Missions in India.* Boston: Congregational, 1874.

Ajayi, J. F. Ade. *Christian Missions in Nigeria 1841-1891.* London: Longmans, Green and Co., 1965.

Band, Edward. *Working Out His Purpose: The History of the English Presbyterian Mission, 1847-1947.* London: Presbyterian, 1948.

Barclay, Wade C. *History of Methodist Missions.* N. Y.: Board of Missions of the Methodist Church, 3 vols., 1949-1957.

Beach, Harlan P. and others. *Protestant Missions in South America.* N. Y.: S.V.M., 1907.

Bede, *A History of the English Church and People.* Baltimore: Penguin, 1976.

Beaver, R. Pierce. *All Loves Excelling. American Protestant Women in World Mission.* Grand Rapids: Eerdmans, 1968.

Berry, L. L. *A Century of Missions of the African Methodist Episcopal Church 1840-1940.* N. Y.: Gutenberg, 1942.

Braga, Erasmo and Grubb, Kenneth. *The Republic of Brazil. A Survey of the Religious Situation.* London: World Dominion, 1932.

Broomhall, Marshall. *The Jubilee Story of the China Inland Mission.* London: Morgan and Scott, 1915.

Brown, Arthur J. *One Hundred Years. A History of the Foreign Mission Work of the Presbyterian Church. U. S. A.* N. Y.: Revell, 1937.

Camargo, G. Baez and Grubb, Kenneth G. *Religion in the Republic of Mexico.* London: World Dominion, 1935.

Cannon, James, III. *History of Southern Methodist Missions.* Nashville: Cokesbury, 1926.

Canton, William, *A History of the British and Foreign Bible Society.* London: John Murray, 5 vols., 1904-1910.

Cary, Otis, *A History of Christianity in Japan.* N. Y.: Revell, 2 vols., 1909.

Cauthen, Baker J., ed. *Advance: A History of Southern Baptist Foreign Missions.* Nashville: Broadman, 1970.

Clarke, W. K. Lowther. *A History of the Society for Promoting Christian Knowledge.* London: S.P.C.K., 1959.

Drach, George, ed., *Our Church Abroad. The Foreign Missions of the Lutheran Church of America.* Phil: United Lutheran, 1926.

Du Plessis, J. *A History of Christian Missions in South Africa.* N. Y.: Longmans, Green, and Co., 1911.

Dvornik, Francis. *Byzantine Missions Among the Slavs.* New Brunswick, N. J.: Rutgers University, 1970.

Dwight, Henry Otis. *The Centennial History of the American Bible Society.* N. Y.: Macmillan, 2 vols., 1916.

Emery, Julia C. *A Century of Endeavor, 1821-1921.* N. Y.: Department of Missions, Protestant Episcopal Church, 1921.

Engelhardt, Zephyrin, *The Missions and Missionaries of California.* Santa Barbara: Mission Santa Barbara, 2 vols., 1929, 1930.

Eusebius, *Ecclesiastical History.* Washington: Catholic University of America, 1965.

Findlay, G. G. and Holdsmith, W. W., *The History of the Wesleyan Methodist Missionary Society.* London: Epworth, 5 vols., 1921-1924.

Foster, John. *After the Apostles: Missionary Preaching of the First Three Centuries.* London: S.C.M., 1951.

————., *To All Nations: Christian Expansion from 1700 to Today.* London: Lutterworth, 1961.

Gonzales, Justo L. *The Development of Christianity in the Latin Caribbean.* Grand Rapids: Eerdmans, 1969.

Goodall, Norman, *A History of the London Missionary Society 1895-1945.*

Groves, C. P., *The Planting of Christianity in Africa 1840-1954.* London: Lutterworth, 4 vols., 1948-1958.

Harvey, G. W. *The Story of Baptist Missions in Foreign Lands.* St. Louis: Chaney R. Barns, 1885.

Held, John A. *European Missions in Texas.* Nashville: Broadman, 1936.

Hewart, Elizabeth G. K. *Vision and Achievement, 1796-1959: a History of the Foreign Missions of the Churches United in the Church of Scotland.* London: Nelson, 1960.

Hogg, William Richey, *Ecumenical Foundations: A History of the International Missionary Council and Its Nineteenth Century Background.* N. Y.: Harper, 1952.

Humphreys, David. *Historical Account of the Incorporated Society for the Propagation of the Gospel in Foreign Parts.* N. Y.: Arno, 1969.

Hutton, J. E. *A History of Moravian Missions,* London: Moravian, 1923.

Kraemer, Hendrick. *From Missionfield to Independent Church: Report on the Decisive Decade in the Growth of Indigenous Churches in Indonesia.* London: S.C.M., 1958.

Latourette, Kenneth Scott. *A History of Christian Missions in China.* N. Y.: Macmillan, 1929.

————., *Christianity in a Revolutionary Age.* N. Y.: Harper and Row, 5 vols., 1958-1962.

Lyall, Leslie T. *A Passion for the Impossible: The China Inland Mission 1865-1965.* Chicago: Moody, 1965.

Mackay, John A. *The Other Spanish Christ. A Study of the Spiritual History of Spain and South America.* London: Student Movement, 1932.

Maclear, G. F., *History of Christian Missions During the Middle Ages.* Cambridge: University, 1863.

McFarland, G. B., ed., *Historical Sketch of Protestant Missions in Siam 1828-1928.* Bangkok: Bangkok Times, 1928.

Moraes, George Mark. *A History of Christianity in India: From Early Times to St. Francis Xavier, AD 52-1542.* Bombay: Manaktalas, 1964.

Murray, A. W. *Missions in Western Polynesia: Historical Sketches 1839-1863.* London: John Snow, 1863.

Park, L. George, *The History of Protestant Missions in Korea 1832-1910.* Pyeng Yang: Union Christian College, 1929.

Pickett, J. Waskom. *Christian Mass Movements in India.* N. Y.: Abingdon, 1933.

Potts, E. Daniel. *British Baptist Missionaries in India 1793-1837.* Cambridge: University, 1967.

Ritter, H. A. *A History of Protestant Missions in Japan.* trans. George E. Albrecht. Tokyo: Methodist, 1898.

Robbins, J. C. *Following the Pioneers: A Story of American Baptist Mission Work in India and Burma.* Phil.: Judson, 1922.

Rutledge, Arthur. *Mission to America: A Century and a Quarter of Southern Baptist Home Missions.* Nashville: Broadman, 1969.

Speer, Robert E. *Missions and Modern History.* N. Y.: Revell, 2 vols., 1904.

Steward, John. *Nestorian Missionary Enterprise: The Story of a Church on Fire.* Edinburgh: Clark, 1928.

Stock, Eugene. *The History of the Church Missionary Society.* London: C.M.S., 4 vols., 1899-1916.

Sudan Interior Mission. *Roots from Dry Ground: The Story of the Sudan Interior Mission.* London: S.I.M., 1966.

Torbet, Robert G. *Venture of Faith: The Story of the American Baptist Foreign Mission Society 1814-1954.* Phil: Judson, 1955.

Tupper, H. A. *The Foreign Missions of the Southern Baptist Convention.* Phil: American Baptist Publication Society, 1880.

Verbeck, Guido H. F. *History of Protestant Missions in Japan.* Yokohama: Meiklejohn, 1883.

Walroud, F. F. *Christian Missions Before the Reformation,* London: S.P.C.K. n.d.

Wells, Kenneth E. *History of Protestant Work in Thailand 1828-1958.* Bangkok: Church of Christ of Thailand, 1958.

Biographies, Autobiographies, Journals, Letters

William Carey

Carey, Eustace. *Memoir of William Carey.* Hartford: Canfield and Roberts, 1837.

Carey, S. Pearce. *William Carey.* N. Y.: Doran, 1923.

Davis, Walter Bruce, *William Carey: Father of Modern Missions.* Chicago: Moody, 1963.

Marshman, John Clark. *The Life and Times of Carey, Marshman and Ward.* London: Longmans, Green, Longmans and Roberts, 2 vols., 1859.

Serampore Letters, Being the Unpublished Correspondence of Carey and Others with John Williams 1800-1816. N. Y.: Putnam's Sons, 1892.

Smith, George. *The Life of William Carey, D.D.* London: John Murray, 1885.

Walker, F. Deaville, *William Carey, Missionary Pioneer and Statesman.* London: Student Christian Movement, 1926.

Alexander Duff

Day, Lal Behari, *Recollections of Alexander Duff. D.D. LL.D.* London: T. Nelson and Sons, 1789.

Duff, W. P. *Memorials of Alexander Duff D.D.* London: James Nisbet, 1890.

Paton, William. *Alexander Duff, Pioneer of Missionary Education.* N. Y.: Doran, n.d.

Smith, George. *The Life of Alexander Duff.* N. Y.: A. C. Armstrong and Sons, 2 vols., n.d.

The Adoniram Judsons

Anderson, Courtney. *To the Golden Shore. The Life of Adoniram Judson.* Boston: Little, Brown, 1956.

Forester, Fanny, *Life of Sarah B. Judson.* London: T. Nelson and Sons, 1873.

Hubbard, Ethel Daniels. *Ann of Ava.* N. Y.: Friendship, 1941.

Judson, Ann H. *An Account of the American Baptist Mission in the Burman Empire: in a Series of Letters Addressed to a Gentleman in London.* London: J. Butterworth and Son, 1823.

Judson, Edward. *The Life of Adoniram Judson.* N. Y.: Anson D. F. Randolph, 1883.

Kendrick, A. C. *The Life and Letters of Mrs. Emily C. Judson.* N. Y.: Sheldon, 1860.

Warburton, Stacy R. *Eastward: The Story of Adoniram Judson.* N. Y.: Round Table, 1937.

Wayland, Francis. *A Memoir of the Life and Labors of the Rev. Adoniram Judson.* N. Y.: Sheldon, 2 vols., 1866.

David Livingstone

Anderson, W. H. *On the Trail of Livingstone.* Mountain View, CA: Pacific, 1919.

Blackie, W. Garden, *The Personal Life of David Livingstone.* Chicago: Revell, n.d.

Campbell, R. J. *Livingstone.* London: Ernest Benn, n.d.

Chamberlin, David. *Some Letters from Livingstone 1840-1872.* Oxford: University, 1940.

Chambliss, J. E. *The Life and Labors of David Livingstone.* Phil.: Hubbard Brothers, 1873.

Fraser, A. Z. *Livingstone and Newstead.* London: John Murray, 1913.

Johnson, H. H., *David Livingstone.* London: Charles H. Kelley, n.d.

Livingstone, David. *Missionary Travels and Researches in Southern Africa.* London: John Murray, 1857.

Livingstone, David and Charles. *Narrative of an Expedition to the Zambesi 1854-1864.* London: John Murray, 1865.

Macnair, James I. *Livingstone's Travels.* N. Y.: Macmillan, 1954.

Monk, William, *Doctor Livingstone's Cambridge Lectures.* Cambridge: Deighton, Bell, 1858.

Northcutt, Cecil. *David Livingstone, His Triumph, Decline and Fall.* Phil.: Westminster, 1973.

Schapera, I. *Livingstone's Missionary Correspondence 1841-1856.* Berkeley: University of California, 1961.

Seaver, George, *David Livingstone: His Life and Letters.* N. Y.: Harper and Brothers, 1957.

Henry Martyn

Padwick, Constance. *Henry Martyn: Confessor of the Faith.* Chicago: Moody, 1950.

Sargent, John. *A Memoir of Rev. Henry Martyn, B.D.* N. Y.: American Tract Society, n.d.

Smith, George. *Henry Martyn.* London: The Religious Tract Society, 1892.

Wilberforce, S., ed. *Journal and Letters of the Rev. Henry Martyn, B.D.* London: R. B. Seeley and W. Burnside, 2 vols., 1837.

The Robert Moffats

Hubbard, Ethel Daniels. *The Moffats.* N. Y.: Friendship, 1944.

Moffat, John S. *The Lives of Robert and Mary Moffat.* London: T. Fisher Unwin, 1886.

Moffat, Robert. *Missionary Labors and Scenes in Southern Africa.* London: John Snow, 1842.

Smith, Edwin W. *Robert Moffat, One of God's Gardeners.* London: Student Christian Movement, 1925.

J. Hudson Taylor

Broomhall, Marshall. *Hudson Taylor.* London: C.I.M., 1929.

————., *Hudson Taylor's Legacy, A Series of Meditations.* London: C.I.M., 1931.

Taylor, Dr. and Mrs. Howard. *Hudson Taylor In Early Years: The Growth of a Soul.* London: C.I.M., 1943.

————. *Hudson Taylor and the China Inland Mission: The Growth of a Work of God.* London: C.I.M., 1943.

————. *Hudson Taylor's Spiritual Secret.* London: C.I.M., 1949.

Taylor, J. Hudson, *A Retrospect.* Phil.: C.I.M., n.d.

Francis Xavier

Brodrick, James. *Saint Francis Xavier.* N. Y.: Wicklow, 1952.

Coleridge, Henry James. *The Life of St. Francis Xavier.* London: Burns and Oates, 2 vols., 1872.

Robertson, Edith Anne. *Francis Xavier.* London: Student Christian Movement, 1930.

Venn, Henry. *The Missionary Life and Labours of Francis Xavier.* London: Longman, Green, Longman, Roberts and Green, 1862.

Others

Bingham, Hiram. *A Residence of Twenty-One Years in the Sandwich Islands.* Hartford: Hezekiah Huntington, 1848.

Broomhall, Marshall, *Robert Morrison, A Master Builder.* London: C.M.S., 1924.

Du Plessis, J. *The Life of Andrew Murray of South Africa.* London: Marshall Brothers, 1919.

Eddy, Sherwood. *Pathfinders of the World Missionary Crusade.* N. Y.: Abingdon-Cokesbury, 1940.

Edwards, Jonathan. *The Life and Diary of David Brainerd.* Chicago: Moody, 1949.

Elliott, Elizabeth, ed. *The Journals of Jim Elliott.* Old Tappan, N. J.: Revell, 1978.

————. *Through Gates of Splendor.* N. Y.: Harper and Brothers, 1957.

Emerton, Ephraim, ed. *The Letters of Saint Boniface.* N. Y.: Columbia University, 1940.

Falconer, James. *John Geddie.* Toronto: Board of Foreign Missions, Presbyterian Church of Canada, 1915.

Gallagher, S. J. trans., ed. *China in the Sixteenth Century: The Journals of Matthew Ricci 1583-1610.* N. Y.: Random House, 1953.

Grenfell, Wilfred. *Forty Years for Labrador.* Boston: Houghton Mifflin, 1932.

Griffis, William Elliott. *Verbeck of Japan.* N. Y.: Revell, 1900.

Grubb, Norman P. *With C. T. Studd in Congo Forests.* Grand Rapids, Zondervan, 1946.

Harrison, Helen Bagby. *The Bagbys of Brazil.* Nashville: Broadman, 1954.

Hemmens, H. L. *George Grenfell, Pioneer to the Congo.* London: Student Christian Movement, 1927.

Hyatt, Irwin T. *Our Ordered Lives Confess: Three Nineteenth-Century American Missionaries in East Shantung.* [Tarleton Perry Crawford, Charlotte Diggs Moon, Calvin Wilson Mateer]. "The Harvard Studies in American-East Asian Relations." Cambridge, Mass.: Harvard University, 1976.

Jessup, Henry Harris. *Fifty-Three Years in Syria.* Chicago: Revell, 2 vols., 1910.

Johnson, Harry H. *George Grenfell and the Congo.* London: Hutchinson, 2 vols., 1928.

Knight, William. *Memoir of the Rev. Henry Venn.* London: Longmans, Green, 1880.

Lawrence, Una Roberts. *Lottie Moon.* Nashville: Sunday School Board, S.B.C., 1927.

Lewis, A. J. *Zinzendorf the Ecumenical Pioneer.* Phil.: Westminster, 1962.

Lull, Ramon. *The Book of the Lover and the Beloved.* London: S.P.C.K., 1928.

Luthuli, Albert. *Let My People Go.* N. Y.: McGraw-Hill, 1962.

MacNutt, Francis Augustus. *Bartholomew de Las Casas, His Life, Apostolate and Writings.* Cleveland: Arthur H. Clark, 1909.

Martin, Marie-Louise. *Kimbangu, An African Prophet and His Church.* Grand Rapids: Eerdmans, 1975.

Matthews, Basil. *John R. Mott, World Citizen.* N. Y.: Harper and Brothers, 1934.

Morrison, E. *Memoirs of the Life and Labours of Robert Morrison.* London: Longman, Orme, Brown, Green, Longmans, 2 vols., 1839.

Nevius, H. S. C. *The Life of John Livingstone Nevius.* Chicago: Revell, 1895.

Page, Jesse. *The Black Bishop, Samuel Adjai Crowther.* N. Y.: Revell, n.d.

Paton, John G. *John G. Paton, Missionary to New Hebrides, An Autobiography.* N. Y.: Revell, 3 parts, 1889, 1898.

Patterson, George. *Missionary Life among the Cannibals: Being the Life of the Rev. John Geddie, D.D. First Missionary to the New Hebrides.* Toronto: James Campbell and Son, 1882.

Peters, Walter H. *The Life of Benedict XV.* Milwaukee: Bruce, 1959.

Prout, Ebenezer. *Memoirs of the Life of the Rev. John Williams, Missionary to Polynesia.* London: John Snow, 1843.

Stevens, George B. *The Life, Letters, and Journal of the Rev. and Hon. Peter Parker, M.D.* Boston: Congregational, 1896.

Stranks, C. J. *The Venerable Bede.* London: S.P.C.K., 1955.

Talbot, C. H. trans., ed. *The Anglo-Saxon Missionaries in Germany.* N. Y.: Sheed and Ward, 1954.

Uchimura, Kanzo. *Diary of a Japanese Convert.* N. Y.: Revell, 1895.

Walker, Robert Sparks. *Torchlight to the Cherokees. The Brainerd Mission.* N. Y.: Macmillan, 1931.

Watt, Mary Caroline. *St. Martin of Tours. The Chronicles of the Sulpicius Severus.* London: Sands, 1928.

White, Newport, J. D., ed. *St. Patrick: His Writings and Life.* N. Y.: Macmillan, 1920.

Zwemer, Samuel M. *Raymund Lull: First Missionary to the Moslems.* N. Y.: Funk and Wagnalls, 1902.

Mission Theory and Practice, Sermons, Tracts

Allen, Roland. *Essential Missionary Principles.* N. Y.: Revell, 1913.

————., *Missionary Methods: St. Paul's or Ours?* Grand Rapids: Eerdmans, 1962 (1912).

————., *The Spontaneous Expansion of the Church and the Causes which Hinder It.* London: Grand Rapids: Eerdmans, 1962 (1927).

Alexander, Calvert, S. J. *The Missionary Dimension: Vatican II and the World Apostolate..* Milwaukee: Brace, 1967.

Anderson, Rufus. *Foreign Missions: Their Relations and Claims.* N. Y.: Charles Scribner, 1869.

Bavinck, J. H. *An Introduction to the Science of Missions.* Phil.: Presbyterian and Reformed, 1964.

Beaver, R. Pierce, ed. *Pioneers in Mission: Early Missionary Ordination, Sermons, Charges, and Introductions.* Grand Rapids: Eerdmans, 1966.

————., ed. *To Advance the Gospel: Selections from the Writings of Rufus Anderson,* Grand Rapids: Eerdmans, 1967.

————., *The Christian World Mission: A Reconsideration.* Calcutta: Baptist Mission, 1957.

————., *The Missionary Between the Times.* Garden City, N. Y.: Doubleday, 1968.

Brown, Arthur J. *The Foreign Missionary.* N. Y.: Revell, 1950.

Burke, Thomas J. M., S. J., ed. *Catholic Missions. Four Great Missionary Encyclicals.* N. Y.: Fordham University, 1957.

Cable, Mildred and French, Francesca. *Ambassadors for Christ.* Chicago: Moody, 1935.

Carey, William, *An Enquiry into the Obligations of Christians to Use Means for the Conversion of the Heathens.* Leicester, Eng.: Ann Ireland, 1792.

Chang, Lit-sen. *Strategy of Missions in the Orient.* Phil.: Presbyterian and Reformed, 1968.

Cook, Harold R. *An Introduction to the Study of Christian Missions*. Chicago: Moody, 1954.

———., *Missionary Life and Work*. Chicago: Moody, 1959.

Danielou, Jean, S. J. *The Salvation of the Nations*. trans. Angeline Bouchard. London: Sheed and Ward, 1949.

Dennis, James S. *Christian Missions and Social Progress*. N. Y.: Revell, 3 vols., 1897.

Duff, Alexander. *India and Indian Missions*. Edinburgh: John Johnston, 1839.

Faunce, W. H. P. *The Social Aspects of Foreign Missions*. N. Y.: Missionary Education Movement, 1914.

Horner, Norman A. *Cross and Crucifix in Mission: A Comparison of Protestant-Catholic Missionary Strategy*. N. Y.: Abingdon, 1965.

Hogg, William Richey, *One World, One Mission*. N. Y.: Friendship, 1960.

Jones, E. Stanley. *Christ at the Round Table*. N. Y.: Grosset and Dunlap, 1928.

Kitagawa, Daisuke. *Race Relations and Christian Missions*. N. Y.: Friendship, 1964.

Lamott, Willis C. *Revolution in Missions*. N. Y.: Macmillan, 1954.

Levai, Blaise., ed. *Revolution in Missions*. Calcutta: Y.M.C.A., 1958.

Lindsell, Harold. *A Christian Philosophy of Missions*. Wheaton, Ill.: Van Kampen Press, 1949.

Laubach, Frank C. *How to Teach One and Win One for Christ. Christ's Plan for Winning the World: Each One Teach and Win One*. Grand Rapids: Zondervan, 1964.

———., *The Silent Billion Speak*. N. Y.: Friendship Press, 1943.

McGavran, Donald. *How Churches Grow*. N. Y.: Friendship, 1955.

———., *The Bridges of God*. N. Y.: Friendship, 1955.

Montgomery, Helen B., *Prayer and Missions*. W. Medford, Ma.: Central Committee on the United Study of Foreign Missions, 1924.

Miller, Donald G. *The Nature and Mission of the Church*. Richmond: John Knox, 1957.

Morgan, E. R. *The Mission of the Church*. London: Centenary, 1946.

Murphy, Edwards L., S. J. *Teach Ye All Nations. The Principles of Catholic Missionary Work*. N. Y.: Benziger Brothers, 1958.

Mott, John R. *The Evangelization of the World in this Generation*. N. Y.: Student Volunteer Movement, 1905.

———., *The Pastor and Modern Missions*. N. Y.: Student Volunteer Movement, 1904.

Neill, Stephen. *Colonialism and Christian Missions.* N. Y.: McGraw-Hill, 1966.

————., *The Unfinished Task.* London: Lutterworth, 1957.

————., *Creative Tension.* London: Edinburgh House, 1958.

Nevius, John L. *Planting and Development of Missionary Churches.* Nutley, N. J.: Presbyterian and Reformed, 1958 (1899).

Newbigin, Lesslie. *One Body, One Gospel, One World: The Christian Mission Today.* London: Edinburgh House, 1958.

Niles, D. T. *Upon the Earth. The Mission of God and the Missionary Enterprise of the Churches.* N. Y.: McGraw-Hill, 1962.

Nida, Eugene A. *Customs and Cultures.* N. Y.: Harper and Row, 1954.

————., *Message and Mission.* N. Y.: Harper and Row, 1960.

Paton, David M. *Christian Missions and the Judgment of God.* London: S.C.M. 1953.

Ray, T. B. *The Highway of Mission Thought.* Nashville: Sunday School Board, S.B.C., 1907.

Schmidlin, Joseph. *Catholic Mission Theory.* Techny, Ill.: Mission, S.V.D., 1931.

Speer, Robert E. *Christianity and the Nations.* N. Y.: Revell, 1910.

————., *Missionary Principles and Practices.* N. Y.: Revell, 1902.

————., *Missions and Politics in Asia.* N. Y.: Revell.

————., *Studies in Missionary Leadership.* Phil.: Westminster, 1914.

Stewart, James S. *Thine Is the Kingdom: The Church's Mission in Our Time.* N. Y.: Charles Scribner's Sons, 1957.

The Staff of the Pope Speaks Magazine, eds. *The Encyclicals of John XXIII.* Washington. T.P.S., 1964.

Vicedom, Georg F. *The Mission of God.* St. Louis: Concordia, 1965 (1958).

Wayland, Francis. *The Moral Dignity of the Missionary Enterprise,* 6th. ed. Edinburgh: James Robertson, 1826.

Warren, Max., ed. *To Apply the Gospel: Selections from the Writings of Henry Venn.* Grand Rapids: Eerdmans, 1971.

————., *The Christian Imperative.* N. Y.: Scribner's, 1955.

————., *The Christian Mission.* London: S.C.M., 1951.

Zinzendorf, Nicholaus Ludwig Count von. *Nine Public Lectures on Important Subjects in Religion.* George W. Forell, trans. and ed. Iowa City: University of Iowa, 1973.

Zwemer, Samuel M. *"Into All the World": The Great Commission, A Vindication and an Interpretation.* Grand Rapids: Zondervan, 1934.

————., *Thinking Missions With Christ.* Grand Rapids: Zondervan, 1934.

Mission Encounter with Non-Christian Religion

Appleton, George. *Glad Encounter: Jesus Christ and the Living Faiths of Men.* London: Edinburgh House, 1959.

Bavinck, John H. *The Church Between Temple and Mosque.* Grand Rapids: Eerdmans, 1966.

————., *The Impact of Christianity on the Non-Christian World.* Grand Rapids: Eerdmans, 1948.

Bouquet, A. C. *Is Christianity the Final Religion?* London: Macmillan, 1921.

————., *The Christian Faith and Non-Christian Religions.* London: James Nisbet, 1958.

————., *The Christian Religion and Its Competitors.* Cambridge: University, 1924.

Braden, Charles S. *Jesus Compared. A Study of Jesus and Other Great Founders of Religions.* Englewood Cliffs, N. J.: Prentice-Hall, 1957.

Cragg, Kenneth. *Sandals at the Mosque. Christian Presence Amid Islam.* N. Y.: Oxford, 1959.

————., *The Call of the Minaret.* N. Y.: Oxford, 1956.

Devanandon, Paul D. *The Gospel and Renascent Hinduism.* London: S.C.M., 1959.

Dewick, E. C. *The Christian Attitude Toward Other Religions.* Cambridge: University, 1953.

Farquhar, John H. *The Crown of Hinduism.* London: Oxford, 1913.

Hocking, William Ernest. *Rethinking Missions. A Laymen's Inquiry After One Hundred Years.* N. Y.: Harper and Brothers, 1932.

————., *Living Religions and a World Faith.* London: Allen and Unwin, 1940.

————., *The Coming World Civilization.* N. Y.: Harper and Brothers, 1956.

Hogg, A. G. *The Christian Message to the Hebrew.* London: S.C.M., 1947.

Jones, E. Stanley. *The Christ of the Indian Road.* N. Y.: Abingdon Press, 1925.

Jurji, Edward J. *The Christian Interpretation of Religion.* N. Y.: Macmillan, 1952.

Kraemer, Hendrick. *Religion and the Christian Faith.* London: Lutterworth, 1956.

————., *The Christian Message in a Non-Christian World.* N. Y.: Harper and Brothers, 1938.

————., *World Cultures and World Religions. The Coming Dialogue.* London: Lutterworth, 1960.

Manikam, Rajah B., ed. *Christianity and the Asian Revolution.* N. Y.: Friendship, 1954.

Moses, David G. *Religious Truth and the Relation between Religions.* Madras: The Christian Literature Society for India, 1950.

Newbigin, Lesslie, *The Finality of Christ.* Richmond: John Knox, 1969.

Niles, D. T. *Buddhism and the Claims of Christ.* Richmond: John Knox, 1967.

————., *The Preacher's Task and the Stone of Stumbling.* N. Y.: Harper and Brothers, 1958.

Perry, Edmund. *The Gospel in Dispute. The Relation of the Christian Faith to Other Missionary Religions.* Garden City, N. Y.: Doubleday, 1958.

Schweitzer, Albert. *Christianity and the Religions of the World.* trans. Johanna Powers. N. Y.: Henry Holt, 1939.

Soper, Edmund Davison. *The Inevitable Choice: Vedanta Philosophy or Christian Gospel.* N. Y.: Abingdon, 1957.

————., *The Philosophy of the Christian World Mission.* N. Y.: Abingdon-Cokesbury, 1943.

Speer, Robert E. *The Finality of Jesus Christ.* N. Y.: Revell, 1933.

The Authority of the Faith. Vol. I in the Madras Series, London: Oxford, 1939.

The Christian Life and Message in Relation to Non-Christian Systems and Life. Vol. I. Jerusalem Meeting, I.M.C., London: Oxford, 1928.

Warren, Max. *The Uniqueness of Jesus Christ.* London: Highway, 1969.

Warneck, John. *The Living Christ and Dying Heathenism.* Grand Rapids: Baker, 1954.

Historic Missionary Proceedings, Periodicals, Reports

Historic Proceedings

Annals of the Propagation of the Faith. N. Y.: Society for the Propagation of the Faith, 1838-1923.

Proceedings of the Board of Missions of the Protestant Episcopal Church in the United States of America, at the Forty-First Annual Meeting, Held in Philadelphia, October 1876. N. Y.: E. S. Dodge, 1876.

Proceedings of the Church Missionary Society for Africa and the East. London, 1805.

Proceedings of the Society for Propagating the Gospel Among the Heathen. Sesqui-Centennial Number . . . 1937. Bethlehem, Penn.: The Society, 1937.

Historic Missionary Periodicals

Church Missionary Intelligencer. Prominent organ of the Church Missionary Society, especially under Henry Venn in the late Nineteenth Century.

International Review of Missions. Published by the D.W.M.E., W.C.C. Founded in 1912 by the Continuing Committee of the Edinburgh World Missionary Conference (1910).

Occasional Bulletin. Published by the Missionary Research Library (now the *Occasional Bulletin of Mission Research* by OMSC).

Practical Anthropology. Succeeded by *Missiology: An International Review*, official organ of A.S.M.

The Missionary Herald (Boston, 1821 ff.). Official organ of the American Board of Commissioners for Foreign Missions.

The Missionary Intelligencer. Published Monthly by the Foreign Christian Missionary Society, Cincinnati, Ohio 1888ff.)

The Missionary Register. Closely Associated with the Church Missionary Society in the early Nineteenth Century.

The New York Missionary Magazine and Repository of Religious Intelligence. N. Y.: 1800-1803.

The Southern Baptist Missionary Journal. Begun in 1846, continued as *the Foreign Mission Journal* (1869-1916), *Home and Foreign Fields,* (1916-1936), *The Commission* (1936 to present).

Early Historic Conferences

Proceedings of the Union Missionary Convention Held in New York, May 4th and 5th, 1854. N. Y.: Taylor and Hogg, 1854.

Ecumenical Missionary Conference, New York 1900, N. Y.: American Tract Society, 2 vols., 1900.

World Missionary Conference, Edinburgh, 1910. N. Y.: Revell, 9 vols., 1910.

Proceedings of the Men's National Missionary Congress of the United States of America. Chicago 1910. N. Y.: Laymen's Missionary Movement, 1910.

International Missionary Council

Jerusalem Meeting of the International Missionary Council, 1928. N. Y.: I.M.C., 8 vols., 1928.

International Missionary Council Meeting at Tambaram, Madras, 1938. N. Y. Oxford, 7 vols., 1939.

Ransom, Charles W., ed. *Renewal and Advance: Christian Witness in a Revolutionary World* (Whitby, 1947). London: Edinburgh House, 1948.

Goodall, Norman, ed. *Missions Under the Cross* (Willingen, 1952). N. Y.: Friendship, 1953.

Orchard, R. K., ed. *The Ghana Assembly of the International Missionary Council.* N. Y.: Friendship, 1958.

Report to the Final Assembly of the International Missionary Council and the Third Assembly of the World Council of Churches. New Delhi, 1961. *Division of World Mission and Evangelism, W.C.C.*

Latham, Robert O. *God For All Men* (Mexico City, 1963). Geneva: W.C.C., 1963.

Bangkok Assembly 1973: Minutes and Reports of the Assembly of the Commission on World Mission and Evangelism. Geneva: W.C.C., 1973.

Inter-Varsity Urbana Student Missionary Conventions

1946. *Completing Christ's Commission,* Chicago: Inter-Varsity, 1947.

1948. *From Every Campus to Every Country.* Chicago: I-V., 1949.

1951. *By All Means—Proclaim Christ.* Chicago: I-V., 1952.

1954. *Changing World—Unchanging Christ.* Chicago: I-V., 1955.

1957. *One Lord, One Church, One World.* Chicago: I-V., 1958.

1961. *Commission, Conflict, Commitment.* Chicago: I-V., 1962.

1964. *Change, Witness, Triumph.* Chicago: I-V., 1965.

1967. *God's Men: From All Nations to All Nations.* Downers Grove: I-V., 1968.

1970. *Christ the Liberator,* Downers Grove: I-V., 1971.

1973. *Jesus Christ, Lord of the Universe, Hope of the World,* Downers Grove: I-V., 1974.

1976. *Declare His Glory Among the Nations.* Downers Grove: I-V., 1977.

Special Mission Conferences

Wheaton Congress, 1966. Lindsell, Harold, ed. *The Church's Worldwide Mission,* Waco, Texas: Word, 1966.

Beaver, R. Pierce, ed. *The Gospel and Frontier Peoples: A Report of a Consultation, December, 1972.* South Pasadena, CA: William Carey Library, 1973.

World Evangelism Congresses

Henry, Carl F. H. and Mooneyham, W. Stanley, eds. *One Race, One World, One Task: World Congress on Evangelism—Berlin, 1966.* Minneapolis: World Wide, 1967.

J. D. Douglas, ed. *Let the Earth Hear His Voice: International Congress on World Evangelism, Lausanne, Switzerland, 1974,* Minneapolis: World Wide, 1975.

Index of Persons

449

Index of Places

453

Index of Subjects

African Methodist Episcopal Church, missions of, 434
Africans, 194, 214, 393, 411, 419
African National Congress, 412, 413, 415
Alexandrian School of Philosophy, 201, 281
American Baptist Convention, 96
American Baptist Foreign Mission Society, 96, 258, 436, 437
American Bible Society, 435
American Board of Commissioners for Foreign Missions, 224, 250, 434
American Society of Missiology, 13, 380
Anglo-Saxons, 211-213, 238
Anglo-Saxon Missionaries, 145, 211, 239, 441
Animistic People, 105, 225
Arabic, 129, 130, 137
Arabs, 190
Archbishop of Canterbury, 207
Armenians, 132, 140, 141, 143, 144
Association of Professors of Missions, 380
Auca Indians, 429

Bangkok World Missionary Conference, 1972-1973, 329, 448
Baptist Missionary Society, (British), 23
Baptists, Missions of, 22, 23, 30, 36, 183, 224, 225, 258, 289, 380, 403, 435, 436
Bengali, 23
Bible Translation, 23, 107, 129, 146, 224, 225, 232, 303, 304, 428, 434
Biblical-Theological Basis of Missions, 14, 21-52, 203-205, 205-210, 268-274, 277-281, 286-289, 290-300, 300-309, 315-316, 316-317, 318-324, 337, 338-350, 365-375, 381-385, 386-390, 391, 420-426, 432-434
Bibliographies, Mission, 431-432
Biographies, Autobiographies, Missionary, 14, 117-157, 437-442
British and Foreign Bible Society, 434
Buddhism, 104, 224, 256, 317-318, 347, 348, 359, 361, 362, 363

457

About the Compiler/Editor

Francis Marquis DuBose is Professor of Missions and Director of Urban Church Studies at Golden Gate Baptist Theological Seminary, Mill Valley, California. Dr. DuBose has served as a pastor in Texas and Superintendent of Missions in Detroit, Michigan. He is a graduate of Baylor University (B.A.), Southwestern Baptist Theological Seminary (B.D.;Th.D.), and has done post-graduate study at Oxford University.

With a special concern for urban problems, Dr. DuBose is active in the San Francisco Conference on Religion, Race, and Social Concern. As a specialist on urban churches he has travelled in 57 countries. He is an active member of the American Society of Missiology and Association of Professors of Missions. He and his wife, Dorothy Anne Sessums, enjoy biking and visiting places of historical interest.